BAMBOO BLADE ⑩

MASAHIRO TOTSUKA
AGURI IGARASHI

Translation: Stephen Paul

Lettering: Terri Delgado

BAMBOO BLADE Vol. 10 © 2009 Masahiro Totsuka, Aguri Igarashi /
SQUARE ENIX CO., LTD. All rights reserved. First published in Japan in
2009 by SQUARE ENIX CO., LTD. English translation rights arranged with
SQUARE ENIX CO., LTD. and Hachette Book Group through Tuttle-Mori
Agency, Inc.

Translation © 2011 by SQUARE ENIX CO., LTD.

Yen Press
Hachette Book Group
237 Park Avenue, New York, NY 10017

www.HachetteBookGroup.com
www.YenPress.com

Yen Press is an imprint of Hachette Book Group, Inc. The Yen Press name
and logo are trademarks of Hachette Book Group, Inc.

First Yen Press Edition: September 2011

ISBN: 978-0-316-18936-1

10 9 8 7 6 5 4 3 2 1

BVG

Printed in the United States of America

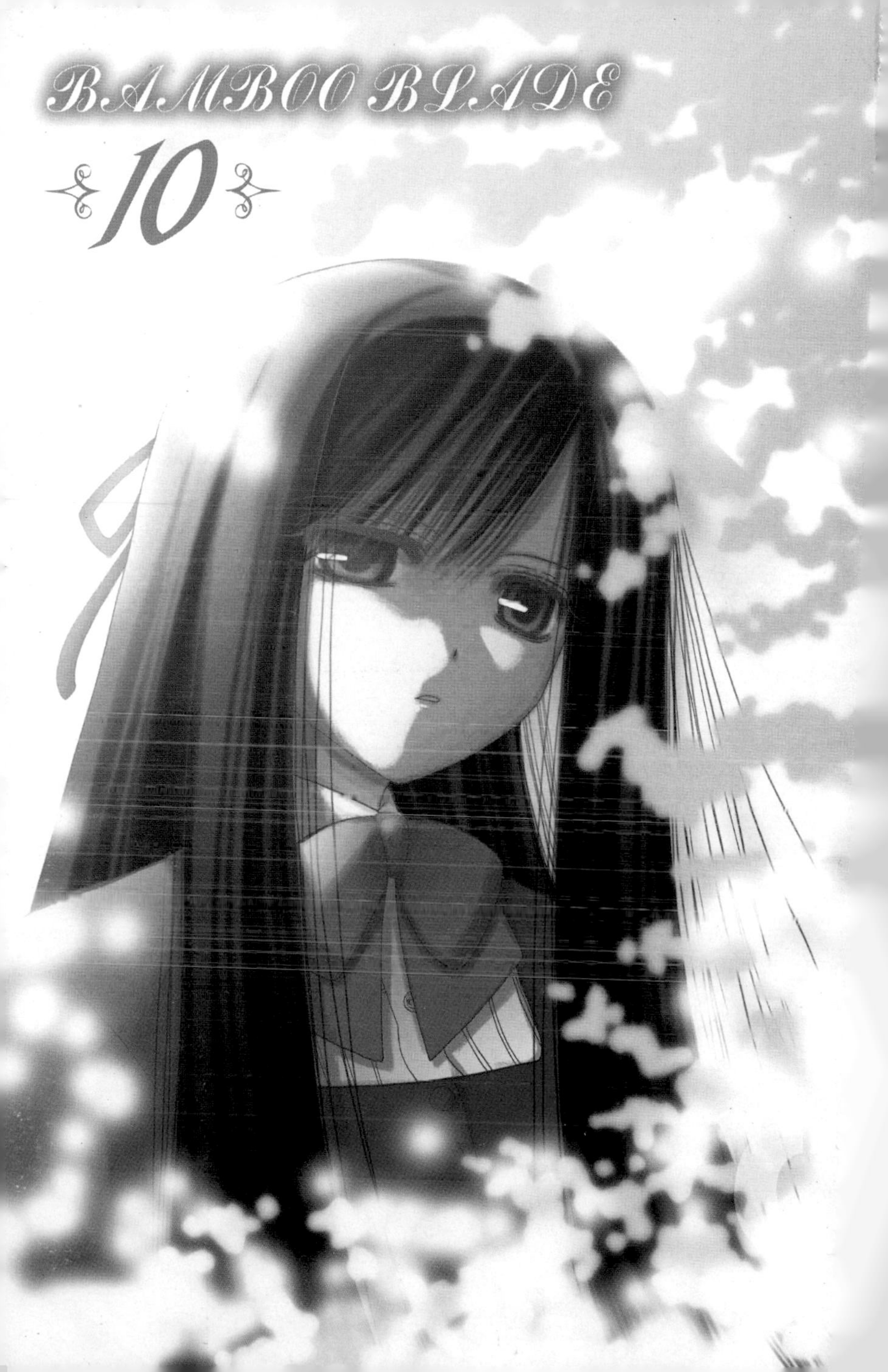
BAMBOO BLADE
10

BAMBOO BLADE 10 CONTENTS

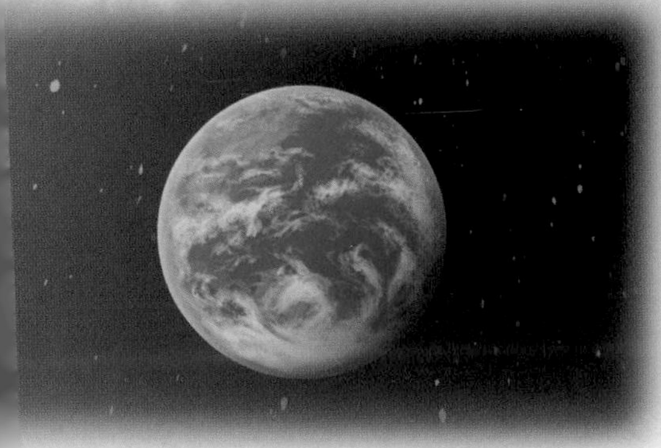

Story: Masahiro Totsuka / Art: Aguri Igarashi

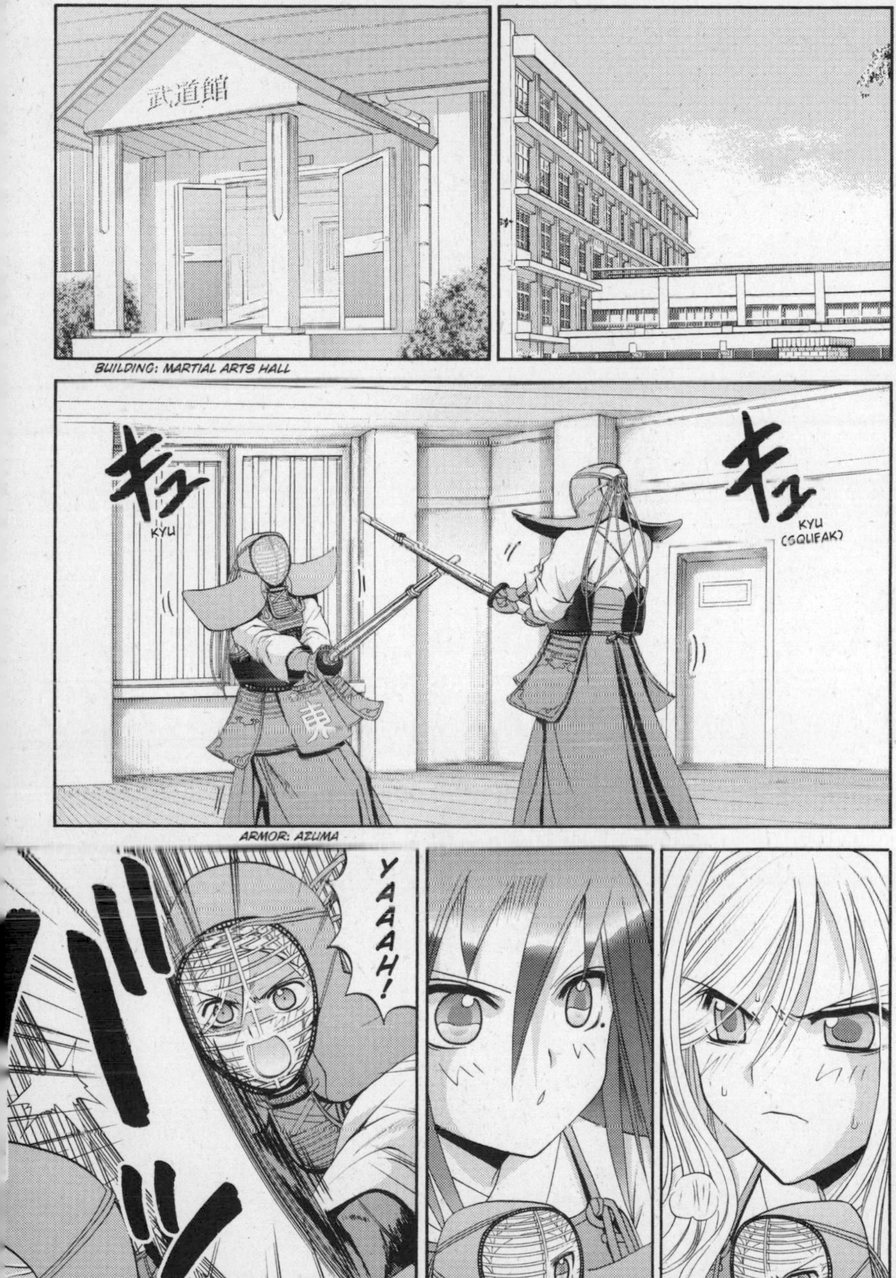
武道館
BUILDING: MARTIAL ARTS HALL
キュ
KYU (SQUIFAK)
キュ
KYU
東
ARMOR: AZUMA
YAAAAH!
BA (WHOOSH)

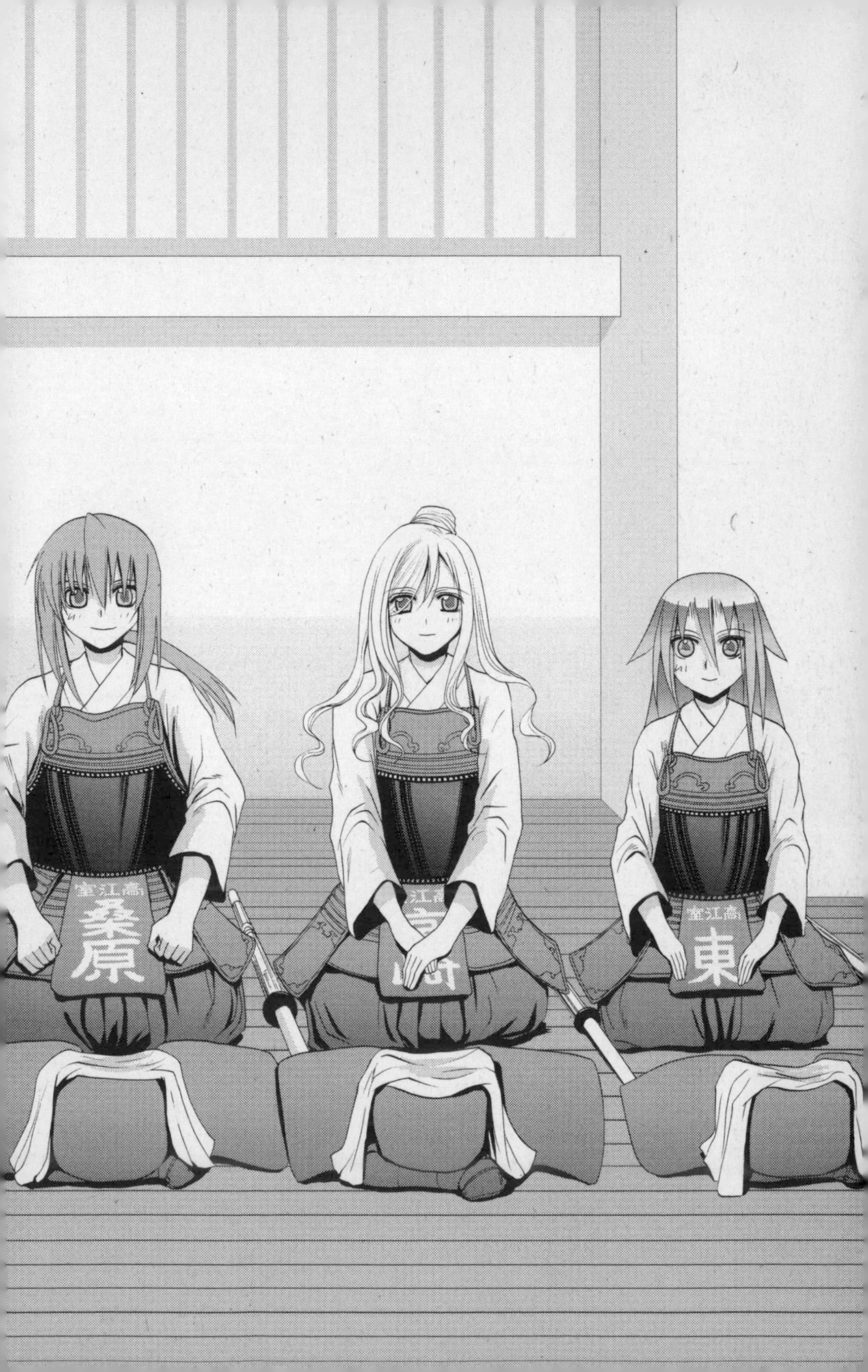
室江高
桑原
室江高
東

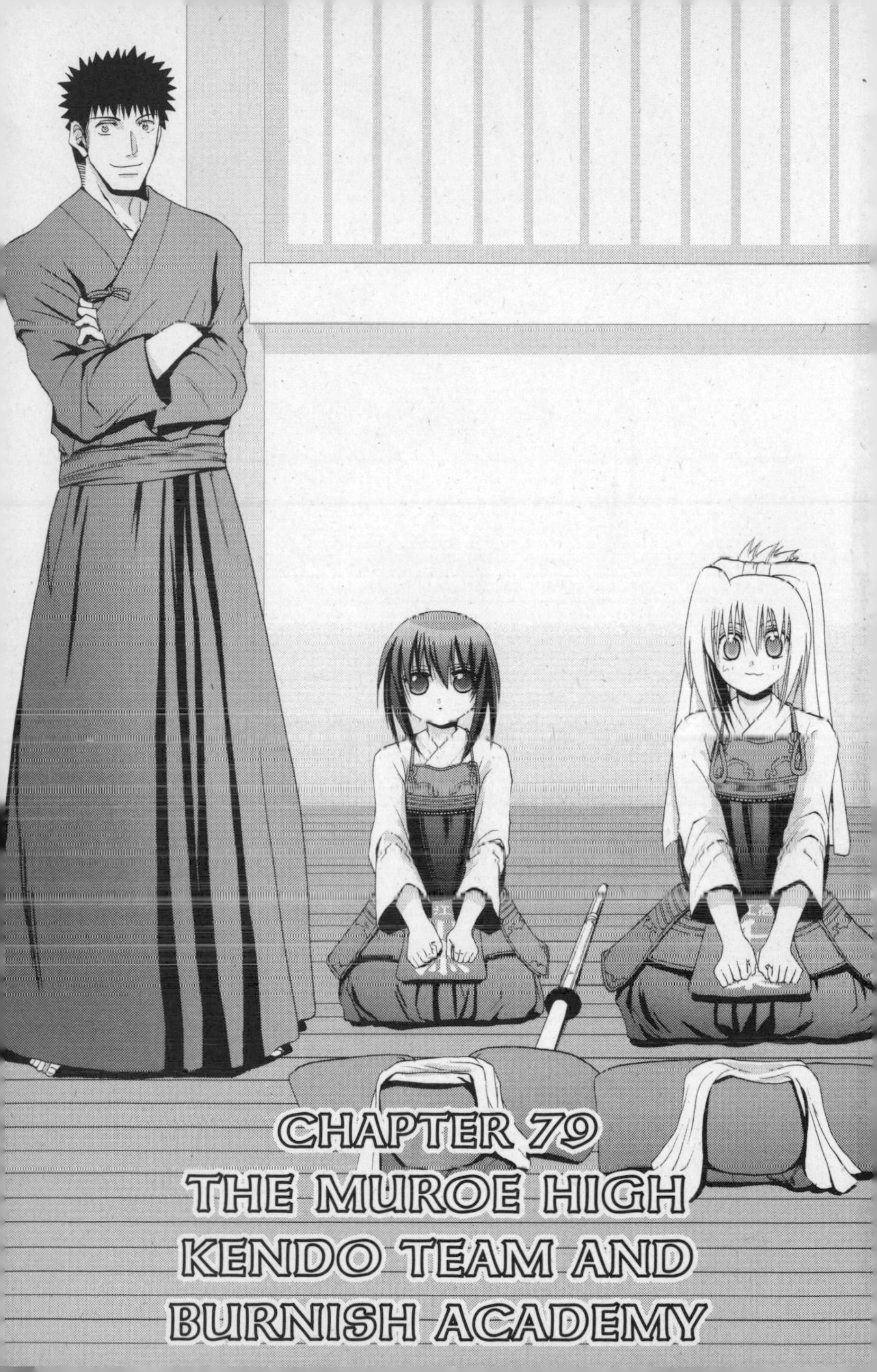
CHAPTER 79
THE MUROE HIGH KENDO TEAM AND BURNISH ACADEMY

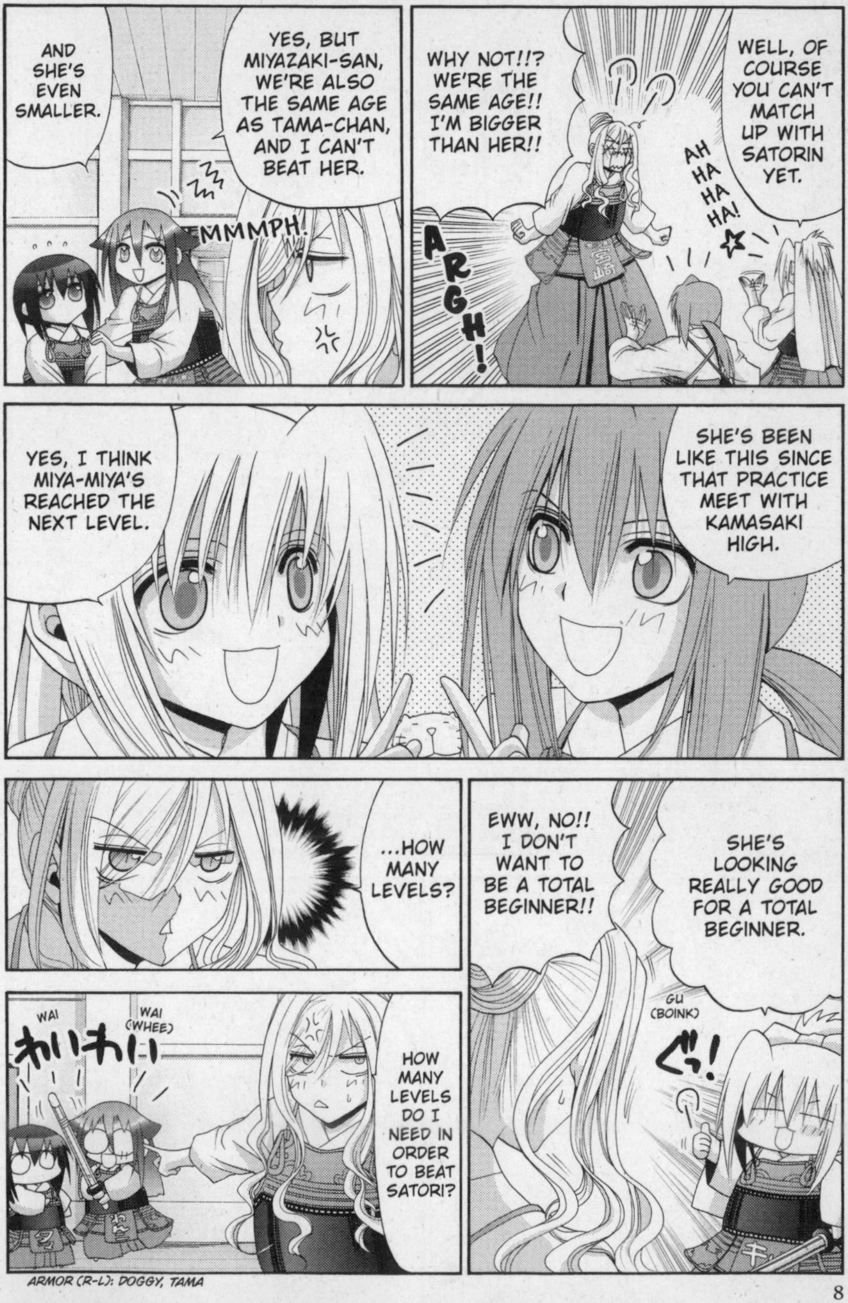
WELL, OF COURSE YOU CAN'T MATCH UP WITH SATORIN YET.
AH HA HA HA!
WHY NOT!!? WE'RE THE SAME AGE!! I'M BIGGER THAN HER!!
ARGH!
YES, BUT MIYAZAKI-SAN, WE'RE ALSO THE SAME AGE AS TAMA-CHAN, AND I CAN'T BEAT HER.
MMMPH!
AND SHE'S EVEN SMALLER.
SHE'S BEEN LIKE THIS SINCE THAT PRACTICE MEET WITH KAMASAKI HIGH.
YES, I THINK MIYA-MIYA'S REACHED THE NEXT LEVEL.
SHE'S LOOKING REALLY GOOD FOR A TOTAL BEGINNER.
EWW, NO!! I DON'T WANT TO BE A TOTAL BEGINNER!!
GU (BOINK)
ぐっ!
...HOW MANY LEVELS?
HOW MANY LEVELS DO I NEED IN ORDER TO BEAT SATORI?
WAI WAI (WHEE)
わいわい

ARMOR (R-L): DOGGY, TAMA

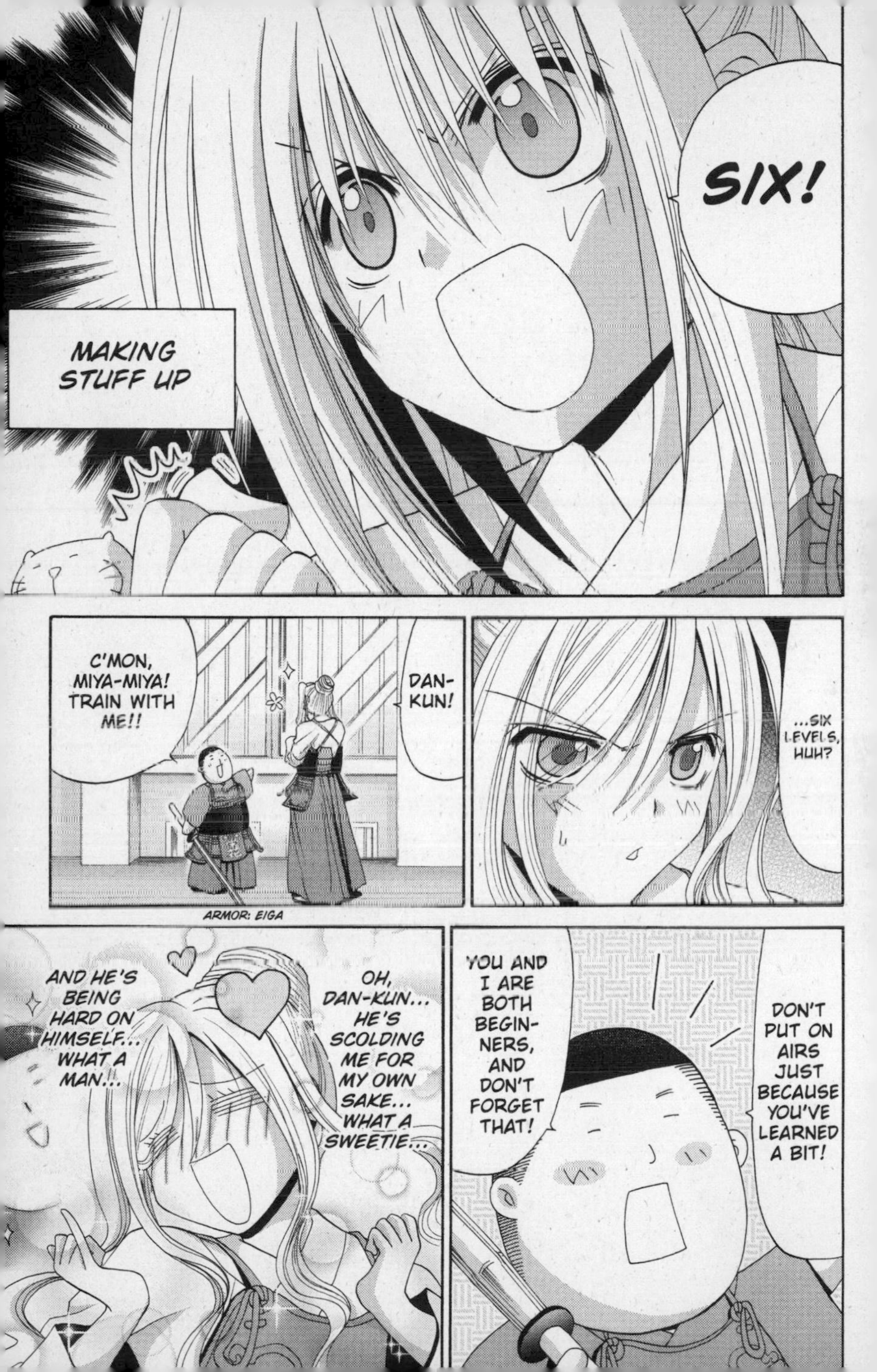
SIX!
MAKING STUFF UP
...SIX LEVELS, HUH?
DAN-KUN!
C'MON, MIYA-MIYA! TRAIN WITH ME!!
ARMOR: EIGA
DON'T PUT ON AIRS JUST BECAUSE YOU'VE LEARNED A BIT!
YOU AND I ARE BOTH BEGINNERS, AND DON'T FORGET THAT!
OH, DAN-KUN... HE'S SCOLDING ME FOR MY OWN SAKE... WHAT A SWEETIE...
AND HE'S BEING HARD ON HIMSELF... WHAT A MAN...

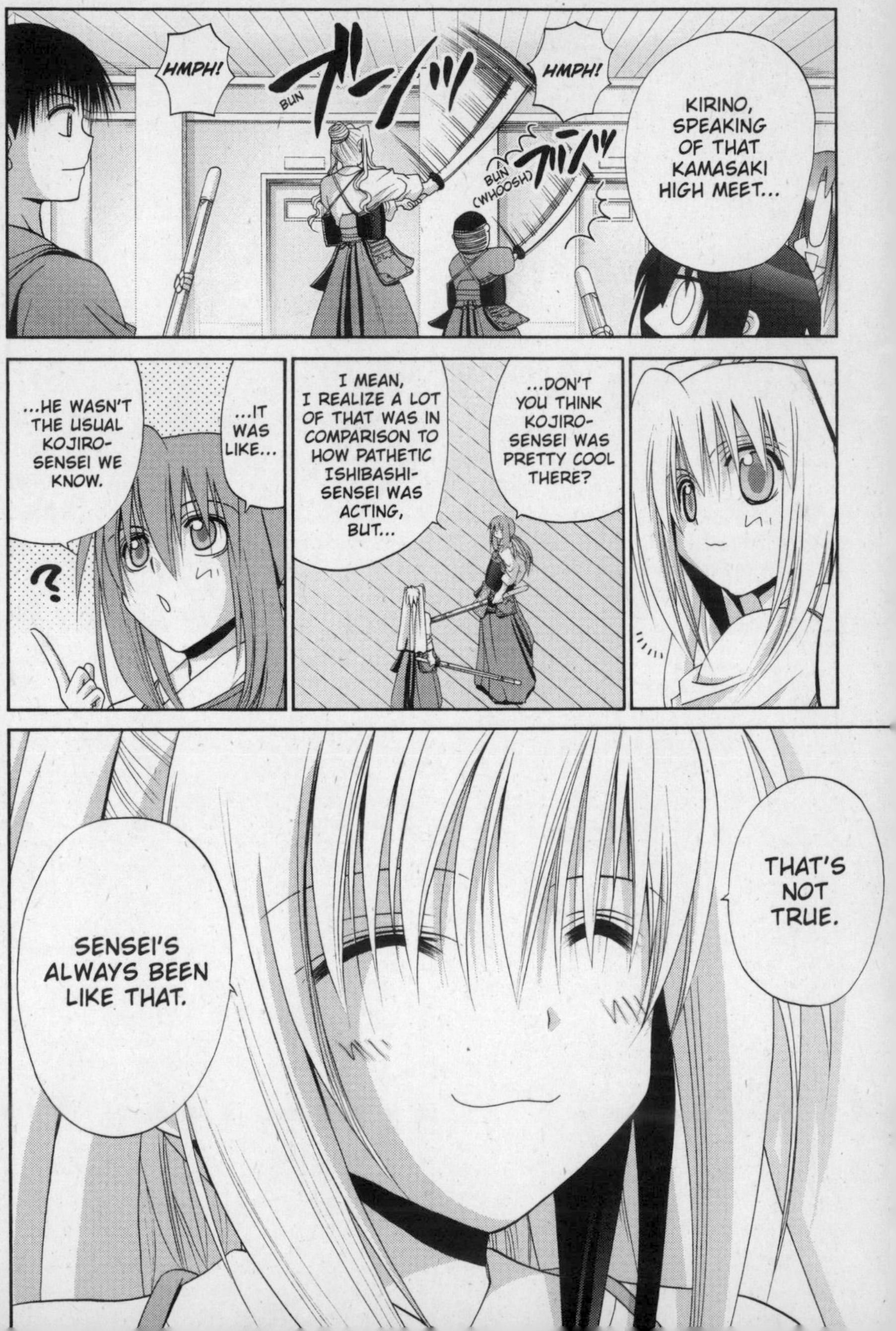
KIRINO, SPEAKING OF THAT KAMASAKI HIGH MEET...
HMPH!
BUN (WHOOSH)
BUN
HMPH!
...DON'T YOU THINK KOJIRO-SENSEI WAS PRETTY COOL THERE?
I MEAN, I REALIZE A LOT OF THAT WAS IN COMPARISON TO HOW PATHETIC ISHIBASHI-SENSEI WAS ACTING, BUT...
...IT WAS LIKE...
...HE WASN'T THE USUAL KOJIRO-SENSEI WE KNOW.
?
THAT'S NOT TRUE.
SENSEI'S ALWAYS BEEN LIKE THAT.

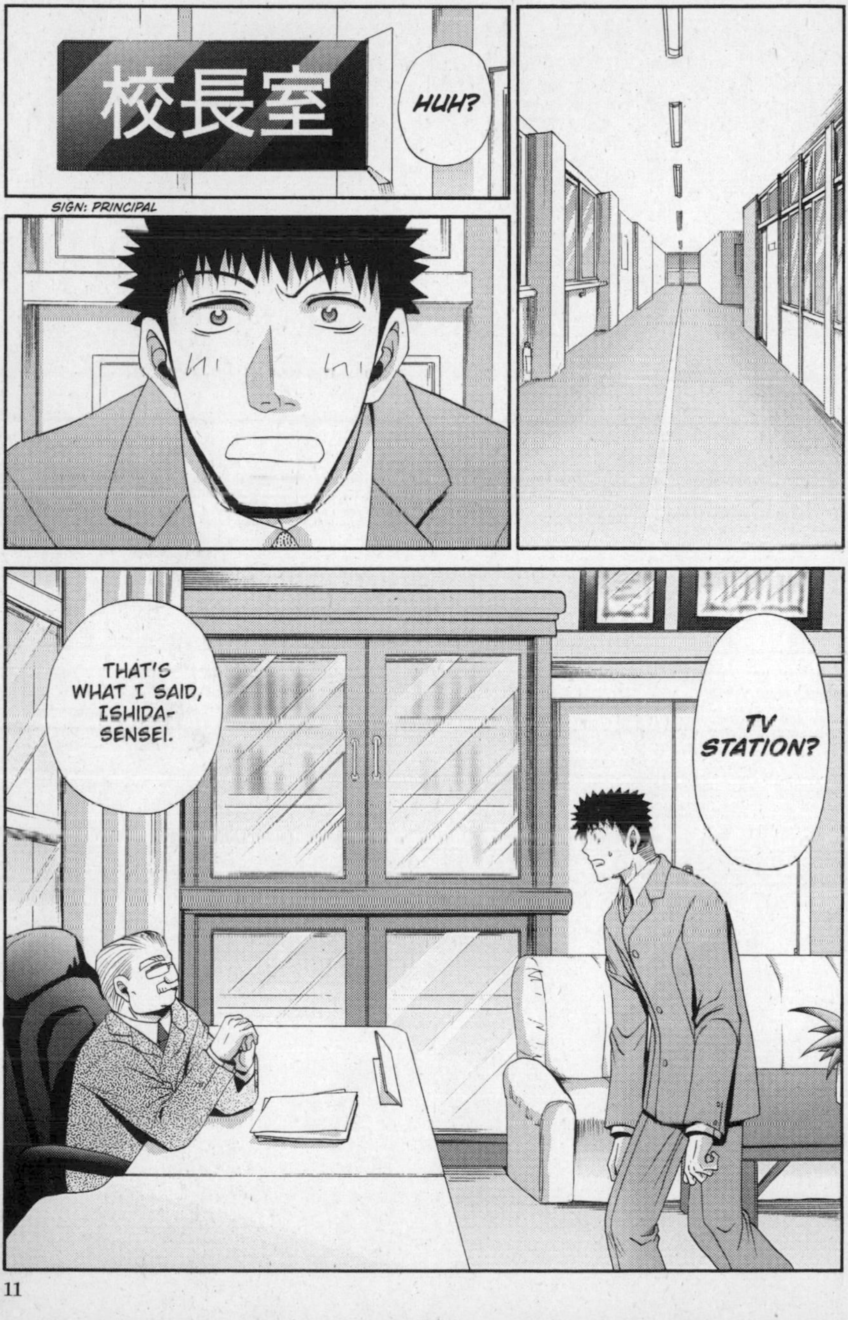
校長室
HUH?
SIGN: PRINCIPAL
TV STATION?
THAT'S WHAT I SAID, ISHIDA-SENSEI.

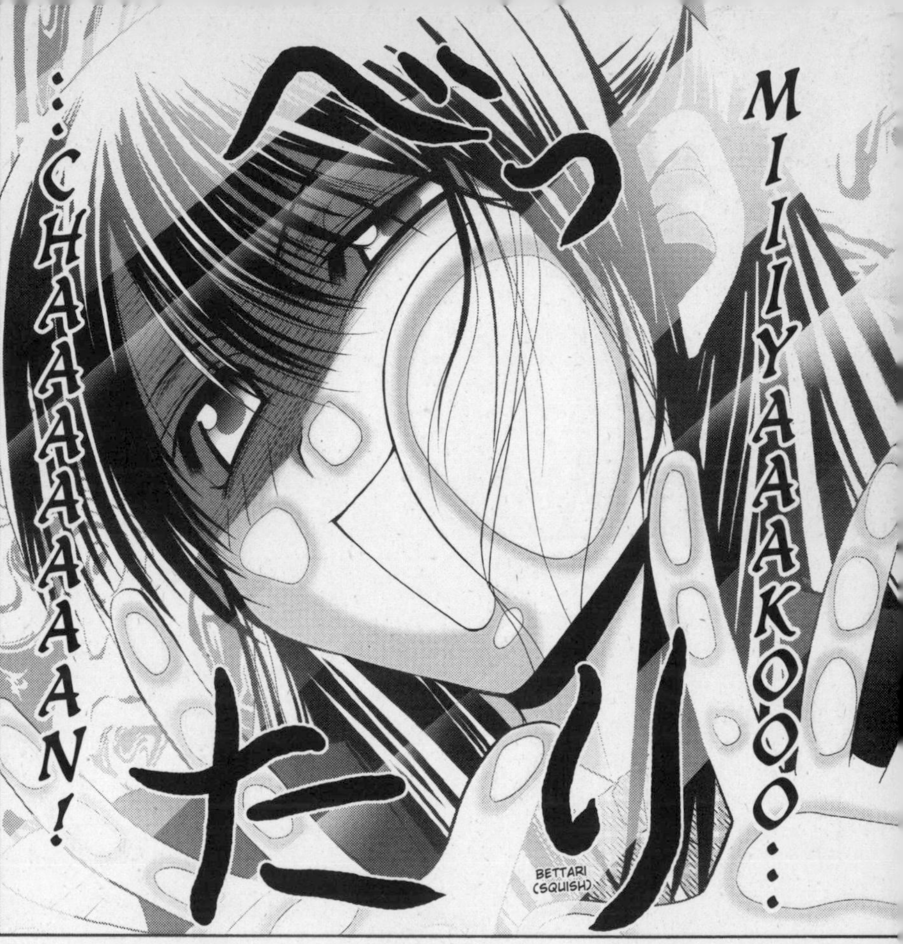
MIIYAAAKOOO...
...CHAAAAAAAN!
BETTARI (SQUISH)

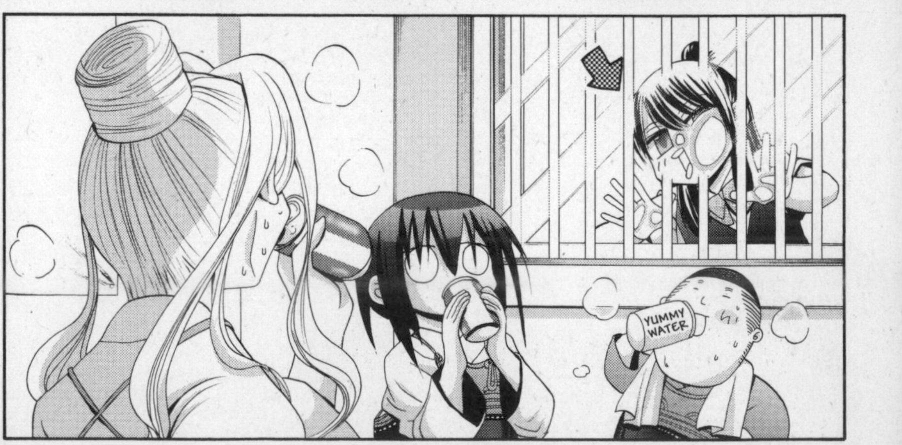
YUMMY WATER

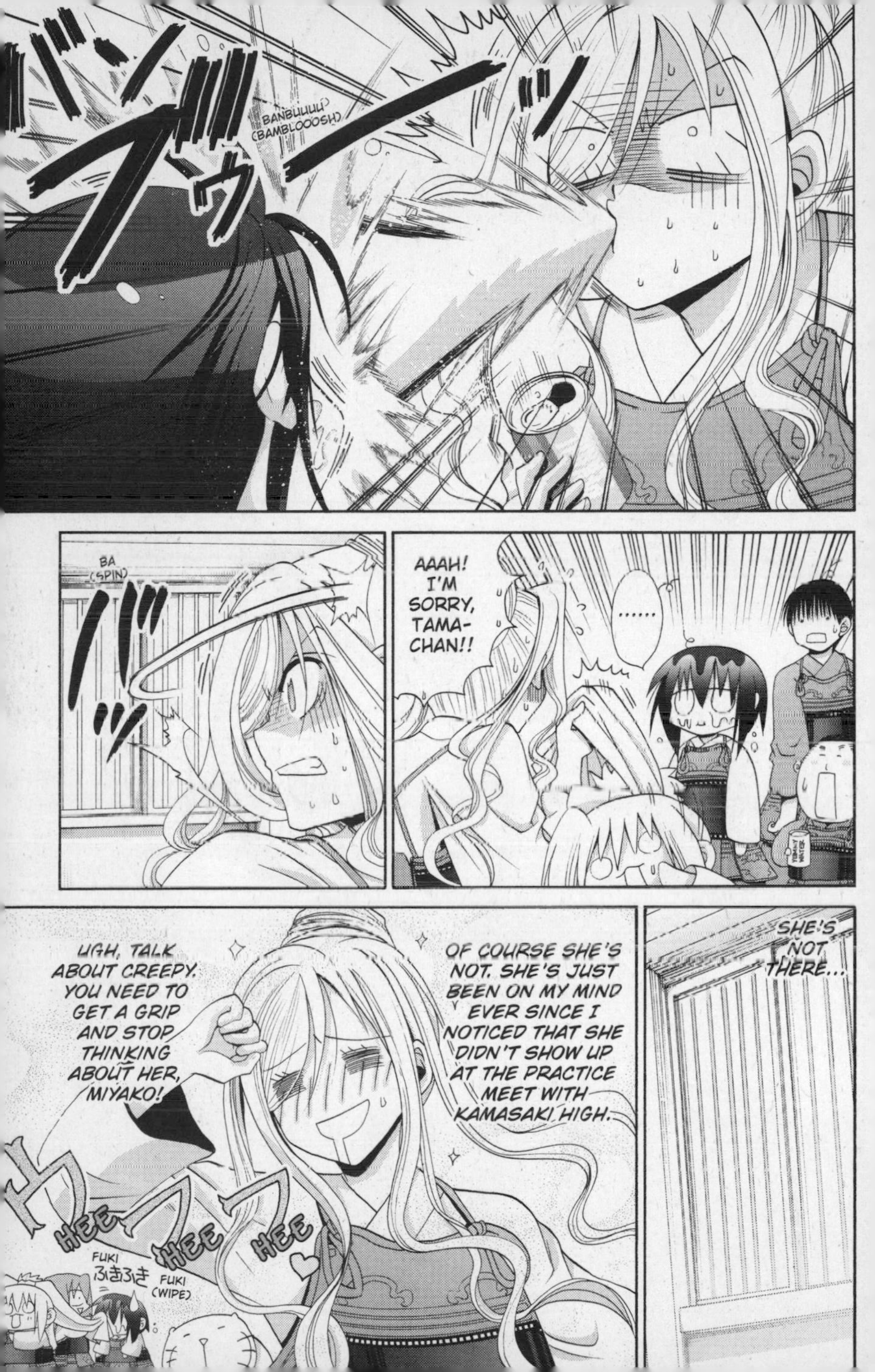
BANBUUUU (BAMBLOOOSH)
AAAH! I'M SORRY, TAMA-CHAN!!
......
BA (SPIN)
SHE'S NOT THERE...
OF COURSE SHE'S NOT. SHE'S JUST BEEN ON MY MIND EVER SINCE I NOTICED THAT SHE DIDN'T SHOW UP AT THE PRACTICE MEET WITH KAMASAKI HIGH.
UGH, TALK ABOUT CREEPY. YOU NEED TO GET A GRIP AND STOP THINKING ABOUT HER, MIYAKO!
HEE HEE HEE
FUKI ふきふき FUKI (WIPE)

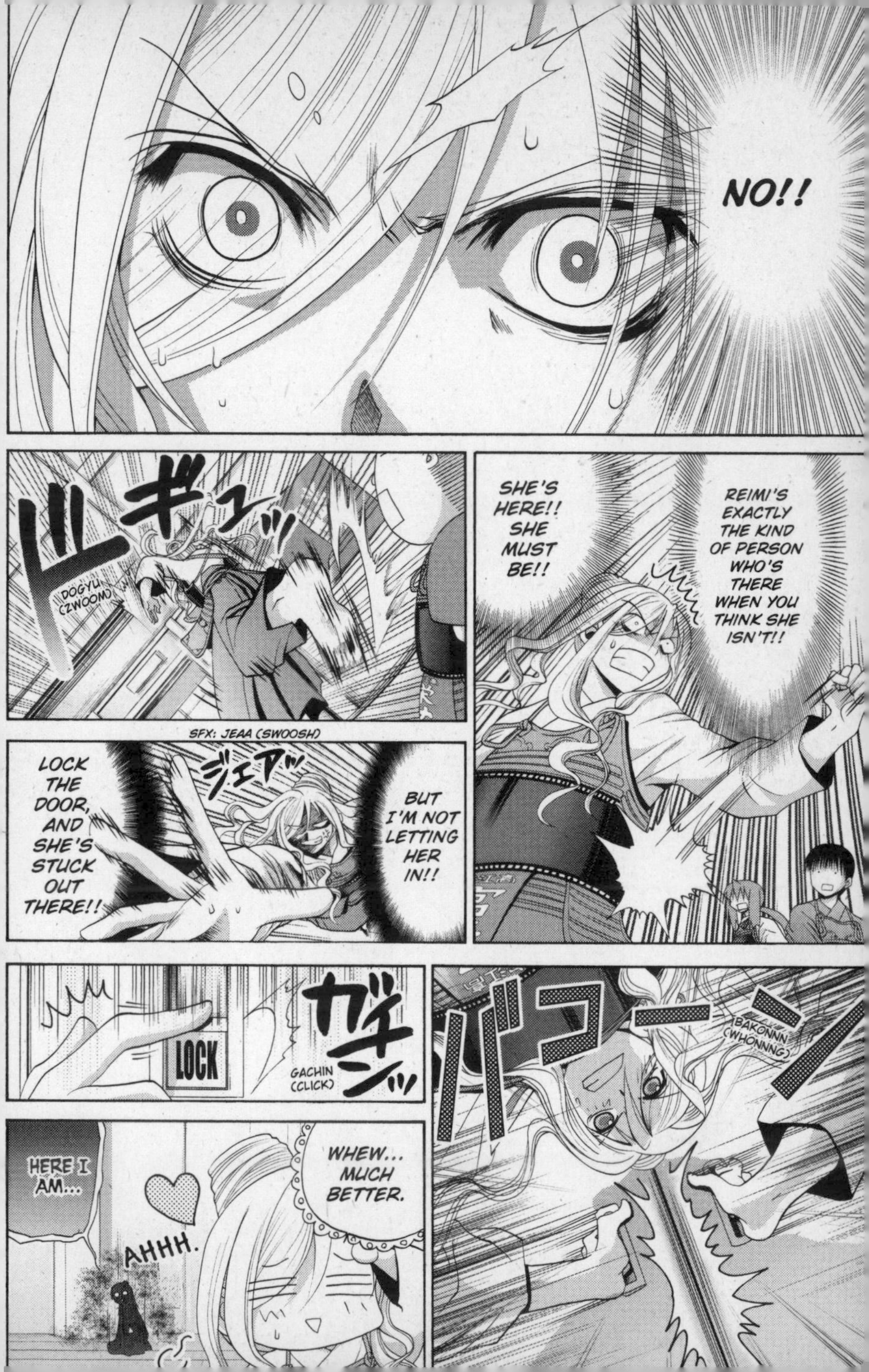
NO!!
REIMI'S EXACTLY THE KIND OF PERSON WHO'S THERE WHEN YOU THINK SHE ISN'T!!
SHE'S HERE!! SHE MUST BE!!
DOGYU (ZWOOM)
SFX: JEAA (SWOOSH)
BUT I'M NOT LETTING HER IN!!
LOCK THE DOOR, AND SHE'S STUCK OUT THERE!!
BAKONNN (WHONNNG)
GACHIN (CLICK)
LOCK
WHEW... MUCH BETTER.
AHHH.
HERE I AM...

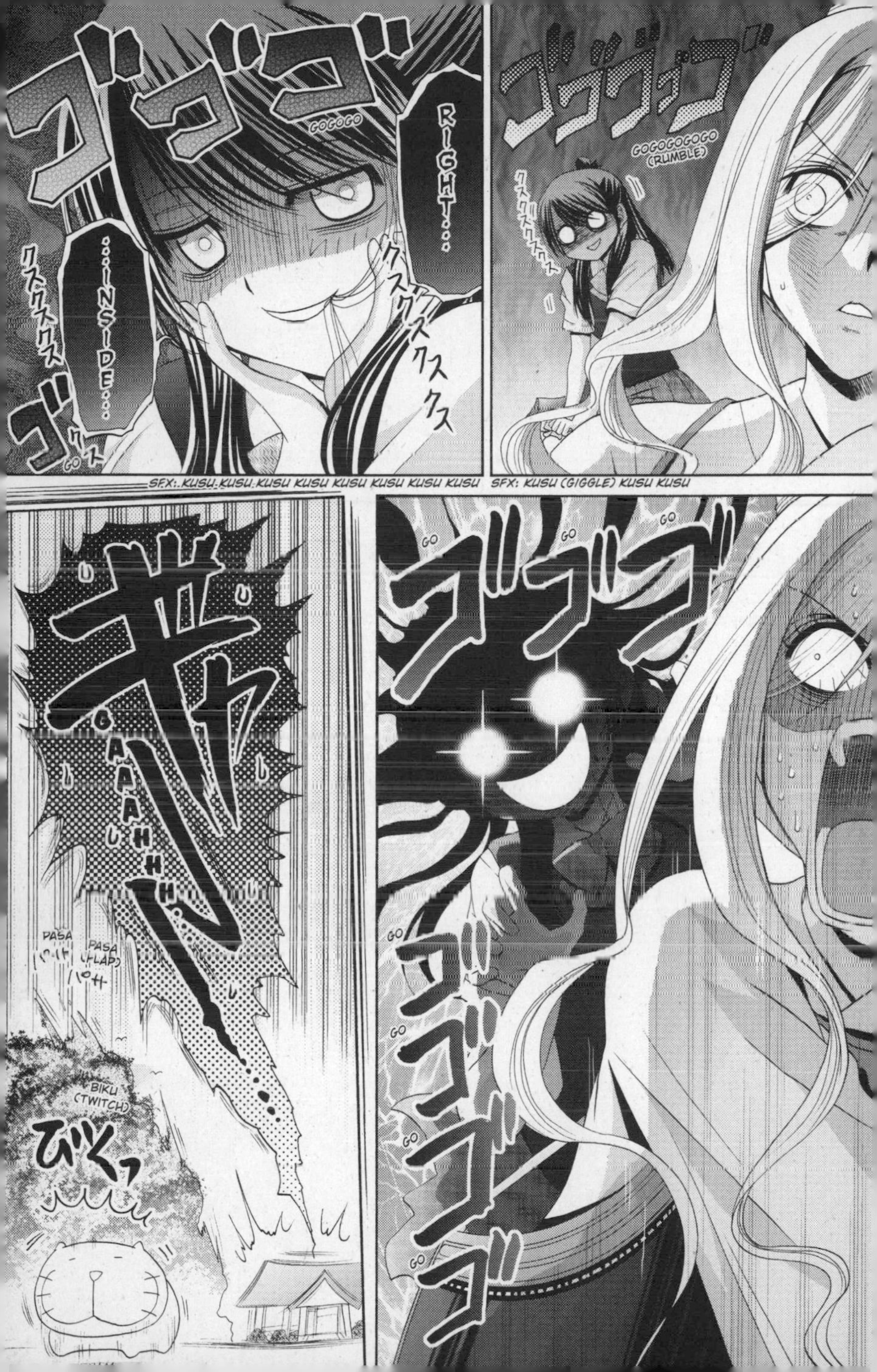
GOGOGOGOGO (RUMBLE)
SFX: KUSU (GIGGLE) KUSU KUSU
GOGOGO
RIGHT...
...INSIDE...
GO
SFX: KUSU KUSU KUSU KUSU KUSU KUSU KUSU KUSU
GO
GO
GO
GO
GO
GO
GO
GAAAHHH...
PASA PASA (FLAP)
BIKU (TWITCH)

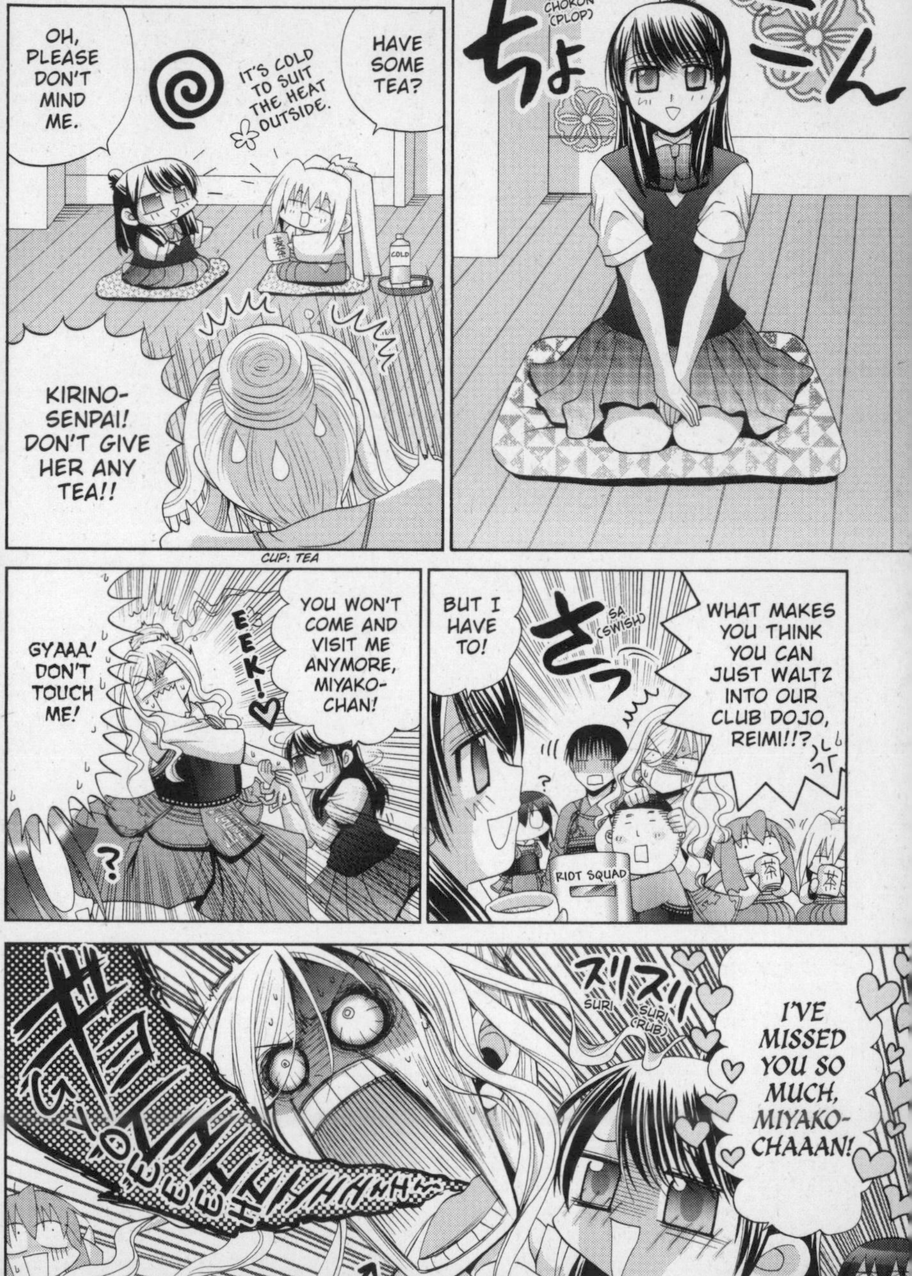
ちょこん
CHOKON (PLOP)
HAVE SOME TEA?
IT'S COLD TO SUIT THE HEAT OUTSIDE.
OH, PLEASE DON'T MIND ME.
KIRINO-SENPAI! DON'T GIVE HER ANY TEA!!
COLD
CUP: TEA
WHAT MAKES YOU THINK YOU CAN JUST WALTZ INTO OUR CLUB DOJO, REIMI!!?
さっ
SA (SWISH)
BUT I HAVE TO!
RIOT SQUAD
茶
茶
YOU WON'T COME AND VISIT ME ANYMORE, MIYAKO-CHAN!
EEK!
GYAAA! DON'T TOUCH ME!
I'VE MISSED YOU SO MUCH, MIYAKO-CHAAAN!
スリスリ
SURI SURI (RUB)
NOTE: MIYA-MIYA

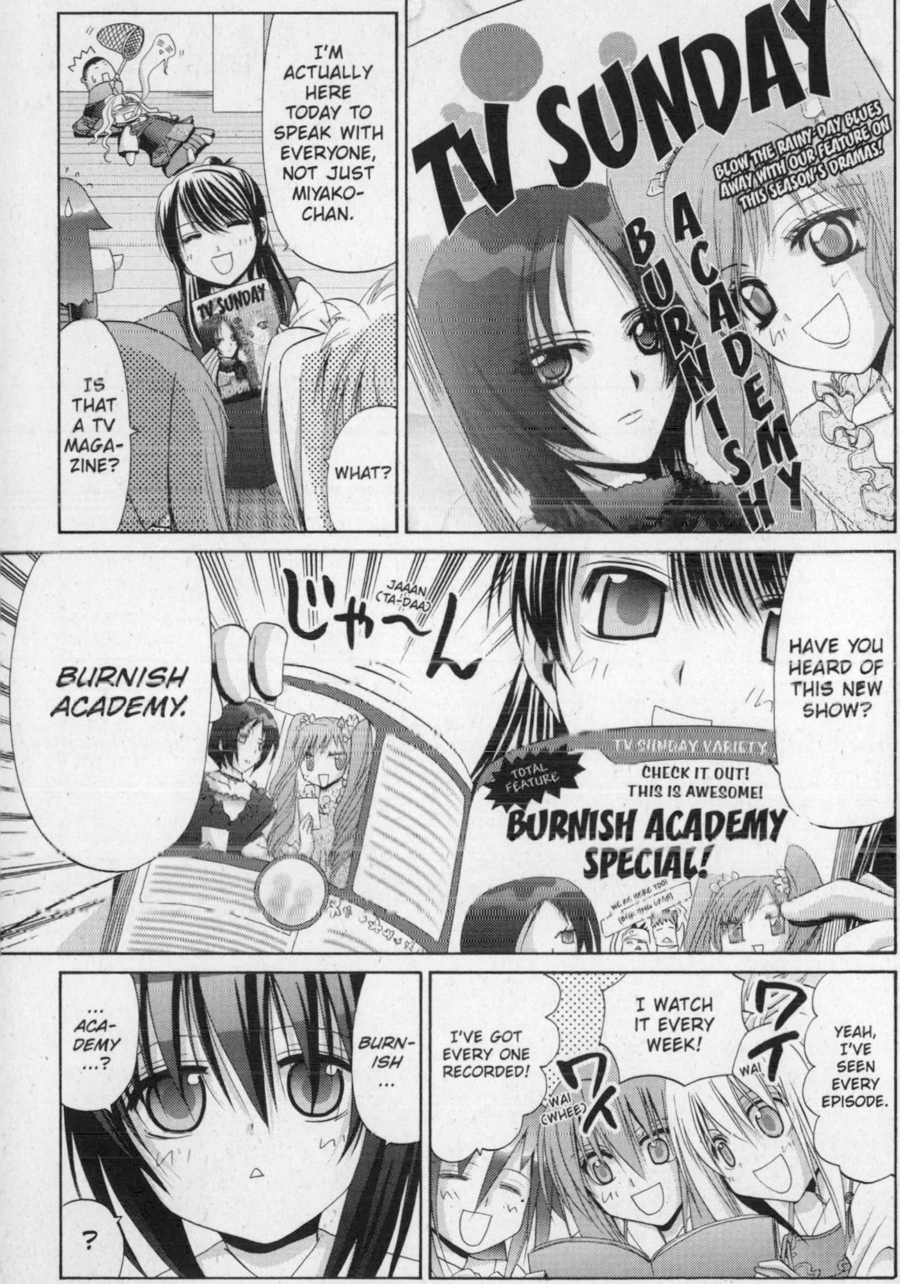
TV SUNDAY
BLOW THE RAINY-DAY BLUES AWAY WITH OUR FEATURE ON THIS SEASON'S DRAMAS!
BURNISH ACADEMY
I'M ACTUALLY HERE TODAY TO SPEAK WITH EVERYONE, NOT JUST MIYAKO-CHAN.
TV SUNDAY
WHAT?
IS THAT A TV MAGAZINE?
HAVE YOU HEARD OF THIS NEW SHOW?
TV SUNDAY VARIETY
TOTAL FEATURE
CHECK IT OUT! THIS IS AWESOME!
BURNISH ACADEMY SPECIAL!
じゃ～ん
JAAAN (TA-DAA)
BURNISH ACADEMY.
YEAH, I'VE SEEN EVERY EPISODE.
ワイ
WAI
I WATCH IT EVERY WEEK!
ワイ
WAI (WHEE)
I'VE GOT EVERY ONE RECORDED!
BURN-ISH ...
... ACA-DEMY ...?
?

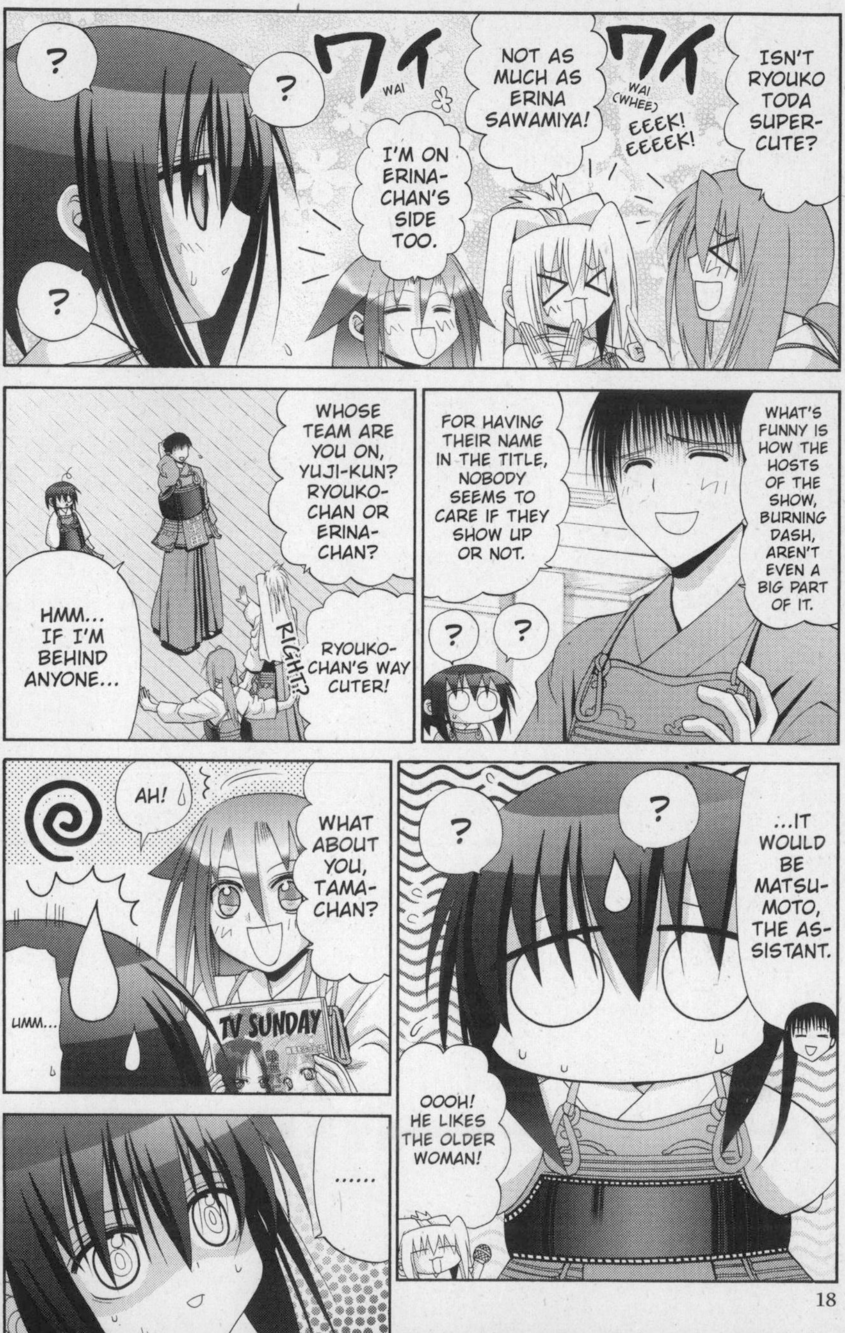
ISN'T RYOUKO TODA SUPER-CUTE?
ワイ
WAI (WHEE)
EEEK! EEEEK!
NOT AS MUCH AS ERINA SAWAMIYA!
I'M ON ERINA-CHAN'S SIDE TOO.
ワイ
WAI
?
?
?
WHAT'S FUNNY IS HOW THE HOSTS OF THE SHOW, BURNING DASH, AREN'T EVEN A BIG PART OF IT.
FOR HAVING THEIR NAME IN THE TITLE, NOBODY SEEMS TO CARE IF THEY SHOW UP OR NOT.
?
?
WHOSE TEAM ARE YOU ON, YUJI-KUN? RYOUKO-CHAN OR ERINA-CHAN?
RYOUKO-CHAN'S WAY CUTER!
RIGHT!?
HMM... IF I'M BEHIND ANYONE...
...IT WOULD BE MATSU-MOTO, THE AS-SISTANT.
?
?
OOOH! HE LIKES THE OLDER WOMAN!
WHAT ABOUT YOU, TAMA-CHAN?
AH!
UMM...
TV SUNDAY
......

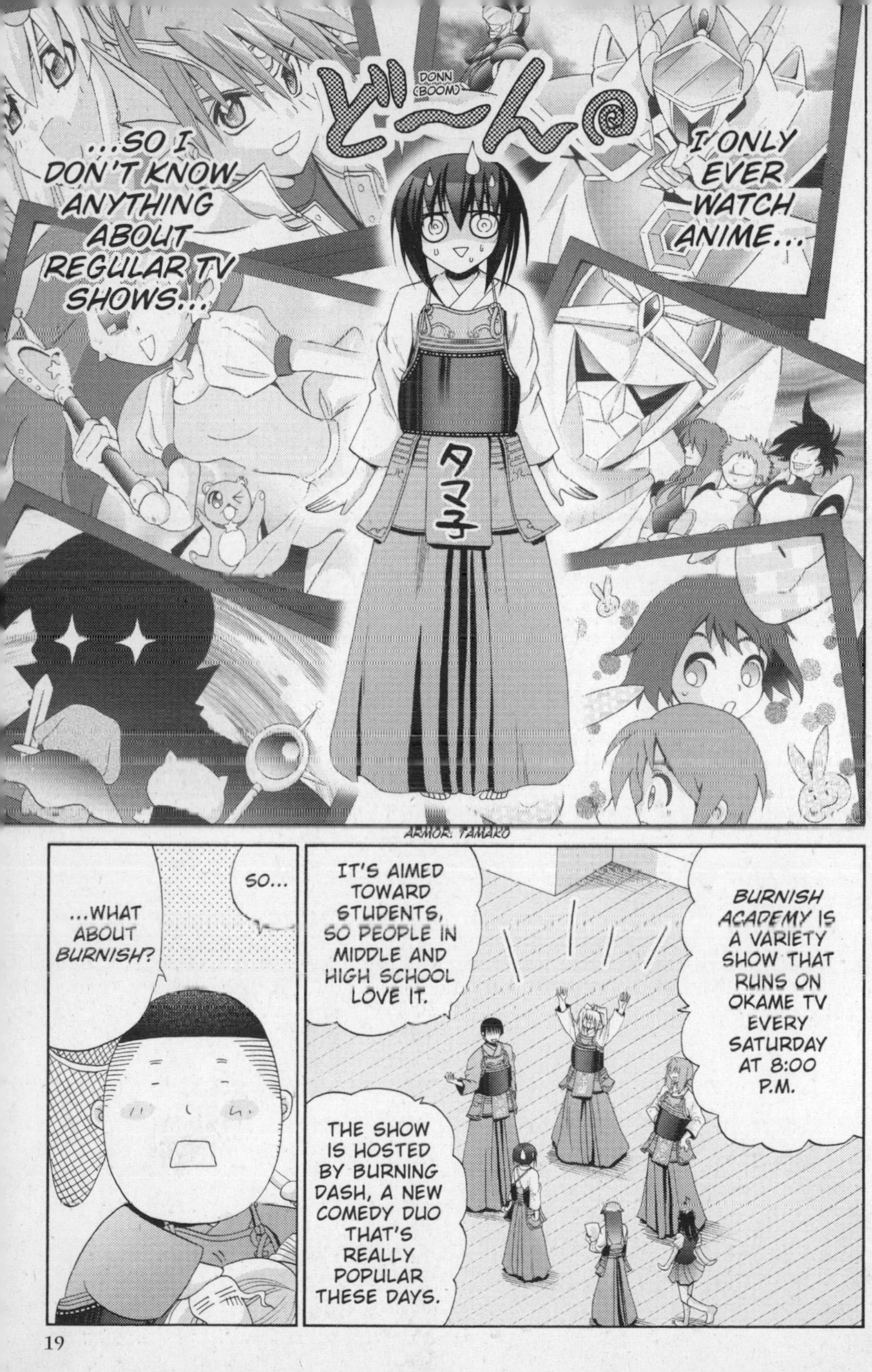
I ONLY EVER WATCH ANIME...
どーん
DONN (BOOM)
...SO I DON'T KNOW ANYTHING ABOUT REGULAR TV SHOWS...
タマ子
ARMOR: TAMAKO
BURNISH ACADEMY IS A VARIETY SHOW THAT RUNS ON OKAME TV EVERY SATURDAY AT 8:00 P.M.
IT'S AIMED TOWARD STUDENTS, SO PEOPLE IN MIDDLE AND HIGH SCHOOL LOVE IT.
THE SHOW IS HOSTED BY BURNING DASH, A NEW COMEDY DUO THAT'S REALLY POPULAR THESE DAYS.
SO...
...WHAT ABOUT BURNISH?

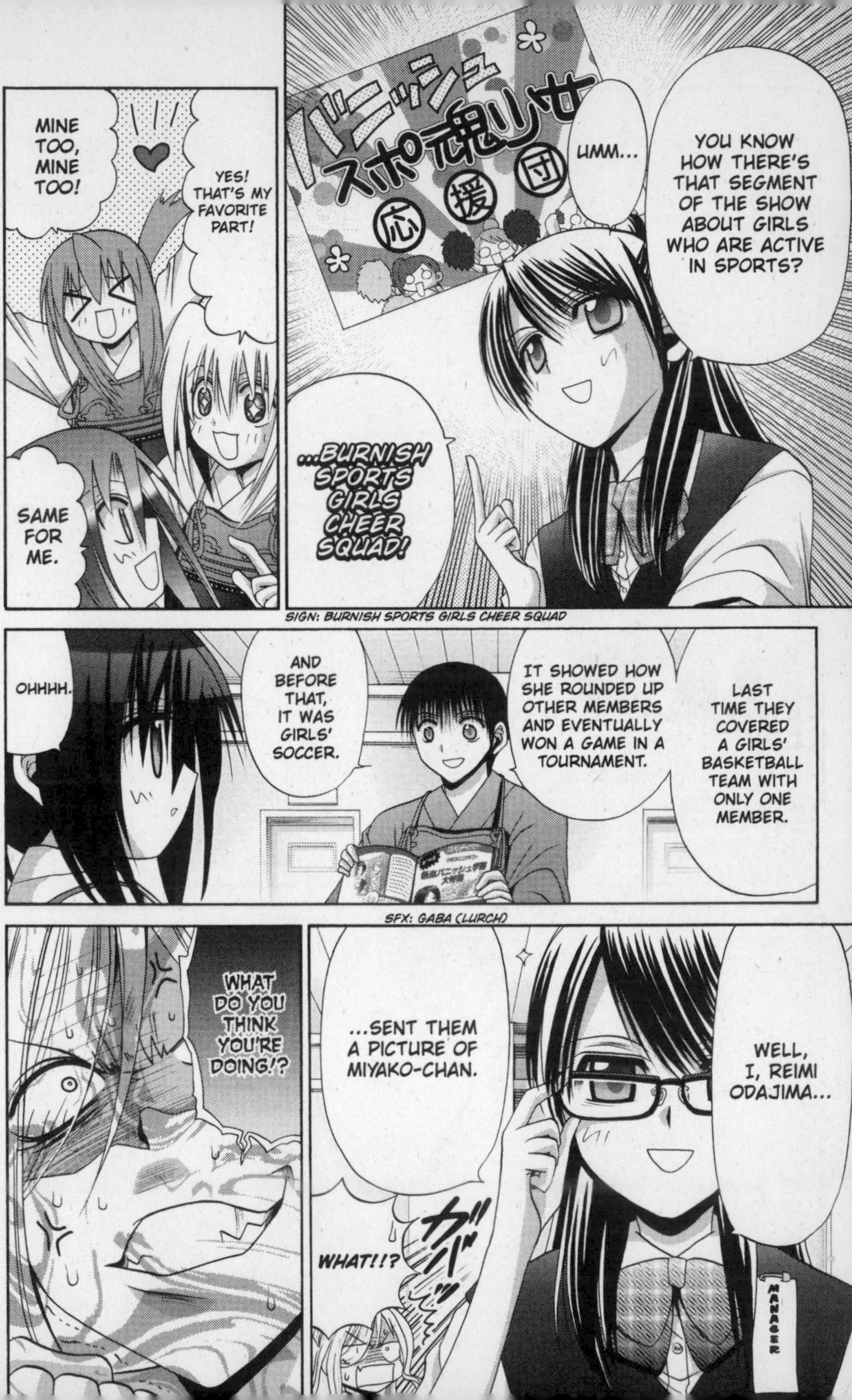
YOU KNOW HOW THERE'S THAT SEGMENT OF THE SHOW ABOUT GIRLS WHO ARE ACTIVE IN SPORTS?
UMM...
...BURNISH SPORTS GIRLS CHEER SQUAD!
YES! THAT'S MY FAVORITE PART!
MINE TOO, MINE TOO!
SAME FOR ME.
SIGN: BURNISH SPORTS GIRLS CHEER SQUAD
LAST TIME THEY COVERED A GIRLS' BASKETBALL TEAM WITH ONLY ONE MEMBER.
IT SHOWED HOW SHE ROUNDED UP OTHER MEMBERS AND EVENTUALLY WON A GAME IN A TOURNAMENT.
AND BEFORE THAT, IT WAS GIRLS' SOCCER.
OHHHH.
SFX: GABA (LURCH)
WELL, I, REIMI ODAJIMA...
...SENT THEM A PICTURE OF MIYAKO-CHAN.
WHAT!!?
MANAGER
WHAT DO YOU THINK YOU'RE DOING!?

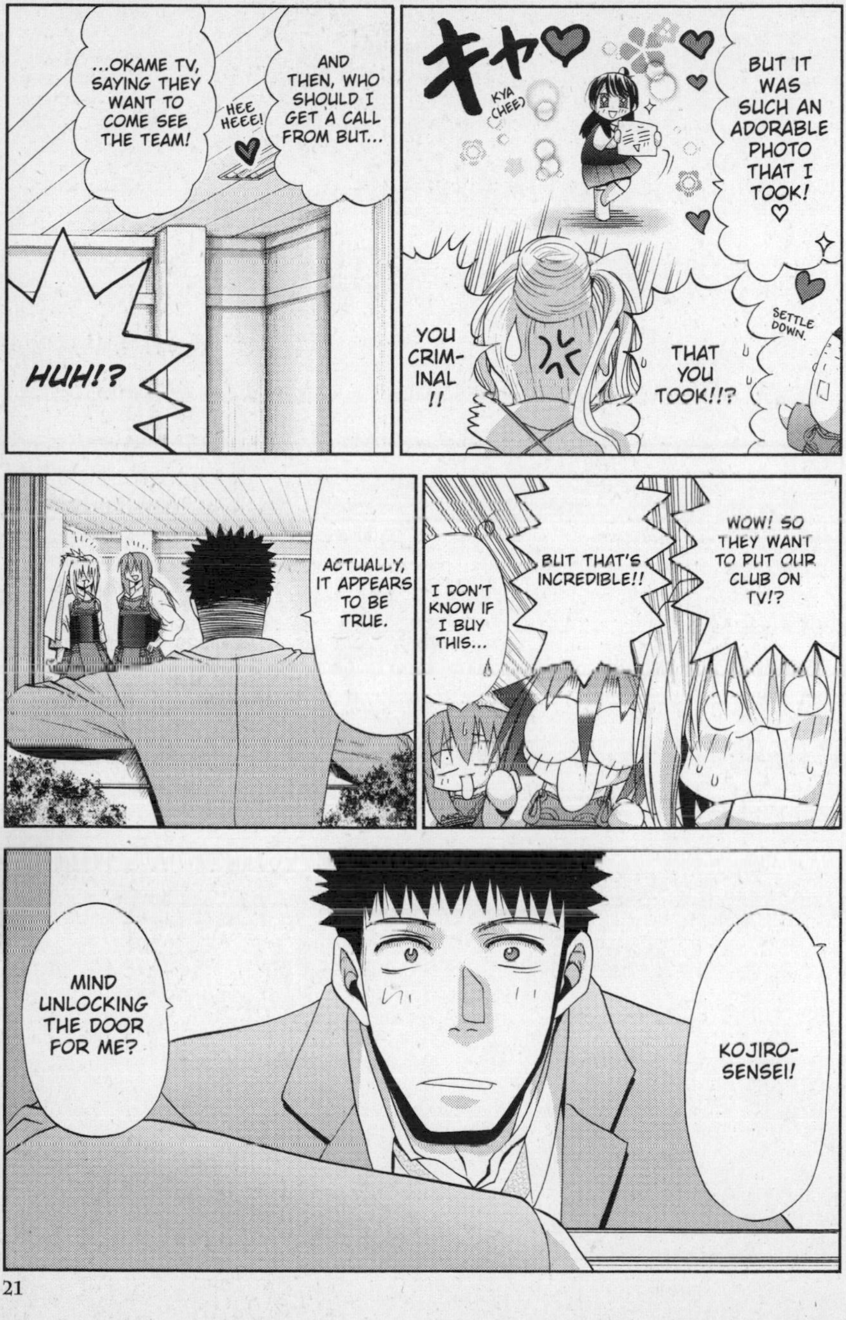
キャ♥
KYA (HEE)
BUT IT WAS SUCH AN ADORABLE PHOTO THAT I TOOK! ♡
SETTLE DOWN.
THAT YOU TOOK!!?
YOU CRIMINAL!!
AND THEN, WHO SHOULD I GET A CALL FROM BUT...
HEE HEEE! ♥
...OKAME TV, SAYING THEY WANT TO COME SEE THE TEAM!
HUH!?
WOW! SO THEY WANT TO PUT OUR CLUB ON TV!?
BUT THAT'S INCREDIBLE!!
I DON'T KNOW IF I BUY THIS...
ACTUALLY, IT APPEARS TO BE TRUE.
KOJIRO-SENSEI!
MIND UNLOCKING THE DOOR FOR ME?

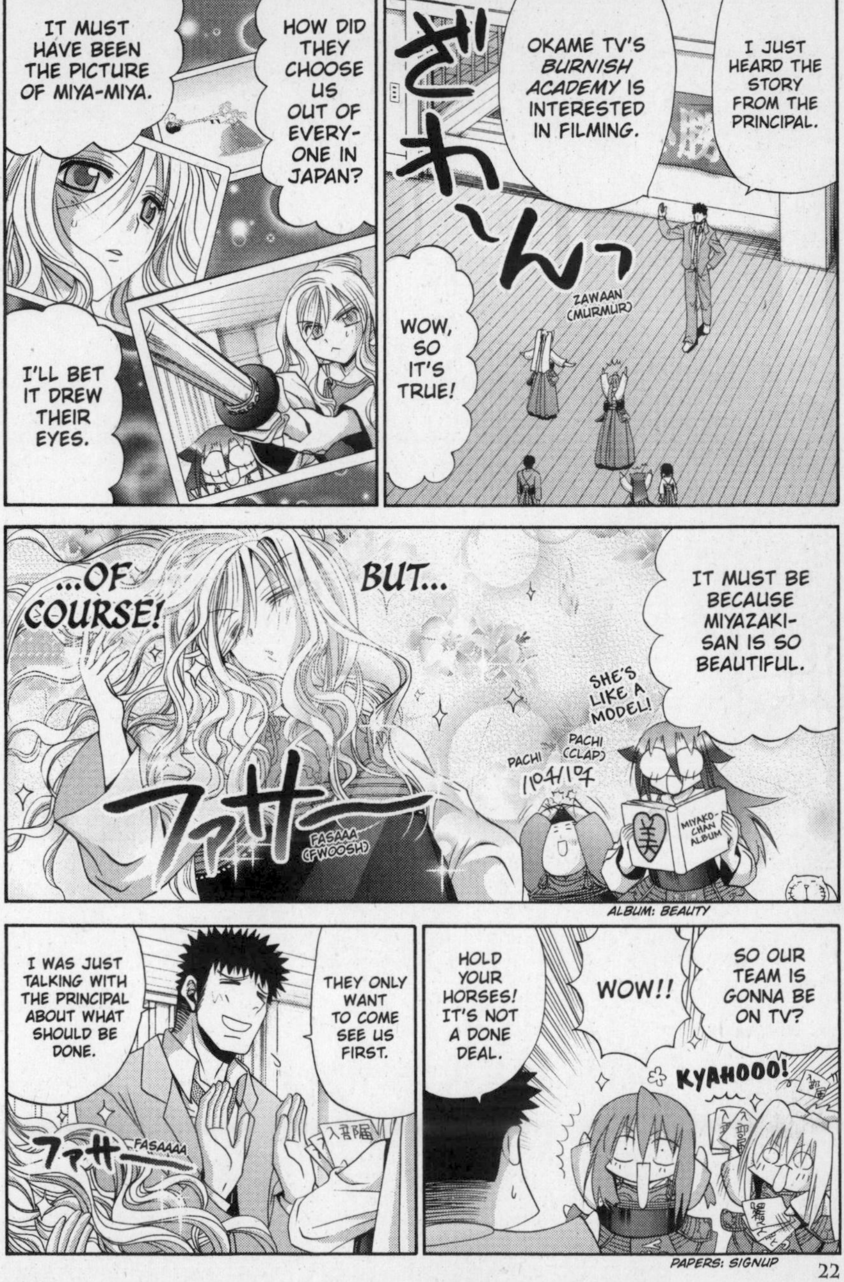
I JUST HEARD THE STORY FROM THE PRINCIPAL.
OKAME TV'S *BURNISH ACADEMY* IS INTERESTED IN FILMING.
ZAWAAN (MURMUR)
WOW, SO IT'S TRUE!
HOW DID THEY CHOOSE US OUT OF EVERY-ONE IN JAPAN?
IT MUST HAVE BEEN THE PICTURE OF MIYA-MIYA.
I'LL BET IT DREW THEIR EYES.
IT MUST BE BECAUSE MIYAZAKI-SAN IS SO BEAUTIFUL.
SHE'S LIKE A MODEL!
PACHI PACHI (CLAP)
MIYAKO-CHAN ALBUM
BUT...
...OF COURSE!
FASAAA (FWOOSH)
ALBUM: BEAUTY
SO OUR TEAM IS GONNA BE ON TV?
WOW!!
KYAHOOO!
HOLD YOUR HORSES! IT'S NOT A DONE DEAL.
THEY ONLY WANT TO COME SEE US FIRST.
I WAS JUST TALKING WITH THE PRINCIPAL ABOUT WHAT SHOULD BE DONE.
FASAAAA
PAPERS: SIGNUP

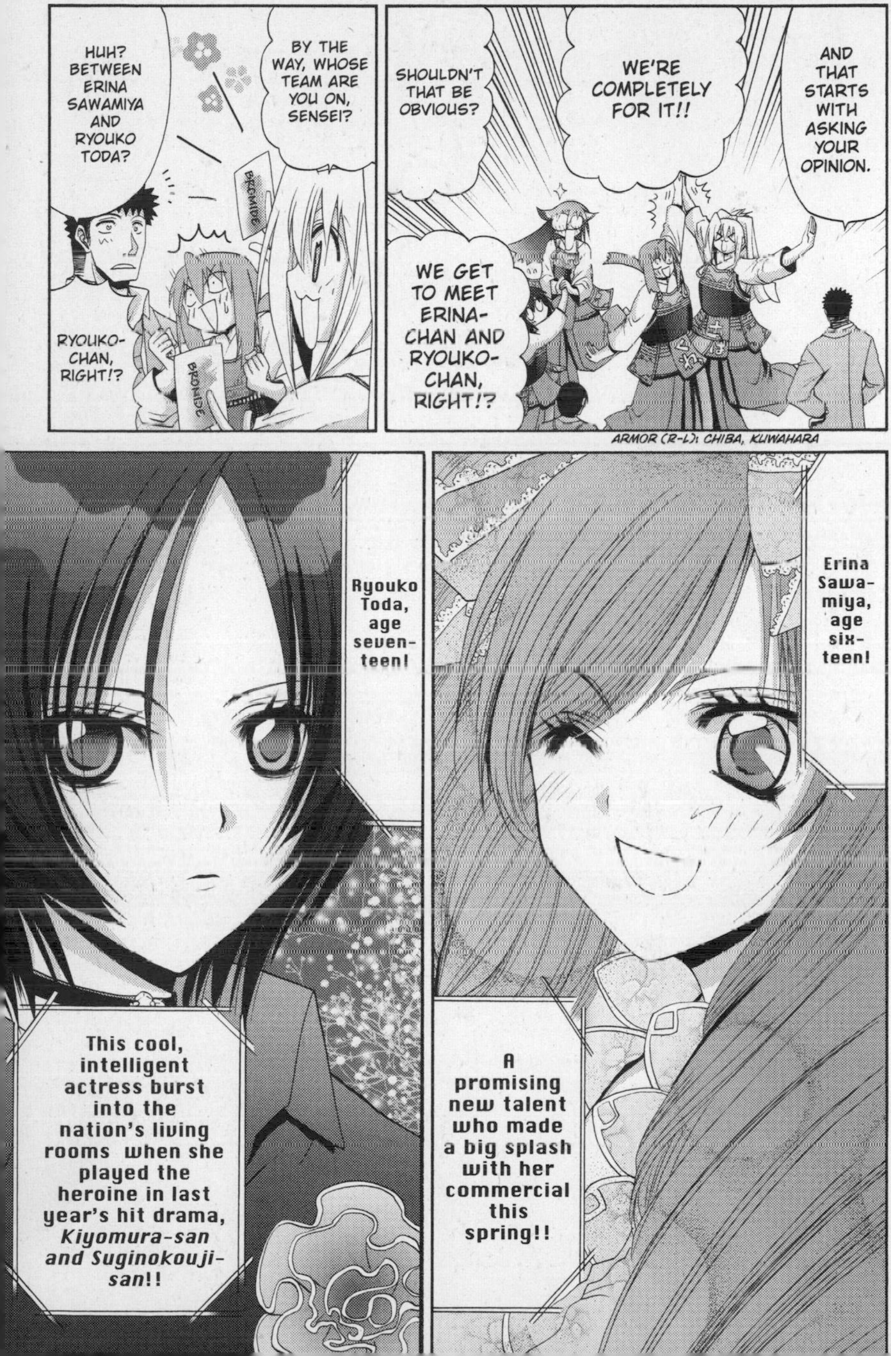
AND THAT STARTS WITH ASKING YOUR OPINION.
WE'RE COMPLETELY FOR IT!!
SHOULDN'T THAT BE OBVIOUS?
WE GET TO MEET ERINA-CHAN AND RYOUKO-CHAN, RIGHT!?
ARMOR (R-L): CHIBA, KUWAHARA
BY THE WAY, WHOSE TEAM ARE YOU ON, SENSEI?
HUH? BETWEEN ERINA SAWAMIYA AND RYOUKO TODA?
BROMIDE
RYOUKO-CHAN, RIGHT!?
BROMIDE
Erina Sawamiya, age sixteen!
A promising new talent who made a big splash with her commercial this spring!!
Ryouko Toda, age seventeen!
This cool, intelligent actress burst into the nation's living rooms when she played the heroine in last year's hit drama, *Kiyomura-san and Suginokouji-san*!!

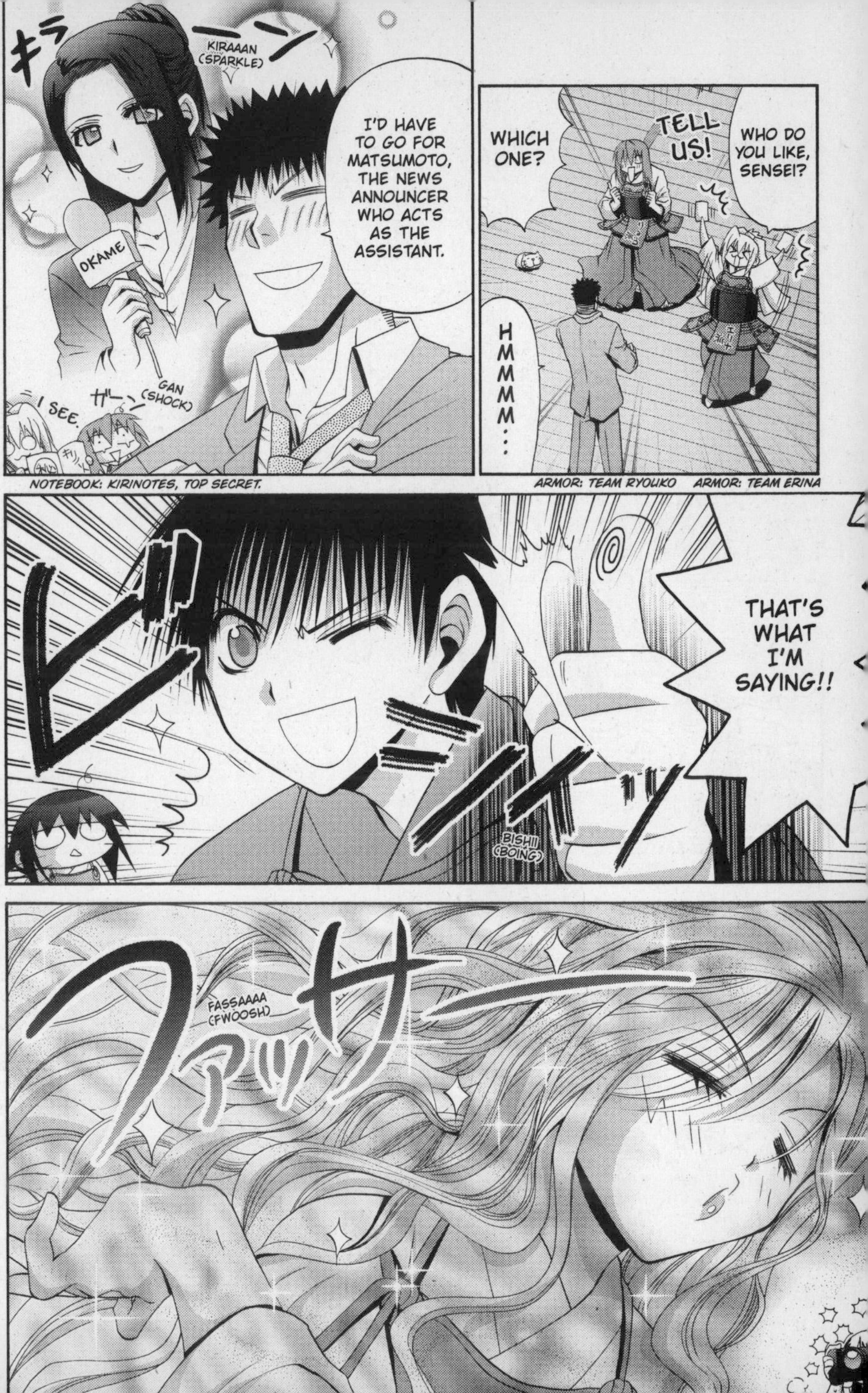
WHO DO YOU LIKE, SENSEI?
TELL US!
WHICH ONE?
HMMMM...
ARMOR: TEAM RYOUKO
ARMOR: TEAM ERINA
KIRAAAN (SPARKLE)
I'D HAVE TO GO FOR MATSUMOTO, THE NEWS ANNOUNCER WHO ACTS AS THE ASSISTANT.
OKAME
GAN (SHOCK)
I SEE.
NOTEBOOK: KIRINOTES, TOP SECRET.
THAT'S WHAT I'M SAYING!!
BISHII (BOING)
FASSAAAA (FWOOSH)

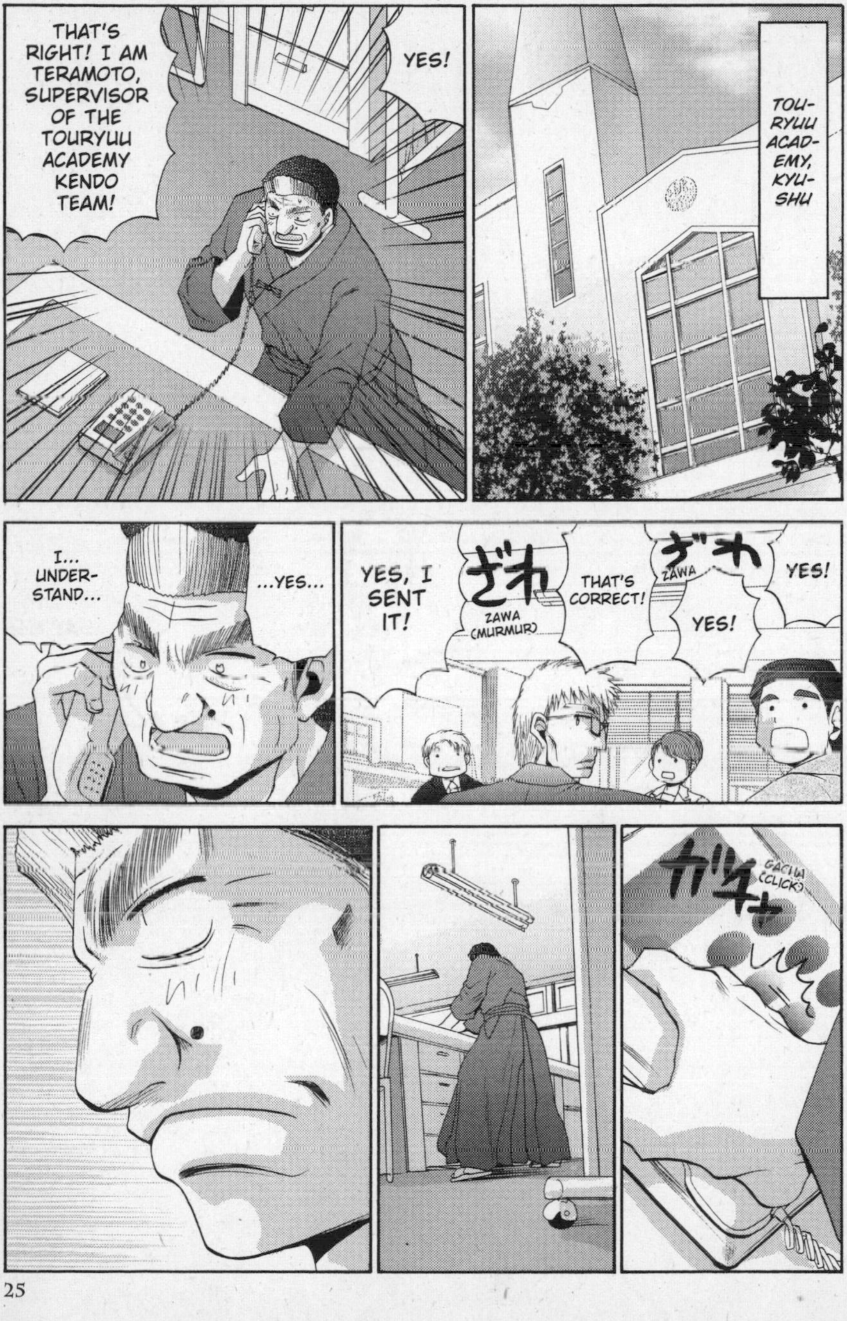
TOURYUU ACADEMY, KYUSHU
YES!
THAT'S RIGHT! I AM TERAMOTO, SUPERVISOR OF THE TOURYUU ACADEMY KENDO TEAM!
YES!
ざわ
ZAWA
YES!
THAT'S CORRECT!
ざわ
ZAWA (MURMUR)
YES, I SENT IT!
...YES...
I... UNDERSTAND...
GACHA (CLICK)

BAMBOO BLADE
バンブーブレード

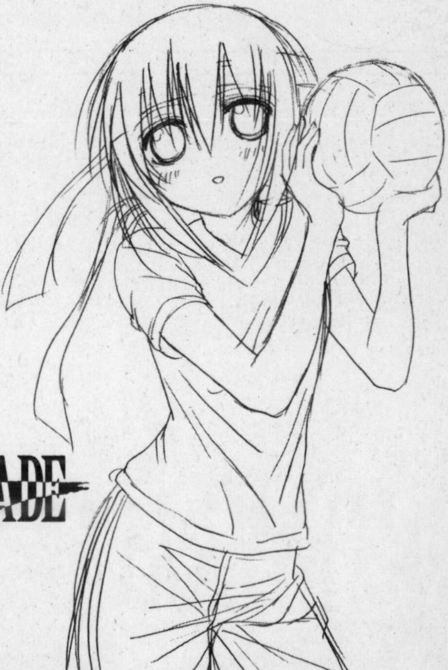

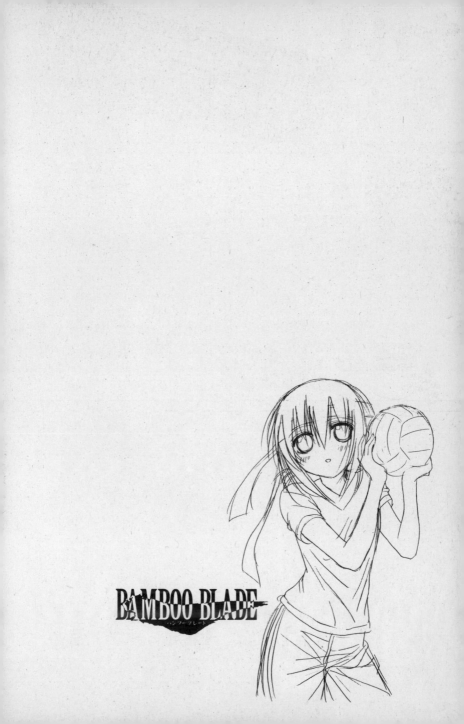

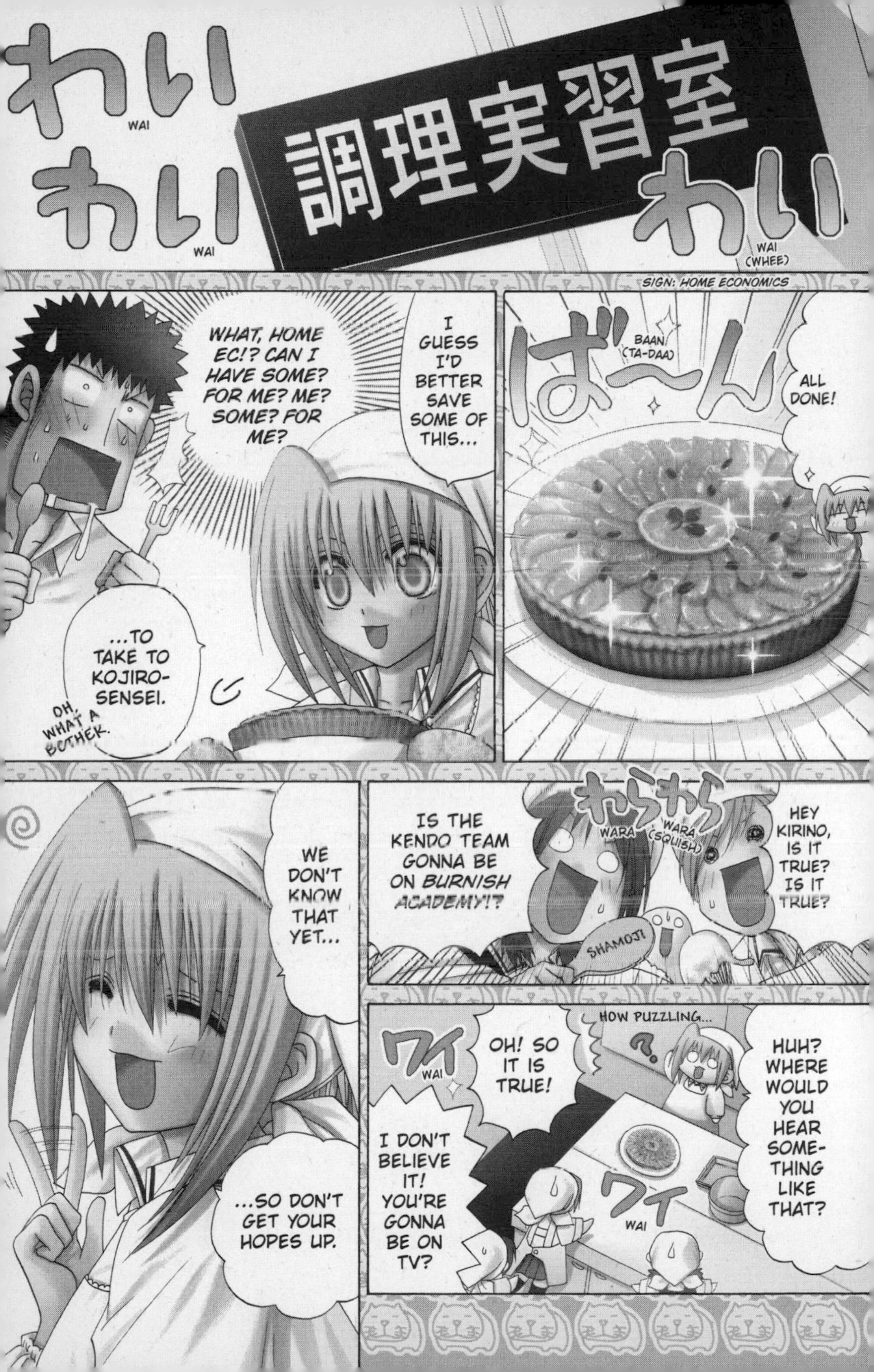

わいわい
WAI
WAI
調理実習室
わい
WAI (WHEE)
SIGN: HOME ECONOMICS
ばーん
BAAN (TA-DAA)
ALL DONE!
I GUESS I'D BETTER SAVE SOME OF THIS...
WHAT, HOME EC!? CAN I HAVE SOME? FOR ME? ME? SOME? FOR ME?
...TO TAKE TO KOJIRO-SENSEI.
OH, WHAT A BOTHER.
HEY KIRINO, IS IT TRUE? IS IT TRUE?
わらわら
WARA WARA (SQUISH)
IS THE KENDO TEAM GONNA BE ON BURNISH ACADEMY!?
SHAMOJI
HUH? WHERE WOULD YOU HEAR SOMETHING LIKE THAT?
HOW PUZZLING...
OH! SO IT IS TRUE!
ワイ
WAI
I DON'T BELIEVE IT! YOU'RE GONNA BE ON TV?
ワイ
WAI
WE DON'T KNOW THAT YET...
...SO DON'T GET YOUR HOPES UP.

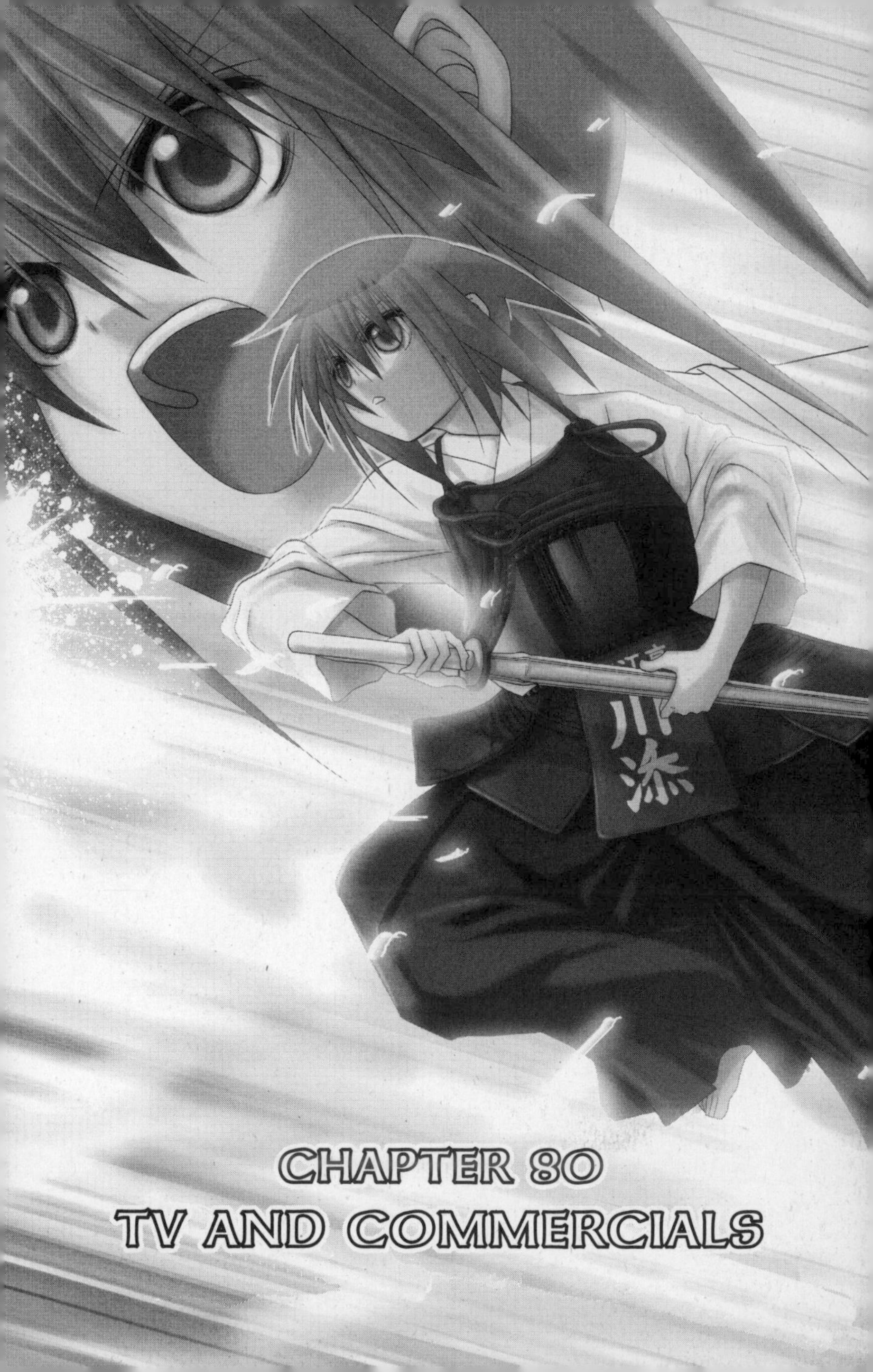
川添

CHAPTER 80
TV AND COMMERCIALS

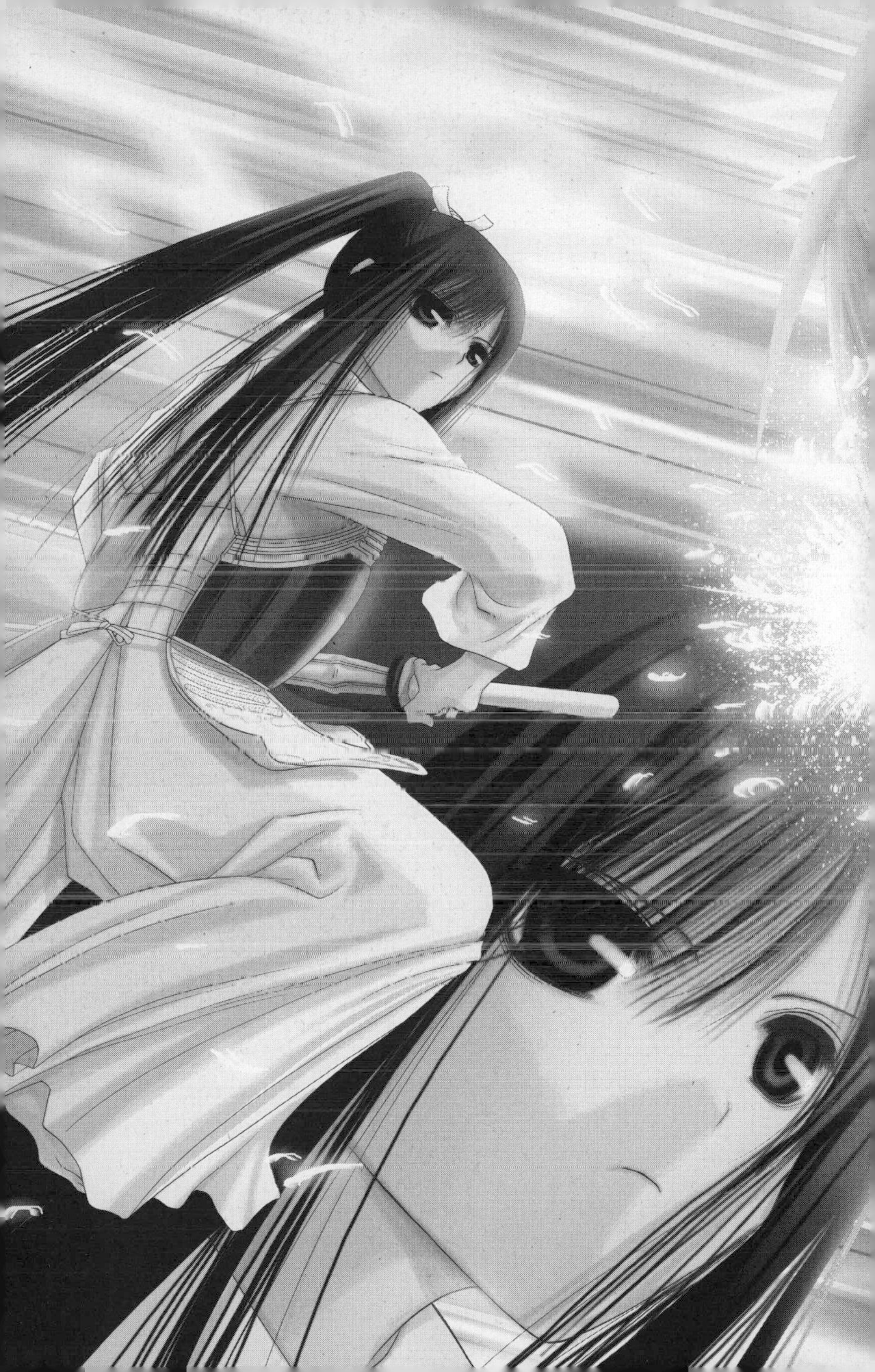

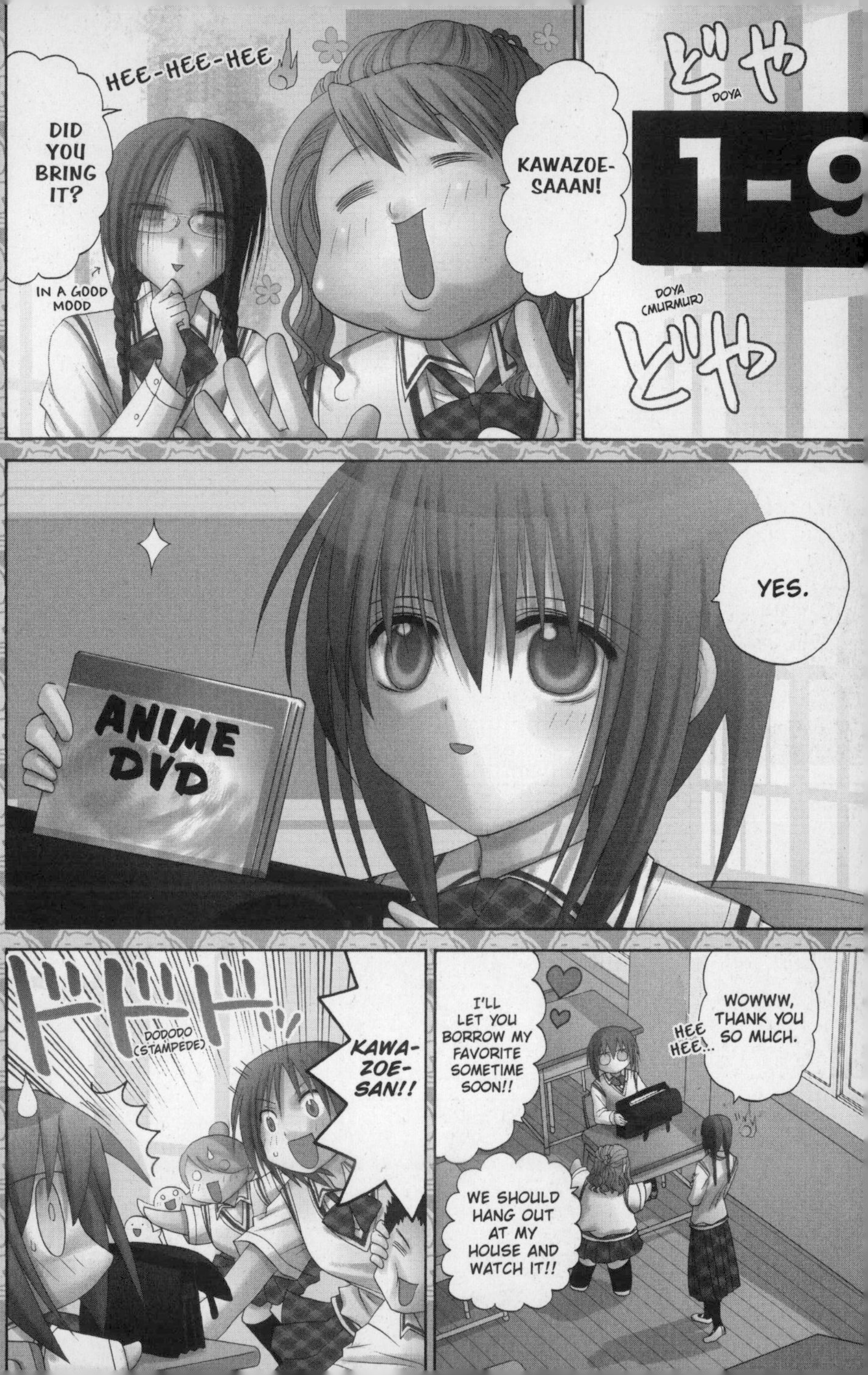
DOYA
1-9
DOYA (MURMUR)
KAWAZOE-SAAAN!
HEE-HEE-HEE
DID YOU BRING IT?
IN A GOOD MOOD
YES.
ANIME DVD
WOWWW, THANK YOU SO MUCH.
HEE HEE...
I'LL LET YOU BORROW MY FAVORITE SOMETIME SOON!!
WE SHOULD HANG OUT AT MY HOUSE AND WATCH IT!!
KAWA-ZOE-SAN!!
DODODO (STAMPEDE)

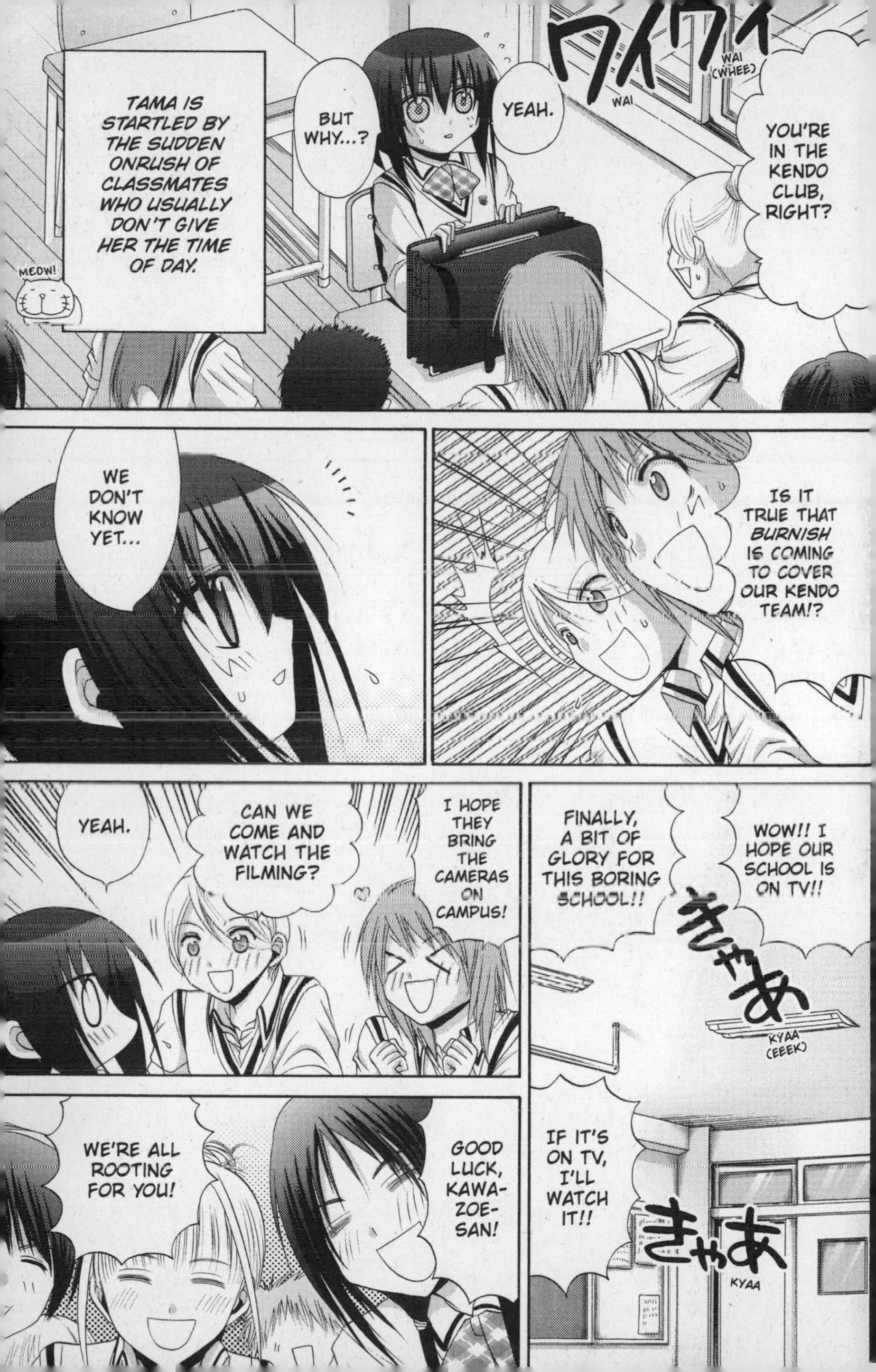
ワイワイ
WAI (WHEE) WAI
YOU'RE IN THE KENDO CLUB, RIGHT?
YEAH.
BUT WHY...?
TAMA IS STARTLED BY THE SUDDEN ONRUSH OF CLASSMATES WHO USUALLY DON'T GIVE HER THE TIME OF DAY.
MEOW!
IS IT TRUE THAT *BURNISH* IS COMING TO COVER OUR KENDO TEAM!?
WE DON'T KNOW YET...
WOW!! I HOPE OUR SCHOOL IS ON TV!!
FINALLY, A BIT OF GLORY FOR THIS BORING SCHOOL!!
きゃあ
KYAA (EEEK)
IF IT'S ON TV, I'LL WATCH IT!!
きゃあ
KYAA
I HOPE THEY BRING THE CAMERAS ON CAMPUS!
CAN WE COME AND WATCH THE FILMING?
YEAH.
GOOD LUCK, KAWAZOE-SAN!
WE'RE ALL ROOTING FOR YOU!

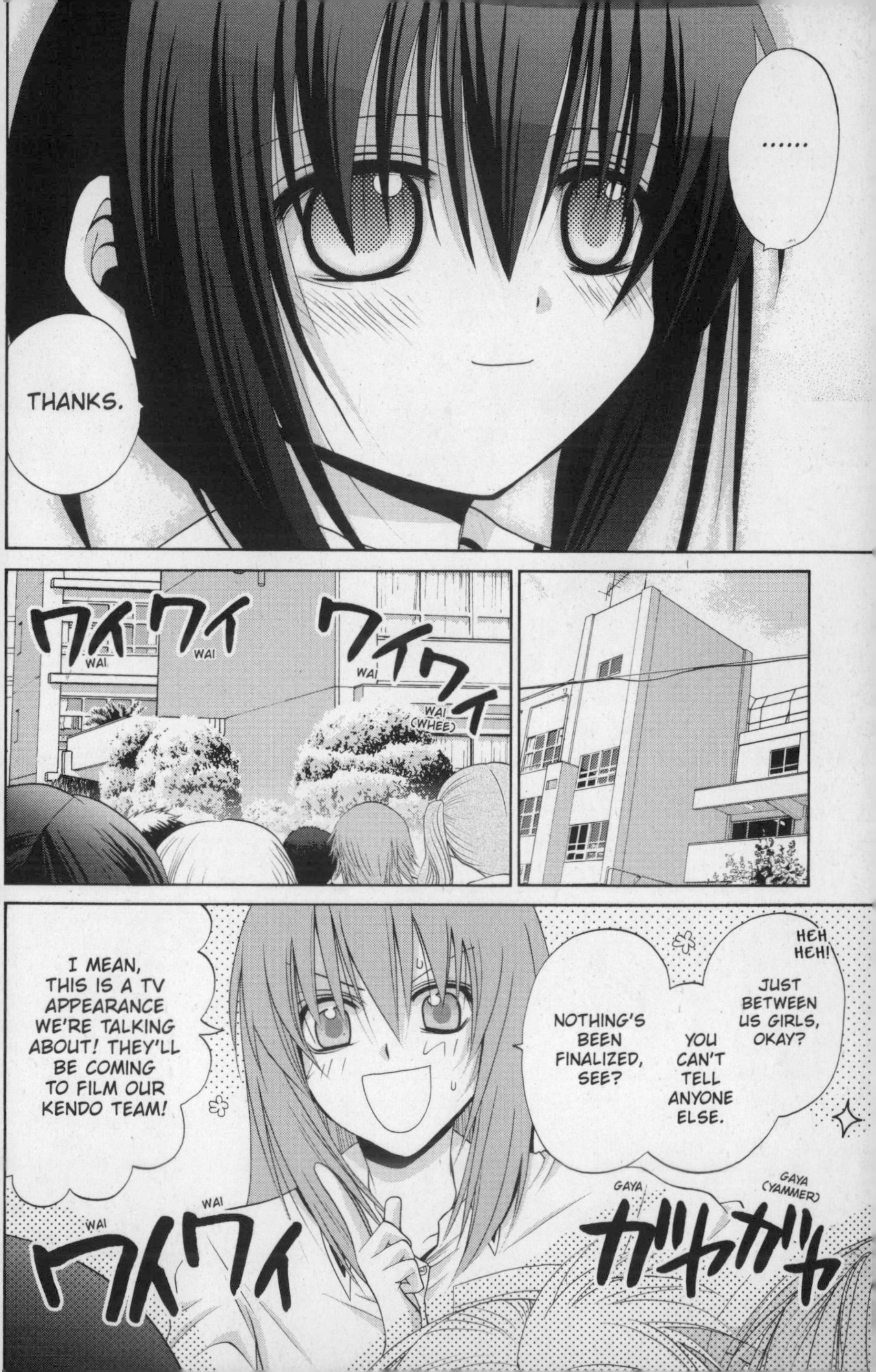
......
THANKS.
ワイワイ
WAI
WAI
ワイワイ
WAI
WAI (WHEE)
HEH HEH!
JUST BETWEEN US GIRLS, OKAY?
YOU CAN'T TELL ANYONE ELSE.
NOTHING'S BEEN FINALIZED, SEE?
I MEAN, THIS IS A TV APPEARANCE WE'RE TALKING ABOUT! THEY'LL BE COMING TO FILM OUR KENDO TEAM!
ガヤガヤ
GAYA
GAYA (YAMMER)
ワイワイ
WAI
WAI

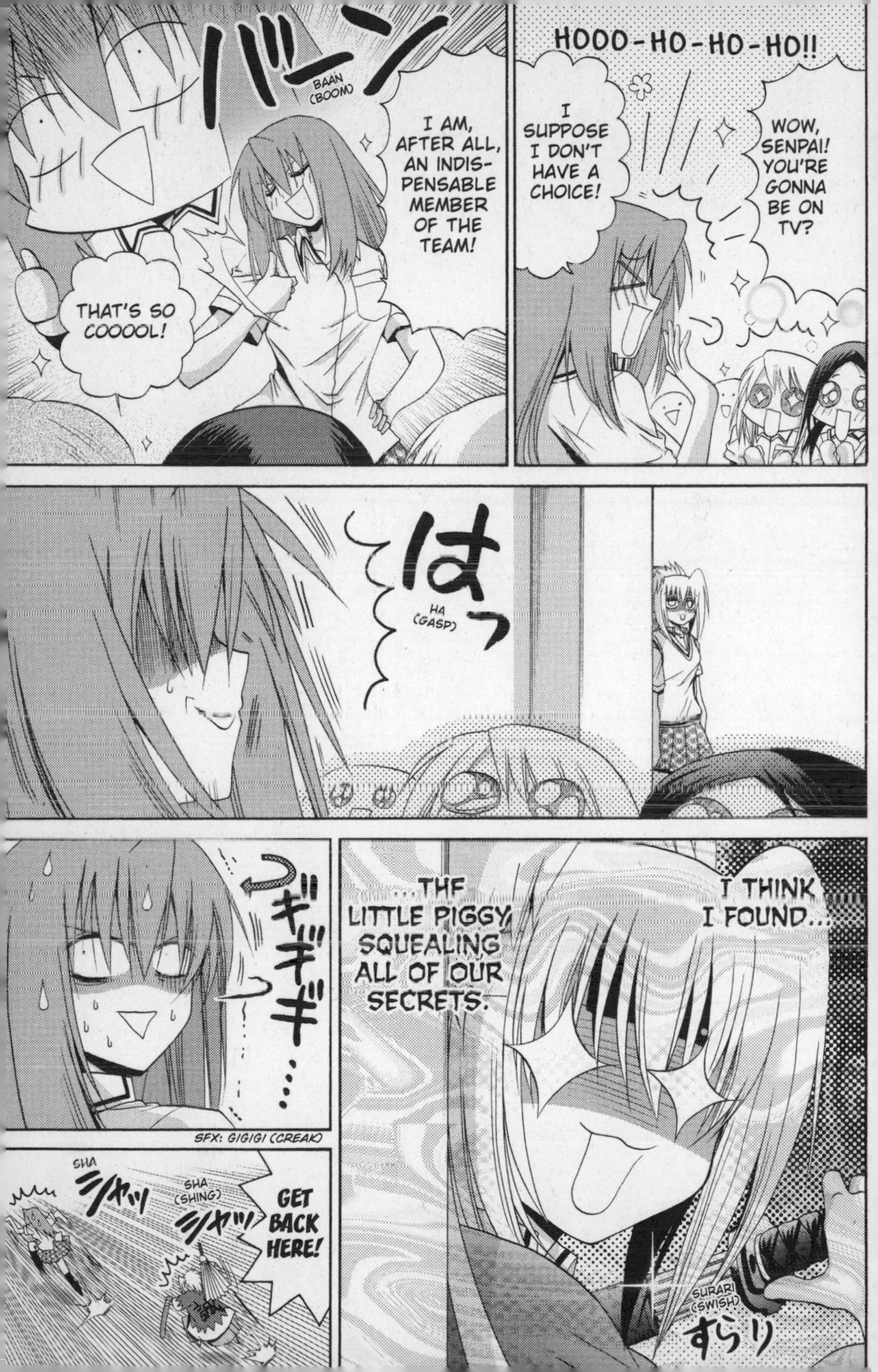
HOOO-HO-HO-HO!!
WOW, SENPAI! YOU'RE GONNA BE ON TV?
I SUPPOSE I DON'T HAVE A CHOICE!
バーン
BAAN (BOOM)
I AM, AFTER ALL, AN INDIS-PENSABLE MEMBER OF THE TEAM!
THAT'S SO COOOOL!
はっ
HA (GASP)
I THINK I FOUND...
...THE LITTLE PIGGY SQUEALING ALL OF OUR SECRETS.
SURARI (SWISH)
すらり
ギギギ…
SFX: GIGIGI (CREAK)
SHA
シャッ
SHA (SHING)
シャッ
GET BACK HERE!

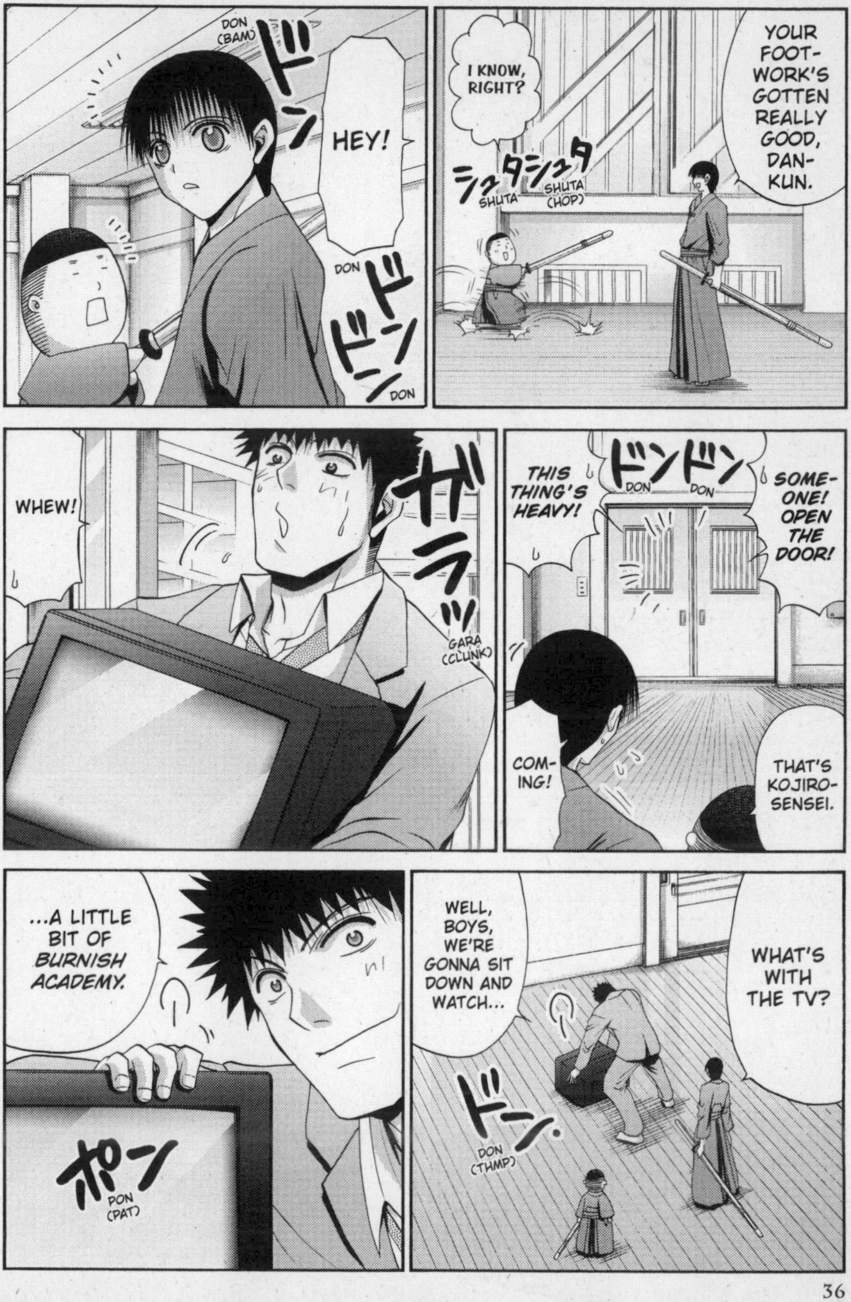
YOUR FOOT-WORK'S GOTTEN REALLY GOOD, DAN-KUN.
I KNOW, RIGHT?
シュタシュタ
SHUTA SHUTA (HOP)
ドン
DON (BAM)
HEY!
ドンドン
DON DON
SOME-ONE! OPEN THE DOOR!
ドンドン
DON DON
THIS THING'S HEAVY!
THAT'S KOJIRO-SENSEI.
COM-ING!
ガラッ
GARA (CLUNK)
WHEW!
WHAT'S WITH THE TV?
WELL, BOYS, WE'RE GONNA SIT DOWN AND WATCH...
ドーン
DON (THMP)
...A LITTLE BIT OF BURNISH ACADEMY.
ポン
PON (PAT)

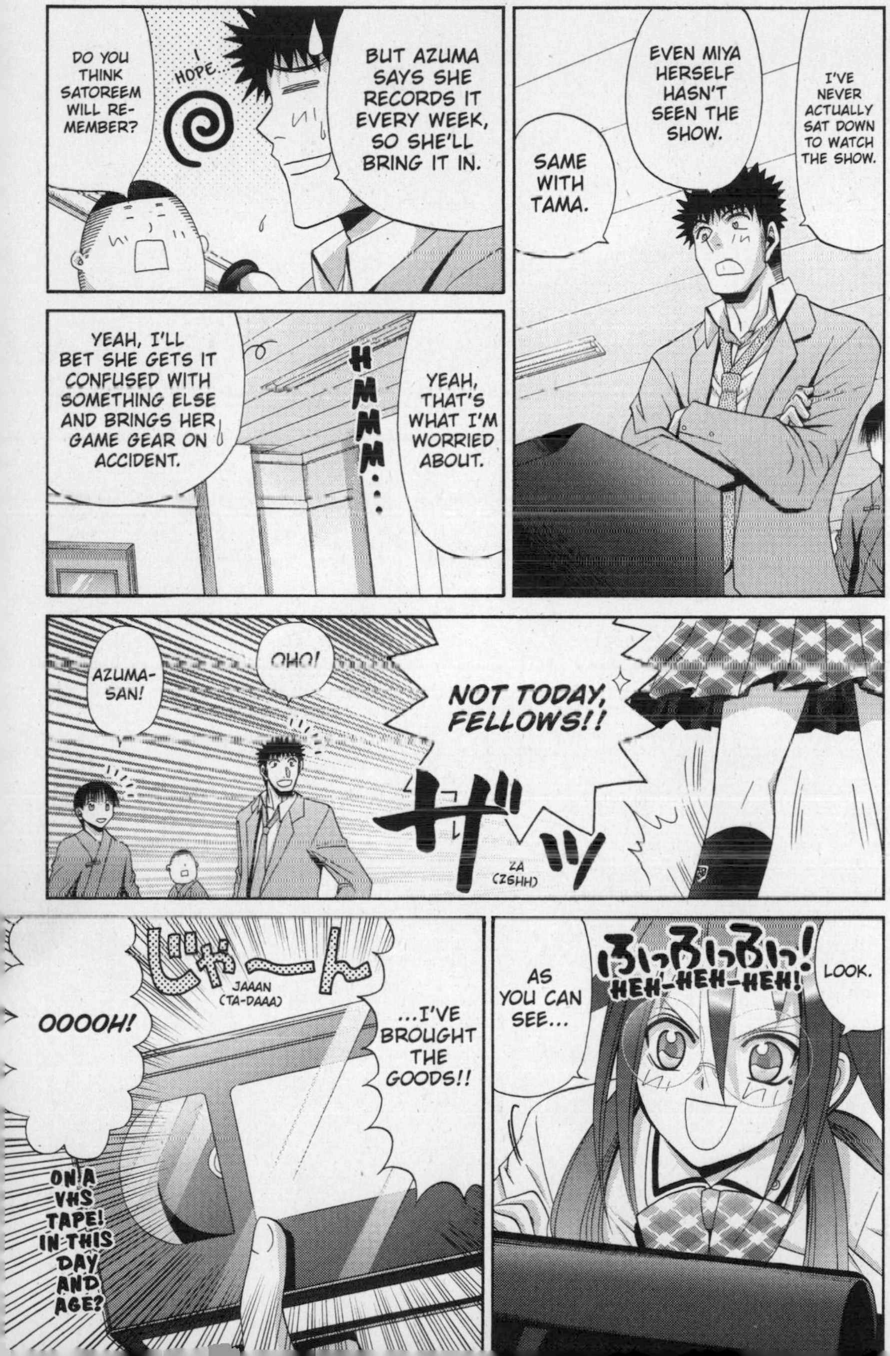

I'VE NEVER ACTUALLY SAT DOWN TO WATCH THE SHOW.
EVEN MIYA HERSELF HASN'T SEEN THE SHOW.
SAME WITH TAMA.
BUT AZUMA SAYS SHE RECORDS IT EVERY WEEK, SO SHE'LL BRING IT IN.
I HOPE...
DO YOU THINK SATOREEM WILL RE-MEMBER?
YEAH, THAT'S WHAT I'M WORRIED ABOUT.
HMMM...
YEAH, I'LL BET SHE GETS IT CONFUSED WITH SOMETHING ELSE AND BRINGS HER GAME GEAR ON ACCIDENT.
NOT TODAY, FELLOWS!!
ザッ
ZA (ZSHH)
OHO!
AZUMA-SAN!
LOOK.
ふっふっふっ!
HEH-HEH-HEH!
AS YOU CAN SEE...
...I'VE BROUGHT THE GOODS!!
じゃーん
JAAAN (TA-DAAA)
OOOOH!
ON A VHS TAPE! IN THIS DAY AND AGE?

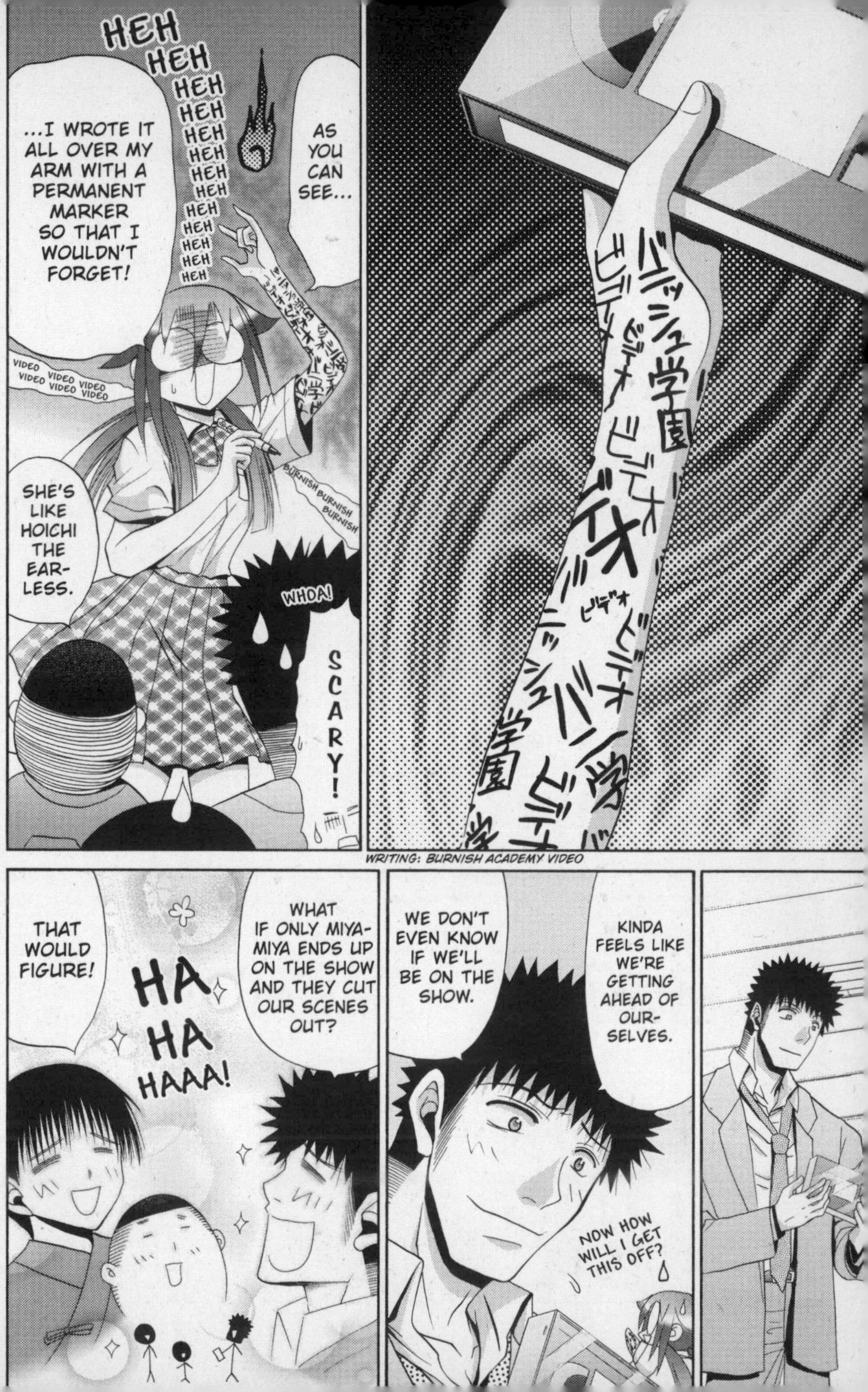
WRITING: BURNISH ACADEMY VIDEO
HEH HEH HEH HEH HEH HEH HEH HEH HEH HEH HEH HEH HEH
AS YOU CAN SEE...
...I WROTE IT ALL OVER MY ARM WITH A PERMANENT MARKER SO THAT I WOULDN'T FORGET!
VIDEO VIDEO VIDEO VIDEO VIDEO VIDEO
BURNISH BURNISH BURNISH BURNISH
SCARY!
WHOA!
SHE'S LIKE HOICHI THE EAR-LESS.
KINDA FEELS LIKE WE'RE GETTING AHEAD OF OUR-SELVES.
WE DON'T EVEN KNOW IF WE'LL BE ON THE SHOW.
NOW HOW WILL I GET THIS OFF?
WHAT IF ONLY MIYA-MIYA ENDS UP ON THE SHOW AND THEY CUT OUR SCENES OUT?
HA HA HAAA!
THAT WOULD FIGURE!

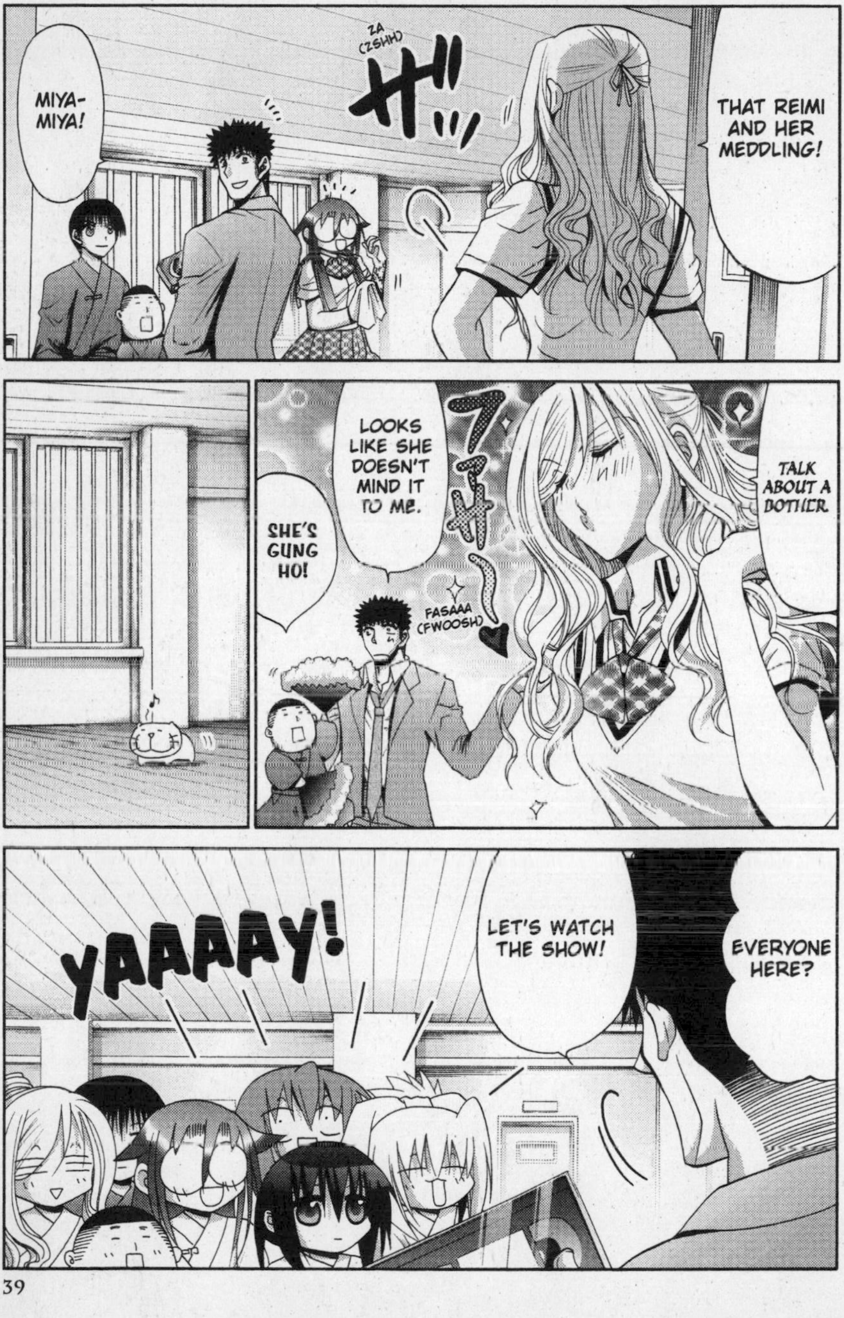
THAT REIMI AND HER MEDDLING!
ZA (ZSHH)
MIYA-MIYA!
TALK ABOUT A BOTHER
LOOKS LIKE SHE DOESN'T MIND IT TO ME.
FASAAA (FWOOSH)
SHE'S GUNG HO!
EVERYONE HERE?
LET'S WATCH THE SHOW!
YAAAAY!

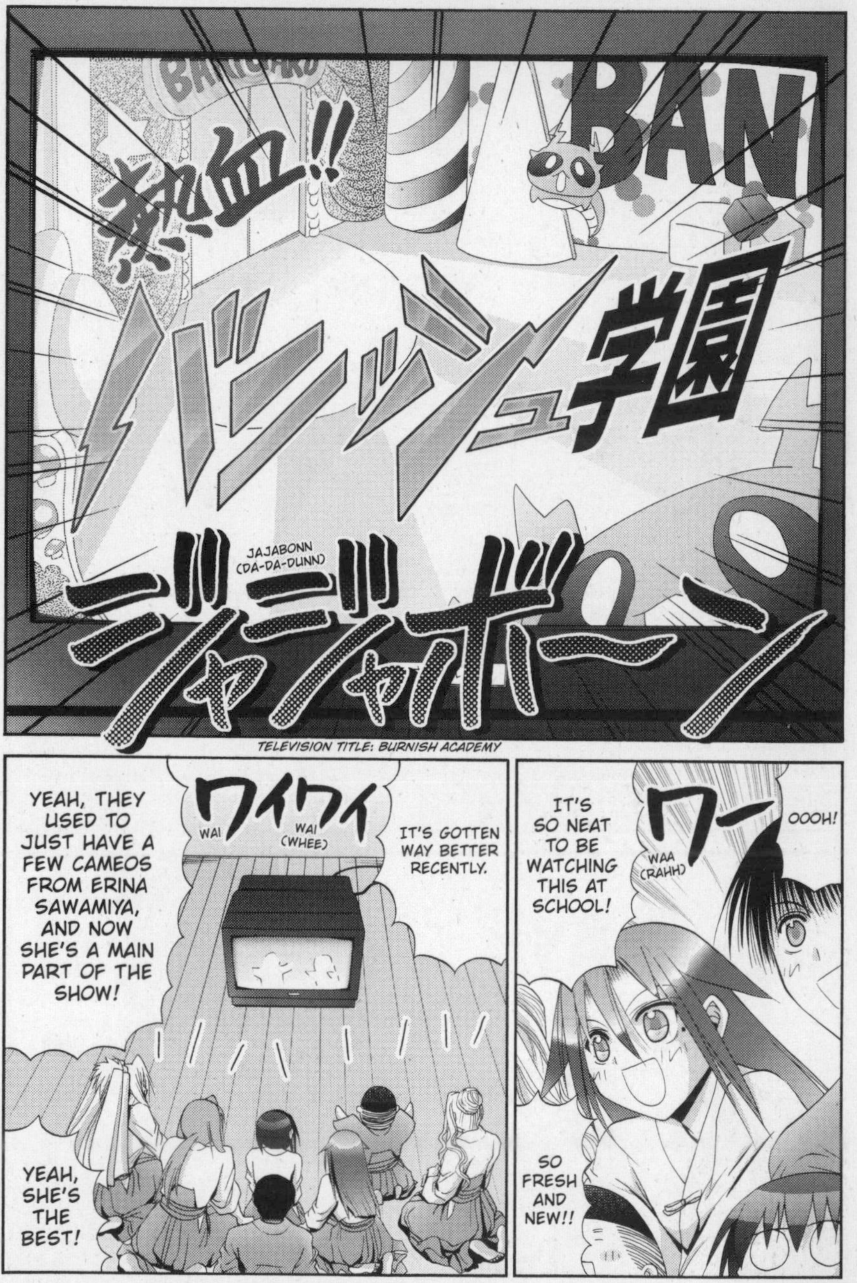

熱血!!
BAN
JAJABONN (DA-DA-DUNN)
ジャジャボーン
TELEVISION TITLE: BURNISH ACADEMY
ワー
WAA (RAHH)
OOOH!
IT'S SO NEAT TO BE WATCHING THIS AT SCHOOL!
SO FRESH AND NEW!!
ワイワイ
WAI WAI (WHEE)
IT'S GOTTEN WAY BETTER RECENTLY.
YEAH, THEY USED TO JUST HAVE A FEW CAMEOS FROM ERINA SAWAMIYA, AND NOW SHE'S A MAIN PART OF THE SHOW!
YEAH, SHE'S THE BEST!

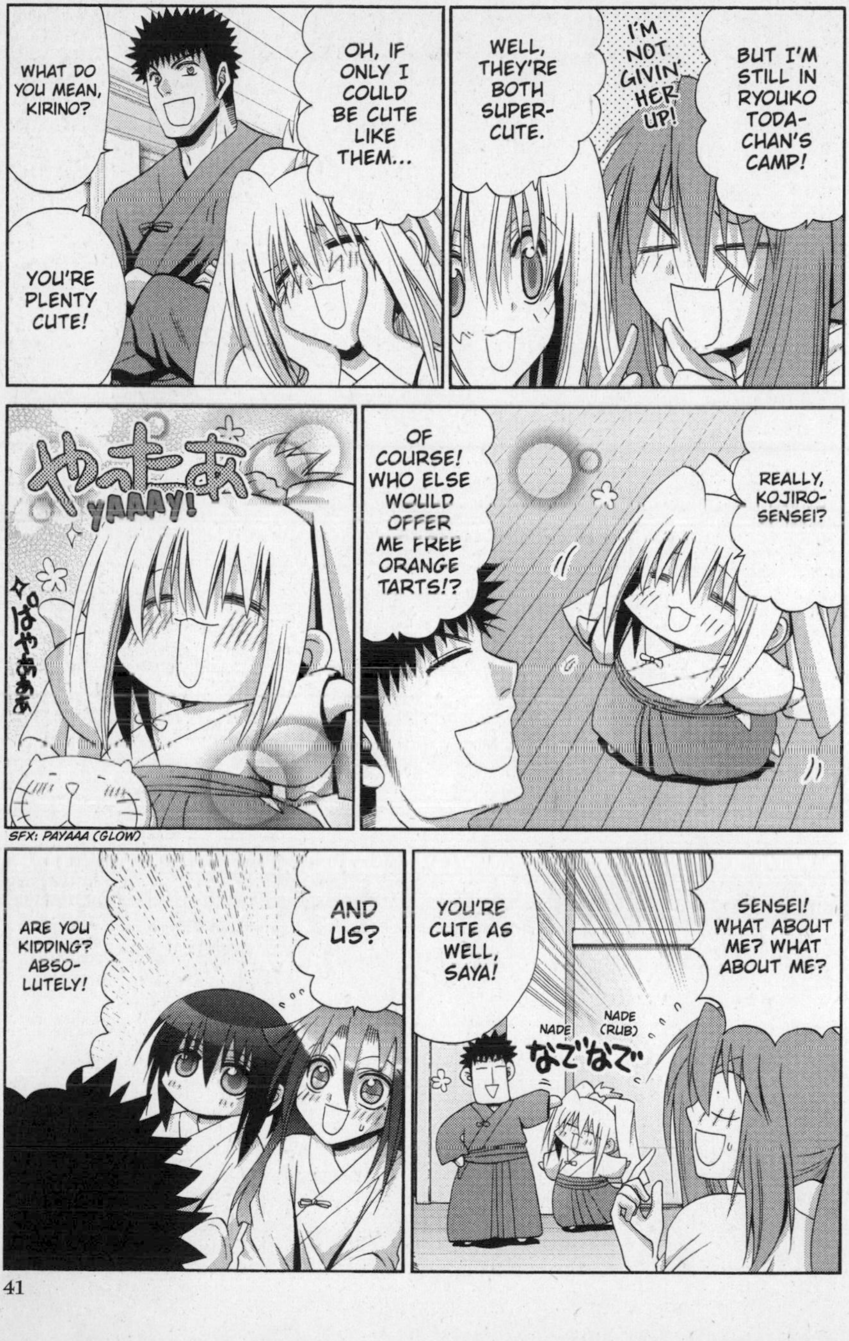
BUT I'M STILL IN RYOUKO TODA-CHAN'S CAMP!
I'M NOT GIVIN' HER UP!
WELL, THEY'RE BOTH SUPER-CUTE.
OH, IF ONLY I COULD BE CUTE LIKE THEM...
WHAT DO YOU MEAN, KIRINO?
YOU'RE PLENTY CUTE!
REALLY, KOJIRO-SENSEI?
OF COURSE! WHO ELSE WOULD OFFER ME FREE ORANGE TARTS!?
やったあ
YAAAY!
SFX: PAYAAA (GLOW)
SENSEI! WHAT ABOUT ME? WHAT ABOUT ME?
なでなで
NADE NADE (RUB)
YOU'RE CUTE AS WELL, SAYA!
AND US?
ARE YOU KIDDING? ABSOLUTELY!

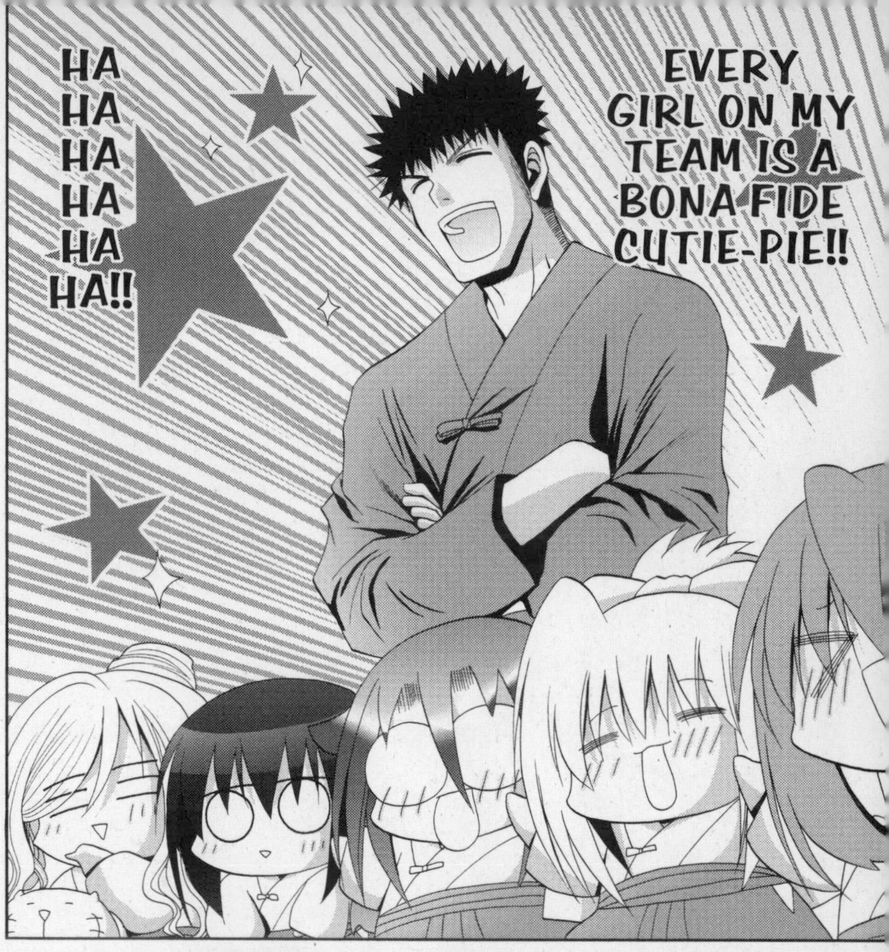
EVERY GIRL ON MY TEAM IS A BONA FIDE CUTIE-PIE!!
HA HA HA HA HA HA HA!!

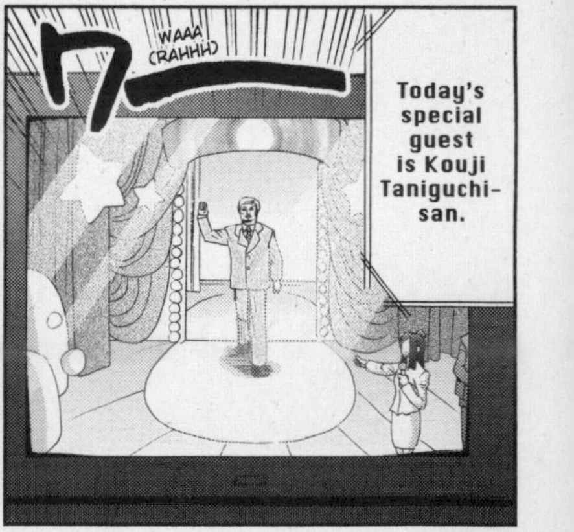
WAAA (RAHHH)
Today's special guest is Kouji Taniguchi-san.

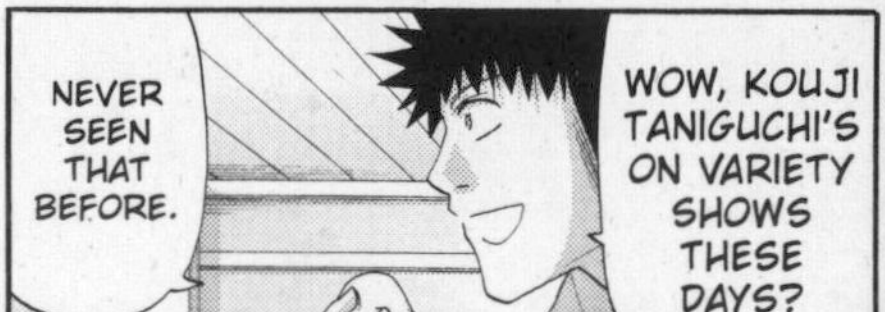
WOW, KOUJI TANIGUCHI'S ON VARIETY SHOWS THESE DAYS?
NEVER SEEN THAT BEFORE.
JUST TO SHILL FOR HIS NEW SHOW.
BUNS
CUP: TEA

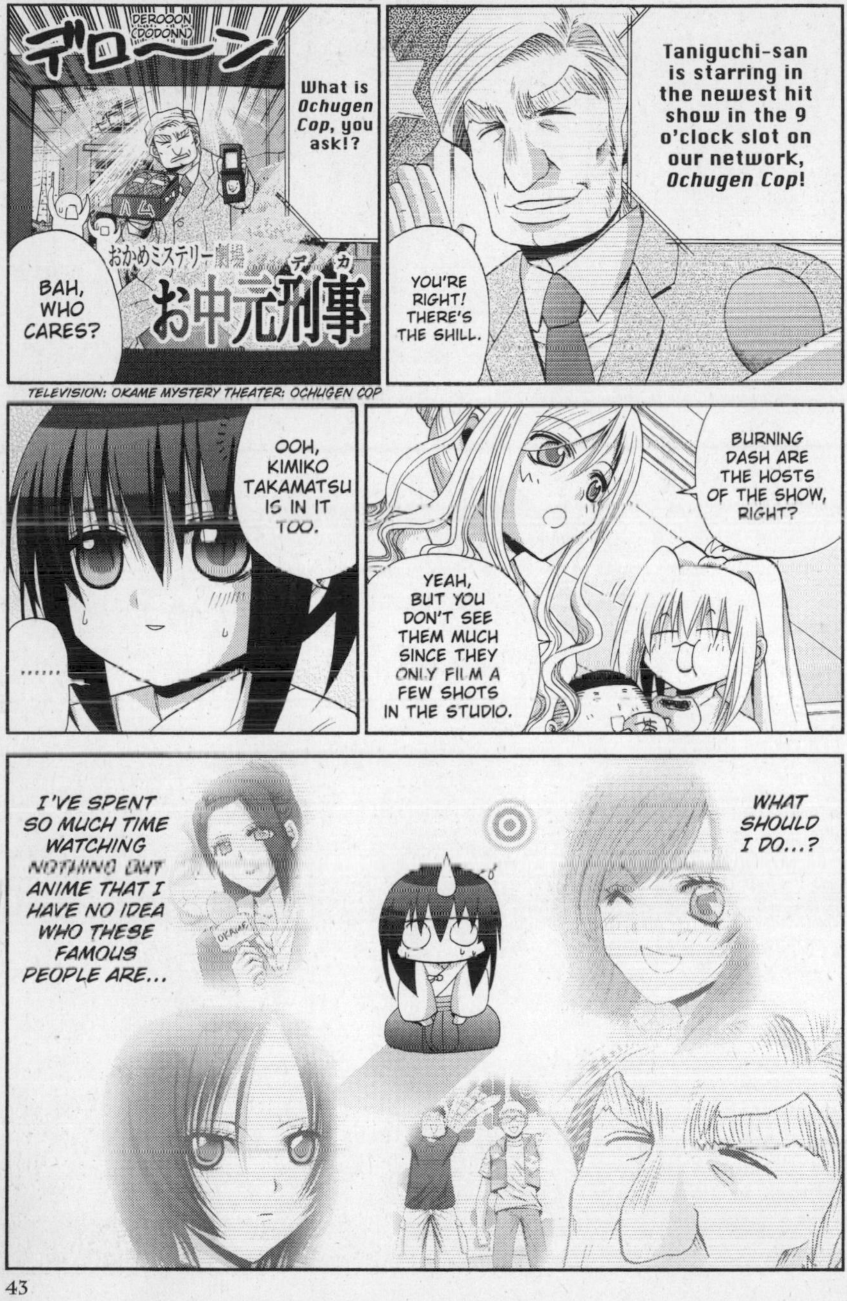
Taniguchi-san is starring in the newest hit show in the 9 o'clock slot on our network, *Ochugen Cop*!
YOU'RE RIGHT! THERE'S THE SHILL.
DEROOON (DODONN)
デローーン
What is *Ochugen Cop*, you ask!?
BAH, WHO CARES?
おかめミステリー劇場
お中元刑事(デカ)
TELEVISION: OKAME MYSTERY THEATER: OCHUGEN COP
BURNING DASH ARE THE HOSTS OF THE SHOW, RIGHT?
YEAH, BUT YOU DON'T SEE THEM MUCH SINCE THEY ONLY FILM A FEW SHOTS IN THE STUDIO.
OOH, KIMIKO TAKAMATSU IS IN IT TOO.
......
WHAT SHOULD I DO...?
I'VE SPENT SO MUCH TIME WATCHING NOTHING BUT ANIME THAT I HAVE NO IDEA WHO THESE FAMOUS PEOPLE ARE...
OKAME

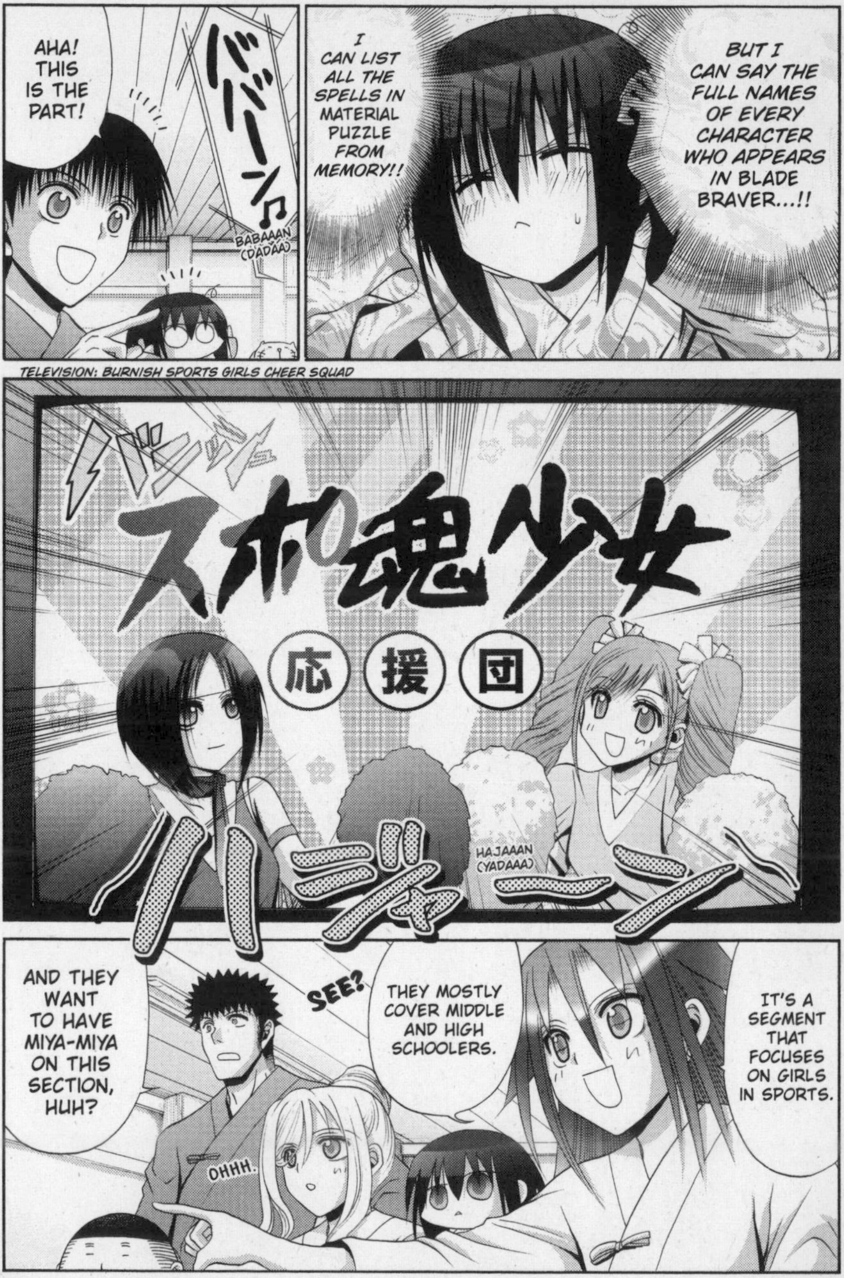
BUT I CAN SAY THE FULL NAMES OF EVERY CHARACTER WHO APPEARS IN BLADE BRAVER...!!
I CAN LIST ALL THE SPELLS IN MATERIAL PUZZLE FROM MEMORY!!
AHA! THIS IS THE PART!
バババーン♫
BABAAAN (DADAA)
TELEVISION: BURNISH SPORTS GIRLS CHEER SQUAD
スポ魂少女
応援団
ハジャーン
HAJAAAN (YADAAA)
IT'S A SEGMENT THAT FOCUSES ON GIRLS IN SPORTS.
THEY MOSTLY COVER MIDDLE AND HIGH SCHOOLERS.
SEE?
AND THEY WANT TO HAVE MIYA-MIYA ON THIS SECTION, HUH?
OHHH.

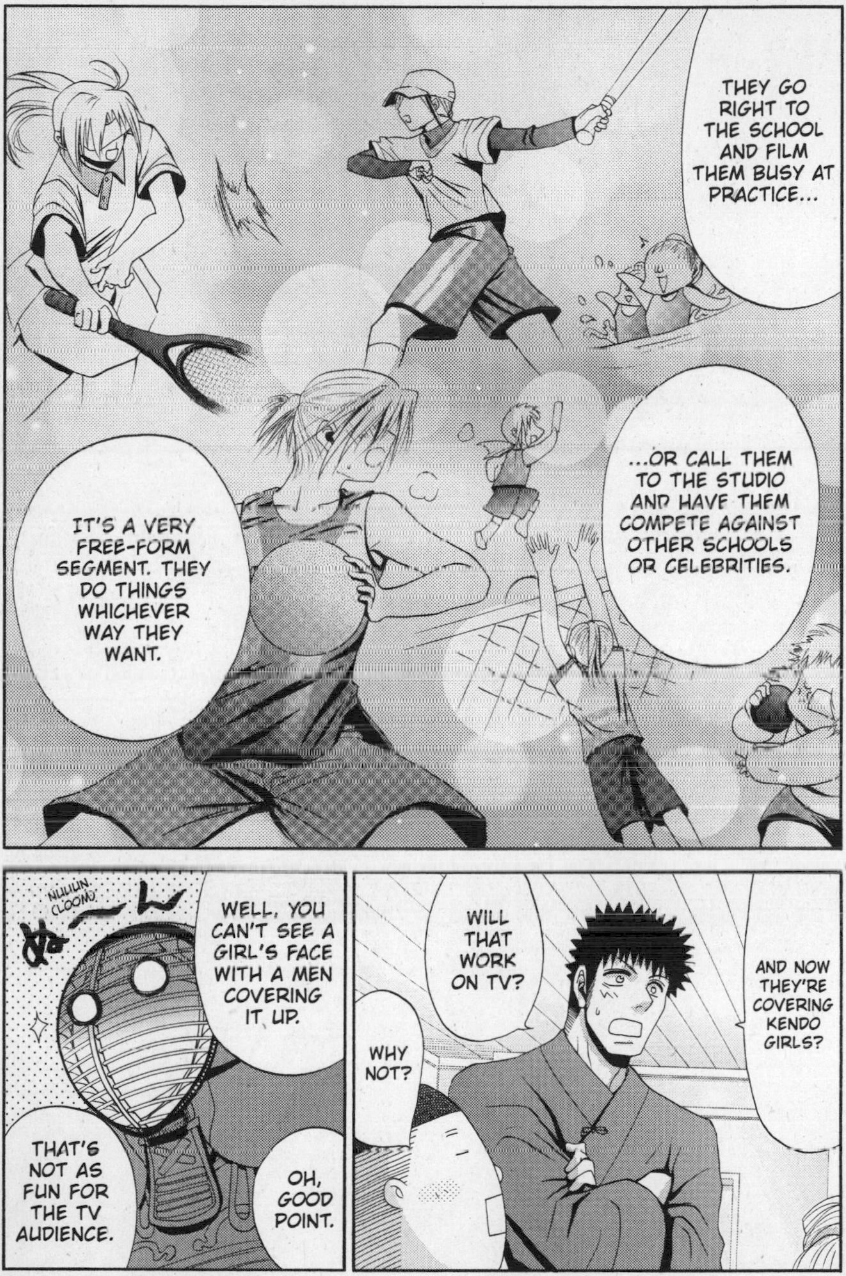
THEY GO RIGHT TO THE SCHOOL AND FILM THEM BUSY AT PRACTICE...
...OR CALL THEM TO THE STUDIO AND HAVE THEM COMPETE AGAINST OTHER SCHOOLS OR CELEBRITIES.
IT'S A VERY FREE-FORM SEGMENT. THEY DO THINGS WHICHEVER WAY THEY WANT.
AND NOW THEY'RE COVERING KENDO GIRLS?
WILL THAT WORK ON TV?
WHY NOT?
WELL, YOU CAN'T SEE A GIRL'S FACE WITH A MEN COVERING IT UP.
NUUUN (LOOM)
OH, GOOD POINT.
THAT'S NOT AS FUN FOR THE TV AUDIENCE.

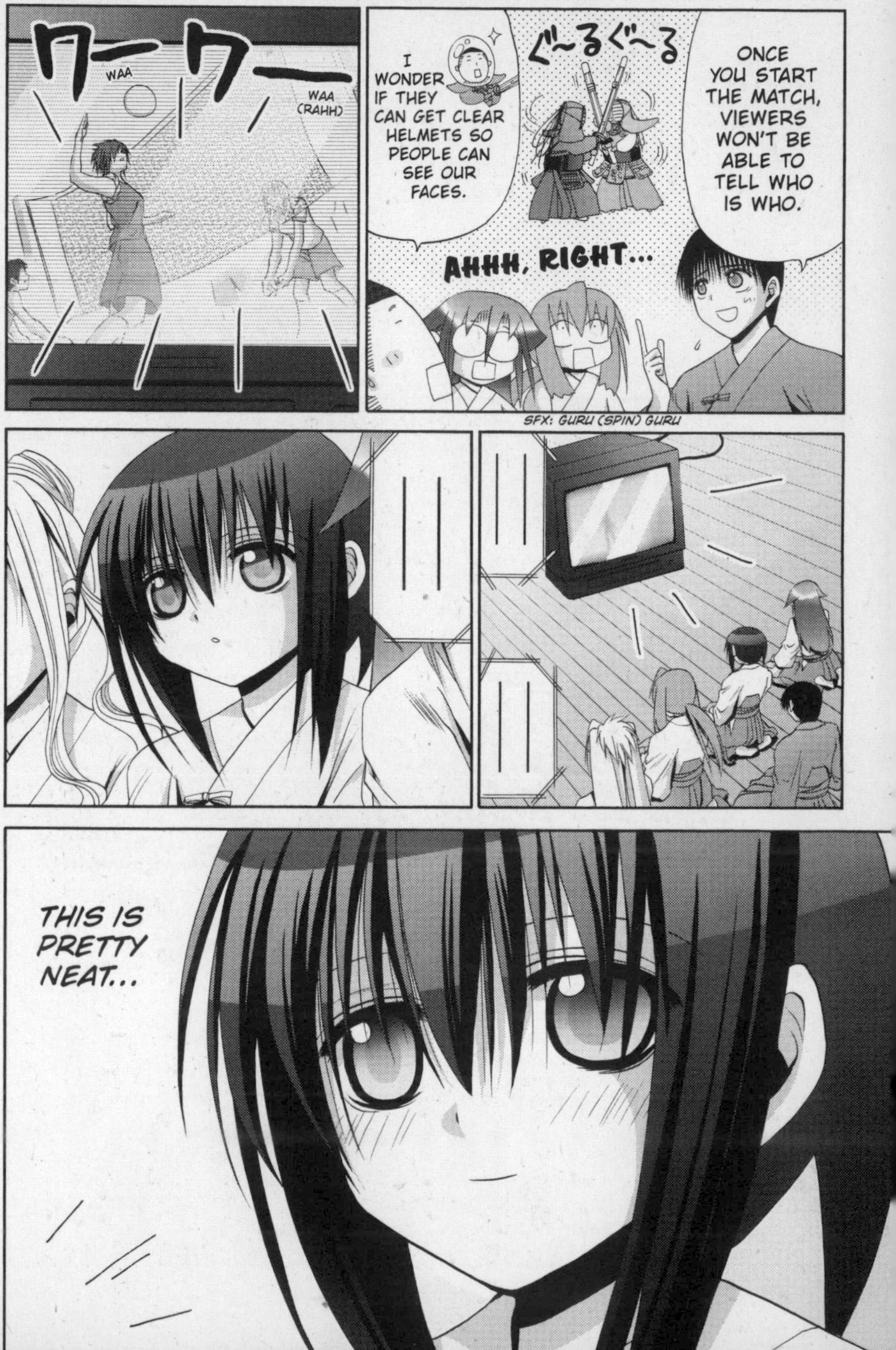
ONCE YOU START THE MATCH, VIEWERS WON'T BE ABLE TO TELL WHO IS WHO.
ぐ〜るぐ〜る
I WONDER IF THEY CAN GET CLEAR HELMETS SO PEOPLE CAN SEE OUR FACES.
AHHH, RIGHT...
SFX: GURU (SPIN) GURU
ワーワー
WAA
WAA (RAHH)
THIS IS PRETTY NEAT...

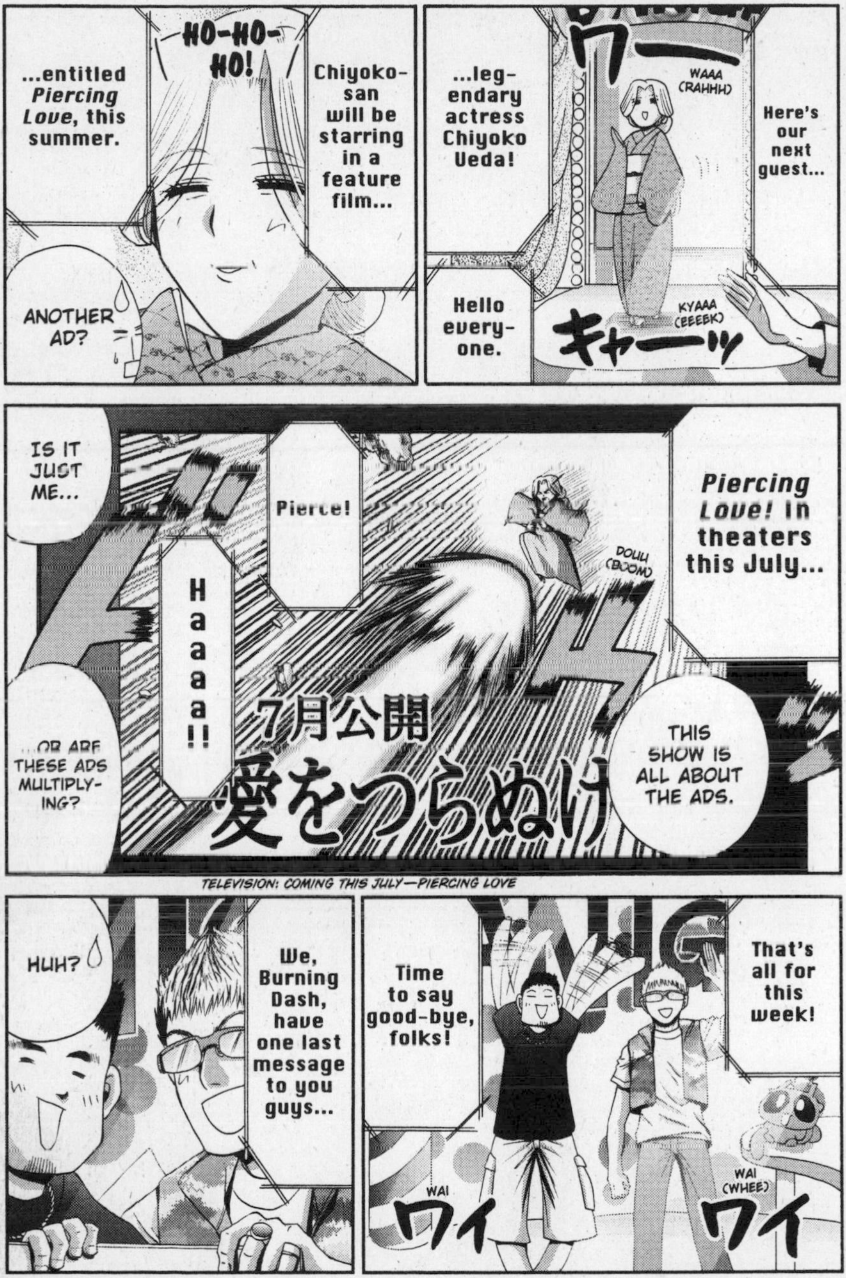
Here's our next guest...
ワー
WAAA (RAHHH)
...legendary actress Chiyoko Ueda!
キャーッ
KYAAA (EEEEK)
Hello everyone.
Chiyoko-san will be starring in a feature film...
HO-HO-HO!
...entitled *Piercing Love*, this summer.
ANOTHER AD?
Piercing Love! In theaters this July...
DOUU (BOOM)
Pierce!
Haaaaa!!
7月公開
愛をつらぬけ
THIS SHOW IS ALL ABOUT THE ADS.
IS IT JUST ME...
...OR ARE THESE ADS MULTIPLYING?
TELEVISION: COMING THIS JULY—PIERCING LOVE
That's all for this week!
Time to say good-bye, folks!
WAI (WHEE)
ワイ
WAI
ワイ
We, Burning Dash, have one last message to you guys...
HUH?

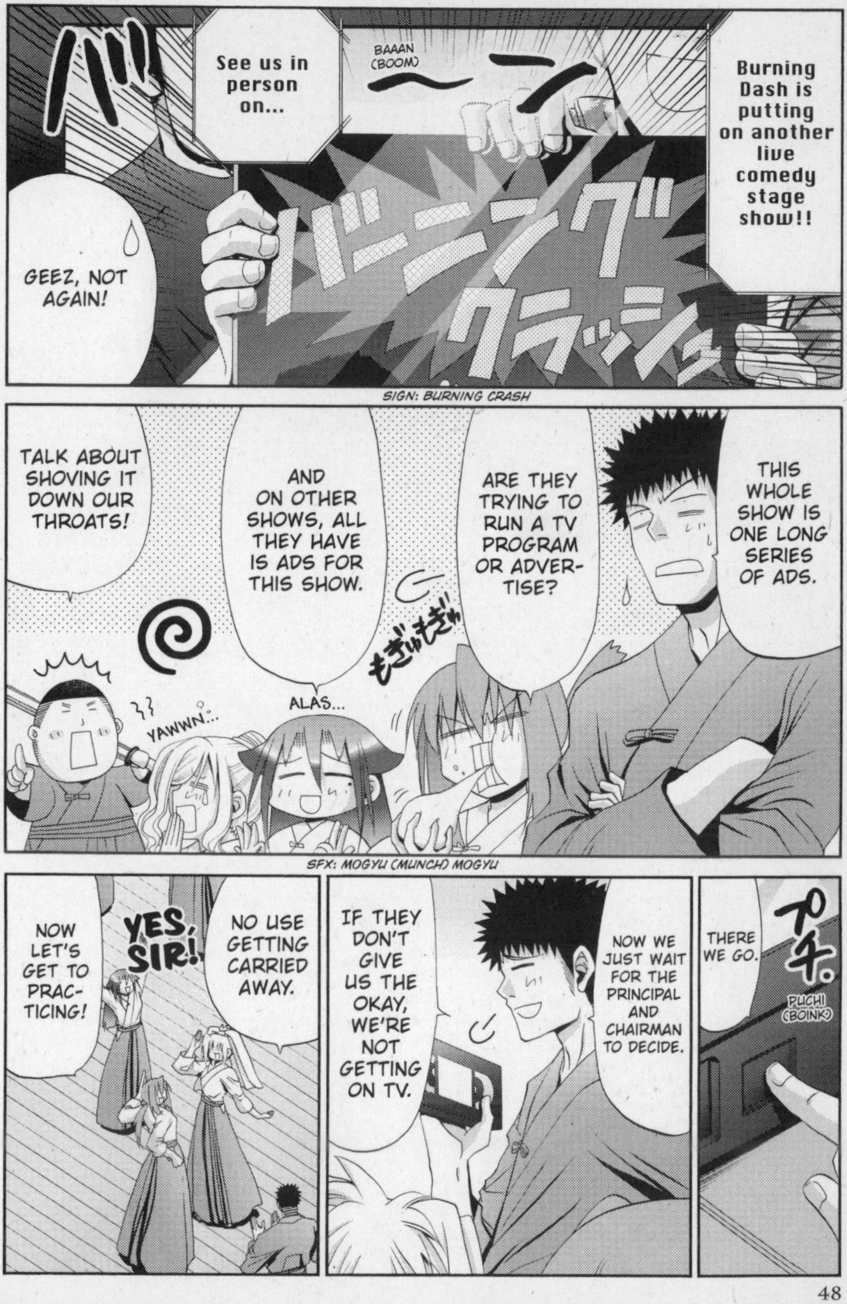
Burning Dash is putting on another live comedy stage show!!
BAAAN (BOOM)
See us in person on...
GEEZ, NOT AGAIN!
SIGN: BURNING CRASH
THIS WHOLE SHOW IS ONE LONG SERIES OF ADS.
ARE THEY TRYING TO RUN A TV PROGRAM OR ADVERTISE?
AND ON OTHER SHOWS, ALL THEY HAVE IS ADS FOR THIS SHOW.
TALK ABOUT SHOVING IT DOWN OUR THROATS!
ALAS...
YAWWN...
SFX: MOGYU (MUNCH) MOGYU
THERE WE GO.
PUCHI (BOINK)
NOW WE JUST WAIT FOR THE PRINCIPAL AND CHAIRMAN TO DECIDE.
IF THEY DON'T GIVE US THE OKAY, WE'RE NOT GETTING ON TV.
NO USE GETTING CARRIED AWAY.
YES, SIR!
NOW LET'S GET TO PRACTICING!

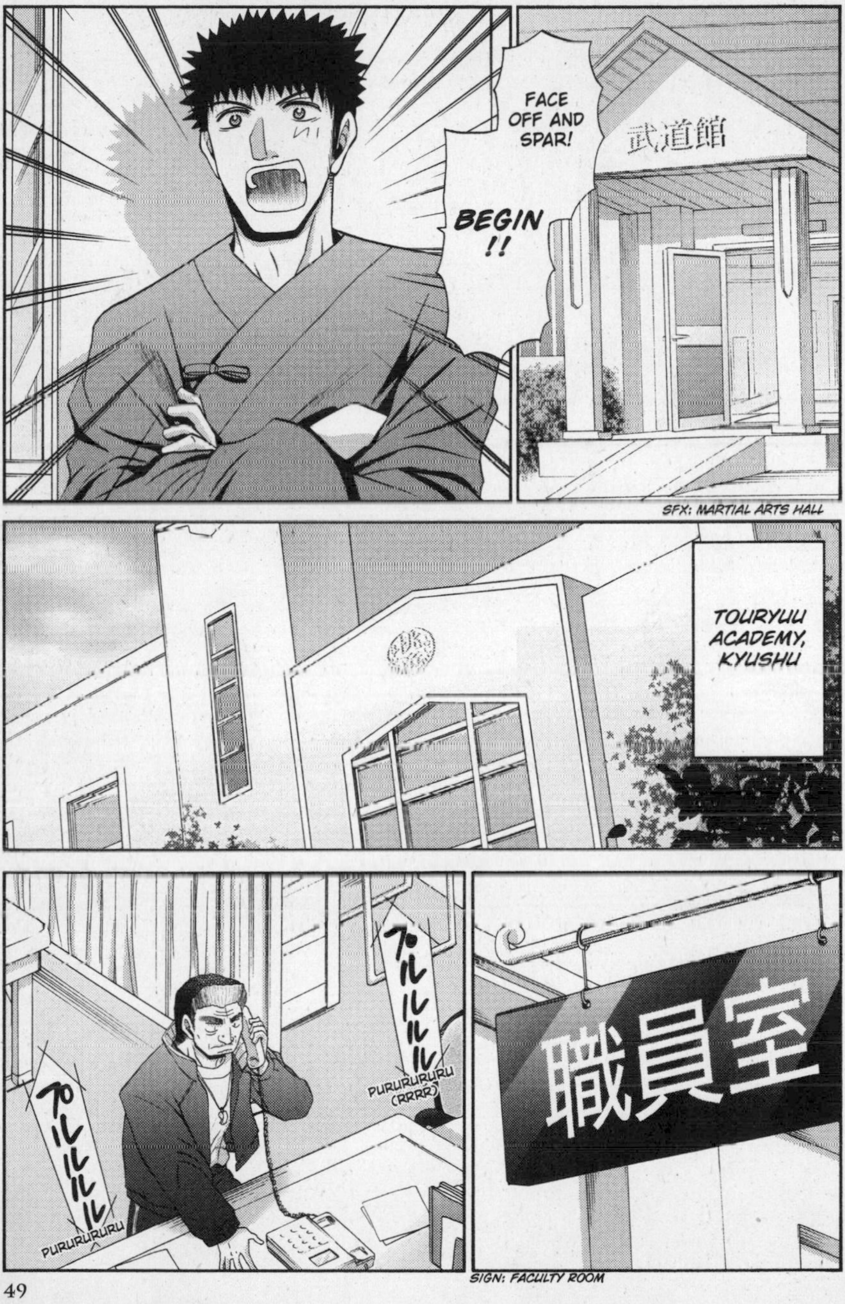
武道館
FACE OFF AND SPAR!
BEGIN !!
TOURYUU ACADEMY, KYUSHU
職員室
プルルルル
PURURURURU (RRRR)
プルルルル
PURURURURU
SFX: MARTIAL ARTS HALL
SIGN: FACULTY ROOM

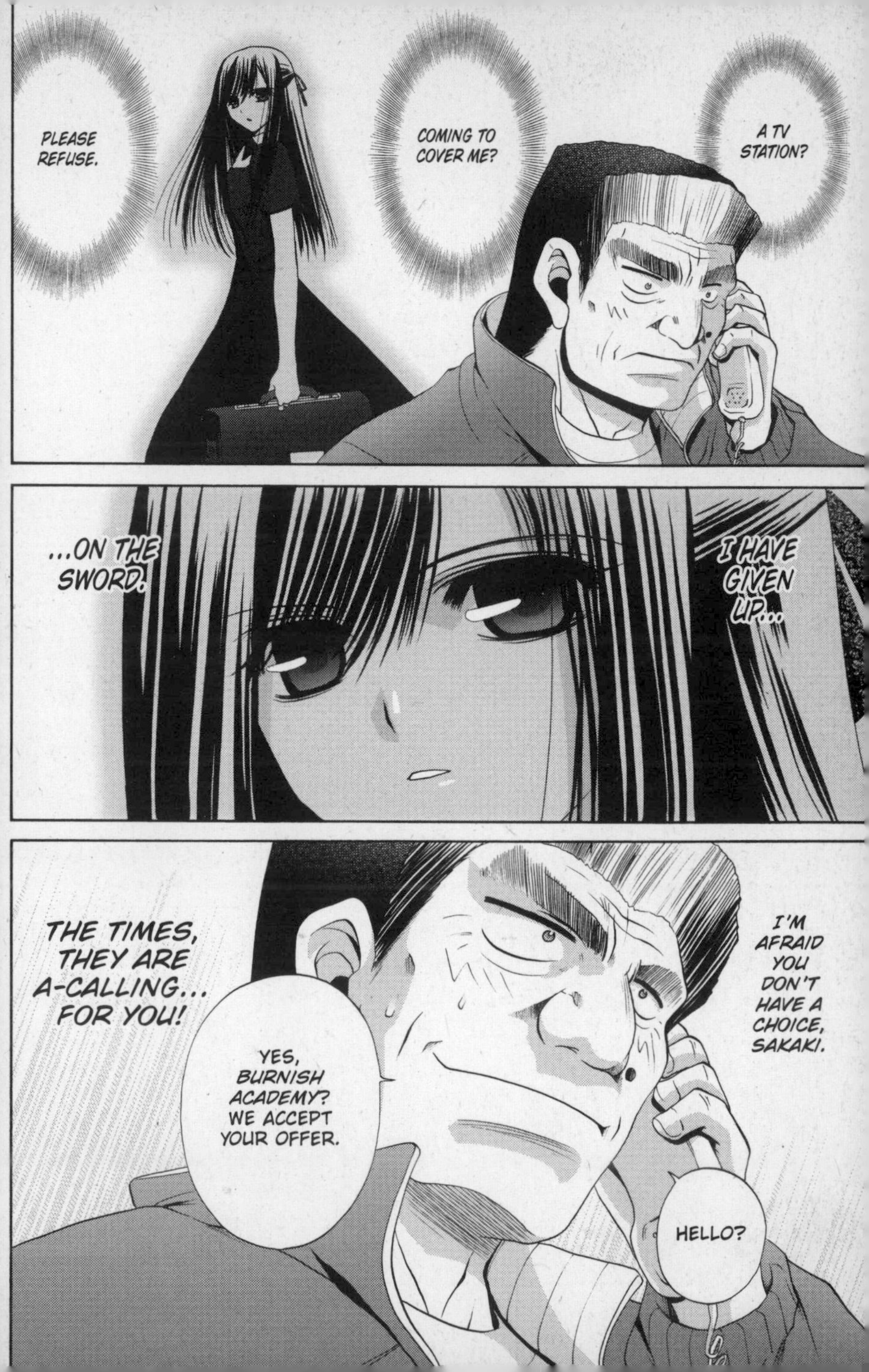
A TV STATION?
COMING TO COVER ME?
PLEASE REFUSE.
I HAVE GIVEN UP...
...ON THE SWORD.
I'M AFRAID YOU DON'T HAVE A CHOICE, SAKAKI.
THE TIMES, THEY ARE A-CALLING... FOR YOU!
YES, BURNISH ACADEMY? WE ACCEPT YOUR OFFER.
HELLO?

BAMBOO BLADE
バンブーブレード

BAMBOO BLADE
バンブーブレード

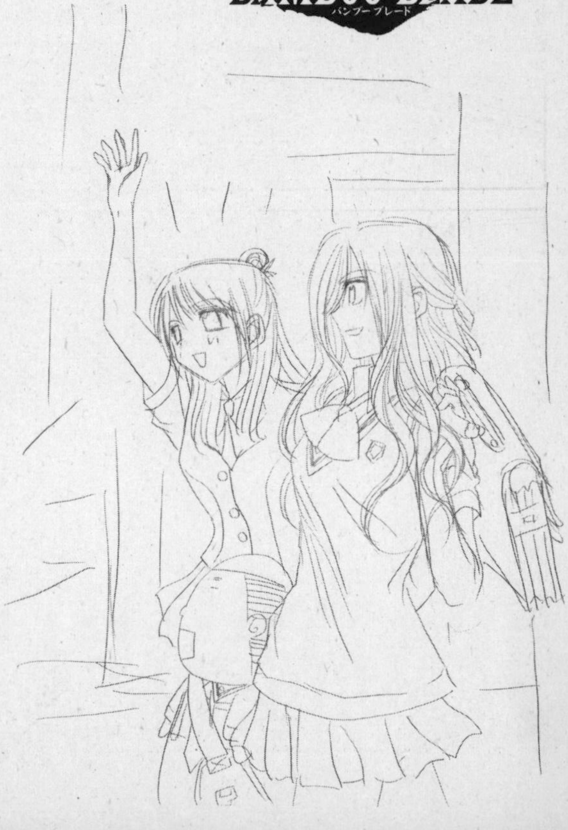

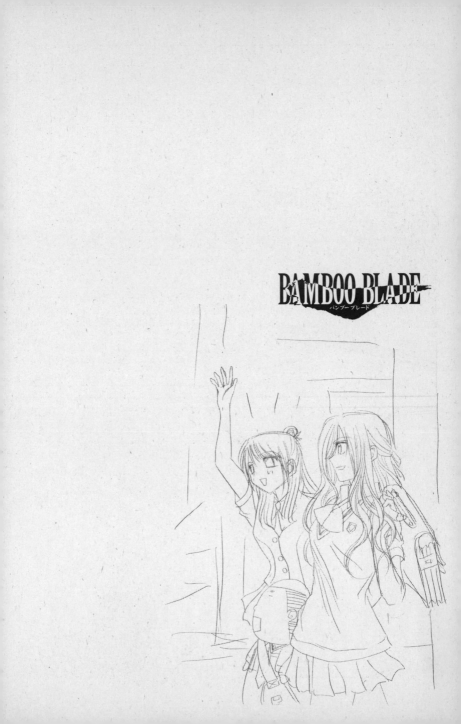

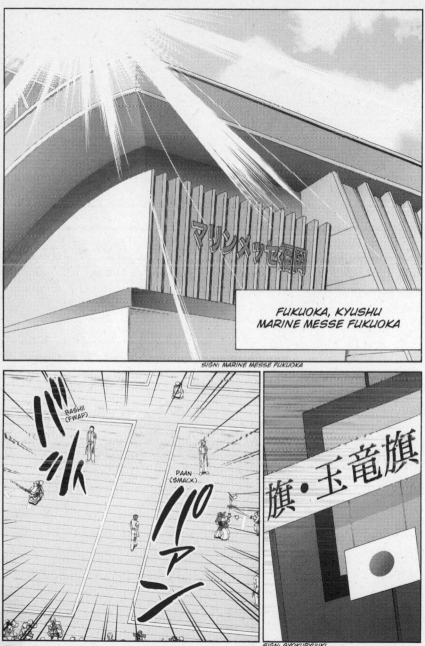

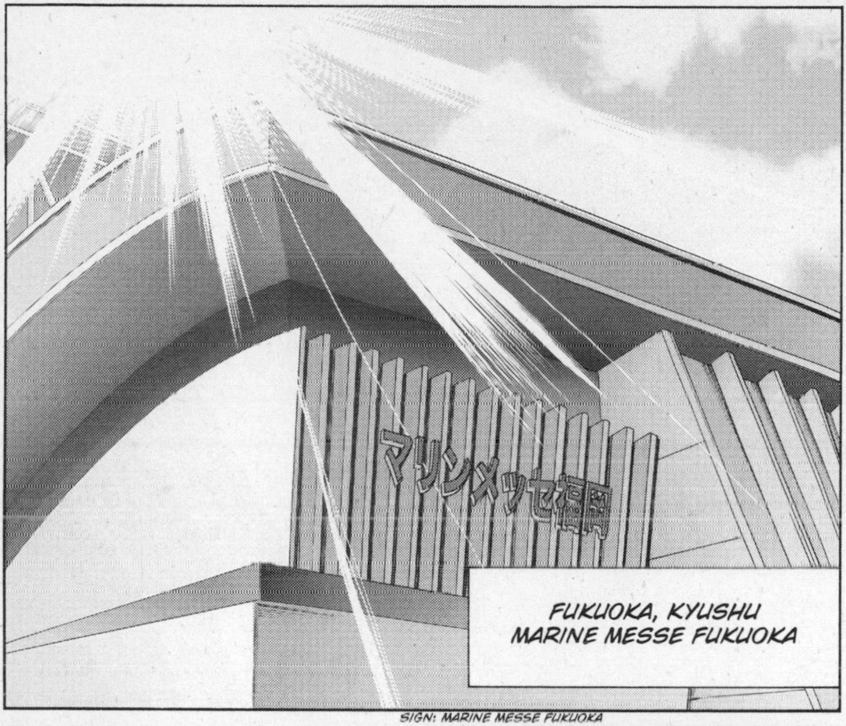
マリンメッセ福岡
FUKUOKA, KYUSHU
MARINE MESSE FUKUOKA

SIGN: MARINE MESSE FUKUOKA

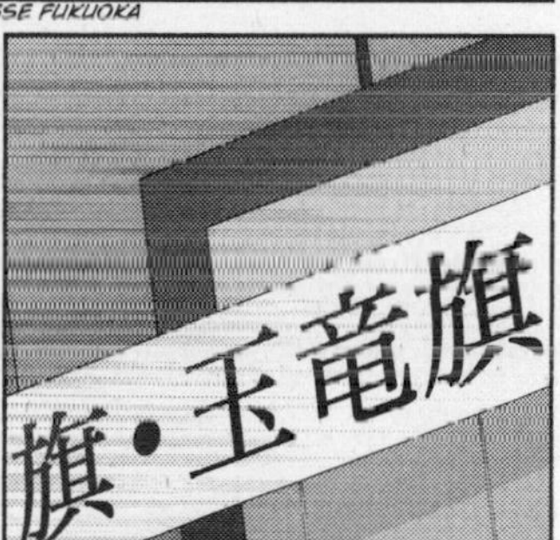
旗・玉竜旗

SIGN: GYOKURYUUKI

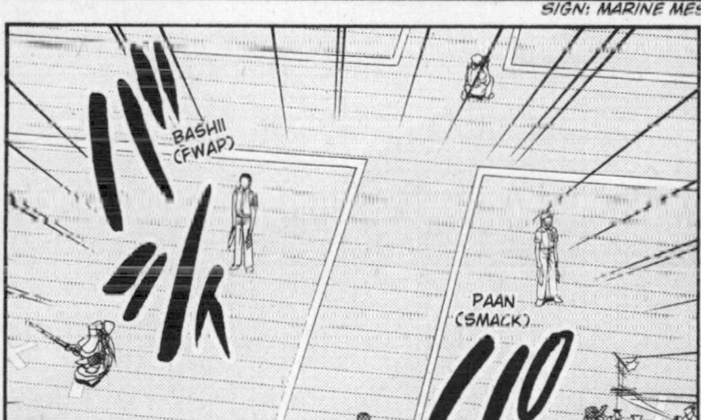
バシッ
BASHII
(FWAP)
PAAN
(SMACK)
パァーン

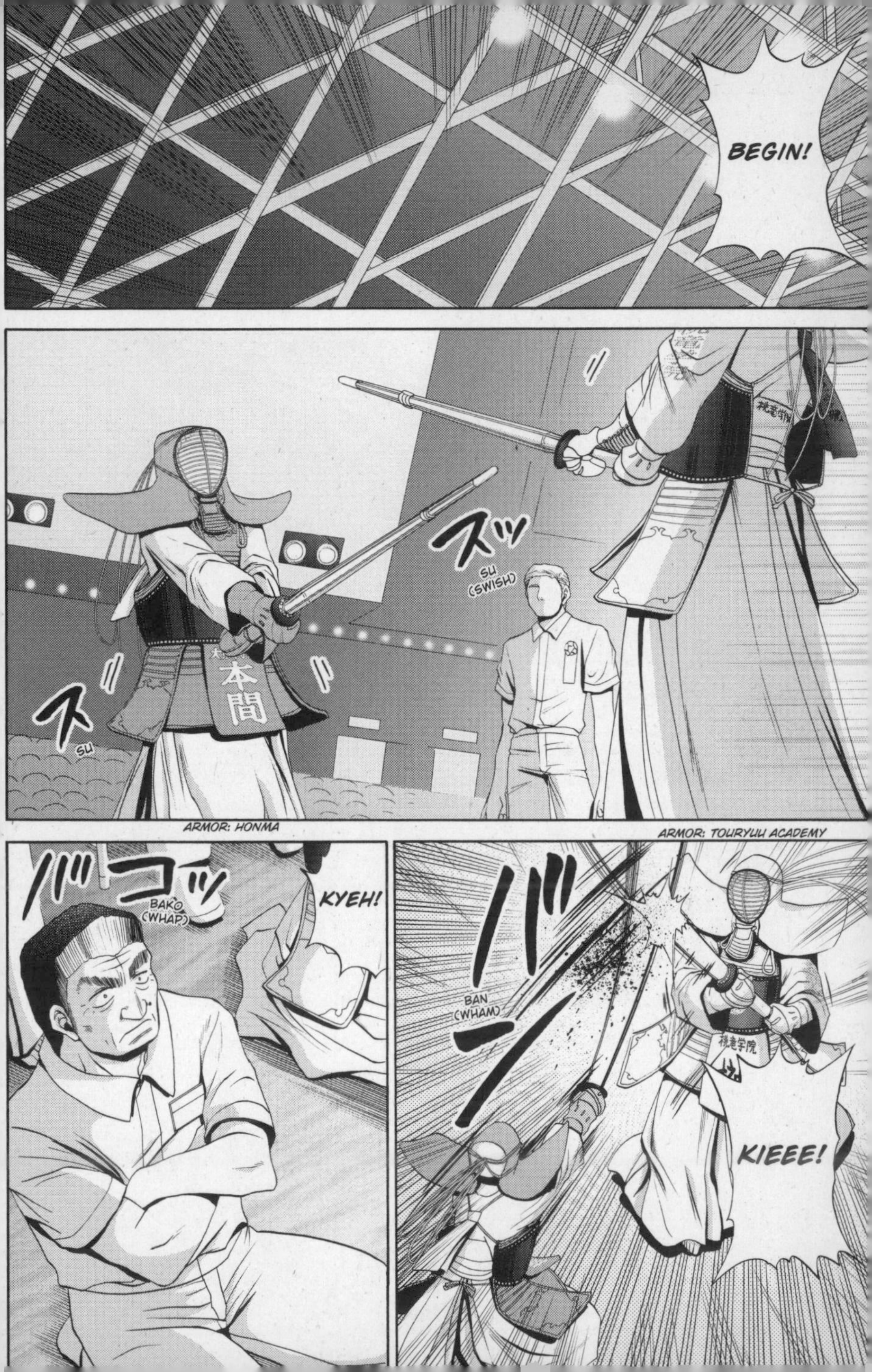
BEGIN!
スッ
SU (SWISH)
本間
ス
SU
ARMOR: TOURYUU ACADEMY
ARMOR: HONMA
バン
BAN (WHAM)
桃竜学院
KIEEE!
バコッ
BAKO (WHAP)
KYEH!

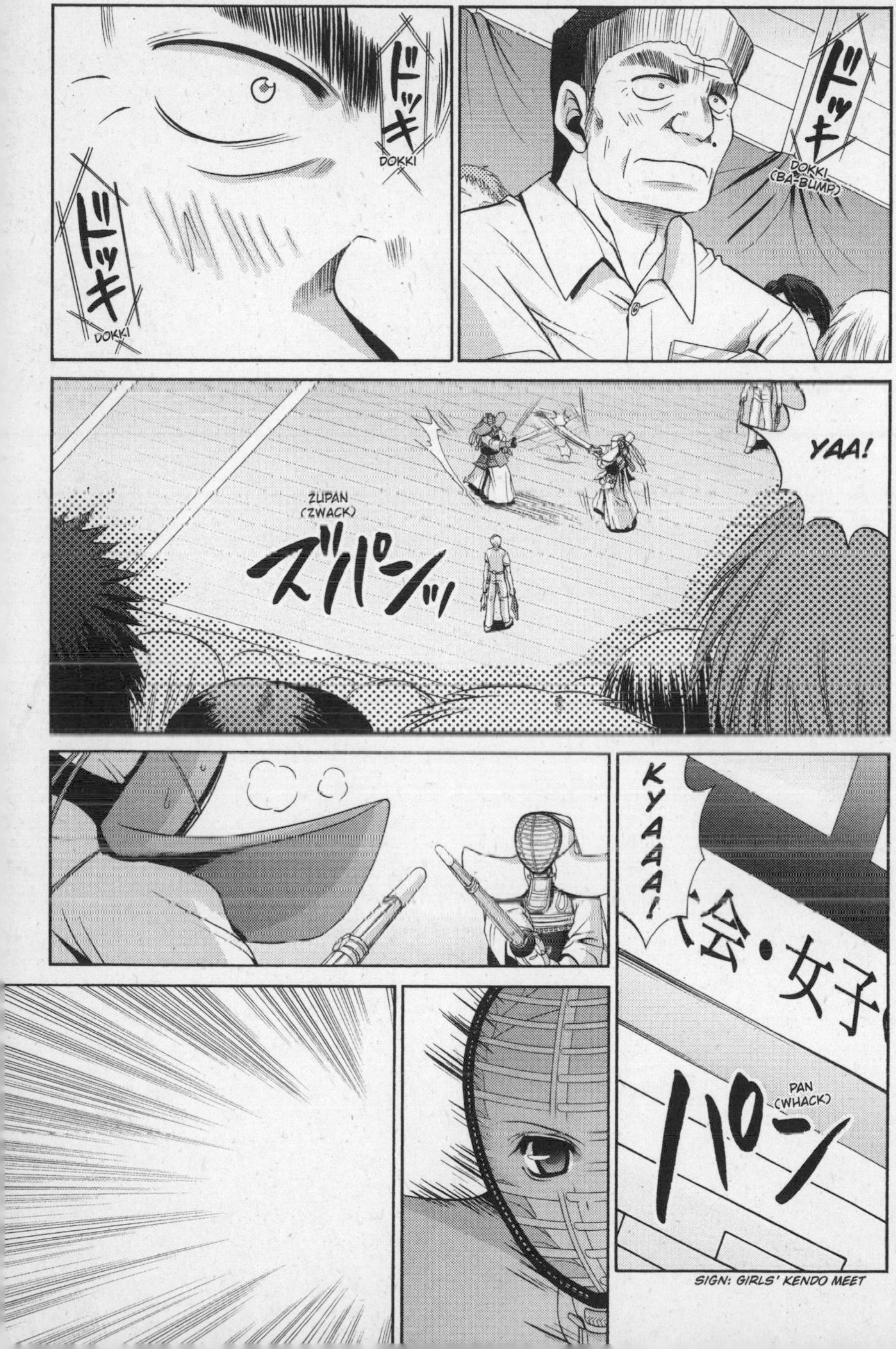
ドッキ
DOKKI (BA-BUMP)
ドッキ
DOKKI
ドッキ
DOKKI
YAA!
ズパンッ
ZUPAN (ZWACK)
KYAAAA!
会・女子
パーン
PAN (WHACK)
SIGN: GIRLS' KENDO MEET

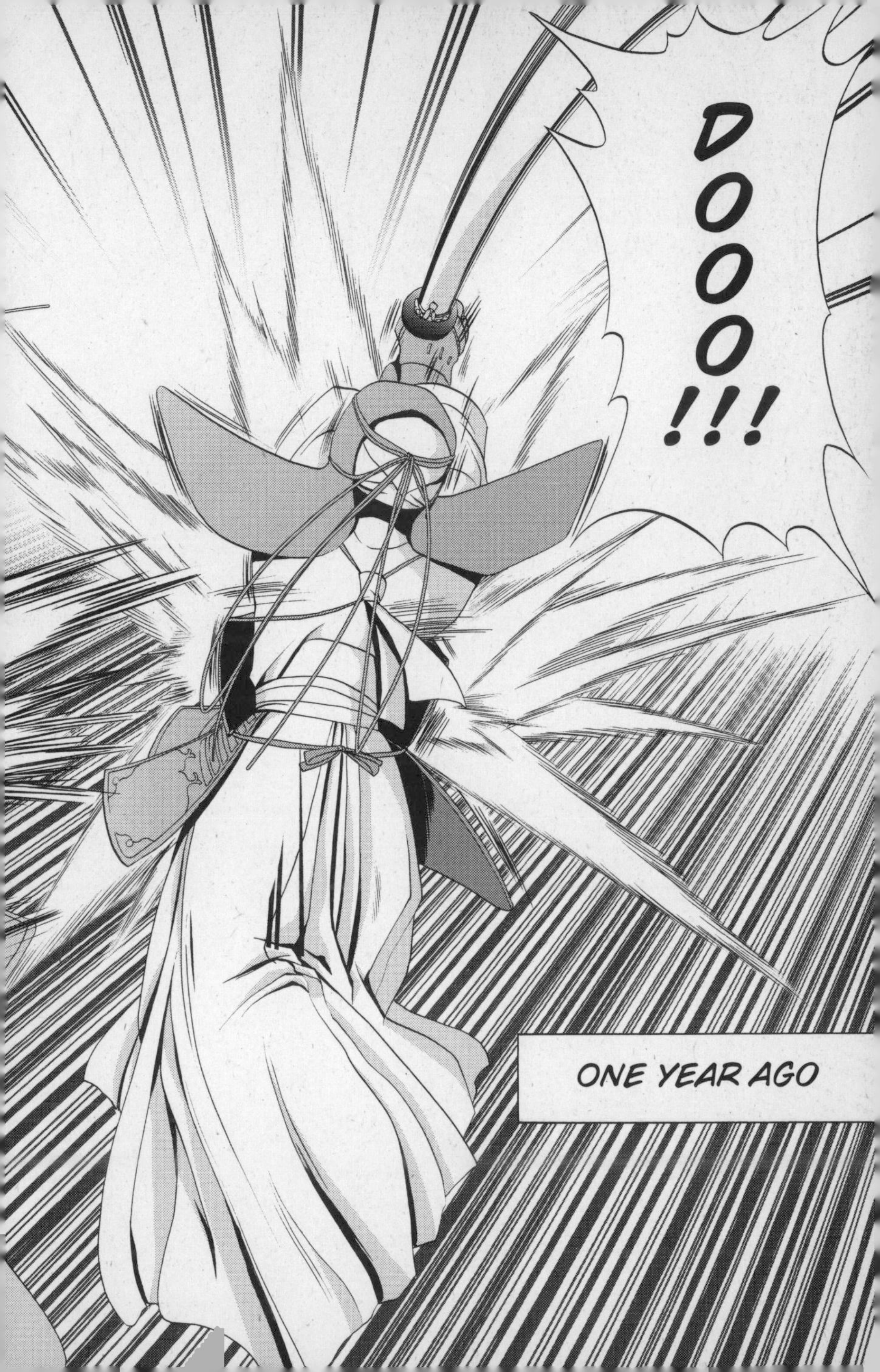
DOOOO!!!
ONE YEAR AGO

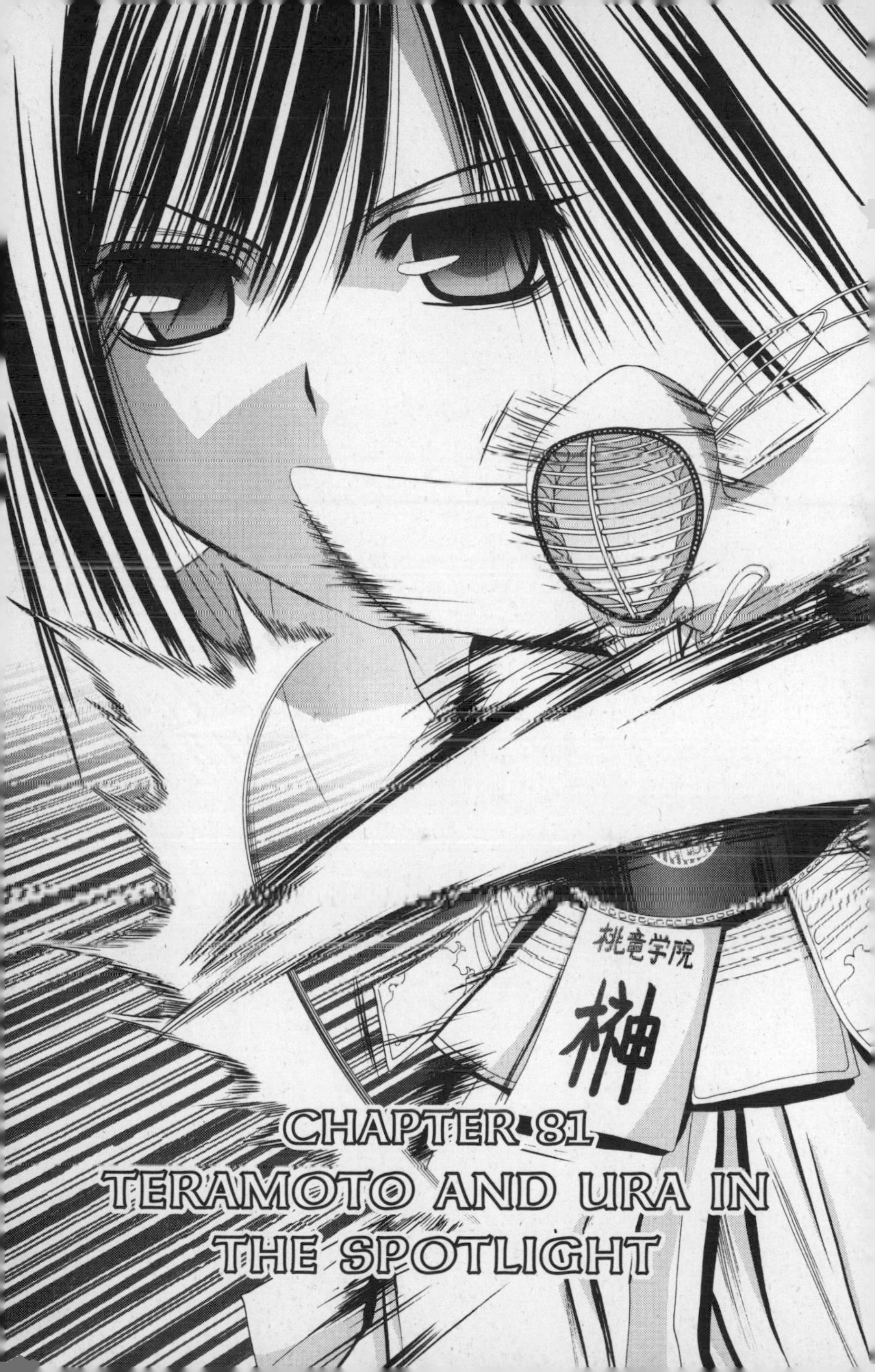
桃竜学院
榊
CHAPTER 81
TERAMOTO AND URA IN THE SPOTLIGHT

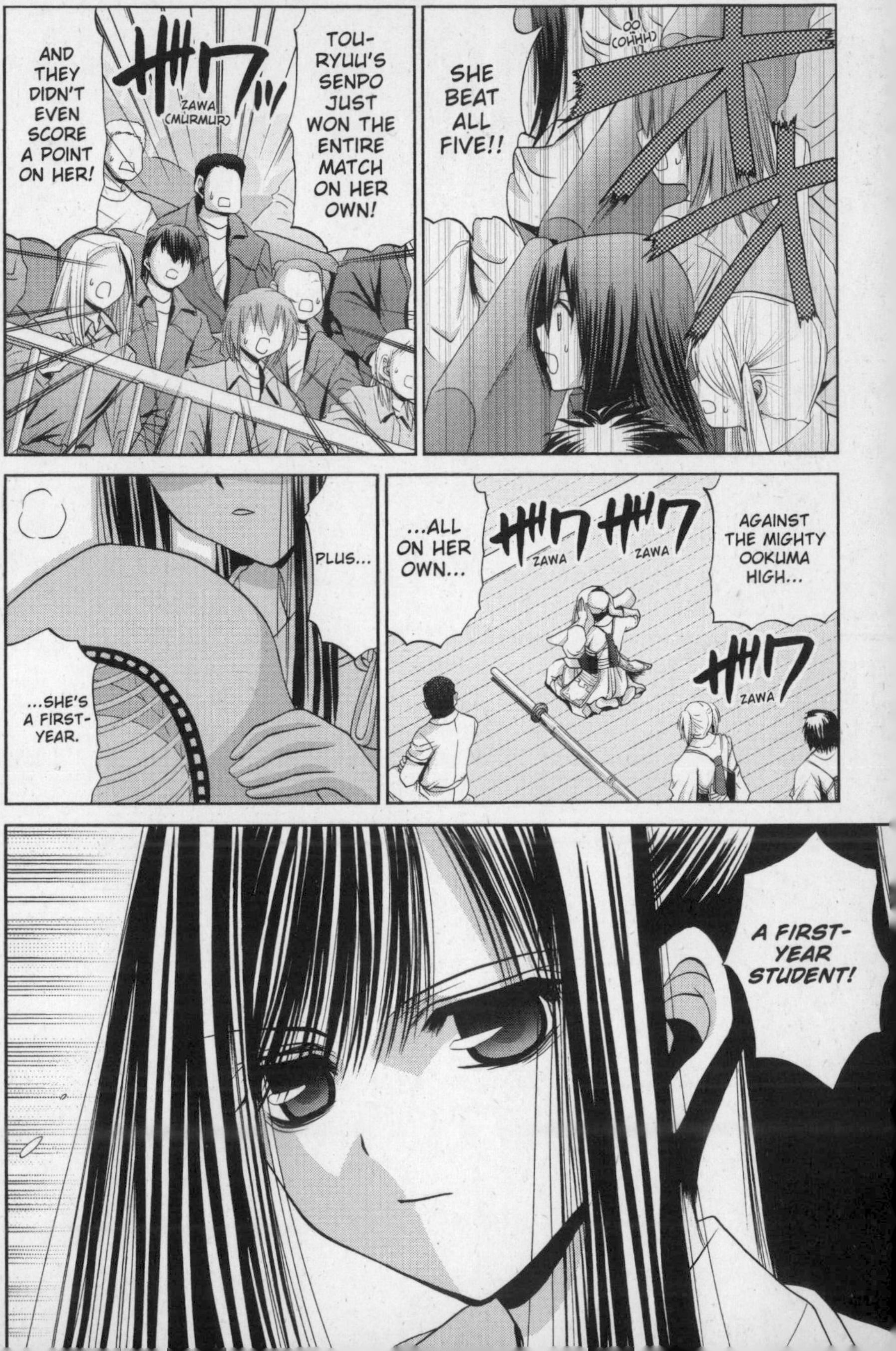
OO (OHHH)
SHE BEAT ALL FIVE!!
TOU-RYUU'S SENPO JUST WON THE ENTIRE MATCH ON HER OWN!
ZAWA (MURMUR)
AND THEY DIDN'T EVEN SCORE A POINT ON HER!
AGAINST THE MIGHTY OOKUMA HIGH...
ZAWA
ZAWA
...ALL ON HER OWN...
ZAWA
PLUS...
...SHE'S A FIRST-YEAR.
A FIRST-YEAR STUDENT!

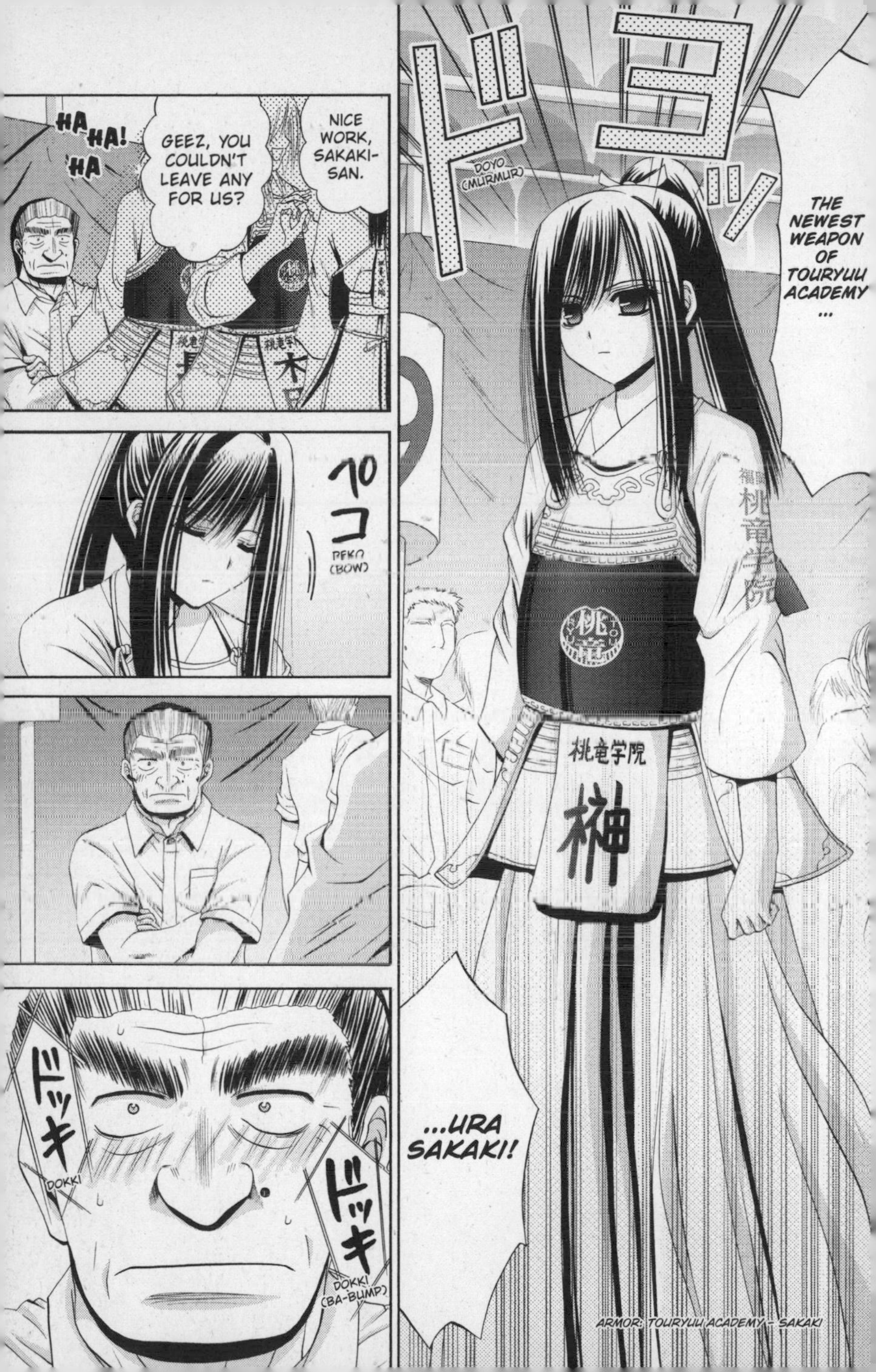
ドヨッ
DOYO (MURMUR)
THE NEWEST WEAPON OF TOURYUU ACADEMY ...
...URA SAKAKI!
ARMOR: TOURYUU ACADEMY - SAKAKI
NICE WORK, SAKAKI-SAN.
GEEZ, YOU COULDN'T LEAVE ANY FOR US?
HA HA! HA
ペコ
PEKO (BOW)
ドッキ
DOKKI
ドッキ
DOKKI (BA-BUMP)

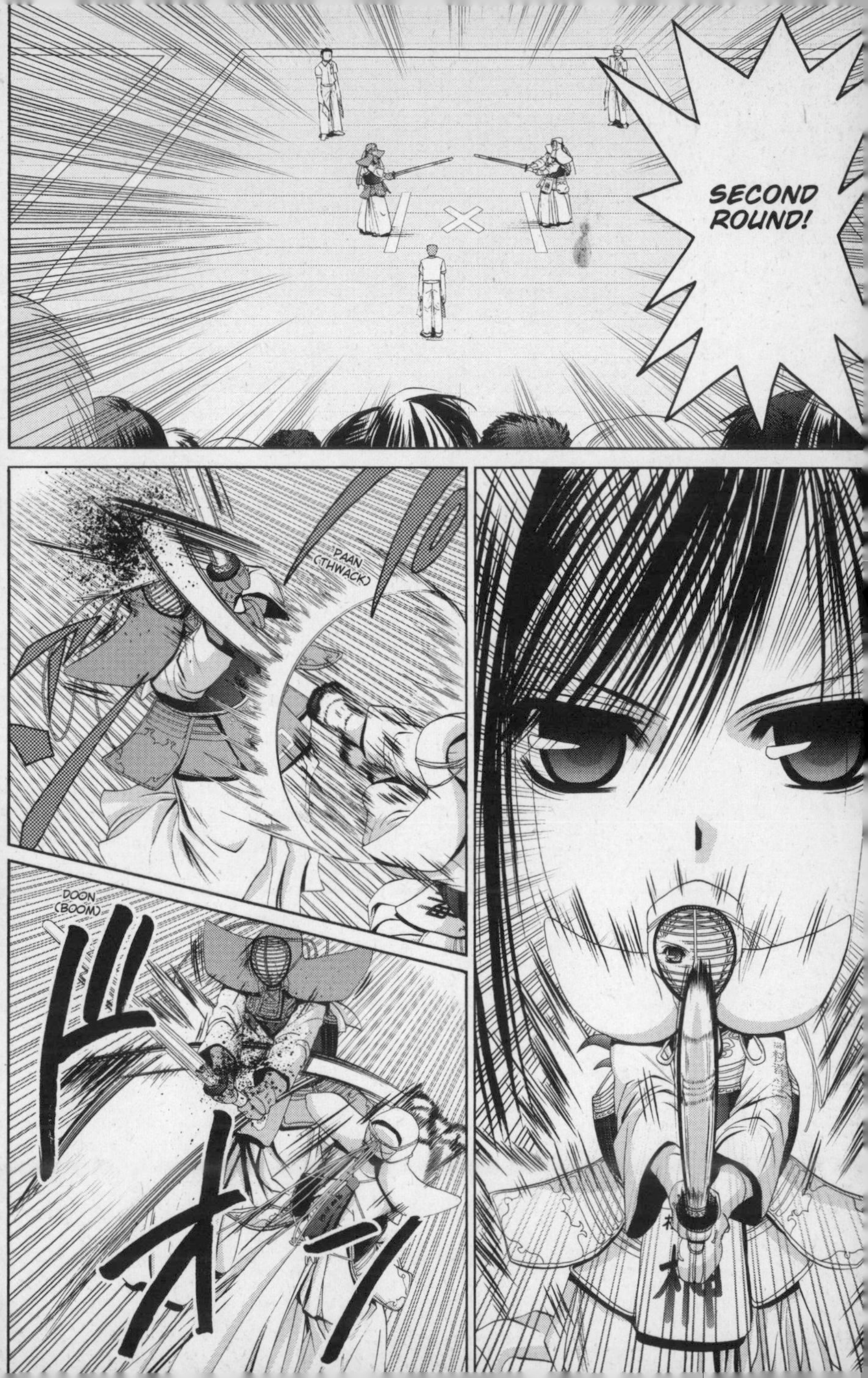
SECOND ROUND!
PAAN (THWACK)
DOON (BOOM)

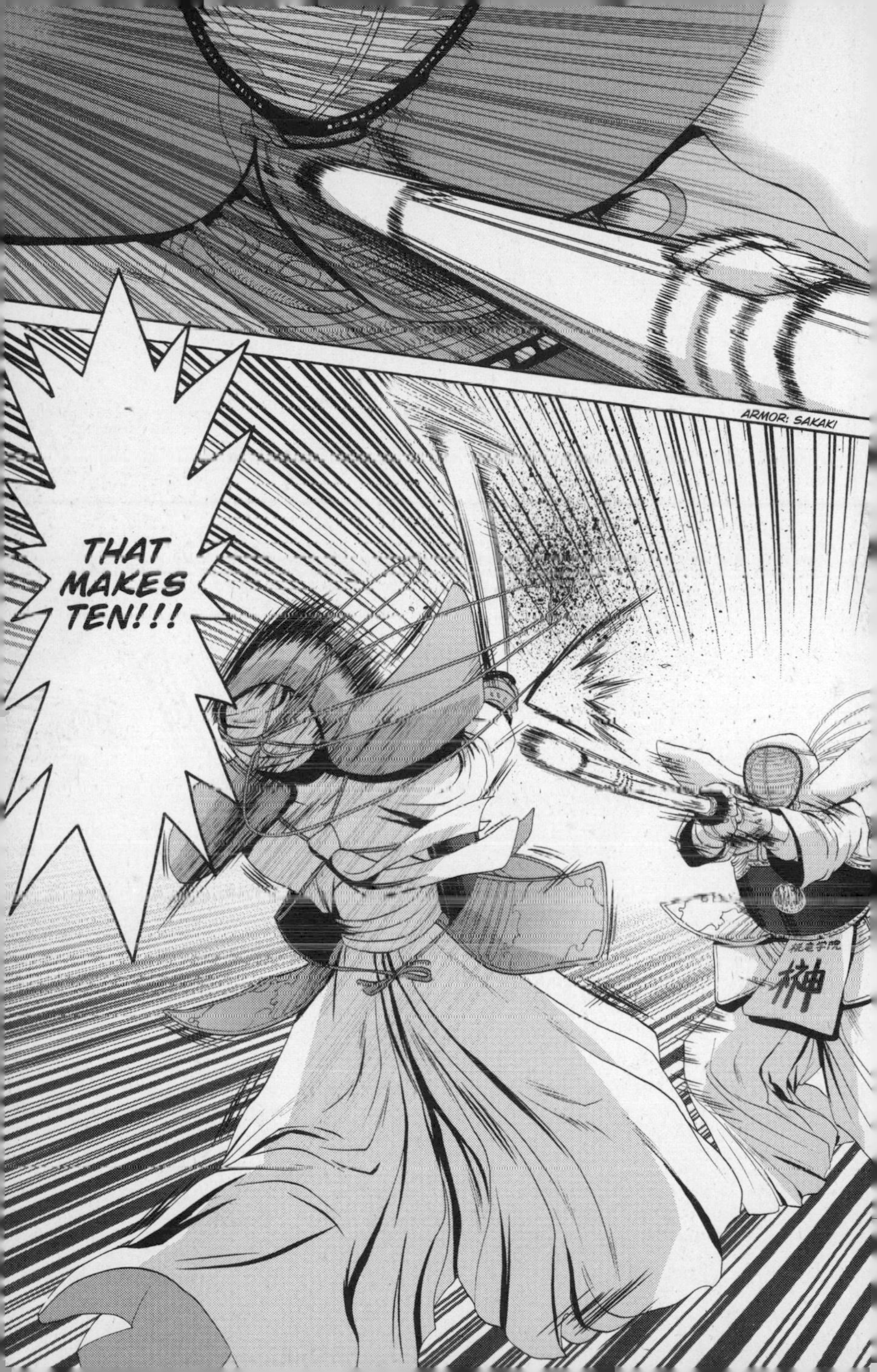
ARMOR: SAKAKI
THAT MAKES TEN!!!
榊

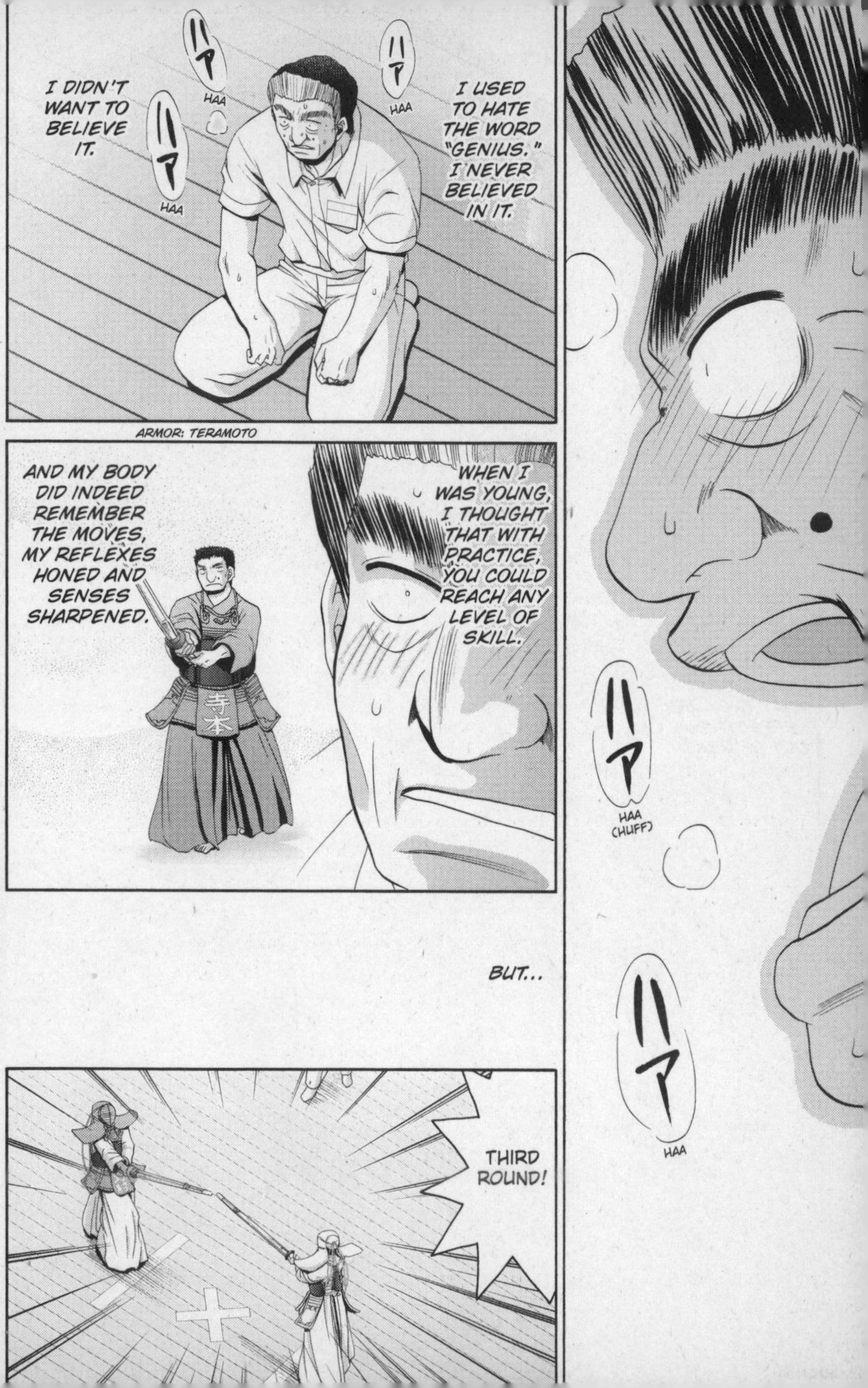
ハア
HAA (HUFF)
ハア
HAA
I USED TO HATE THE WORD "GENIUS." I NEVER BELIEVED IN IT.
ハア
HAA
ハア
HAA
ハア
HAA
I DIDN'T WANT TO BELIEVE IT.
ARMOR: TERAMOTO
WHEN I WAS YOUNG, I THOUGHT THAT WITH PRACTICE, YOU COULD REACH ANY LEVEL OF SKILL.
AND MY BODY DID INDEED REMEMBER THE MOVES, MY REFLEXES HONED AND SENSES SHARPENED.
寺本
BUT...
THIRD ROUND!

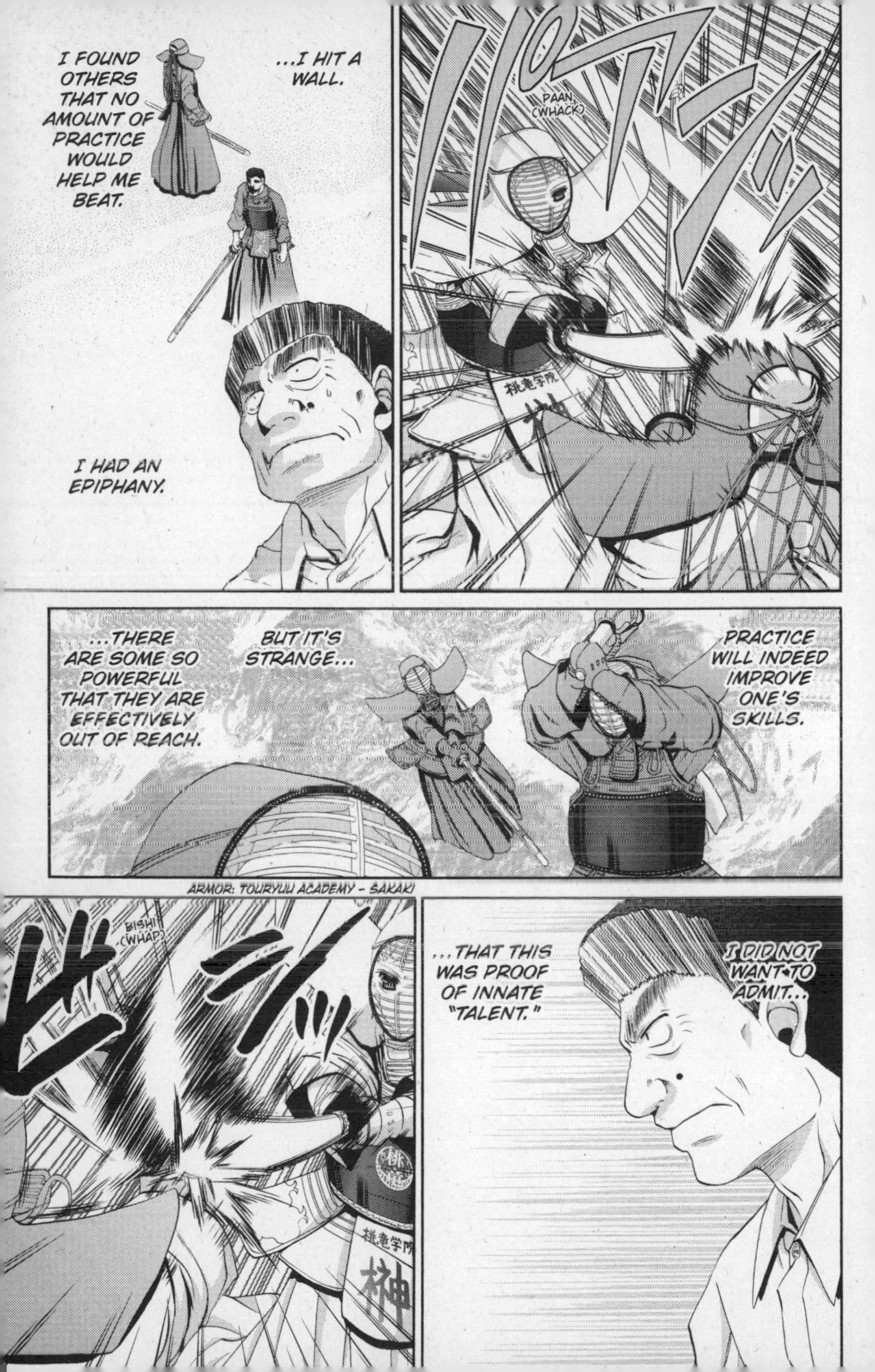
PAAN (WHACK)
...I HIT A WALL.
I FOUND OTHERS THAT NO AMOUNT OF PRACTICE WOULD HELP ME BEAT.
I HAD AN EPIPHANY.
PRACTICE WILL INDEED IMPROVE ONE'S SKILLS.
BUT IT'S STRANGE...
...THERE ARE SOME SO POWERFUL THAT THEY ARE EFFECTIVELY OUT OF REACH.
ARMOR: TOURYUU ACADEMY - SAKAKI
I DID NOT WANT TO ADMIT...
...THAT THIS WAS PROOF OF INNATE "TALENT."
BISHI (WHAP)

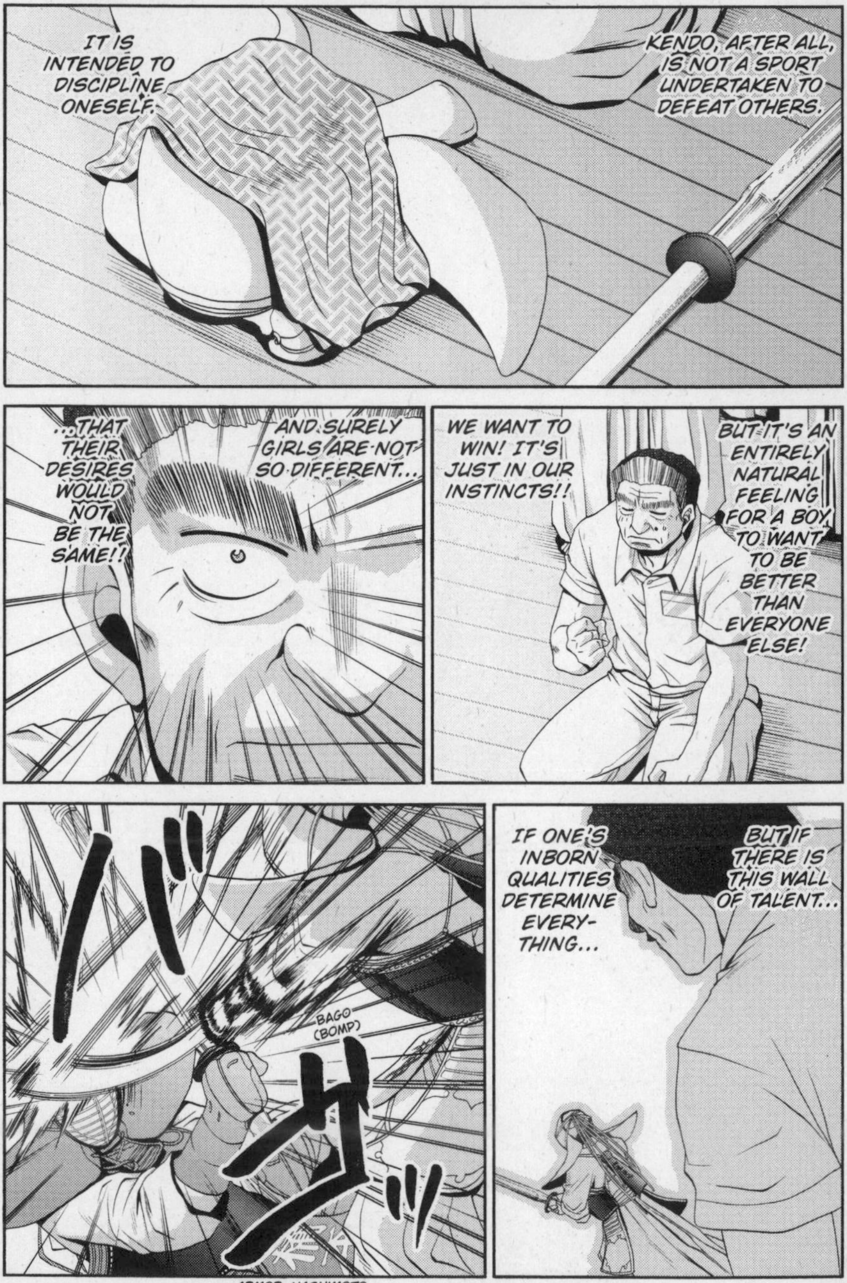
KENDO, AFTER ALL, IS NOT A SPORT UNDERTAKEN TO DEFEAT OTHERS.
IT IS INTENDED TO DISCIPLINE ONESELF.
BUT IT'S AN ENTIRELY NATURAL FEELING FOR A BOY TO WANT TO BE BETTER THAN EVERYONE ELSE!
WE WANT TO WIN! IT'S JUST IN OUR INSTINCTS!!
AND SURELY GIRLS ARE NOT SO DIFFERENT...
...THAT THEIR DESIRES WOULD NOT BE THE SAME!!
BUT IF THERE IS THIS WALL OF TALENT...
IF ONE'S INBORN QUALITIES DETERMINE EVERY-THING...
BAGO (BOMP)
ARMOR: HASHIMOTO

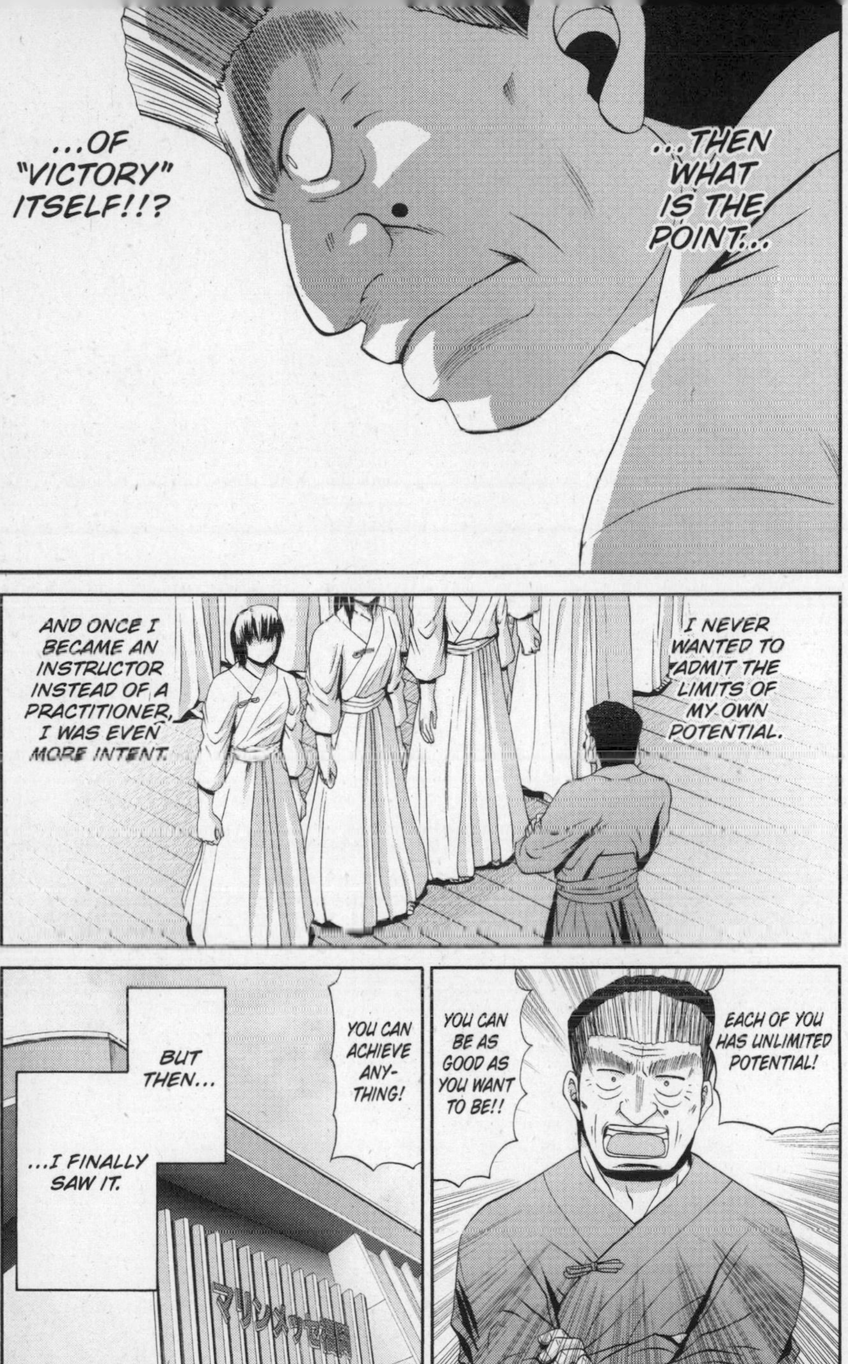
...THEN WHAT IS THE POINT...
...OF "VICTORY" ITSELF!!?
I NEVER WANTED TO ADMIT THE LIMITS OF MY OWN POTENTIAL.
AND ONCE I BECAME AN INSTRUCTOR INSTEAD OF A PRACTITIONER, I WAS EVEN MORE INTENT.
EACH OF YOU HAS UNLIMITED POTENTIAL!
YOU CAN BE AS GOOD AS YOU WANT TO BE!!
YOU CAN ACHIEVE ANY-THING!
BUT THEN...
...I FINALLY SAW IT.
SIGN: MARINE MESSE FUKUOKA

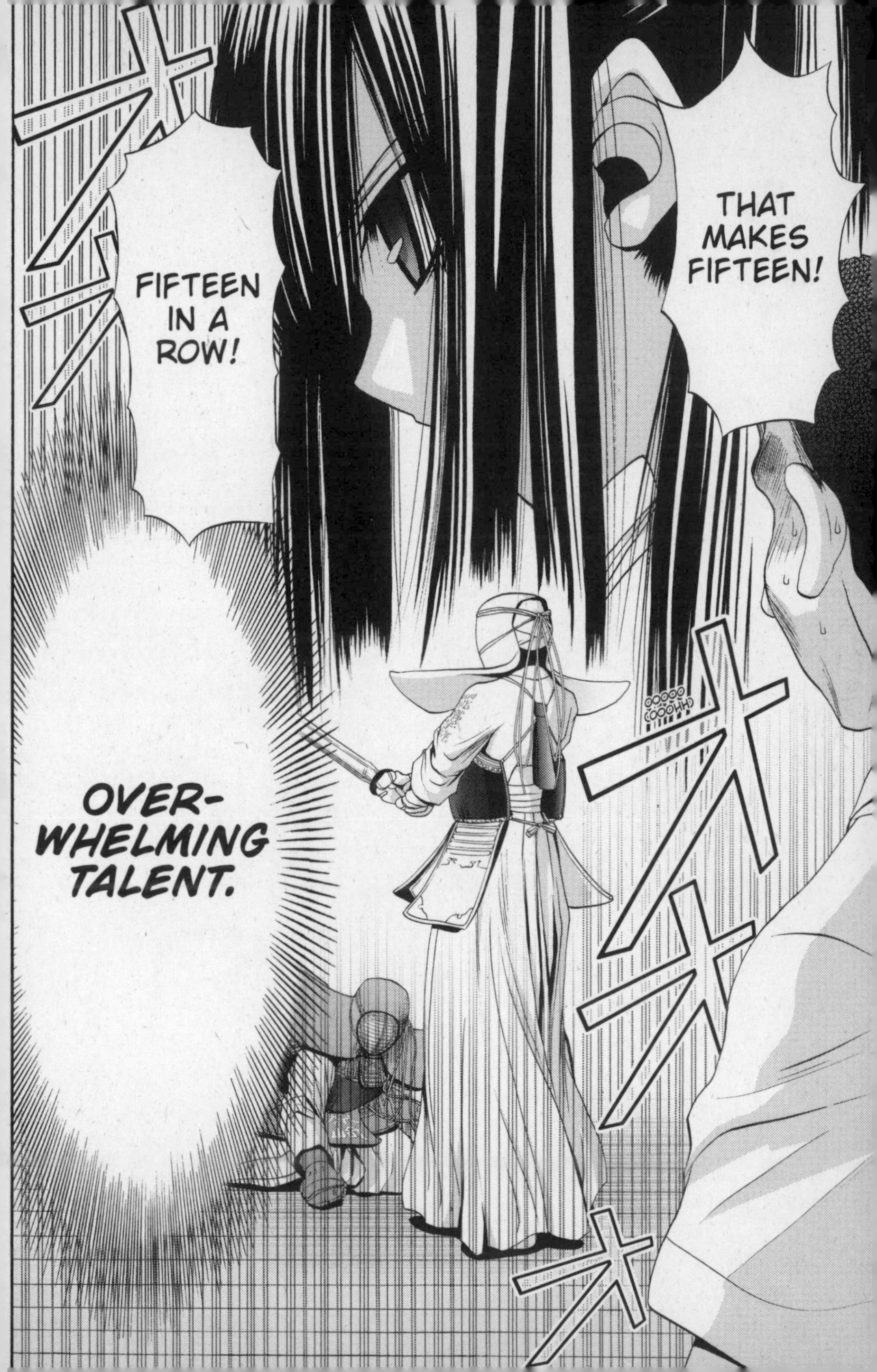
THAT MAKES FIFTEEN!
FIFTEEN IN A ROW!
OOOOOOOOOHH
OVER-WHELMING TALENT.

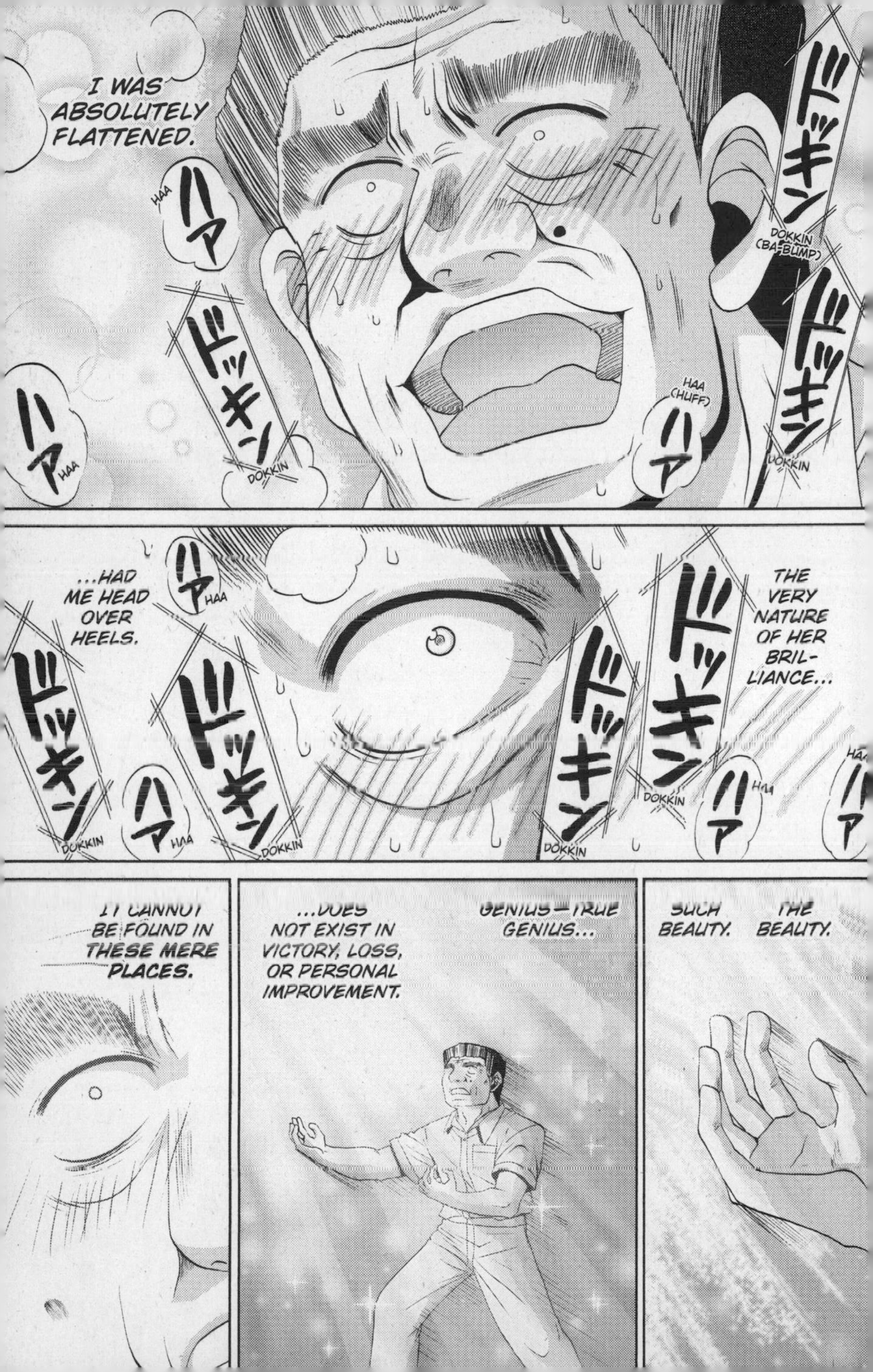
ドッキン
DOKKIN (BA-BUMP)
ドッキン
DOKKIN
HAA (HUFF)
ハア
I WAS ABSOLUTELY FLATTENED.
HAA
ハア
ドッキン
DOKKIN
ハア
HAA
HAA
ハア
ハア
HAA
THE VERY NATURE OF HER BRIL-LIANCE...
ドッキン
DOKKIN
ドッキン
DOKKIN
...HAD ME HEAD OVER HEELS.
ハア
HAA
ドッキン
DOKKIN
ハア
HAA
ドッキン
DOKKIN
THE BEAUTY.
SUCH BEAUTY.
GENIUS—TRUE GENIUS...
...DOES NOT EXIST IN VICTORY, LOSS, OR PERSONAL IMPROVEMENT.
IT CANNOT BE FOUND IN THESE MERE PLACES.

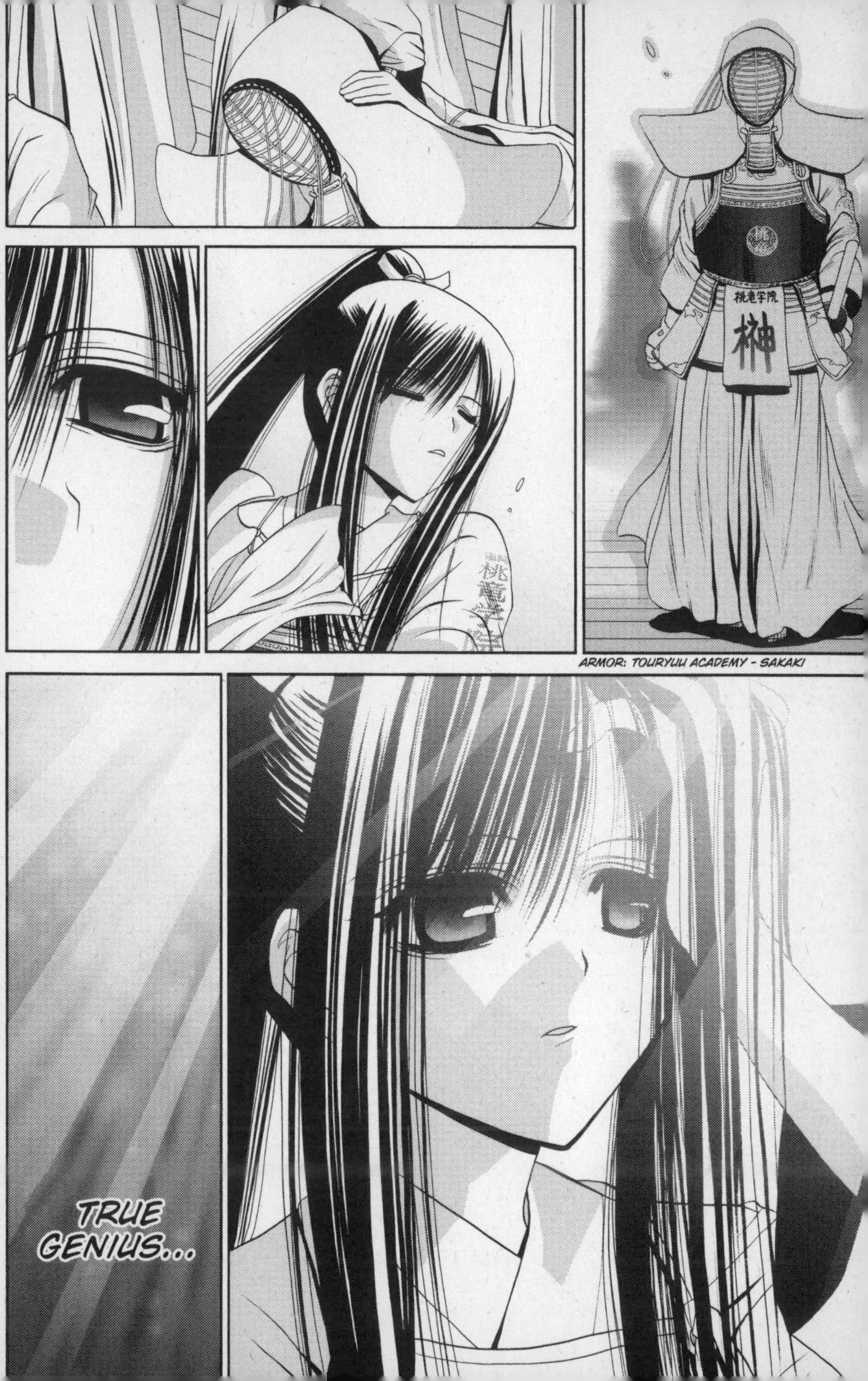
桃竜学院
榊
ARMOR: TOURYUU ACADEMY - SAKAKI
TRUE GENIUS...

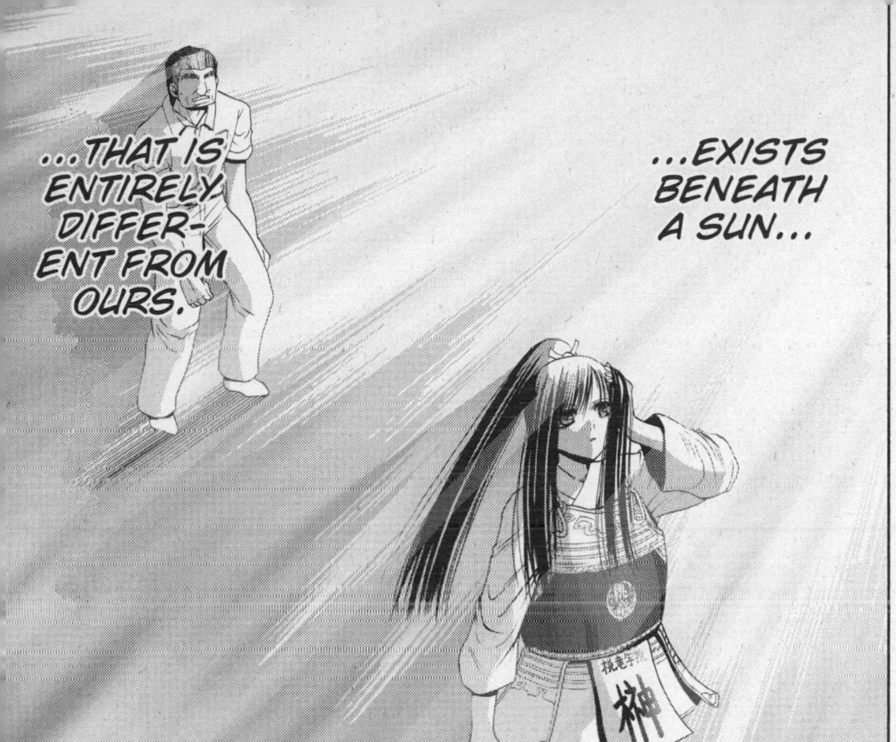
...EXISTS BENEATH A SUN...
...THAT IS ENTIRELY DIFFER-ENT FROM OURS.

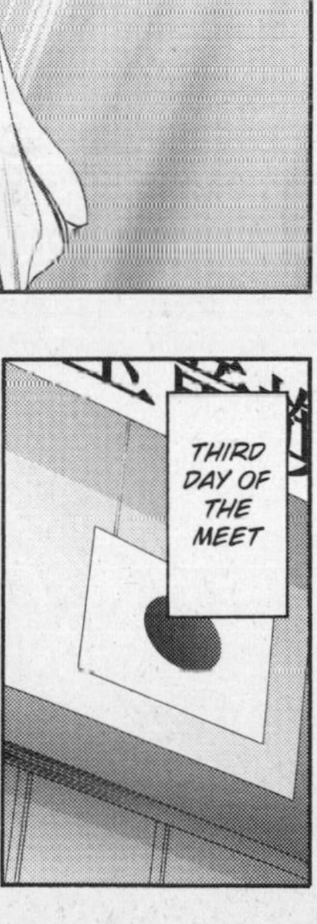
THIRD DAY OF THE MEET

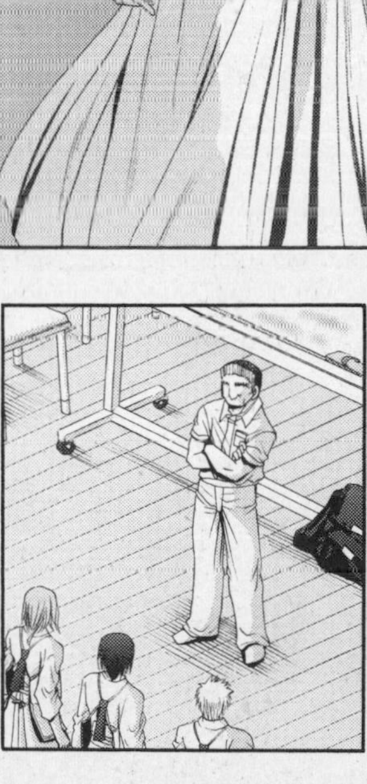

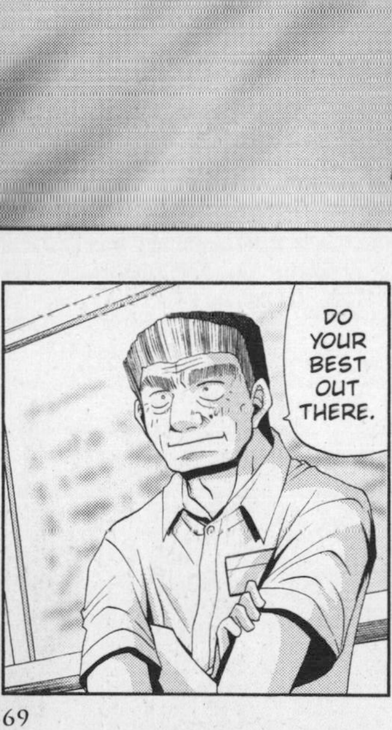
DO YOUR BEST OUT THERE.

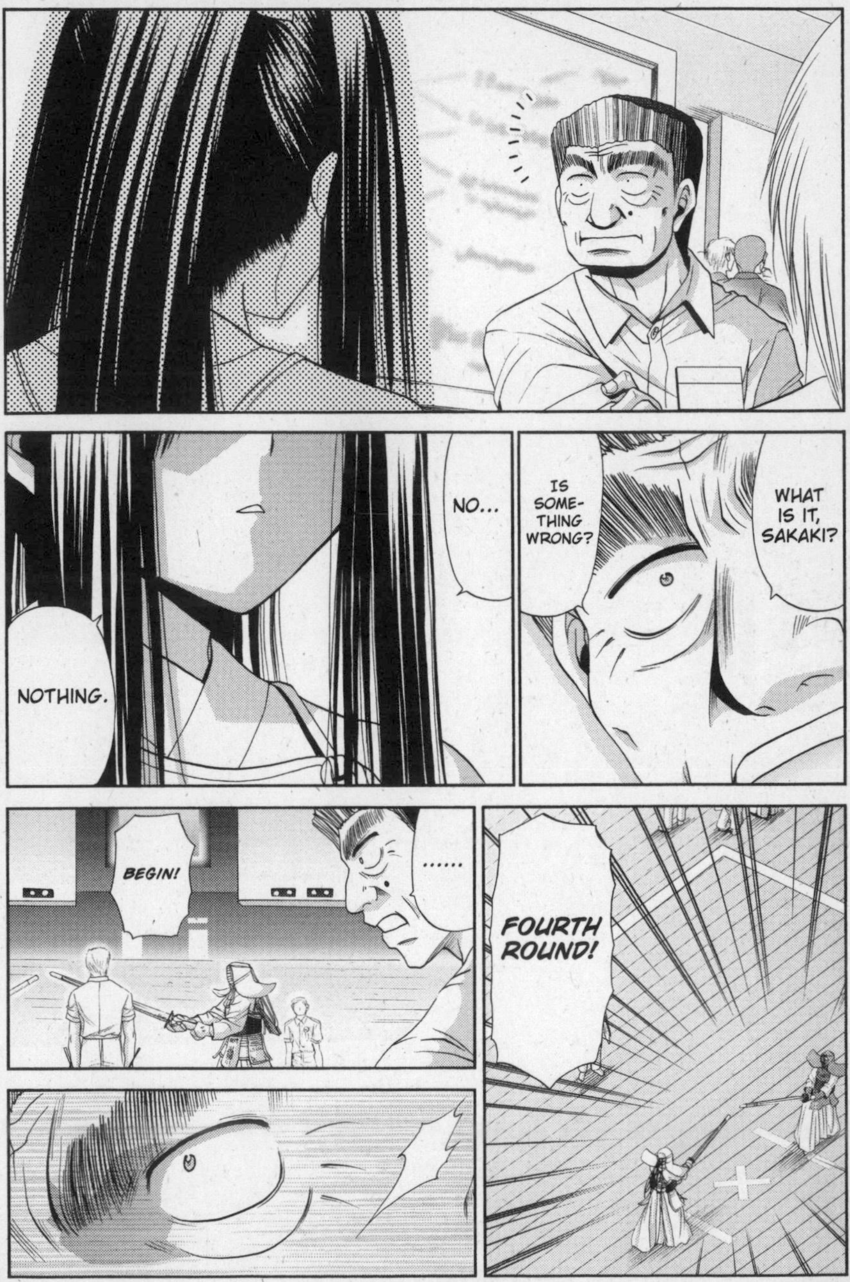
WHAT IS IT, SAKAKI?
IS SOME-THING WRONG?
NO...
NOTHING.
FOURTH ROUND!
......
BEGIN!

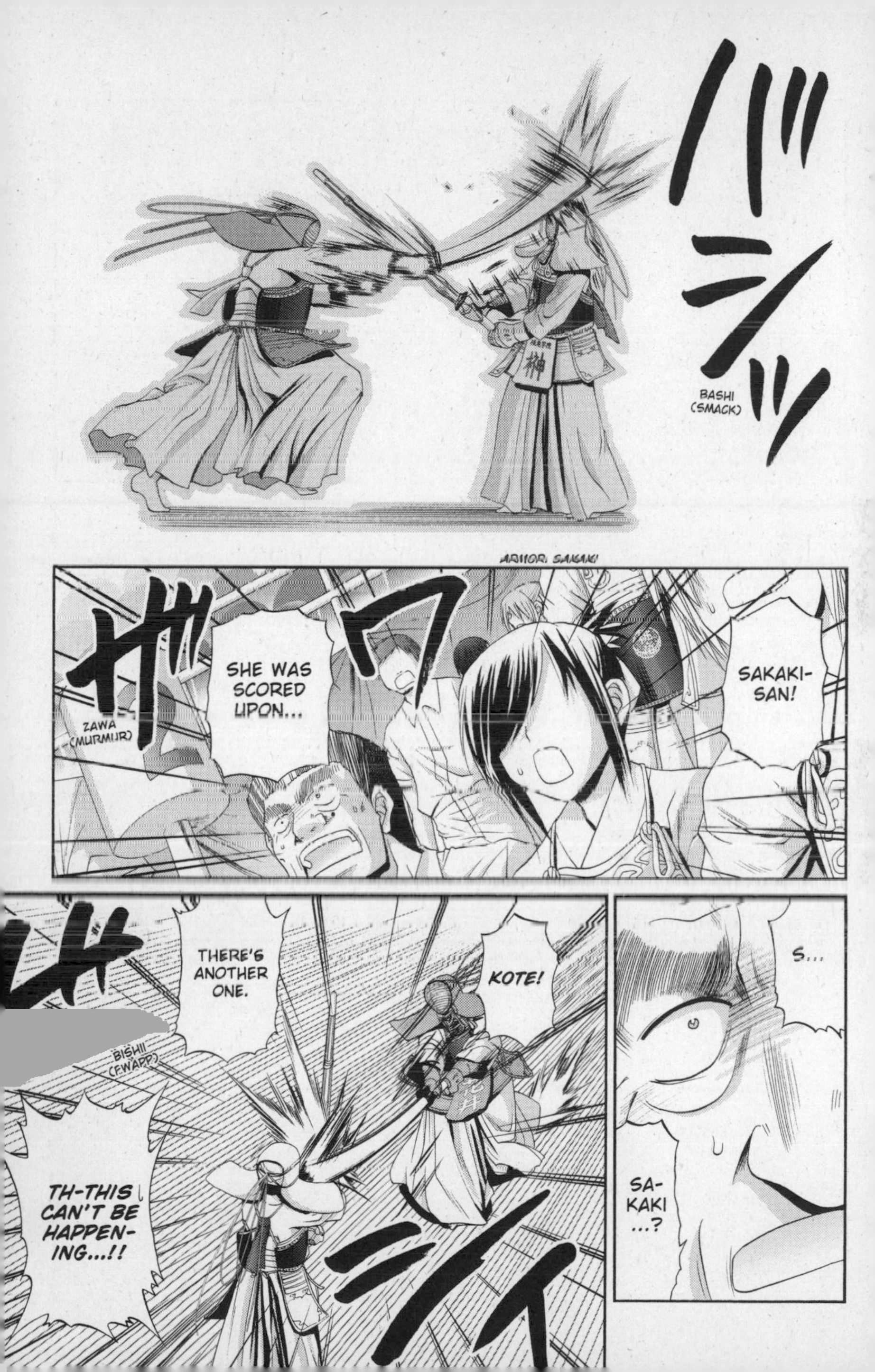
BASHI (SMACK)
ARMOR: SAKAKI
SAKAKI-SAN!
SHE WAS SCORED UPON...
ZAWA (MURMUR)
S...
SA-KAKI ...?
KOTE!
THERE'S ANOTHER ONE.
BISHII (F'WAPP)
TH-THIS CAN'T BE HAPPEN-ING...!!

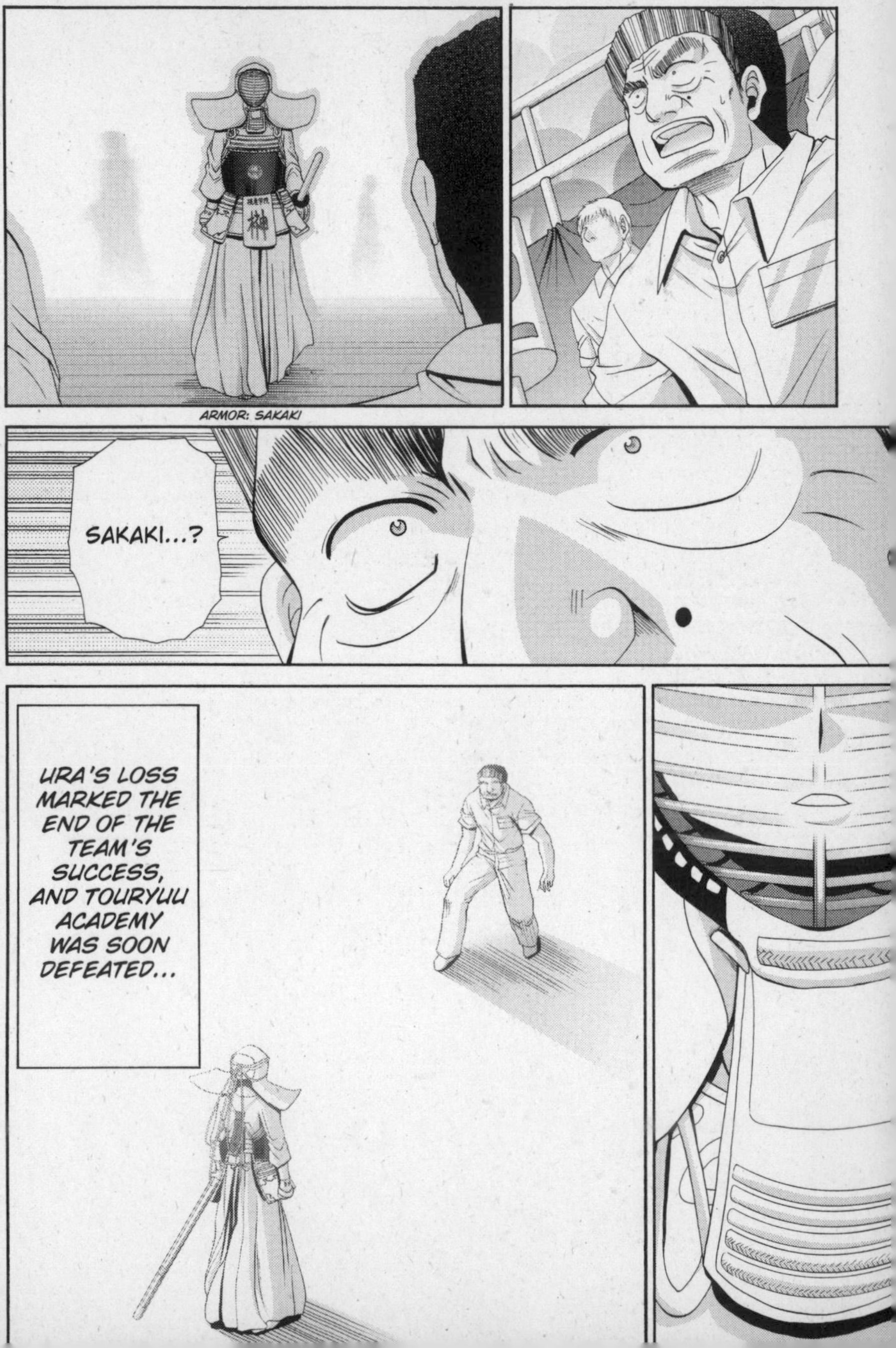
ARMOR: SAKAKI
SAKAKI...?
URA'S LOSS MARKED THE END OF THE TEAM'S SUCCESS, AND TOURYUU ACADEMY WAS SOON DEFEATED...

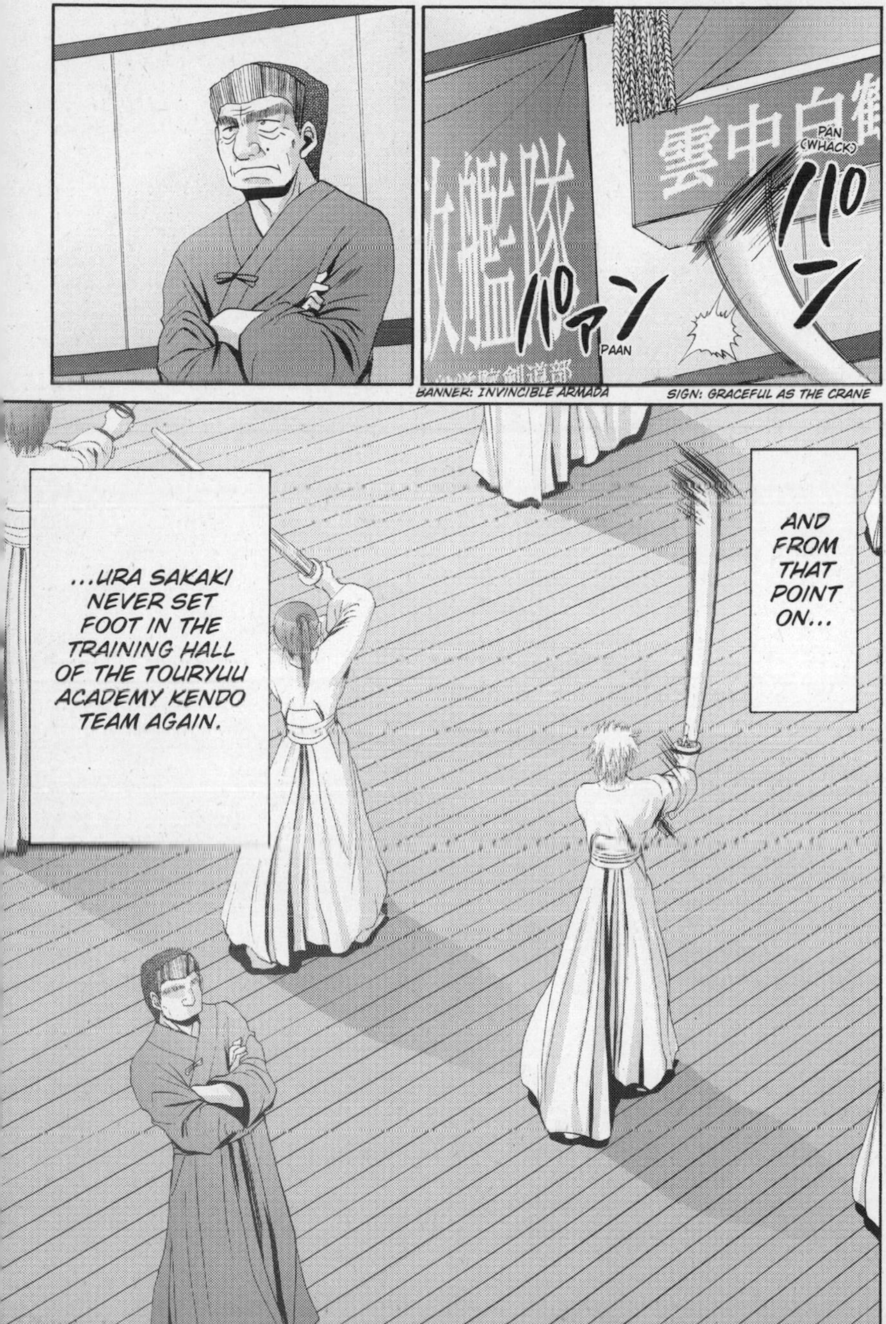
雲中白
PAN
(WHACK)
パン
パァン
PAAN
BANNER: INVINCIBLE ARMADA
SIGN: GRACEFUL AS THE CRANE
AND FROM THAT POINT ON...
...URA SAKAKI NEVER SET FOOT IN THE TRAINING HALL OF THE TOURYUU ACADEMY KENDO TEAM AGAIN.

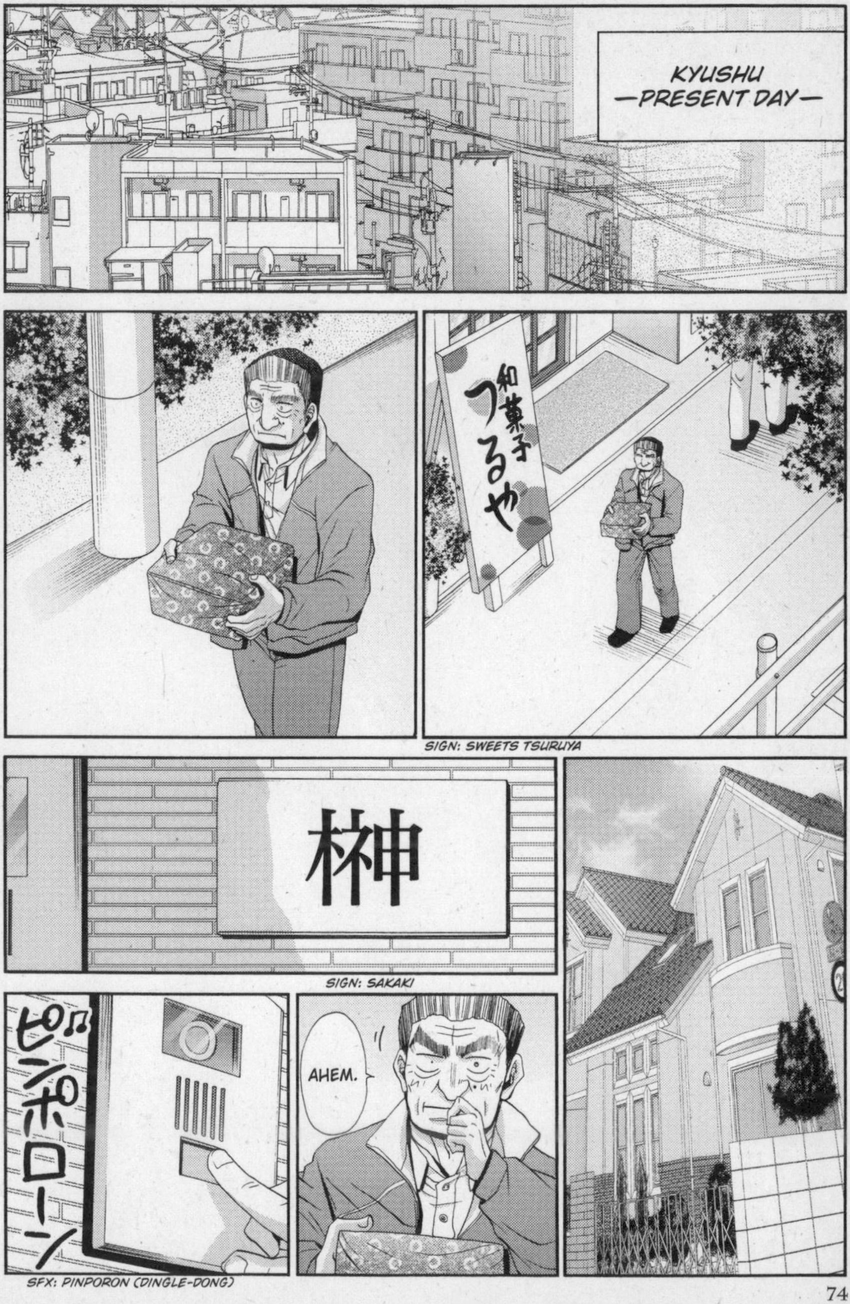
KYUSHU
—PRESENT DAY—
和菓子
つるや
SIGN: SWEETS TSURUYA
榊
SIGN: SAKAKI
AHEM.
ピンポローン♪
SFX: PINPORON (DINGLE-DONG)

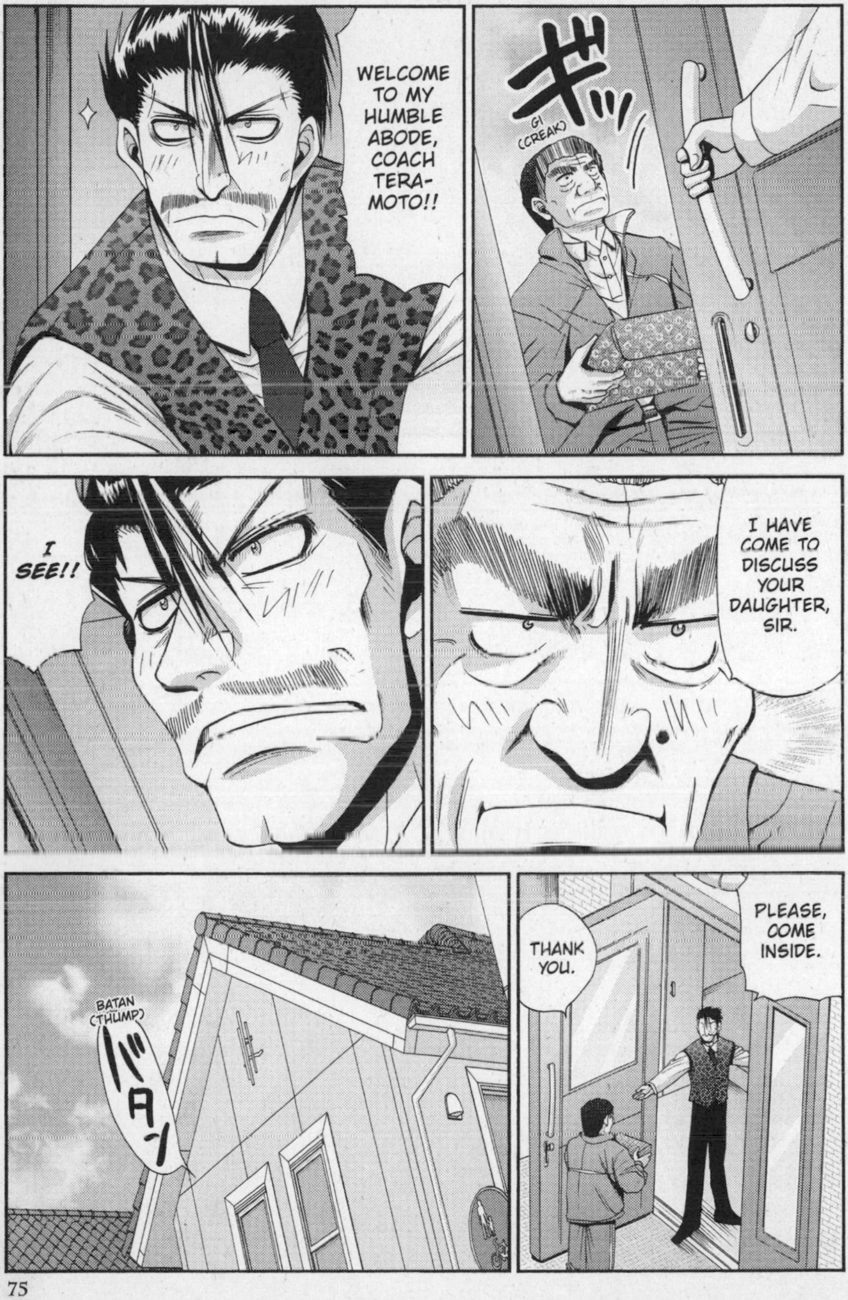
ギッ
GI (CREAK)
WELCOME TO MY HUMBLE ABODE, COACH TERA-MOTO!!
I HAVE COME TO DISCUSS YOUR DAUGHTER, SIR.
I SEE!!
PLEASE, COME INSIDE.
THANK YOU.
バタン
BATAN (THUMP)

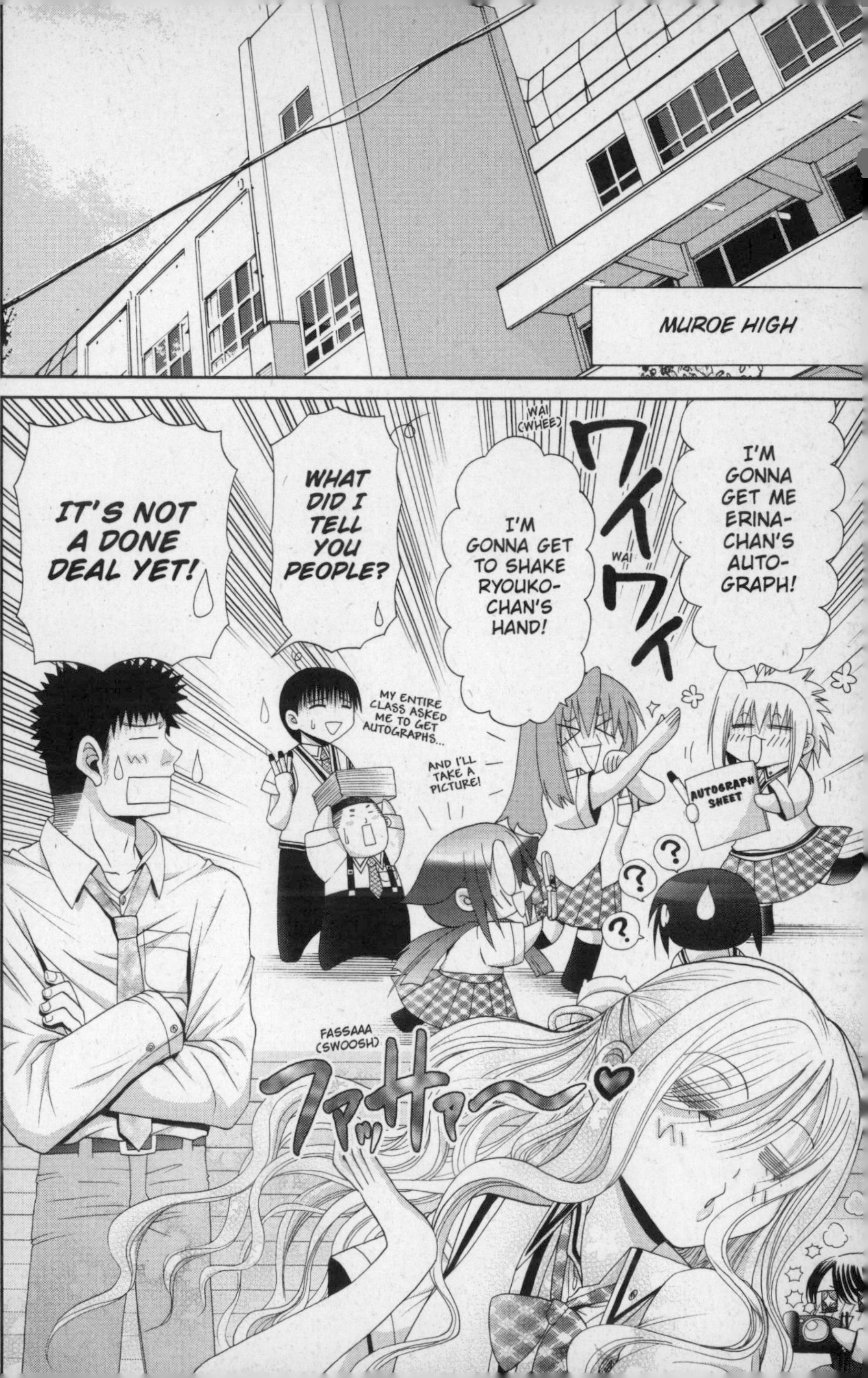
MUROE HIGH
I'M GONNA GET ME ERINA-CHAN'S AUTOGRAPH!
WAI (WHEE)
WAI
I'M GONNA GET TO SHAKE RYOUKO-CHAN'S HAND!
WHAT DID I TELL YOU PEOPLE?
IT'S NOT A DONE DEAL YET!
AUTOGRAPH SHEET
MY ENTIRE CLASS ASKED ME TO GET AUTOGRAPHS...
AND I'LL TAKE A PICTURE!
FASSAAA (SWOOSH)

BAMBOO BLADE

バンブーブレード

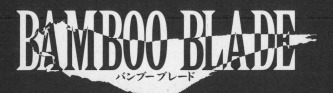

BAMBOO BLADE
バンブーブレード

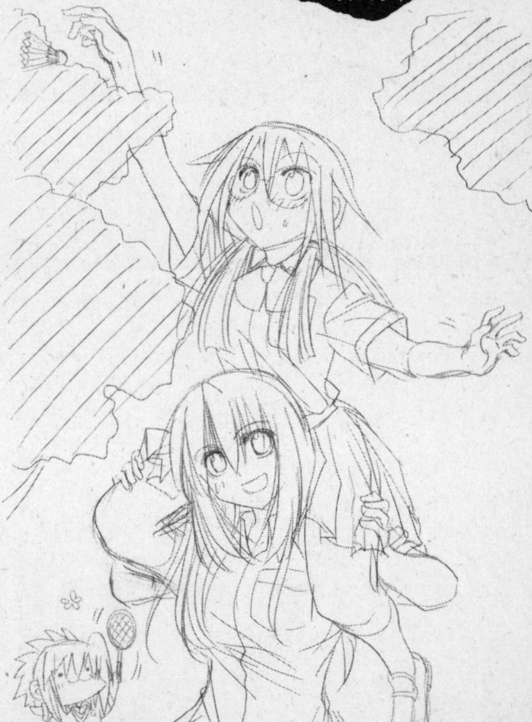

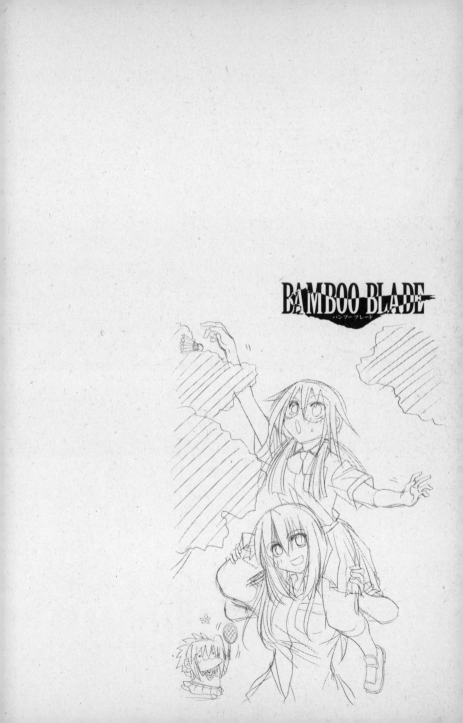

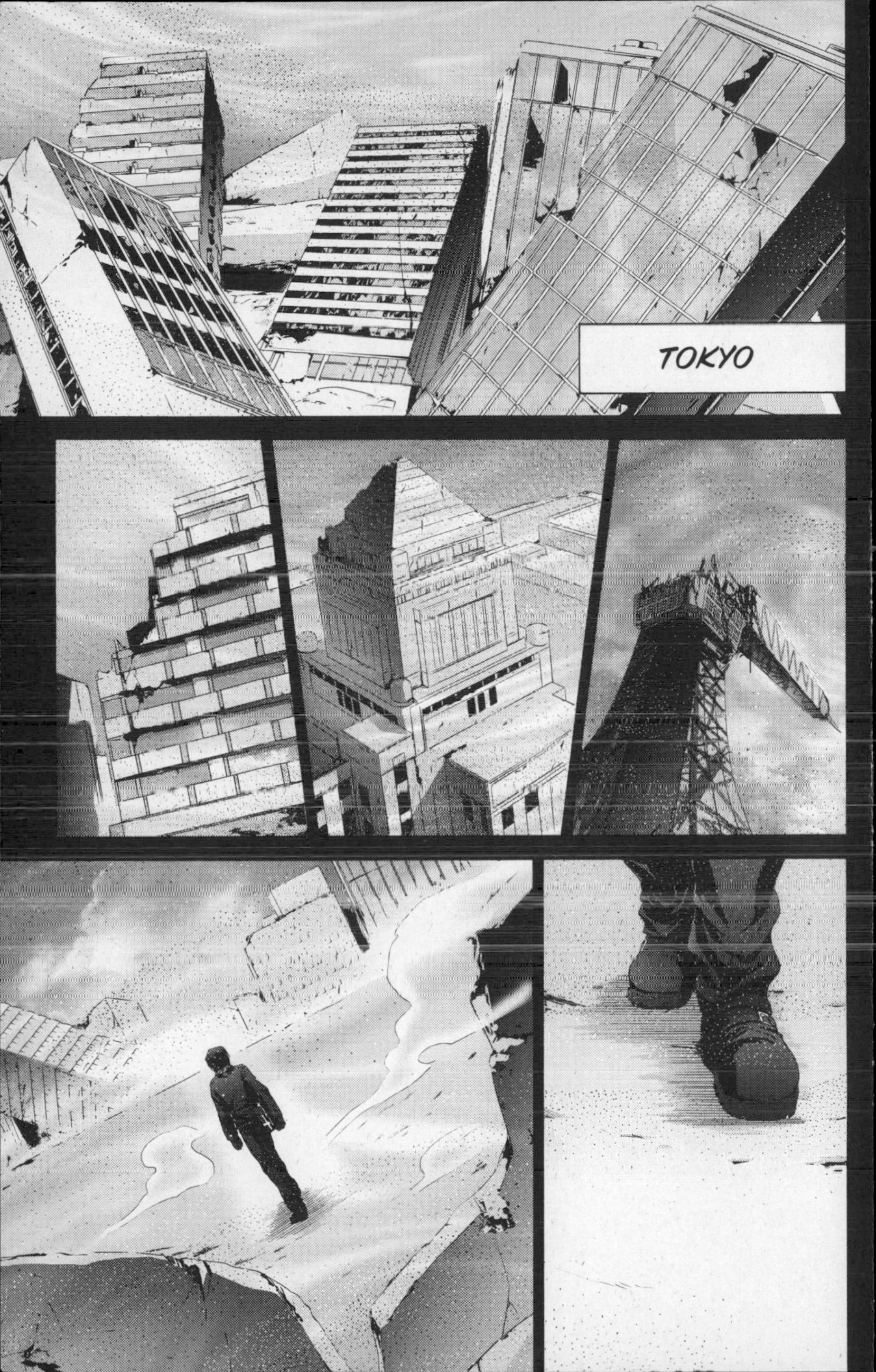
TOKYO

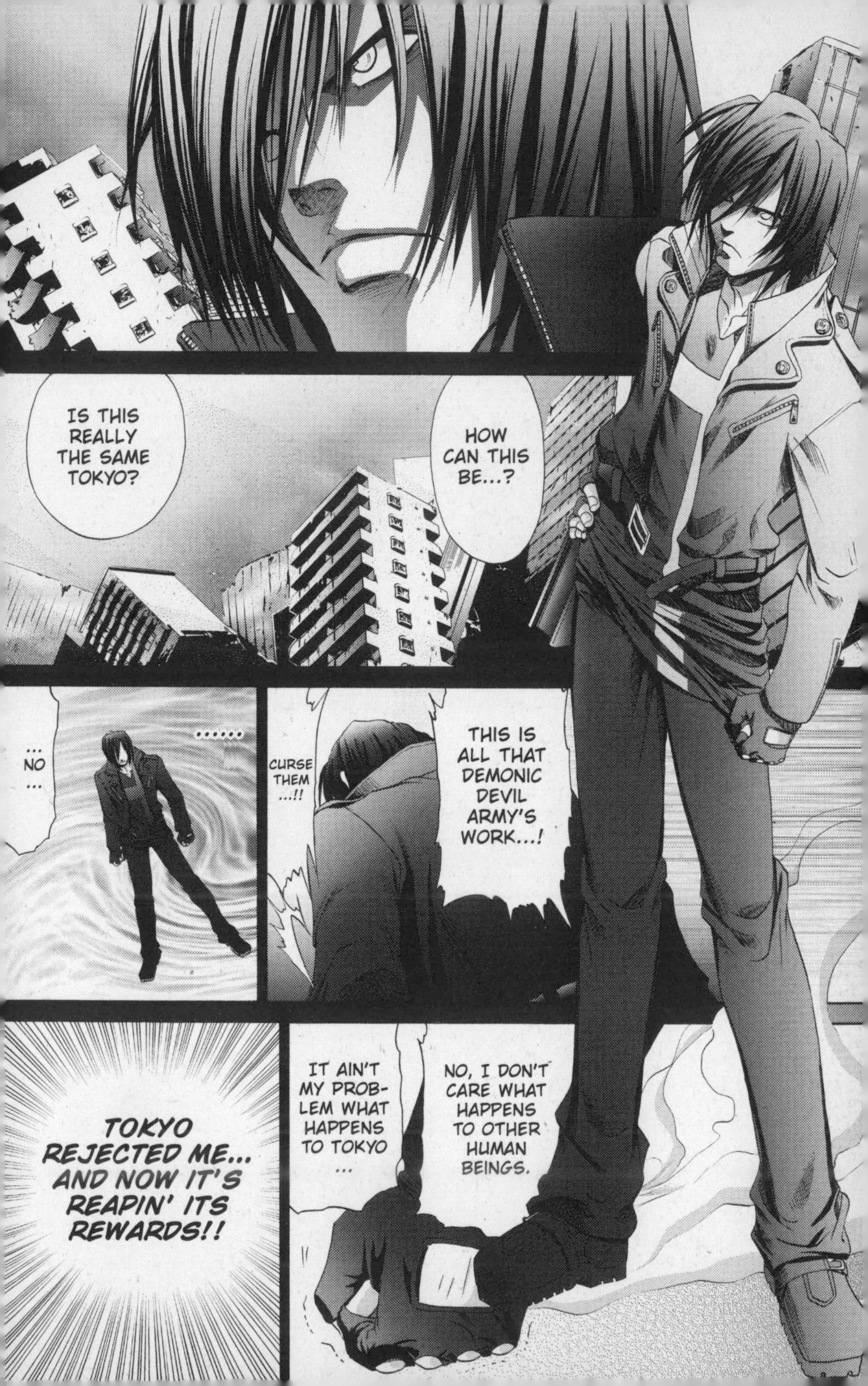
HOW CAN THIS BE...?
IS THIS REALLY THE SAME TOKYO?
THIS IS ALL THAT DEMONIC DEVIL ARMY'S WORK...!
CURSE THEM ...!!
......
... NO ...
NO, I DON'T CARE WHAT HAPPENS TO OTHER HUMAN BEINGS.
IT AIN'T MY PROB-LEM WHAT HAPPENS TO TOKYO ...
TOKYO REJECTED ME... AND NOW IT'S REAPIN' ITS REWARDS!!

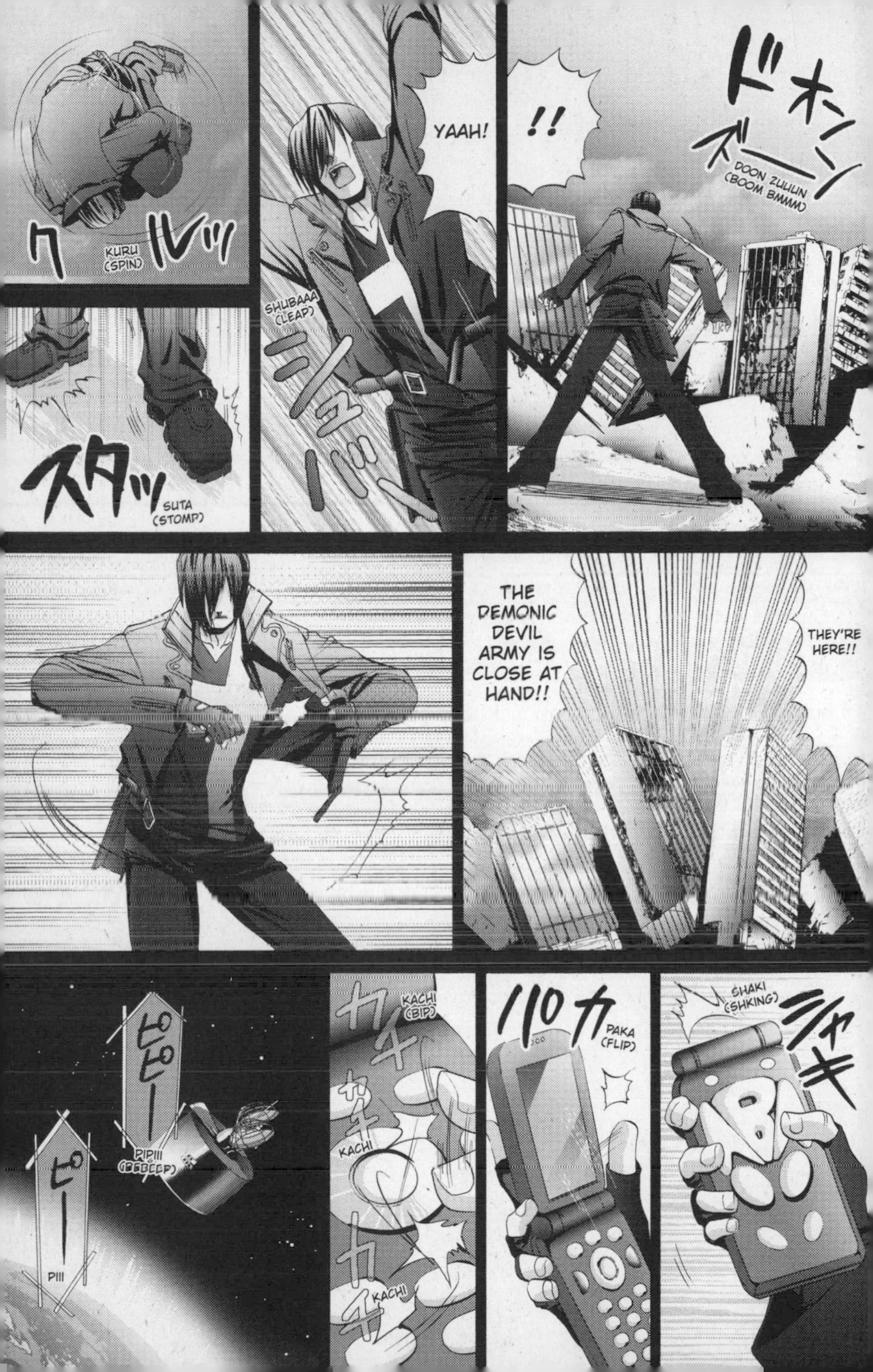
!!
ドオン
ズーン
DOON ZUUUN
(BOOM BMMM)
YAAH!
SHUBAAA
(LEAP)
クルッ
KURU
(SPIN)
スタッ
SUTA
(STOMP)
THE DEMONIC DEVIL ARMY IS CLOSE AT HAND!!
THEY'RE HERE!!
シャキ
SHAKI
(SHKING)
パカ
PAKA
(FLIP)
KACHI
(BIP)
KACHI
KACHI
ピピー
PIPIII
(BEEEEEP)
ピー
PIII

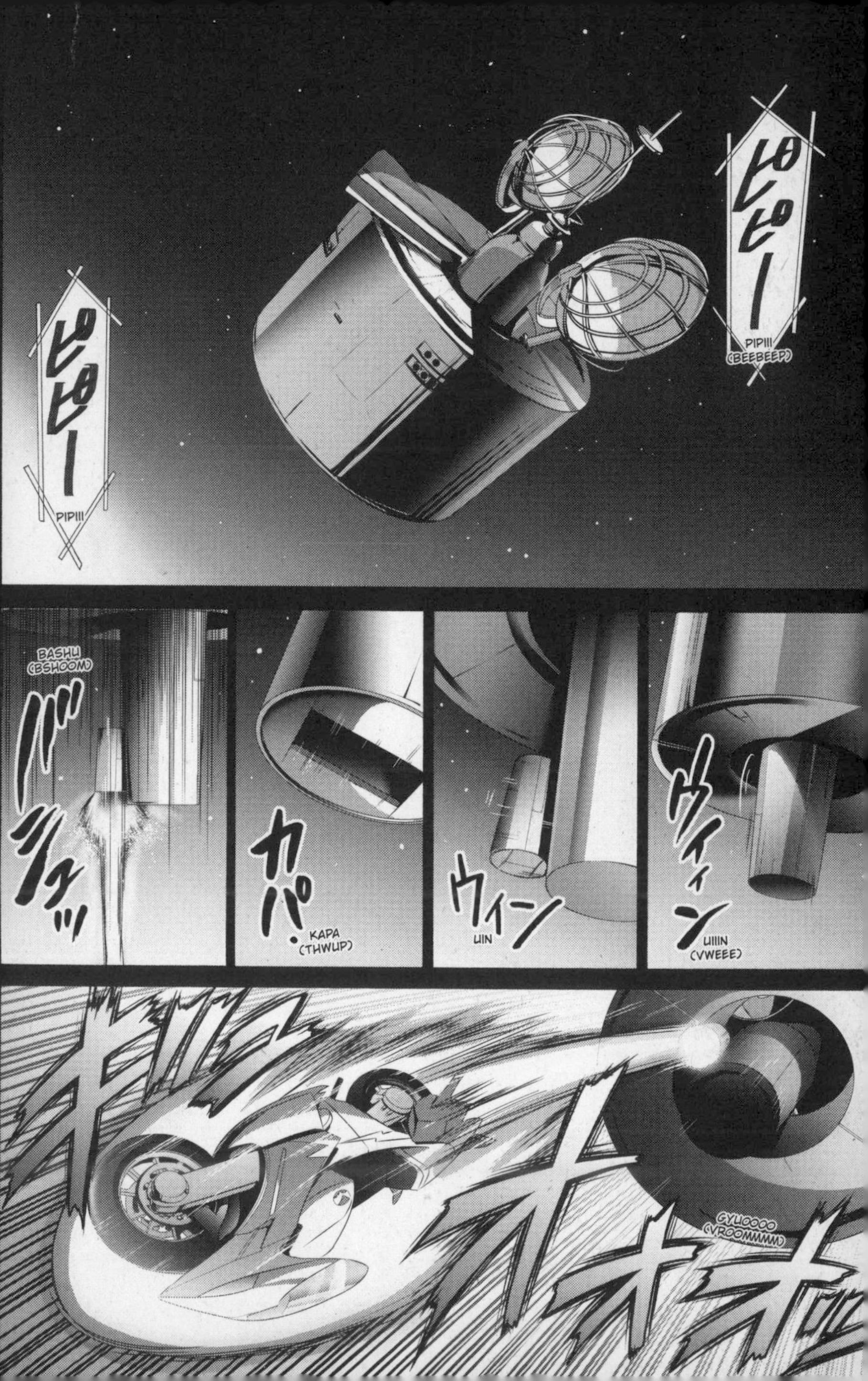
ピピピー
PIPIII (BEEBEEP)
ピピピー
PIPIII
ヴィィン
UIIIN (VWEEE)
ウィーン
UIN
カパ
KAPA (THWUP)
バシュッ
BASHU (BSHOOM)
GYUOOOO (VROOMMMM)

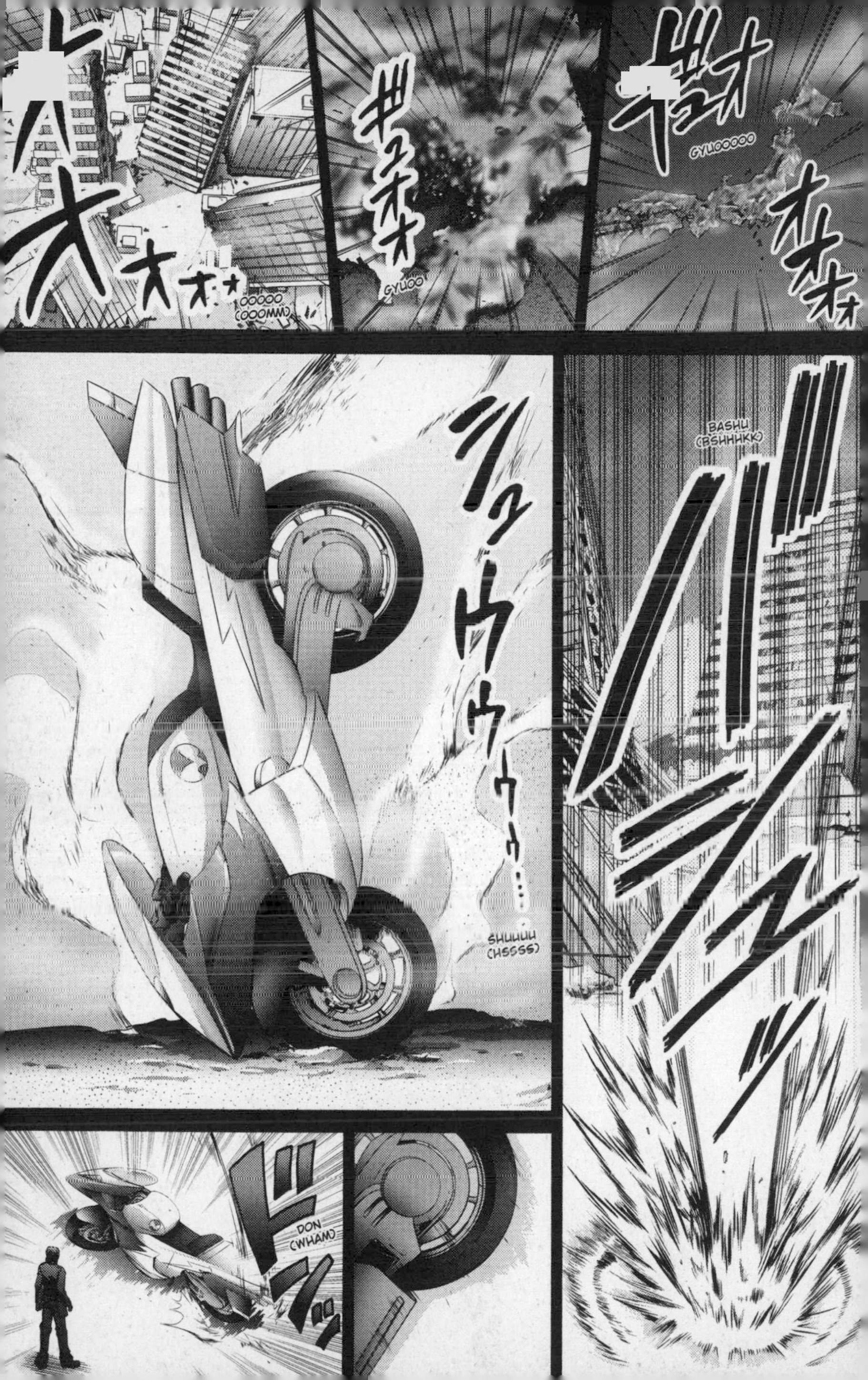

GYUOOOOO
GYUOO
OOOOO (OOOMM)
BASHU (BSHHHKK)
SHUUUU (HSSSS)
DON (WHAM)

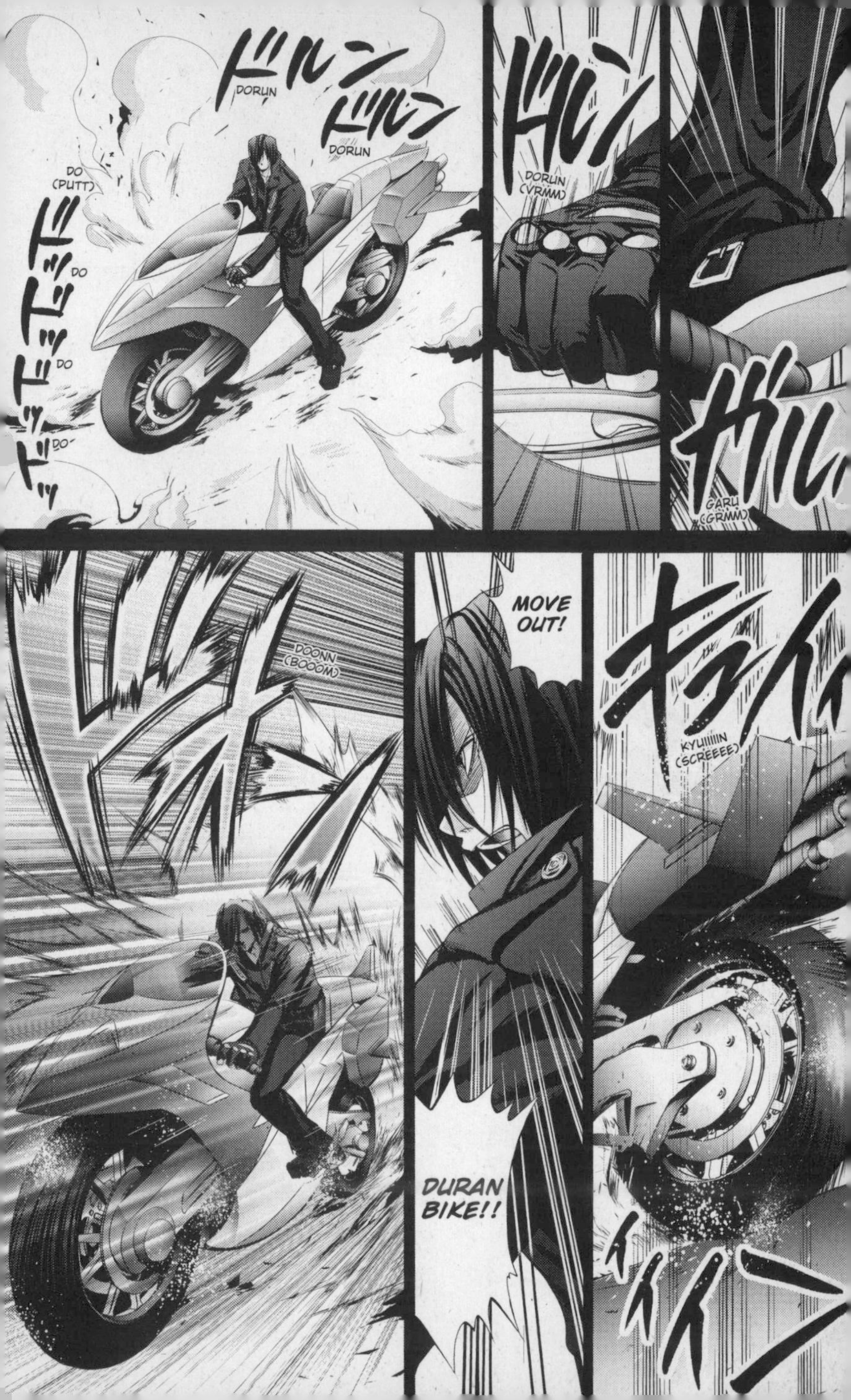
GARU (GRMM)
DORUN (VRMM)
DORUN
DORUN
DO (PUTT)
DO
DO
DO-
KYUIIIIIN (SCREEEE)
MOVE OUT!
DURAN BIKE!!
DOONN (BOOOM)

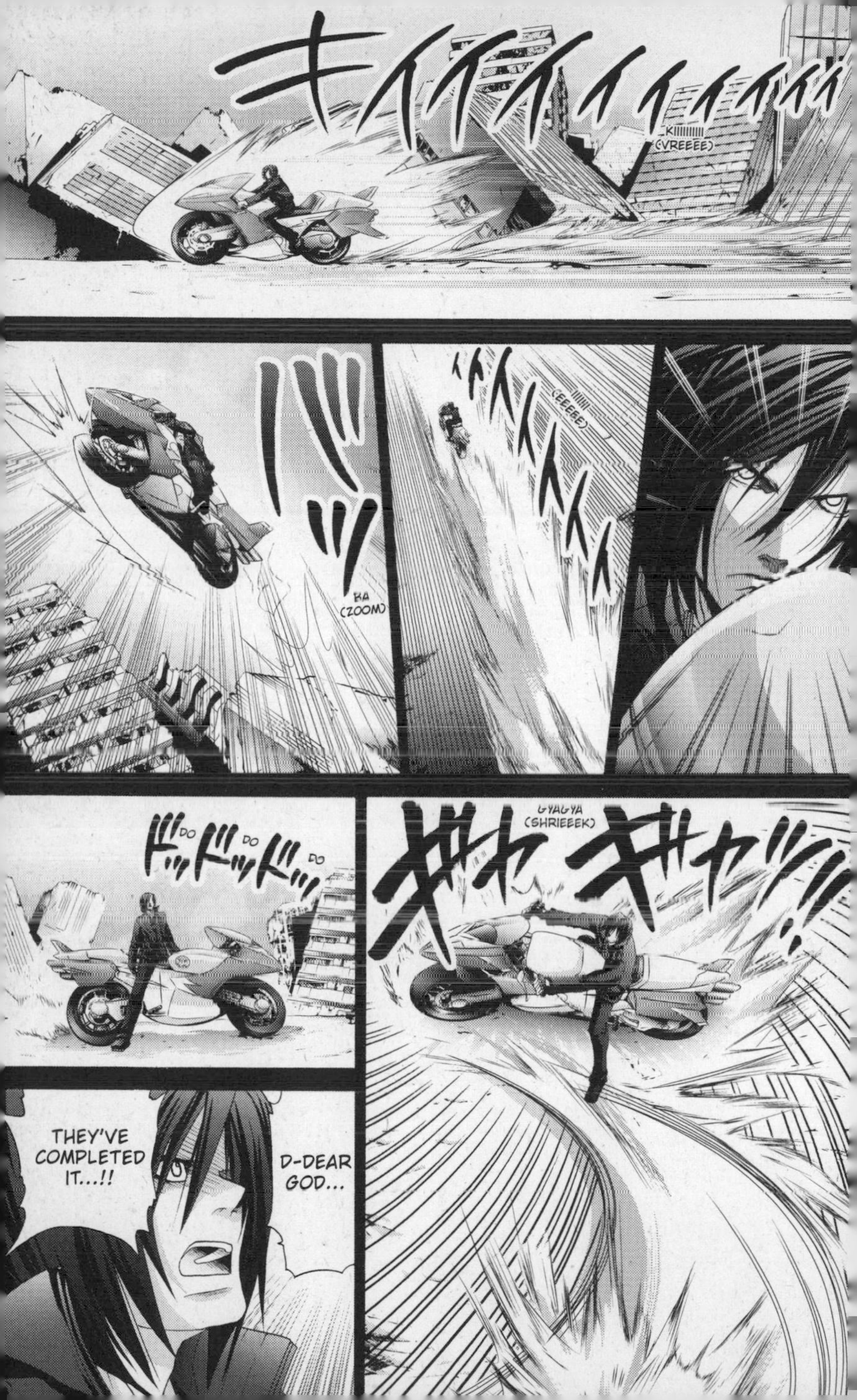

KIIIIIIII
(VREEEE)
IIIIIII
(EEEEE)
BA
(ZOOM)
GYAGYA
(SHRIEEEK)
DO DO DO
D-DEAR GOD...
THEY'VE COMPLETED IT...!!

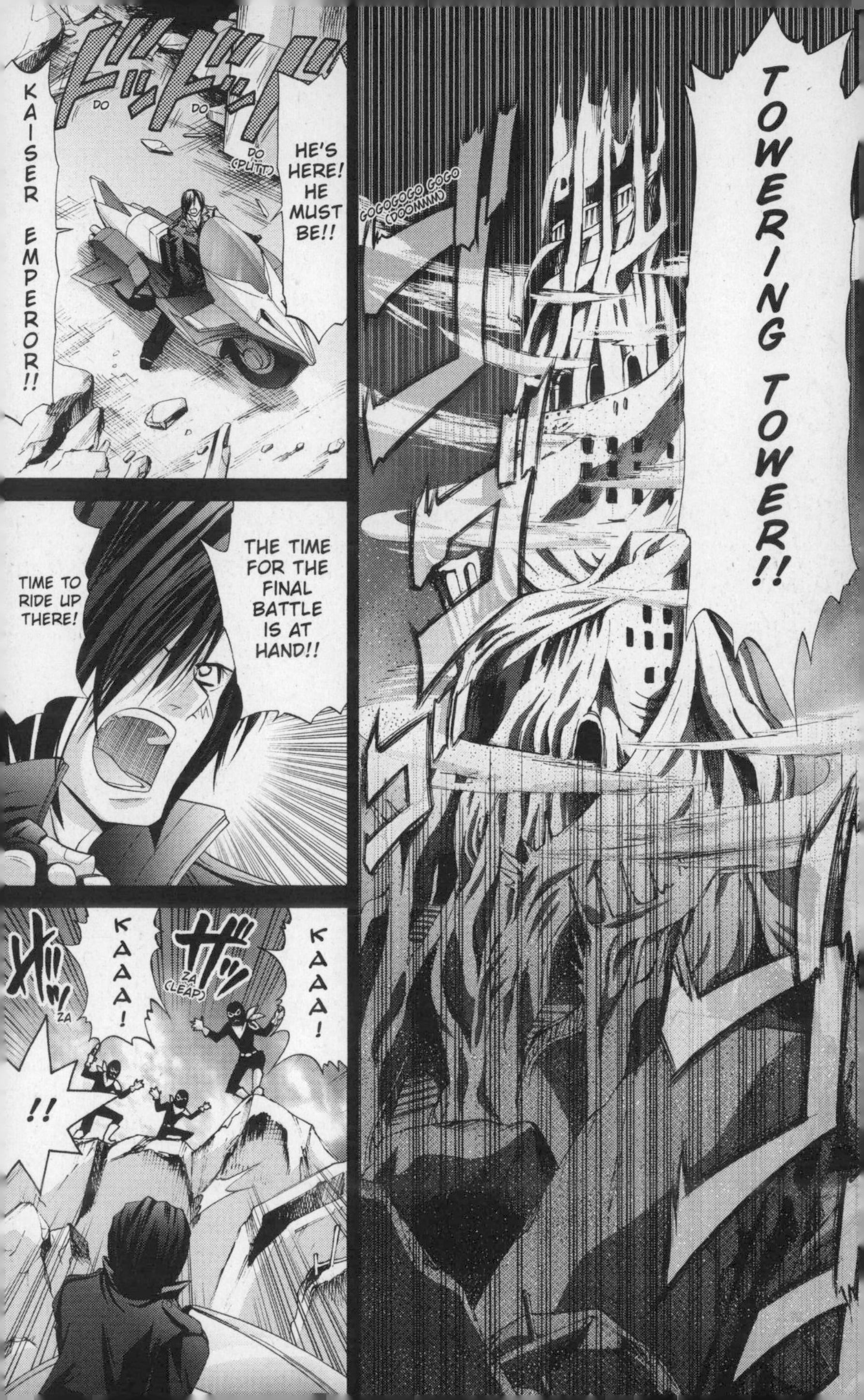
TOWERING TOWER!!
GOGOGOGO GOGO (DOOMMM)
HE'S HERE! HE MUST BE!!
DO (PLÜTT)
DO
DO
KAISER EMPEROR!!
THE TIME FOR THE FINAL BATTLE IS AT HAND!!
TIME TO RIDE UP THERE!
KAAAA!
ZA (LEAP)
KAAAA!
ZA
!!

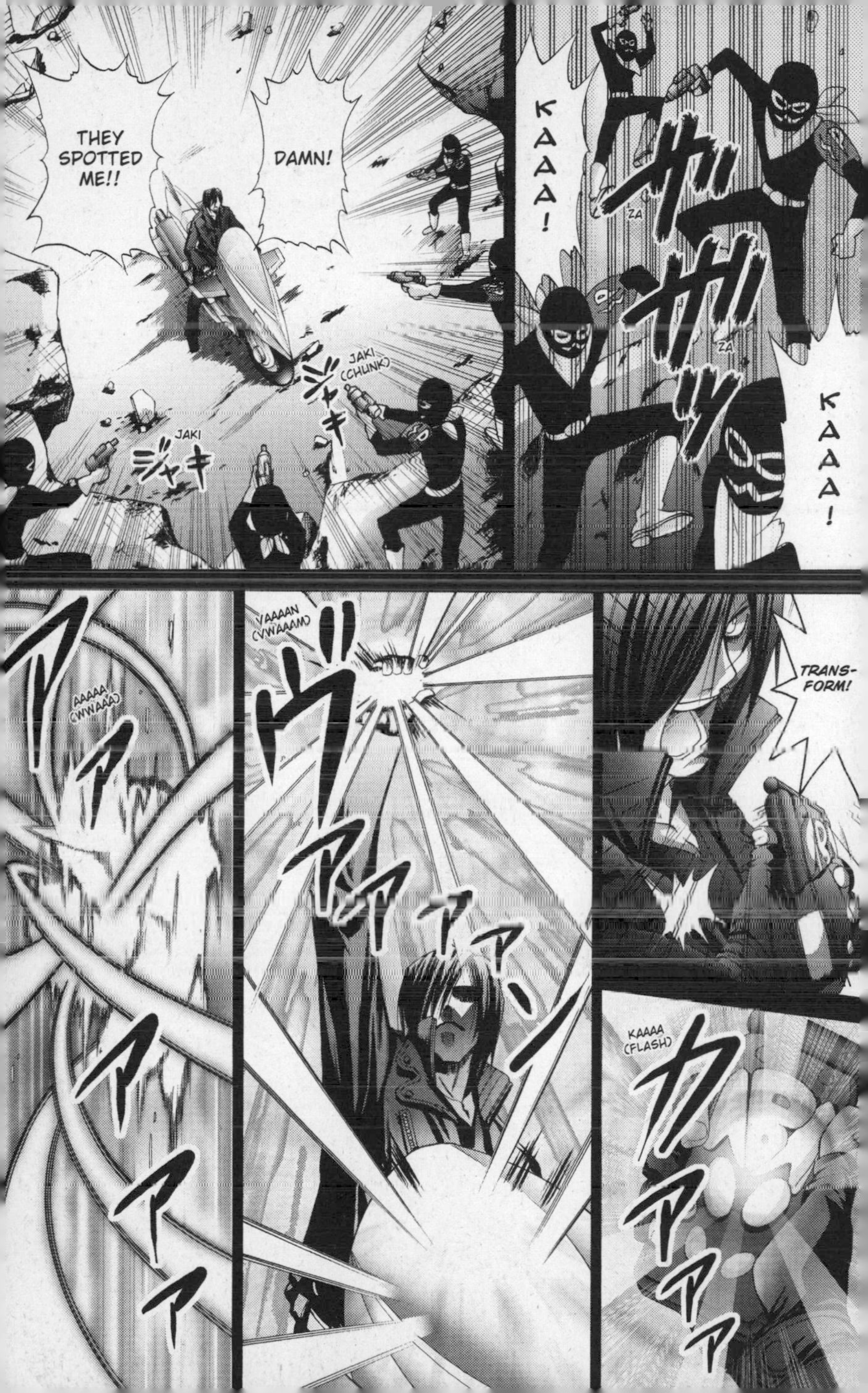
KAAAA!
ZA
ZA
KAAAA!
DAMN!
THEY SPOTTED ME!!
JAKI (CHUNK)
JAKI
TRANS-FORM!
KAAAA (FLASH)
VAAAAN (VWAAAM)
AAAAA (WWAAA)

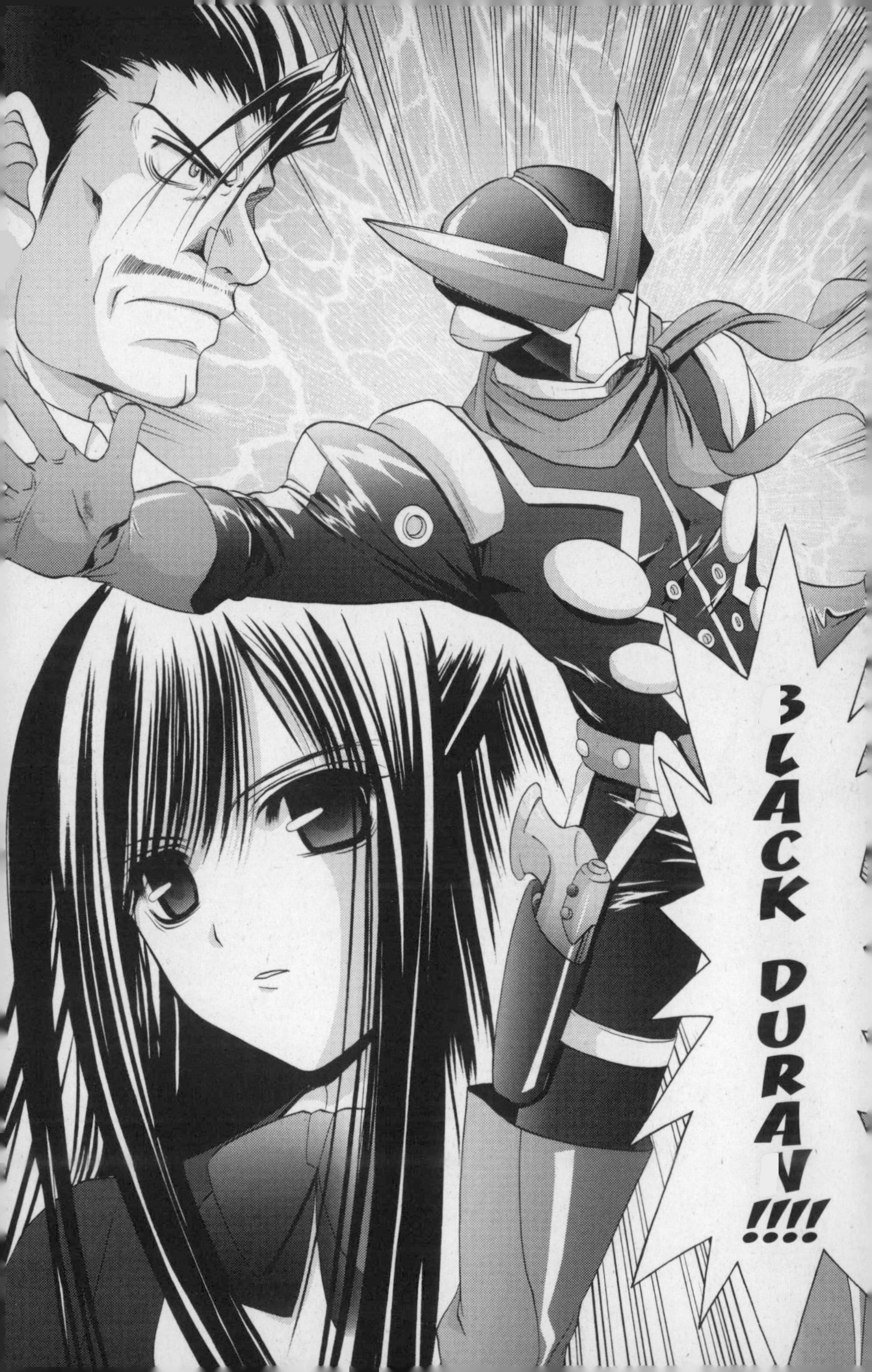
BLACK DURAV!!!!

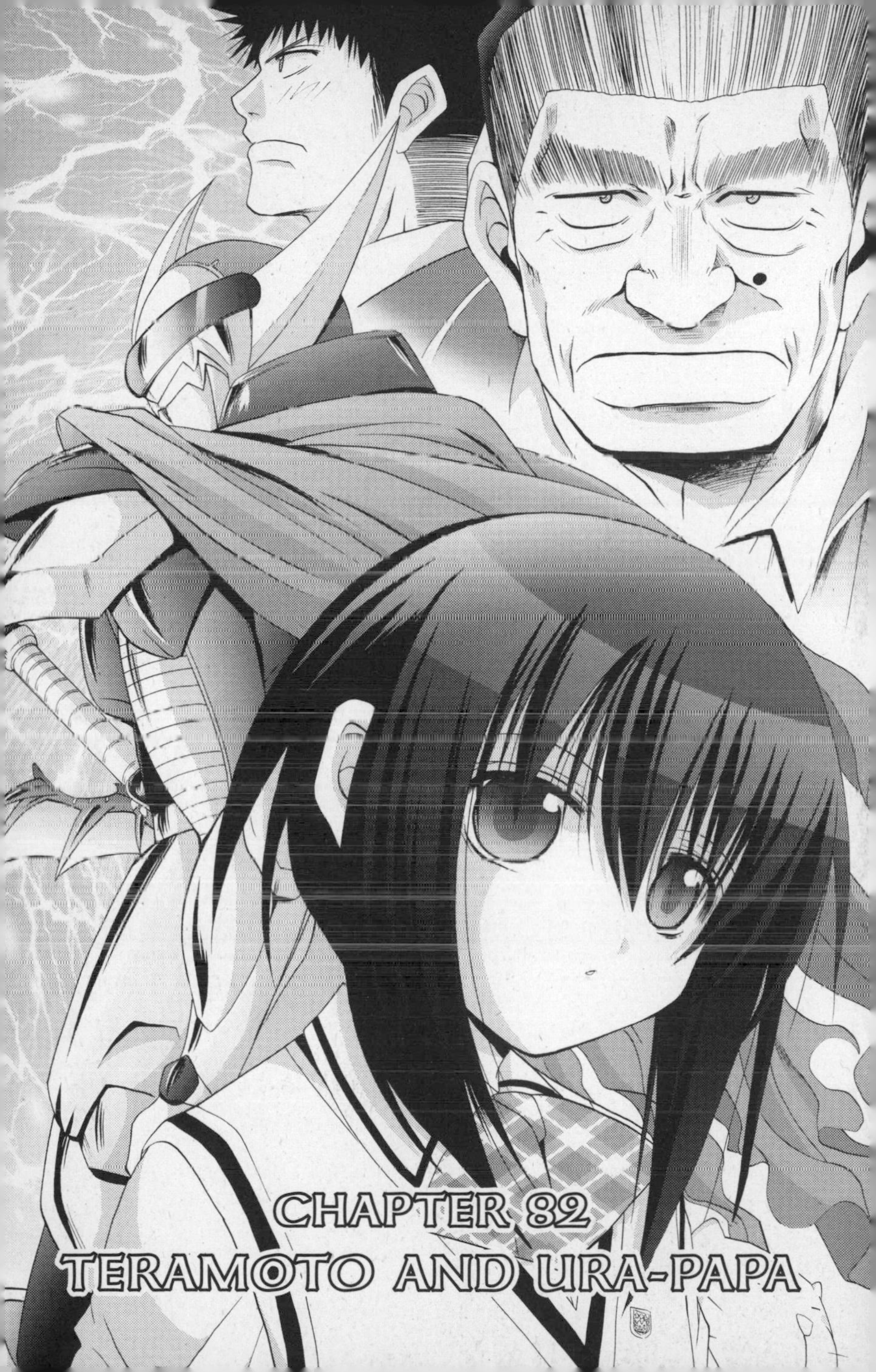
CHAPTER 82
TERAMOTO AND URA-PAPA

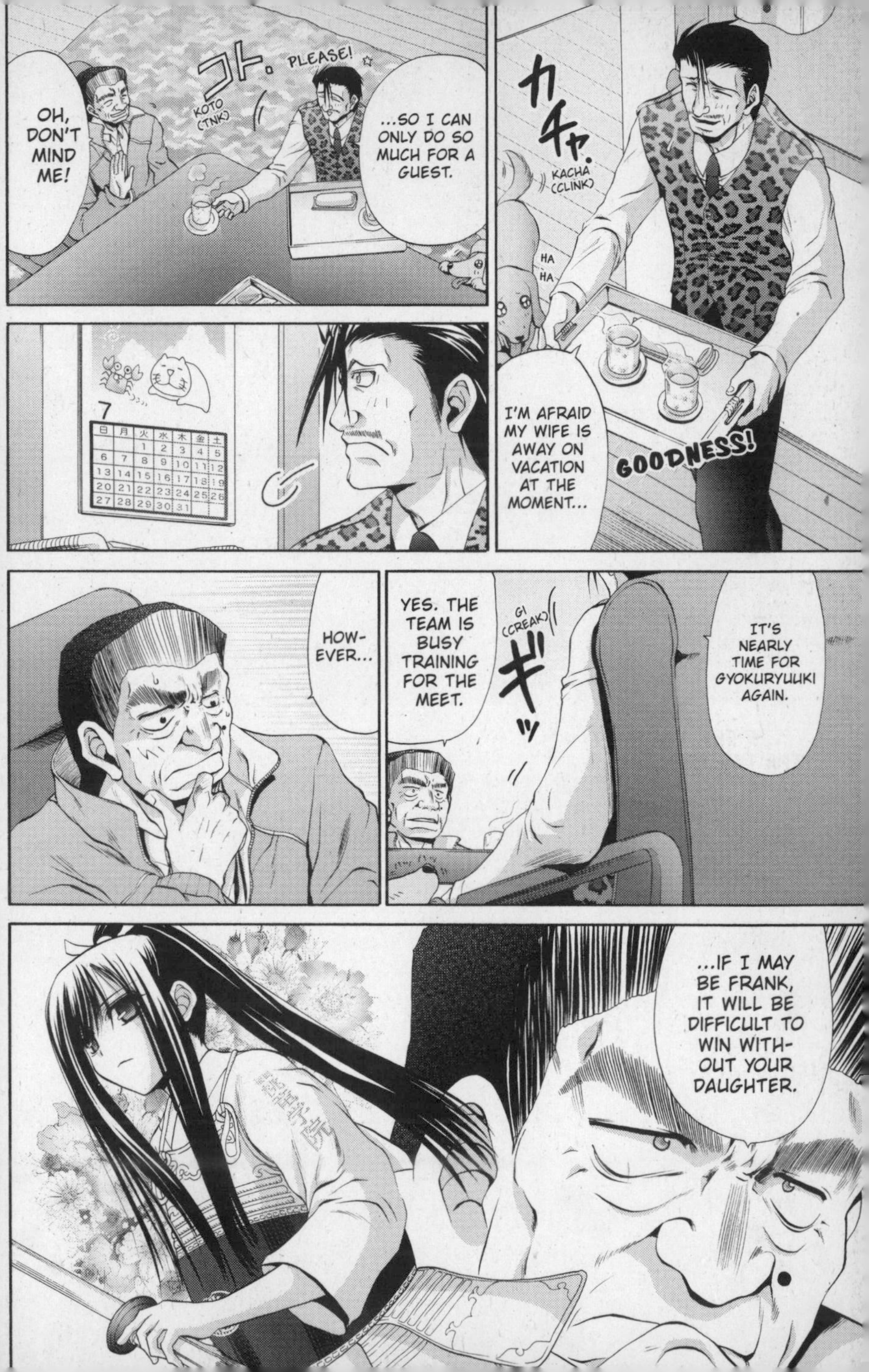
カチャ
KACHA (CLINK)
HA HA
I'M AFRAID MY WIFE IS AWAY ON VACATION AT THE MOMENT...
GOODNESS!
...SO I CAN ONLY DO SO MUCH FOR A GUEST.
PLEASE!
コト
KOTO (TNK)
OH, DON'T MIND ME!
7
日 月 火 水 木 金 土
1 2 3 4 5
6 7 8 9 10 11 12
13 14 15 16 17 18 19
20 21 22 23 24 25 26
27 28 29 30 31
IT'S NEARLY TIME FOR GYOKURYUUKI AGAIN.
ギッ
GI (CREAK)
YES. THE TEAM IS BUSY TRAINING FOR THE MEET.
HOW-EVER...
...IF I MAY BE FRANK, IT WILL BE DIFFICULT TO WIN WITH-OUT YOUR DAUGHTER.

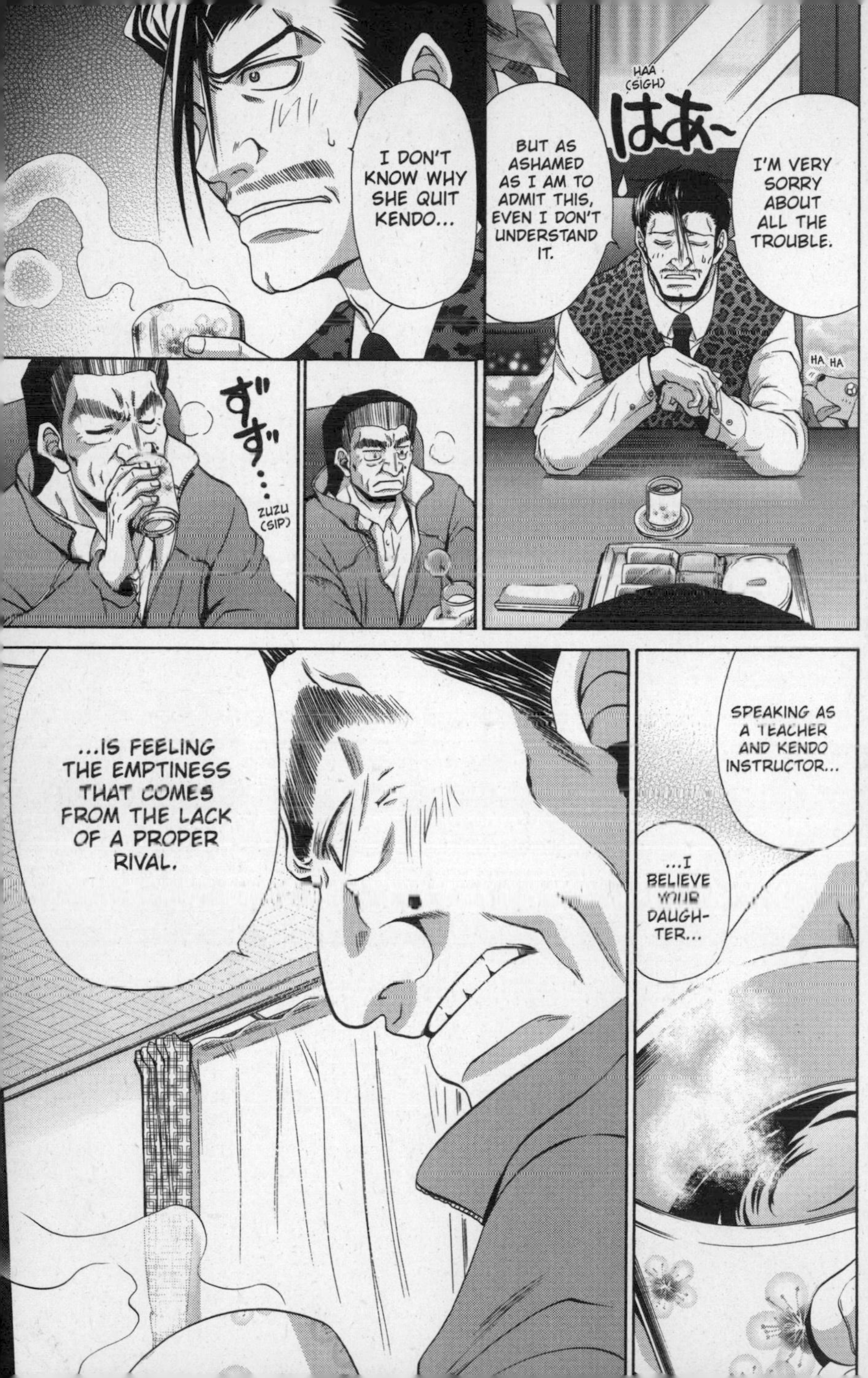
HAA (SIGH)
はあ~
I'M VERY SORRY ABOUT ALL THE TROUBLE.
BUT AS ASHAMED AS I AM TO ADMIT THIS, EVEN I DON'T UNDERSTAND IT.
HA HA
I DON'T KNOW WHY SHE QUIT KENDO...
ずず…
ZUZU (SIP)
SPEAKING AS A TEACHER AND KENDO INSTRUCTOR...
...I BELIEVE YOUR DAUGHTER...
...IS FEELING THE EMPTINESS THAT COMES FROM THE LACK OF A PROPER RIVAL.

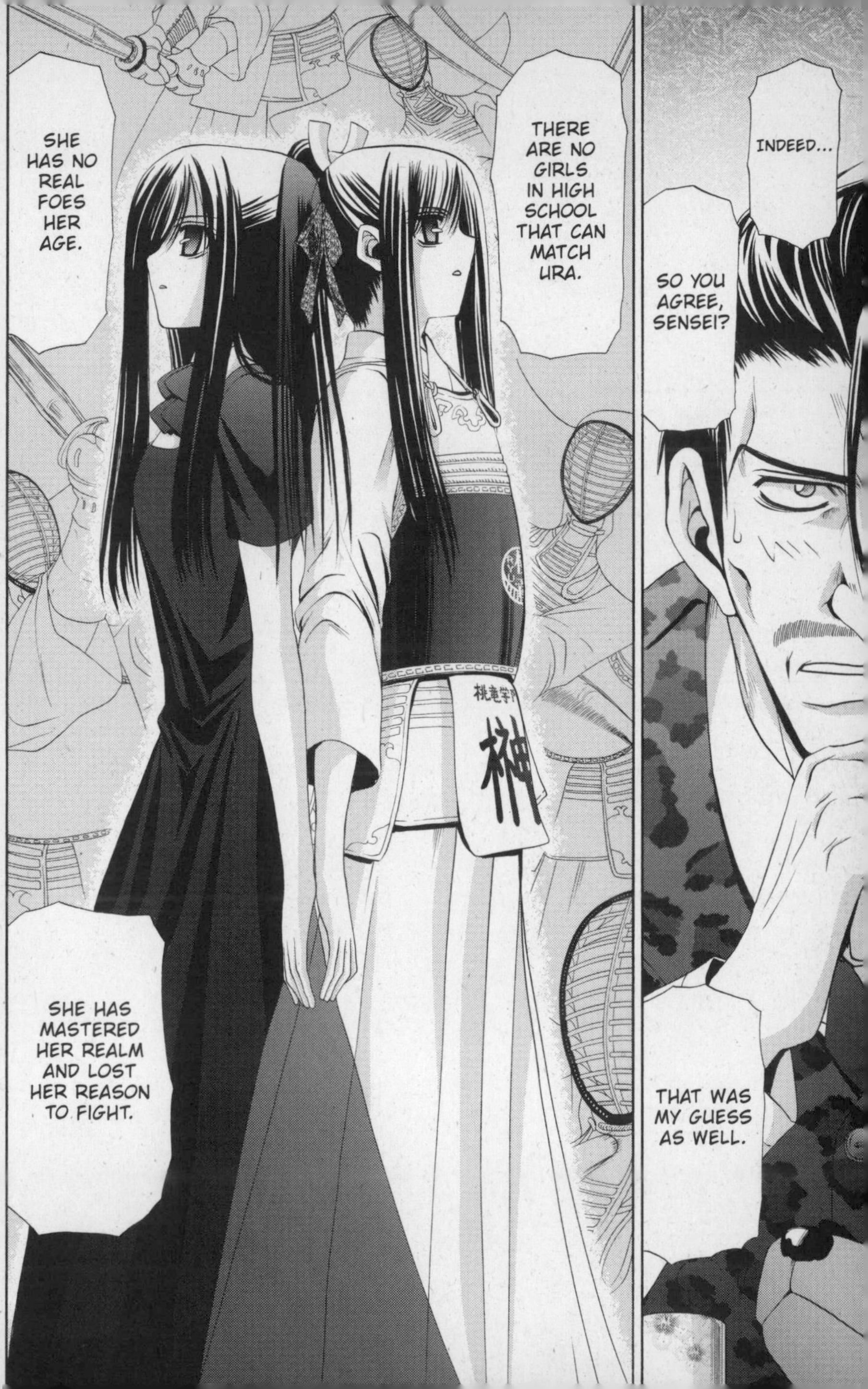
INDEED...
SO YOU AGREE, SENSEI?
THAT WAS MY GUESS AS WELL.
THERE ARE NO GIRLS IN HIGH SCHOOL THAT CAN MATCH URA.
SHE HAS NO REAL FOES HER AGE.
SHE HAS MASTERED HER REALM AND LOST HER REASON TO FIGHT.

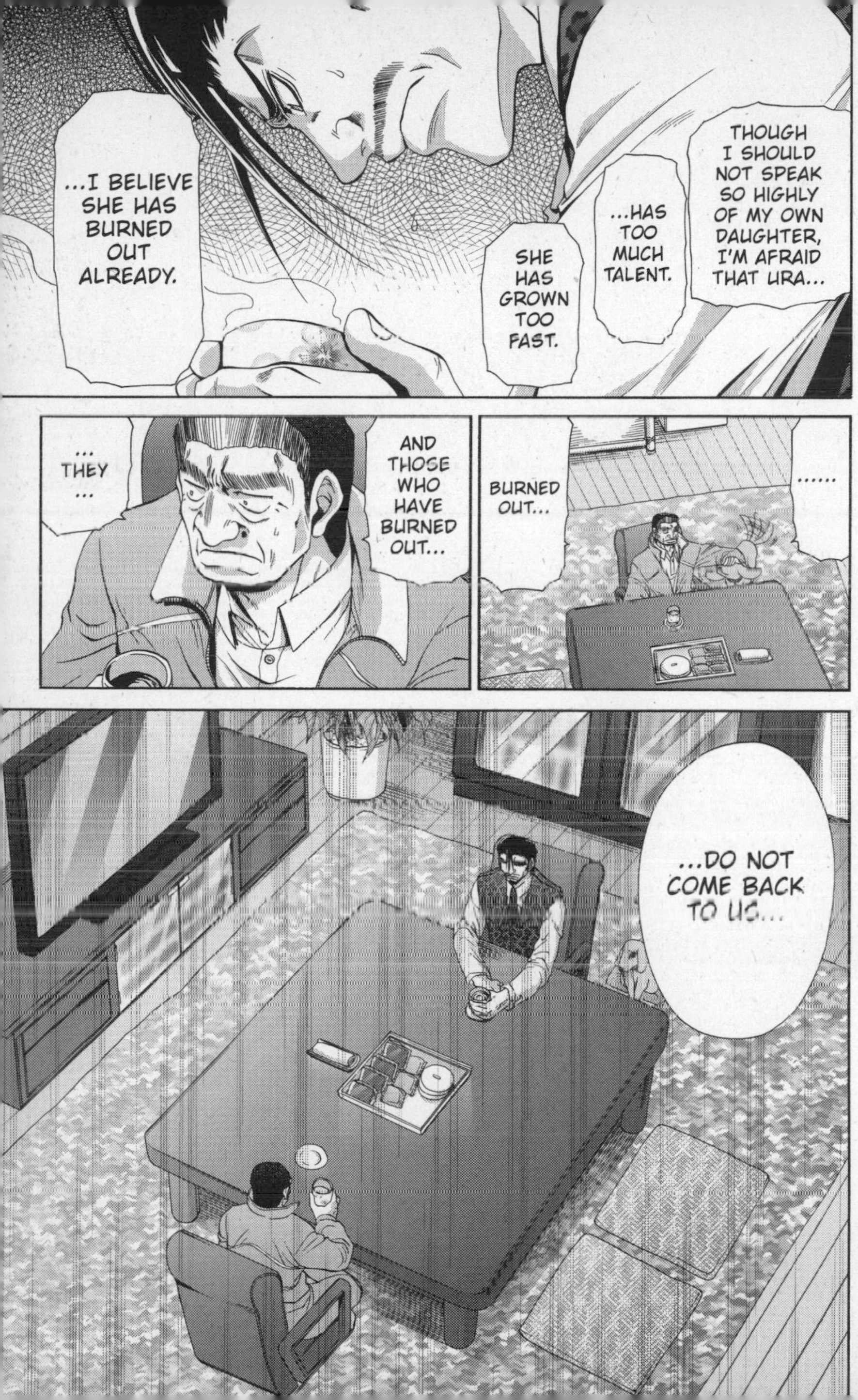
THOUGH I SHOULD NOT SPEAK SO HIGHLY OF MY OWN DAUGHTER, I'M AFRAID THAT URA...
...HAS TOO MUCH TALENT.
SHE HAS GROWN TOO FAST.
...I BELIEVE SHE HAS BURNED OUT ALREADY.
......
BURNED OUT...
AND THOSE WHO HAVE BURNED OUT...
...THEY...
...DO NOT COME BACK TO US...

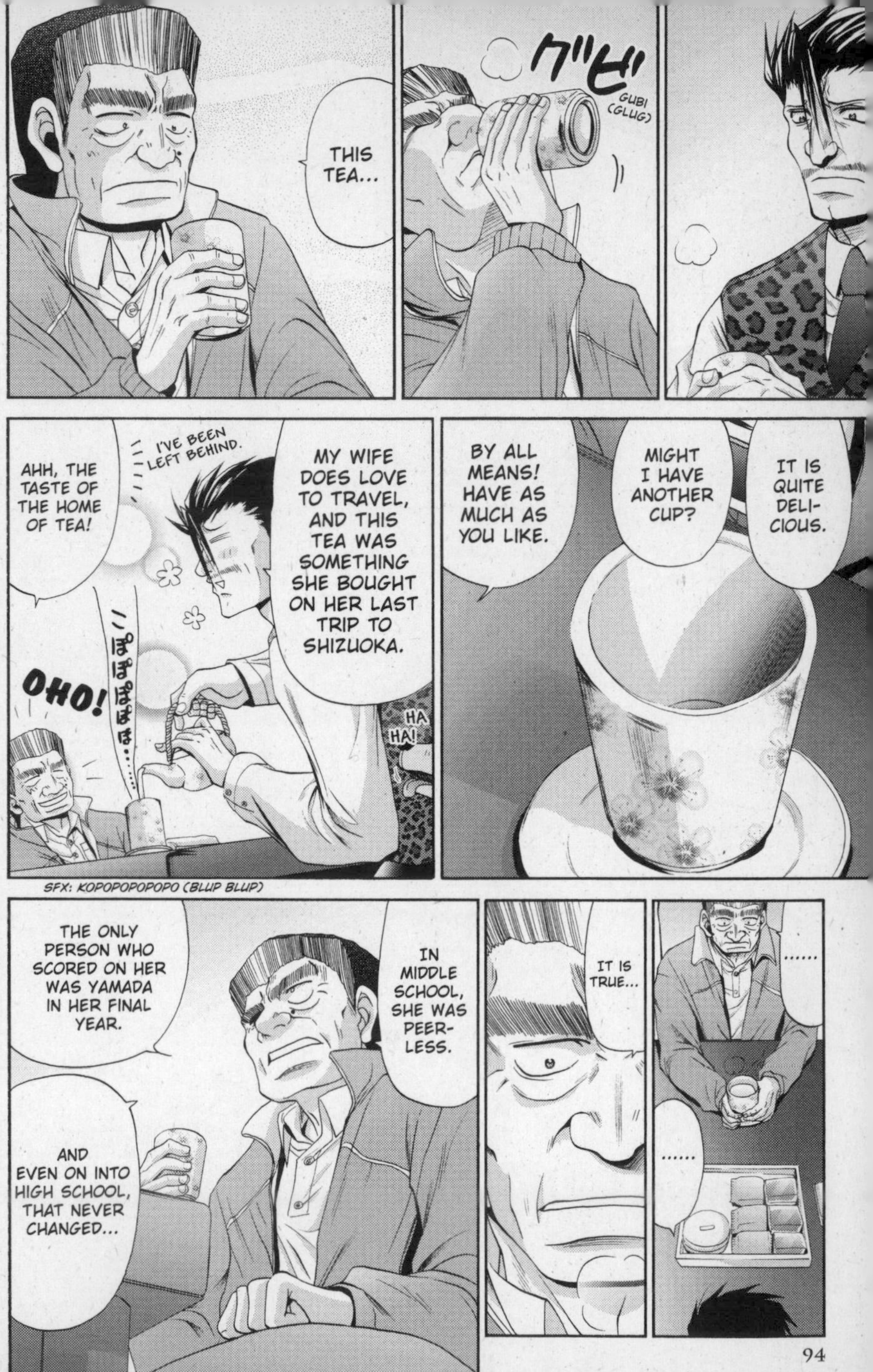
グビ
GUBI (GLUG)
THIS TEA...
IT IS QUITE DELI-CIOUS.
MIGHT I HAVE ANOTHER CUP?
BY ALL MEANS! HAVE AS MUCH AS YOU LIKE.
MY WIFE DOES LOVE TO TRAVEL, AND THIS TEA WAS SOMETHING SHE BOUGHT ON HER LAST TRIP TO SHIZUOKA.
I'VE BEEN LEFT BEHIND.
AHH, THE TASTE OF THE HOME OF TEA!
HA HA!
こぽぽぽぽぽ……
OHO!
SFX: KOPOPOPOPOPO (BLUP BLUP)
......
......
IT IS TRUE...
IN MIDDLE SCHOOL, SHE WAS PEER-LESS.
THE ONLY PERSON WHO SCORED ON HER WAS YAMADA IN HER FINAL YEAR.
AND EVEN ON INTO HIGH SCHOOL, THAT NEVER CHANGED...

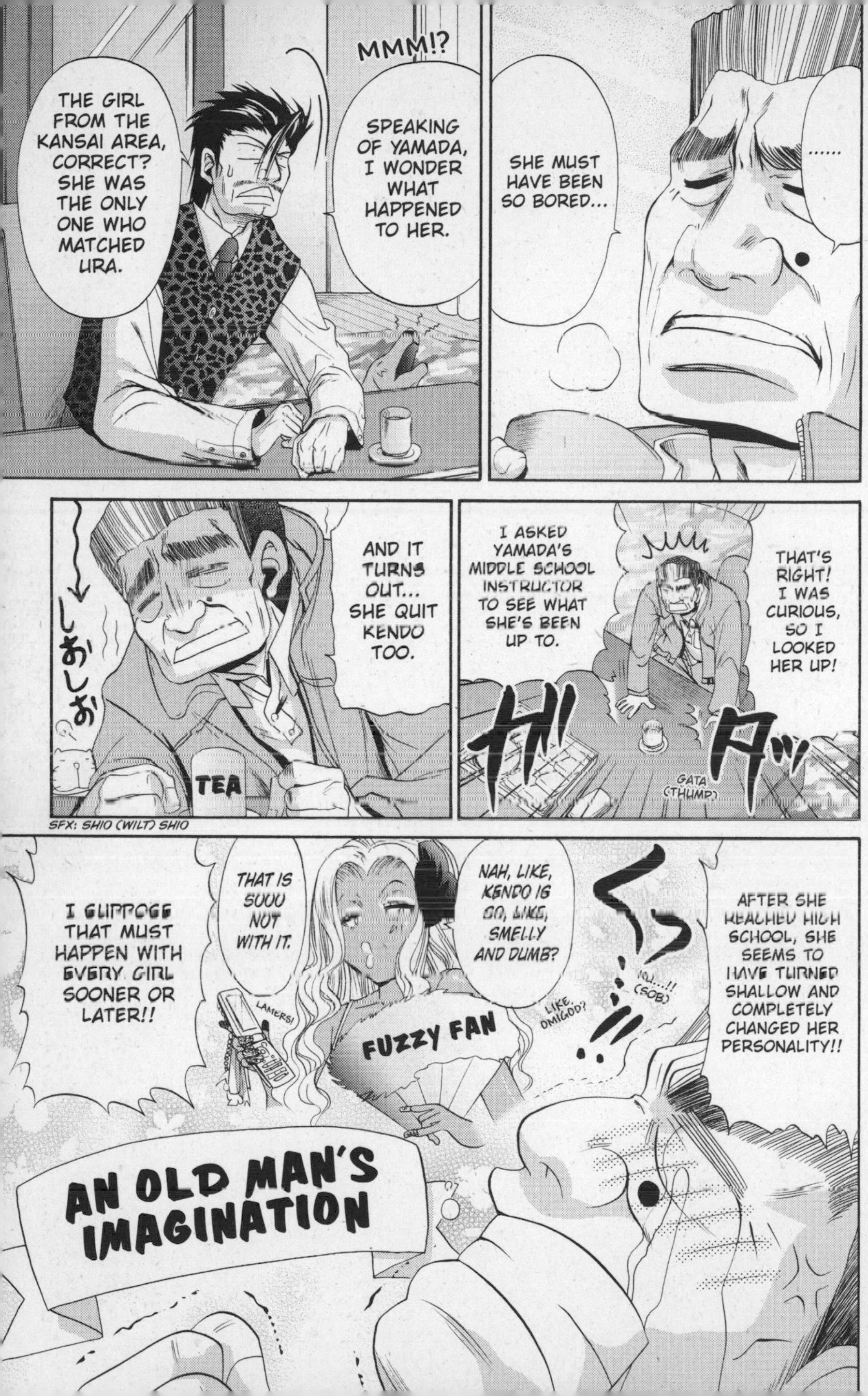
......
SHE MUST HAVE BEEN SO BORED...
MMM!?
SPEAKING OF YAMADA, I WONDER WHAT HAPPENED TO HER.
THE GIRL FROM THE KANSAI AREA, CORRECT? SHE WAS THE ONLY ONE WHO MATCHED URA.
THAT'S RIGHT! I WAS CURIOUS, SO I LOOKED HER UP!
I ASKED YAMADA'S MIDDLE SCHOOL INSTRUCTOR TO SEE WHAT SHE'S BEEN UP TO.
GATA (THUMP)
AND IT TURNS OUT... SHE QUIT KENDO TOO.
しおしお
TEA
SFX: SHIO (WILT) SHIO
AFTER SHE REACHED HIGH SCHOOL, SHE SEEMS TO HAVE TURNED SHALLOW AND COMPLETELY CHANGED HER PERSONALITY!!
KU...!! (SOB)
NAH, LIKE, KENDO IS SO, LIKE, SMELLY AND DUMB?
LIKE, OMIGOD?
FUZZY FAN
THAT IS SOOO NOT WITH IT.
LAMERS!
I SUPPOSE THAT MUST HAPPEN WITH EVERY GIRL SOONER OR LATER!!
AN OLD MAN'S IMAGINATION

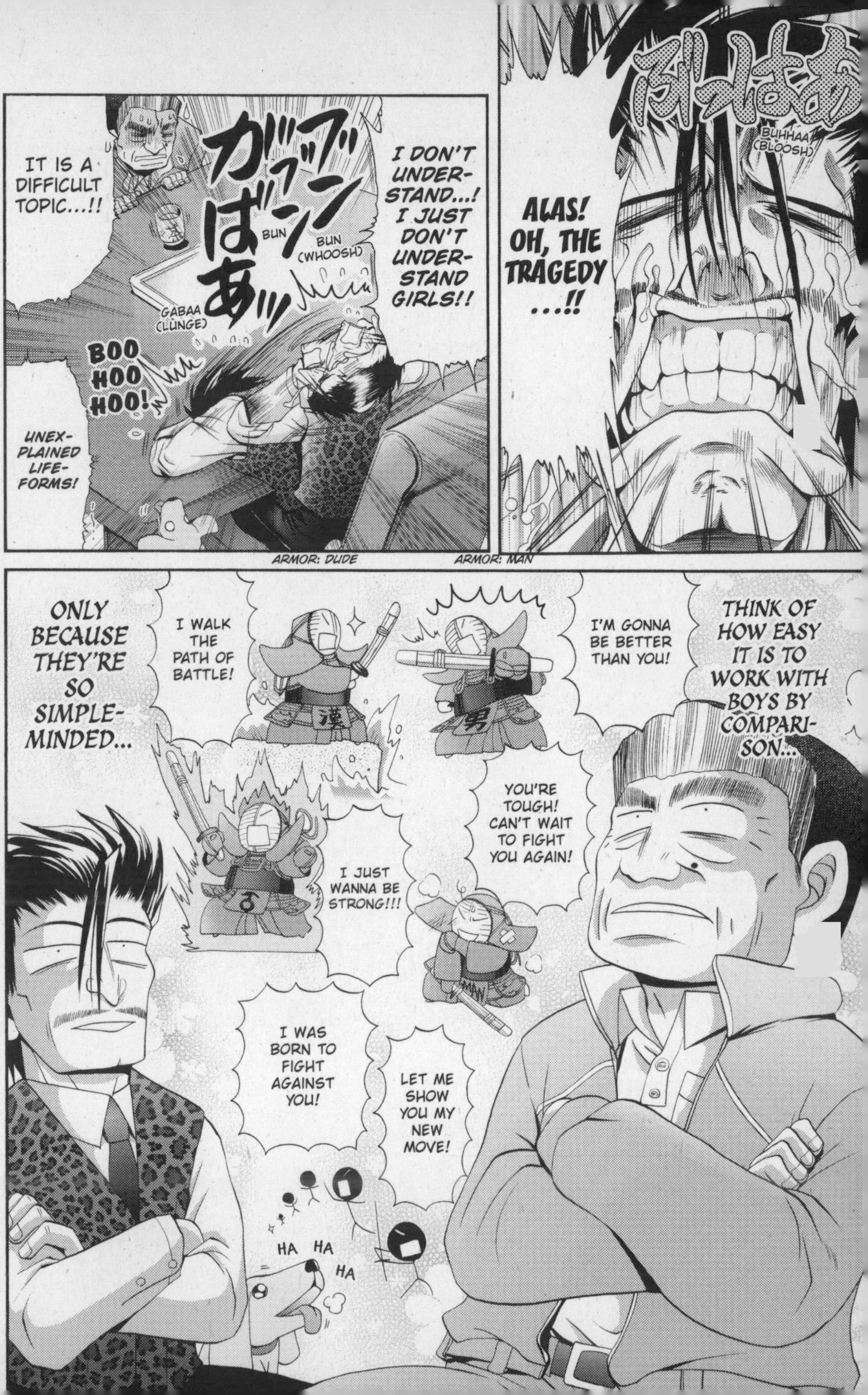

BUHHAA (BLOOSH)
ALAS! OH, THE TRAGEDY ...!!
I DON'T UNDERSTAND...! I JUST DON'T UNDERSTAND GIRLS!!
BUN BUN (WHOOSH)
IT IS A DIFFICULT TOPIC...!!
GABAA (LUNGE)
BOO HOO HOO!
UNEXPLAINED LIFE-FORMS!
ARMOR: MAN
ARMOR: DUDE
THINK OF HOW EASY IT IS TO WORK WITH BOYS BY COMPARISON...
I'M GONNA BE BETTER THAN YOU!
I WALK THE PATH OF BATTLE!
ONLY BECAUSE THEY'RE SO SIMPLE-MINDED...
YOU'RE TOUGH! CAN'T WAIT TO FIGHT YOU AGAIN!
I JUST WANNA BE STRONG!!!
LET ME SHOW YOU MY NEW MOVE!
I WAS BORN TO FIGHT AGAINST YOU!
HA HA HA

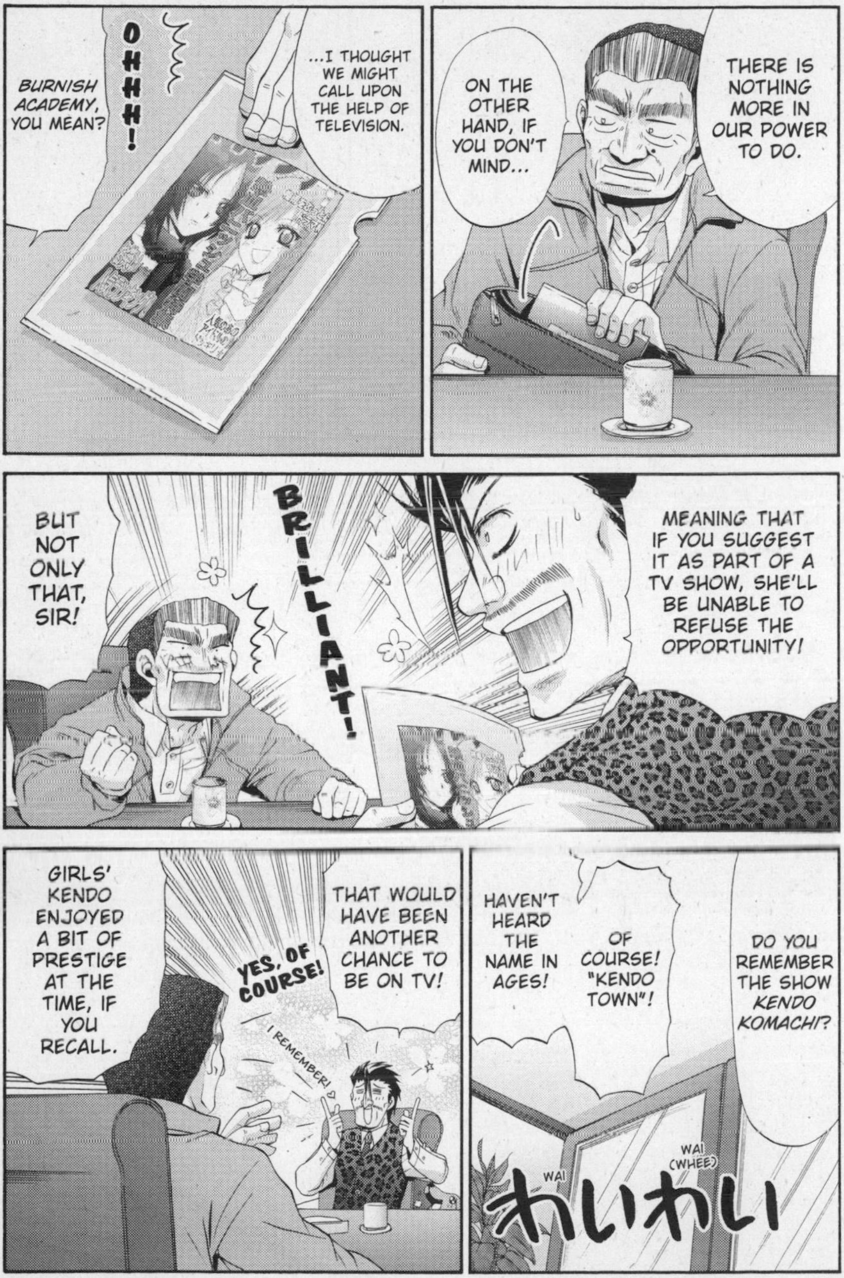
THERE IS NOTHING MORE IN OUR POWER TO DO.
ON THE OTHER HAND, IF YOU DON'T MIND...
...I THOUGHT WE MIGHT CALL UPON THE HELP OF TELEVISION.
OHHHH!
BURNISH ACADEMY, YOU MEAN?
MEANING THAT IF YOU SUGGEST IT AS PART OF A TV SHOW, SHE'LL BE UNABLE TO REFUSE THE OPPORTUNITY!
BRILLIANT!
BUT NOT ONLY THAT, SIR!
DO YOU REMEMBER THE SHOW *KENDO KOMACHI*?
OF COURSE! "KENDO TOWN"!
HAVEN'T HEARD THE NAME IN AGES!
WAI (WHEE)
WAI
わいわい
THAT WOULD HAVE BEEN ANOTHER CHANCE TO BE ON TV!
YES, OF COURSE!
I REMEMBER!
GIRLS' KENDO ENJOYED A BIT OF PRESTIGE AT THE TIME, IF YOU RECALL.

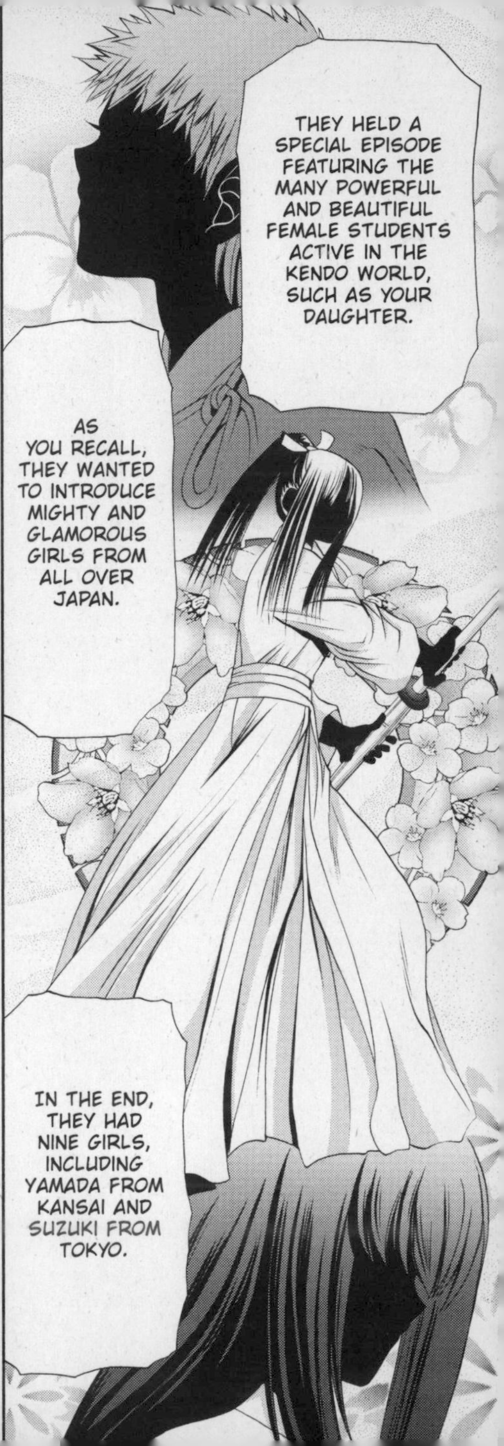
THEY HELD A SPECIAL EPISODE FEATURING THE MANY POWERFUL AND BEAUTIFUL FEMALE STUDENTS ACTIVE IN THE KENDO WORLD, SUCH AS YOUR DAUGHTER.
AS YOU RECALL, THEY WANTED TO INTRODUCE MIGHTY AND GLAMOROUS GIRLS FROM ALL OVER JAPAN.
IN THE END, THEY HAD NINE GIRLS, INCLUDING YAMADA FROM KANSAI AND SUZUKI FROM TOKYO.
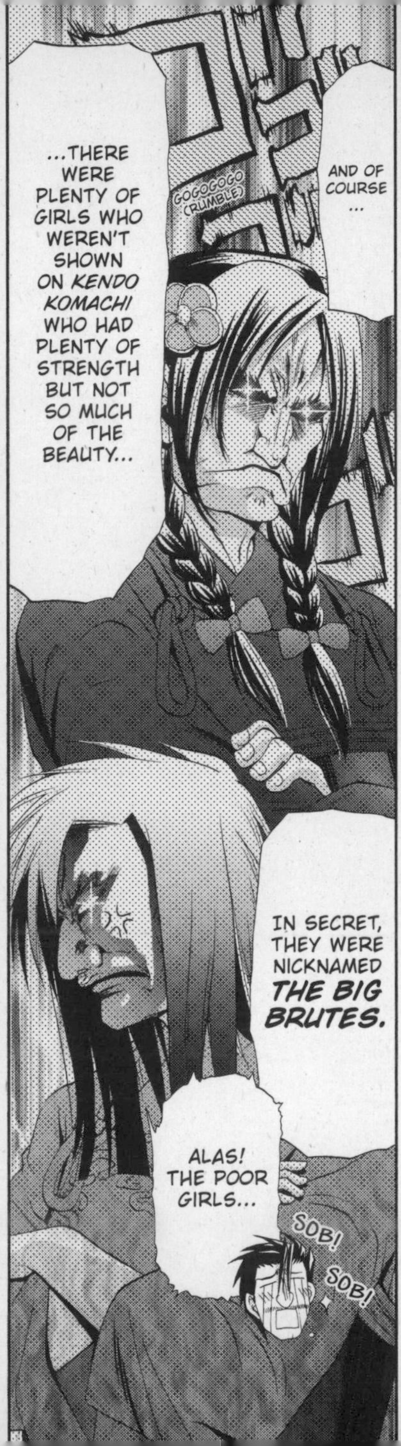
AND OF COURSE ...
GOGOGOGO (RUMBLE)
...THERE WERE PLENTY OF GIRLS WHO WEREN'T SHOWN ON *KENDO KOMACHI* WHO HAD PLENTY OF STRENGTH BUT NOT SO MUCH OF THE BEAUTY...
IN SECRET, THEY WERE NICKNAMED **THE BIG BRUTES.**
ALAS! THE POOR GIRLS...
SOB!
SOB!

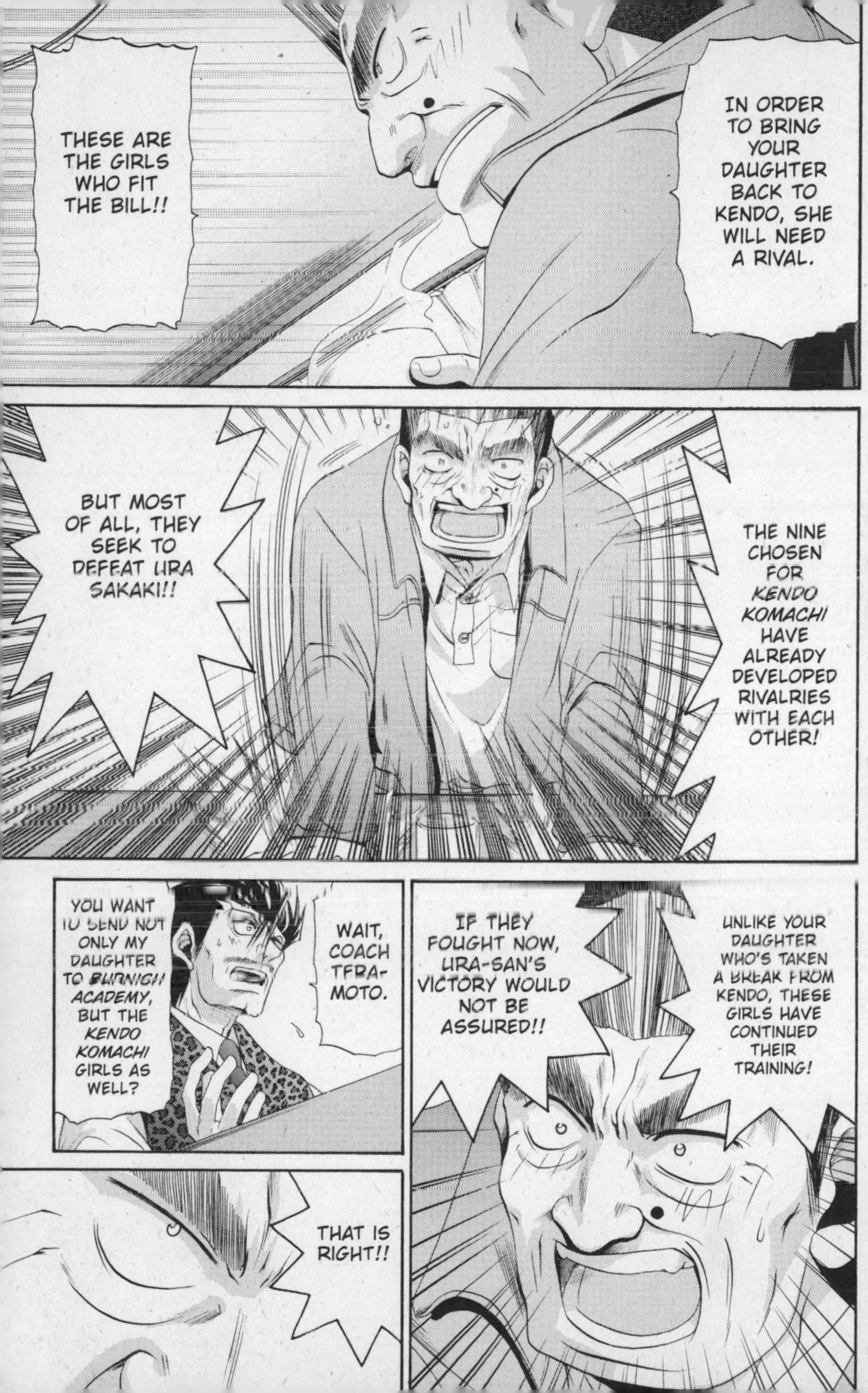
IN ORDER TO BRING YOUR DAUGHTER BACK TO KENDO, SHE WILL NEED A RIVAL.
THESE ARE THE GIRLS WHO FIT THE BILL!!
THE NINE CHOSEN FOR *KENDO KOMACHI* HAVE ALREADY DEVELOPED RIVALRIES WITH EACH OTHER!
BUT MOST OF ALL, THEY SEEK TO DEFEAT URA SAKAKI!!
UNLIKE YOUR DAUGHTER WHO'S TAKEN A BREAK FROM KENDO, THESE GIRLS HAVE CONTINUED THEIR TRAINING!
IF THEY FOUGHT NOW, URA-SAN'S VICTORY WOULD NOT BE ASSURED!!
WAIT, COACH TERA-MOTO.
YOU WANT TO SEND NOT ONLY MY DAUGHTER TO *BURNICHI ACADEMY*, BUT THE *KENDO KOMACHI* GIRLS AS WELL?
THAT IS RIGHT!!

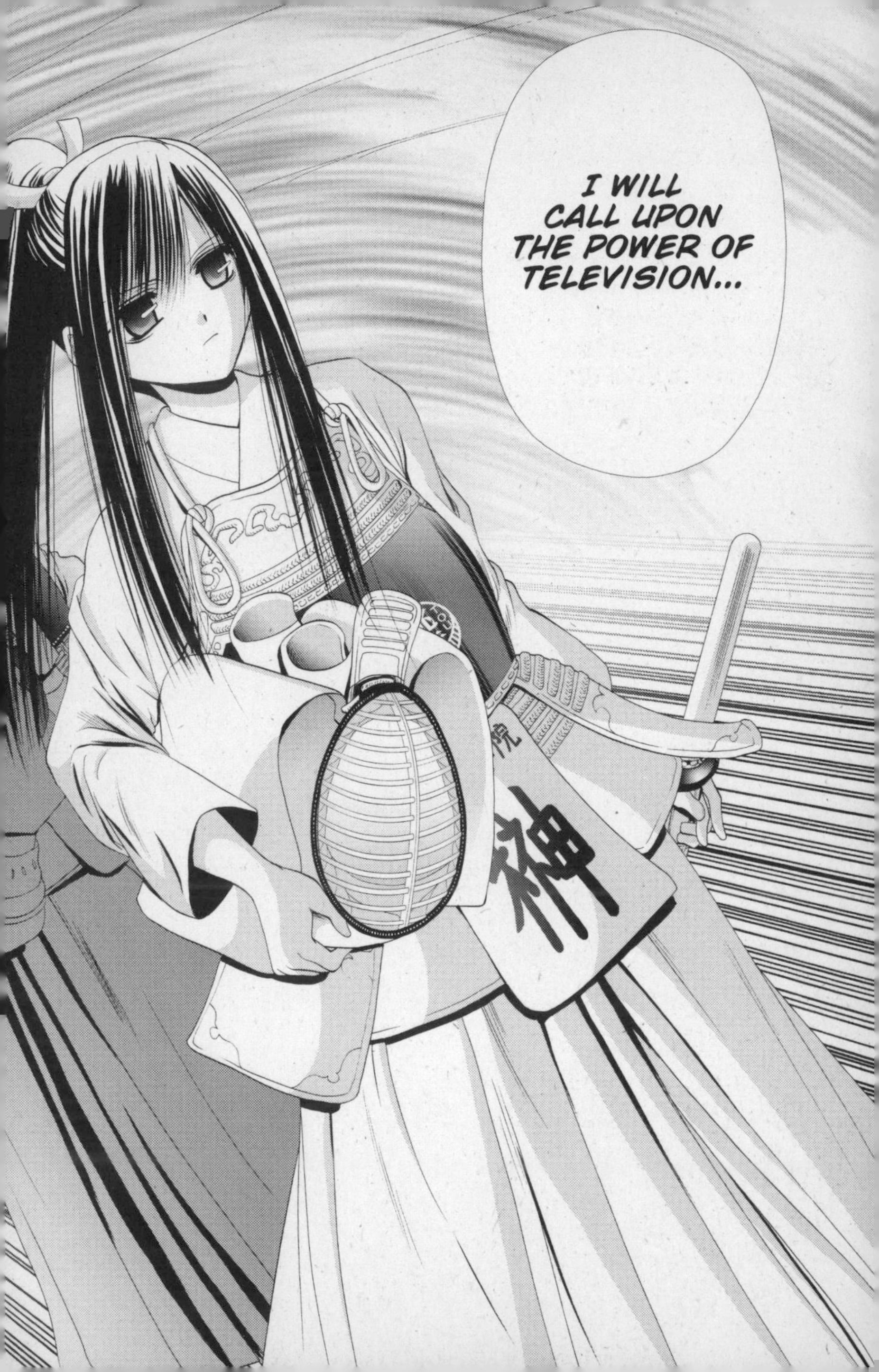
I WILL CALL UPON THE POWER OF TELEVISION...
神

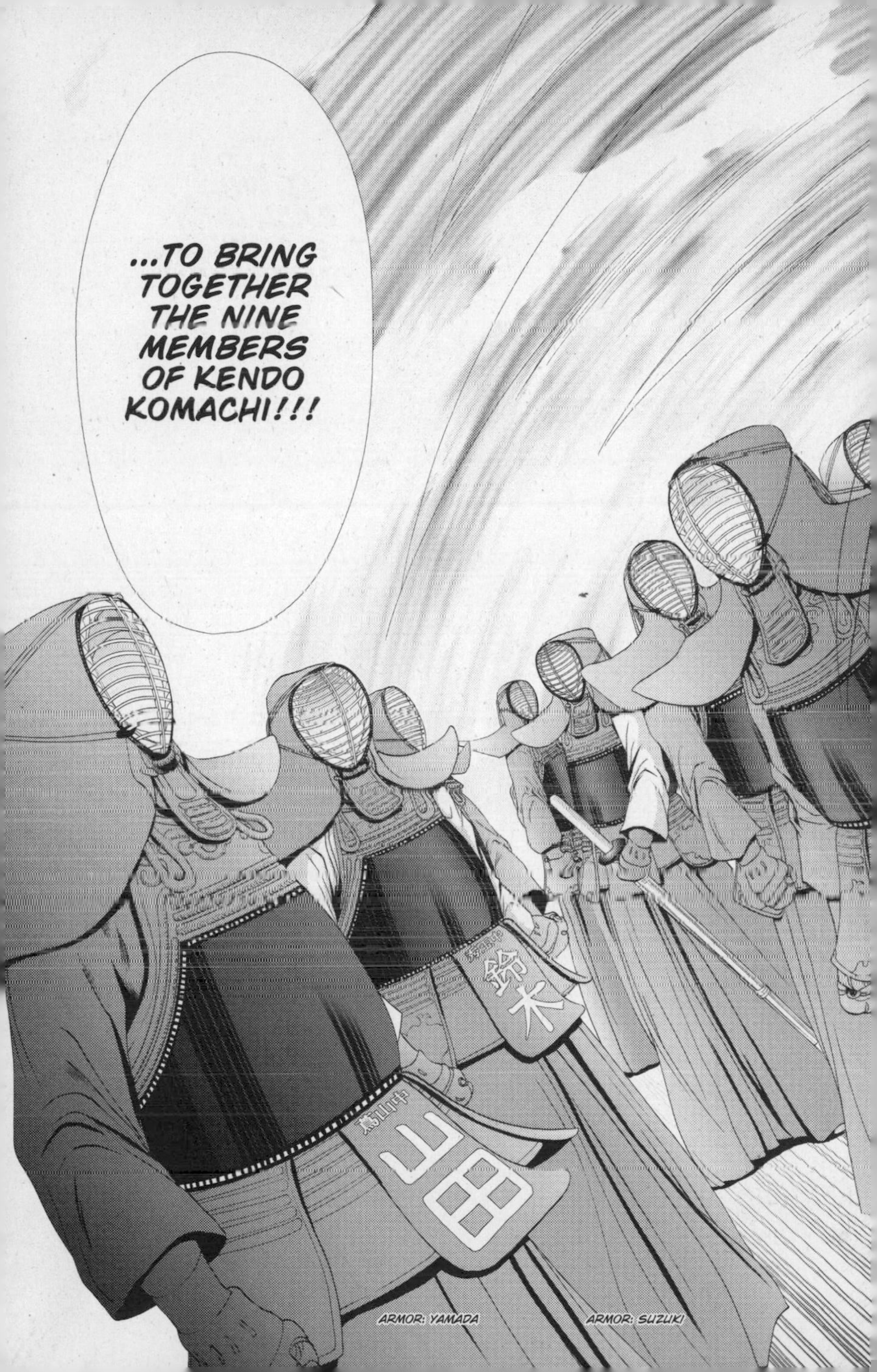
...TO BRING TOGETHER THE NINE MEMBERS OF KENDO KOMACHI!!!
鈴木
山田
ARMOR: YAMADA
ARMOR: SUZUKI

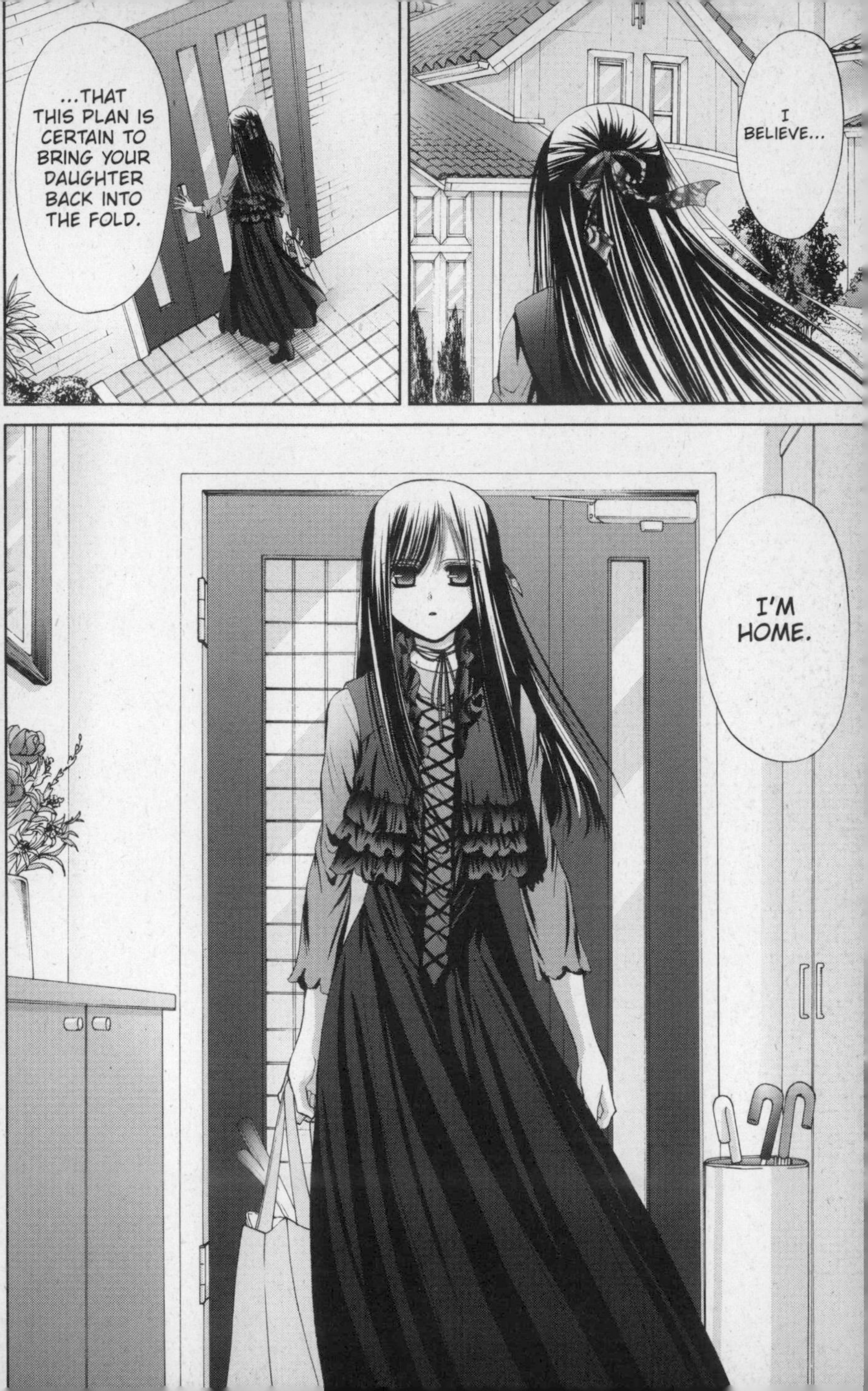
I BELIEVE...
...THAT THIS PLAN IS CERTAIN TO BRING YOUR DAUGHTER BACK INTO THE FOLD.
I'M HOME.

BAMBOO BLADE
バンブーブレード

BAMBOO BLADE
バンブーブレード

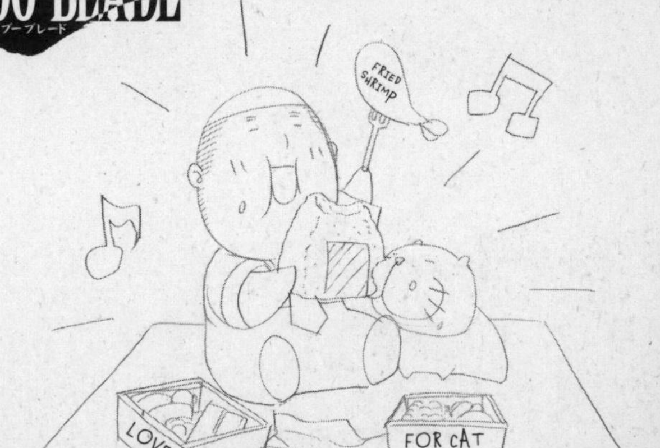
FRIED SHRIMP
LOVE
FOR CAT

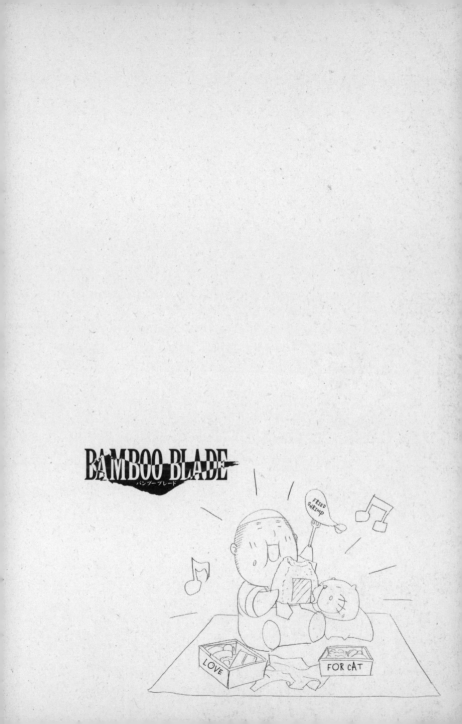

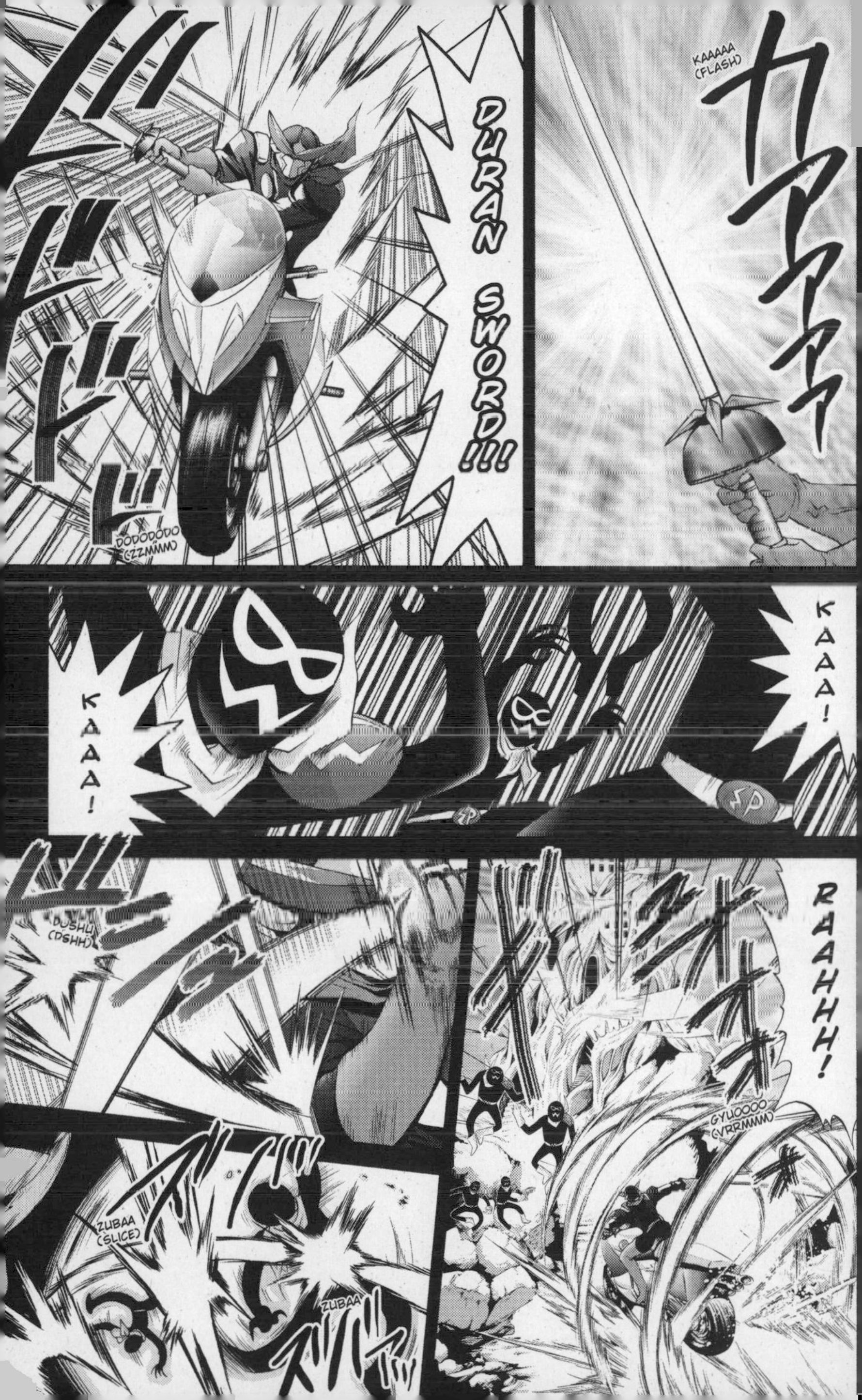
KAAAAA (FLASH)
DURAN SWORD!!!
DODODODO (ZZMMM)
KAAAA!
KAAAA!
RAAHHH!
GYUOOOO (VRRMMM)
DUSHU (DSHH)
ZUBAA (SLICE)
ZUBAA

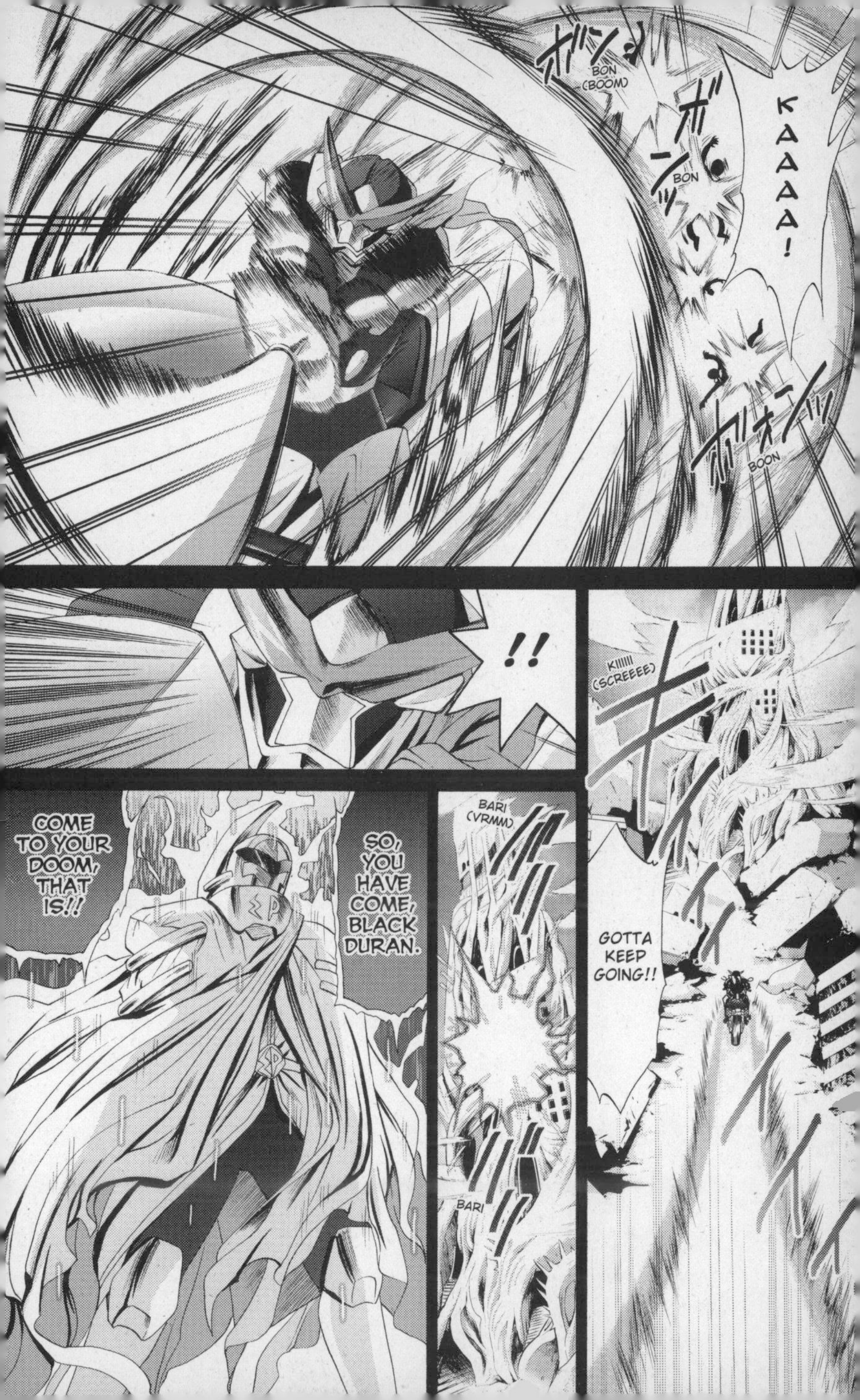
KAAAA!
BON (BOOM)
BON
BOON
KIIIII (SCREEEE)
GOTTA KEEP GOING!!
!!
BARI (VRMM)
BARI
SO, YOU HAVE COME, BLACK DURAN.
COME TO YOUR DOOM, THAT IS!!

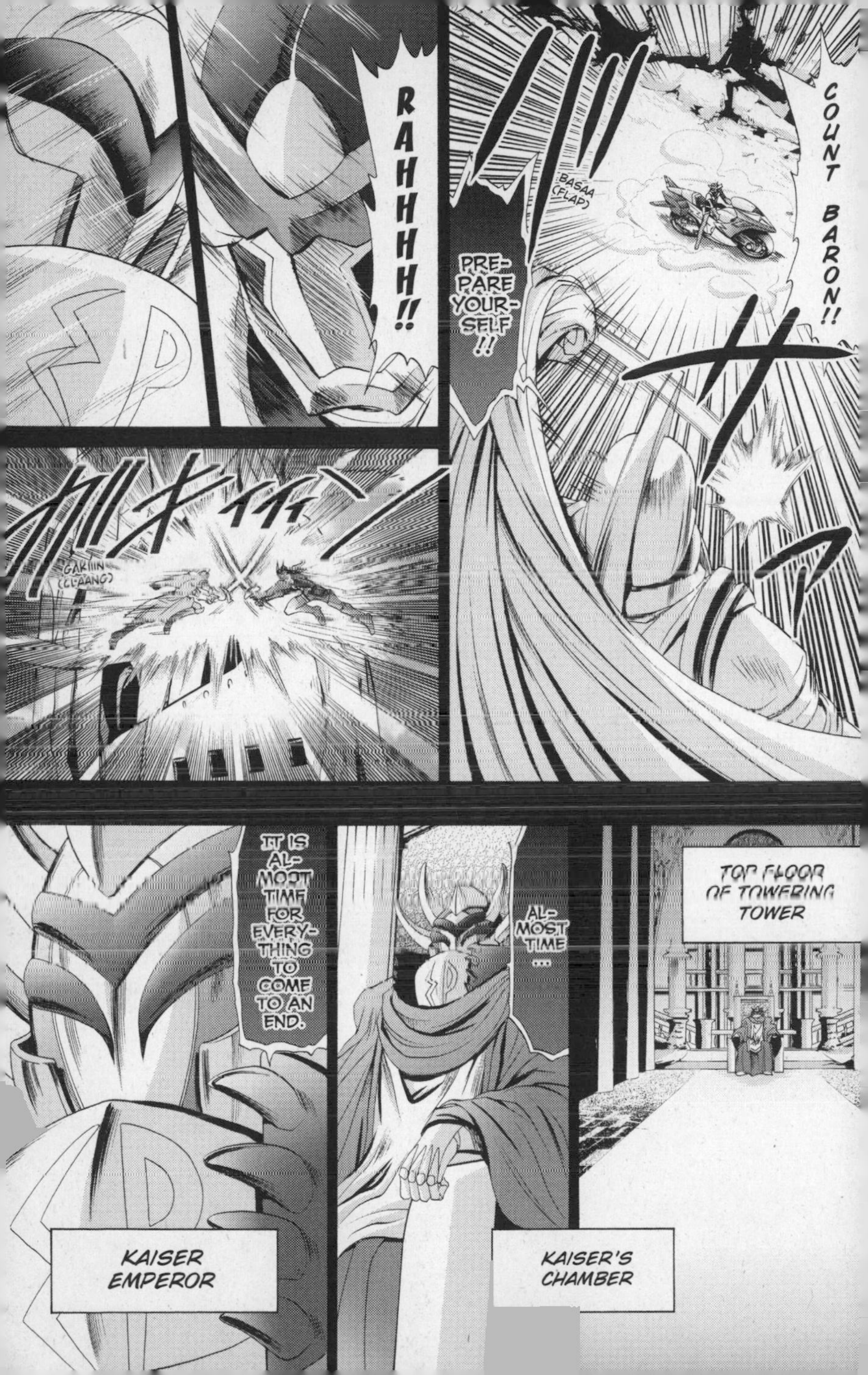
COUNT BARON!!
BASAA (FLAP)
PRE-PARE YOUR-SELF!!
RAHHHHH!!
GAKIIIN (CL-AANG)
TOP FLOOR OF TOWERING TOWER
KAISER'S CHAMBER
AL-MOST TIME...
IT IS AL-MOST TIME FOR EVERY-THING TO COME TO AN END.
KAISER EMPEROR

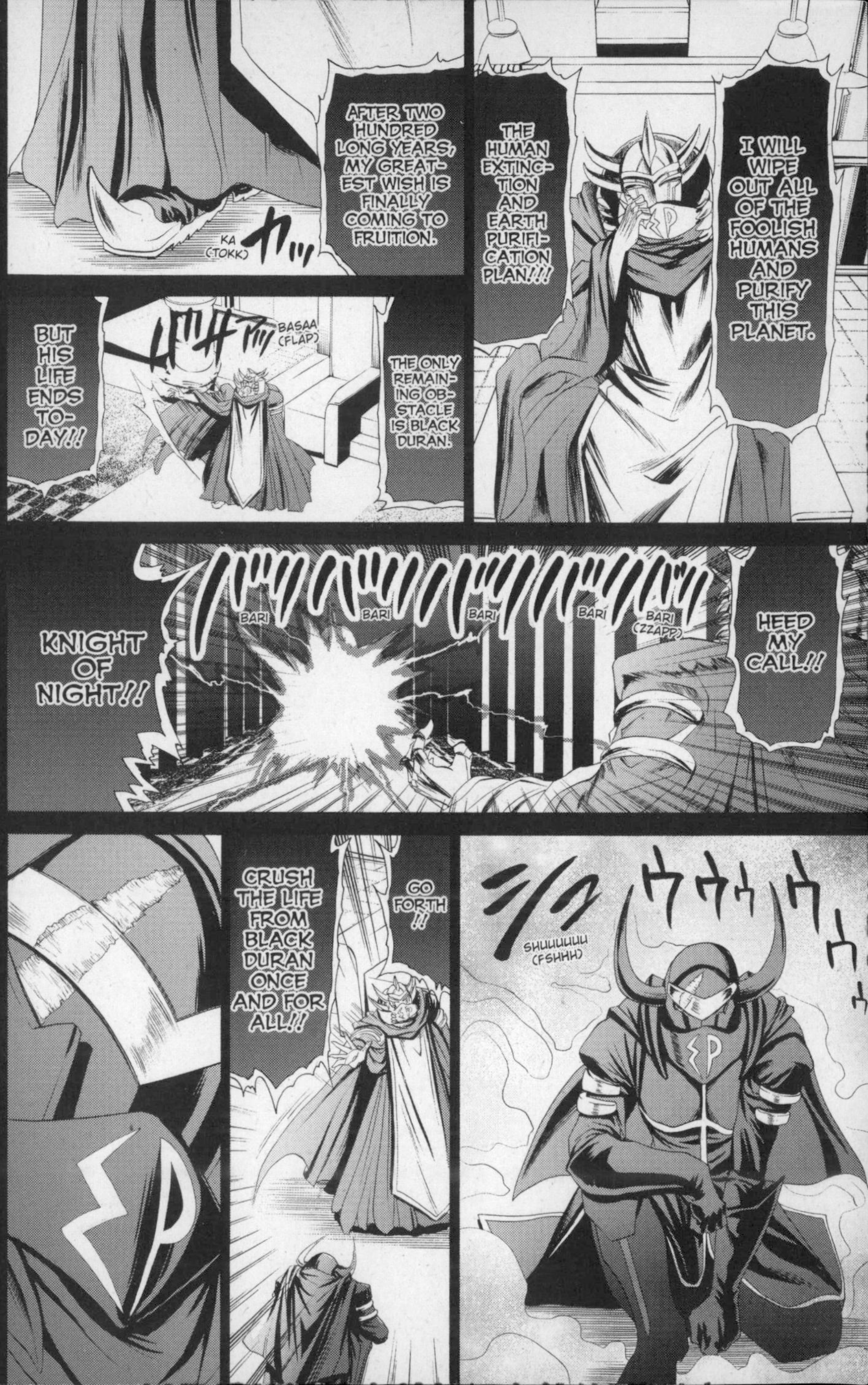

I WILL WIPE OUT ALL OF THE FOOLISH HUMANS AND PURIFY THIS PLANET.
THE HUMAN EXTINCTION AND EARTH PURIFICATION PLAN!!!
AFTER TWO HUNDRED LONG YEARS, MY GREATEST WISH IS FINALLY COMING TO FRUITION.
KA (TOKK)
BASAA (FLAP)
THE ONLY REMAINING OBSTACLE IS BLACK DURAN.
BUT HIS LIFE ENDS TODAY!!
HEED MY CALL!!
BARI (ZZAPP)
BARI
BARI
BARI
BARI
KNIGHT OF NIGHT!!
SHUUUUUUU (FSHHH)
GO FORTH!!
CRUSH THE LIFE FROM BLACK DURAN ONCE AND FOR ALL!!

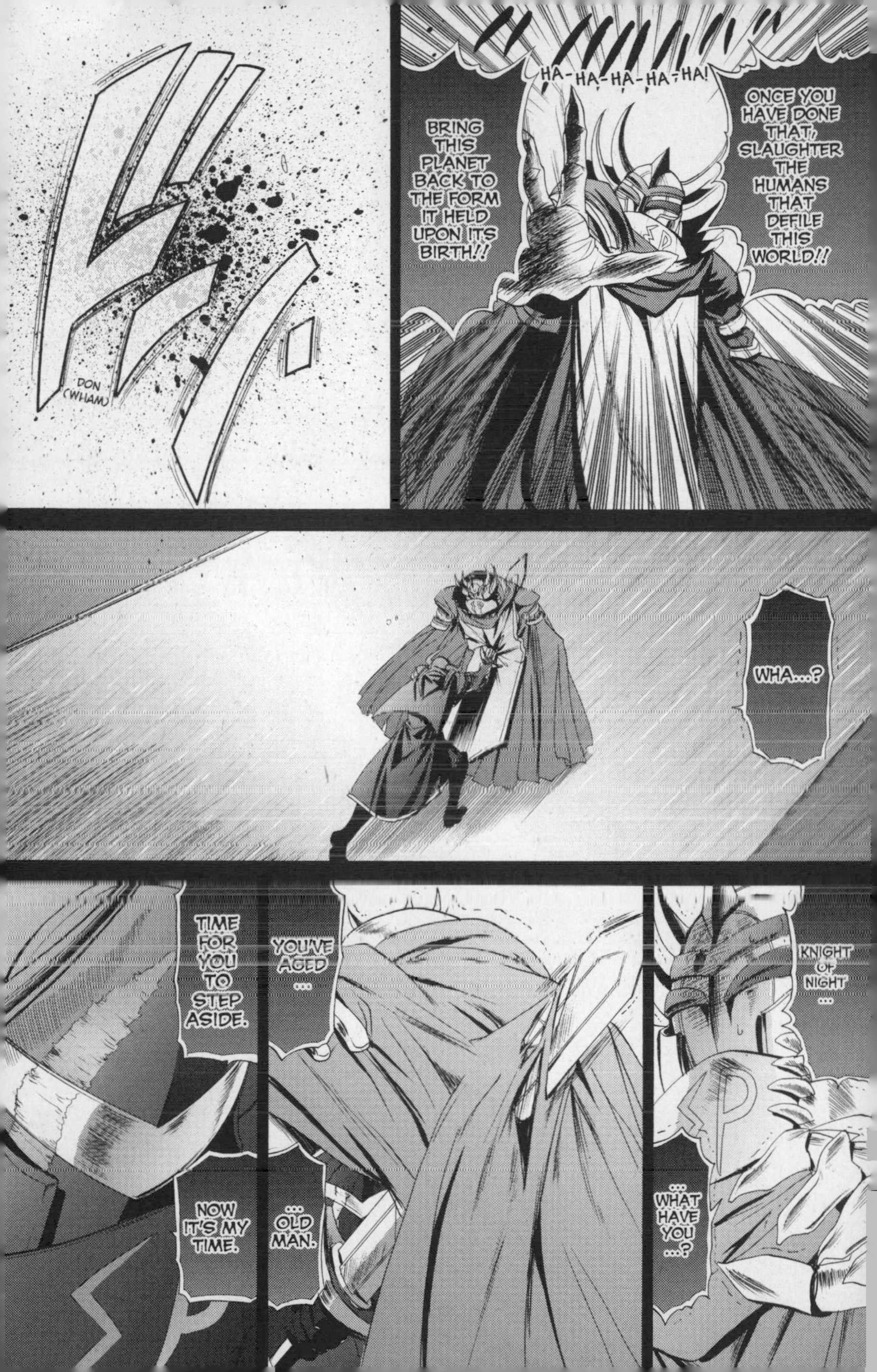
HA-HA-HA-HA-HA!
BRING THIS PLANET BACK TO THE FORM IT HELD UPON ITS BIRTH!!
ONCE YOU HAVE DONE THAT, SLAUGHTER THE HUMANS THAT DEFILE THIS WORLD!!
DON (WHAM)
WHA...?
KNIGHT OF NIGHT ...
... WHAT HAVE YOU ...?
YOU'VE AGED ...
... OLD MAN.
TIME FOR YOU TO STEP ASIDE.
NOW IT'S MY TIME.

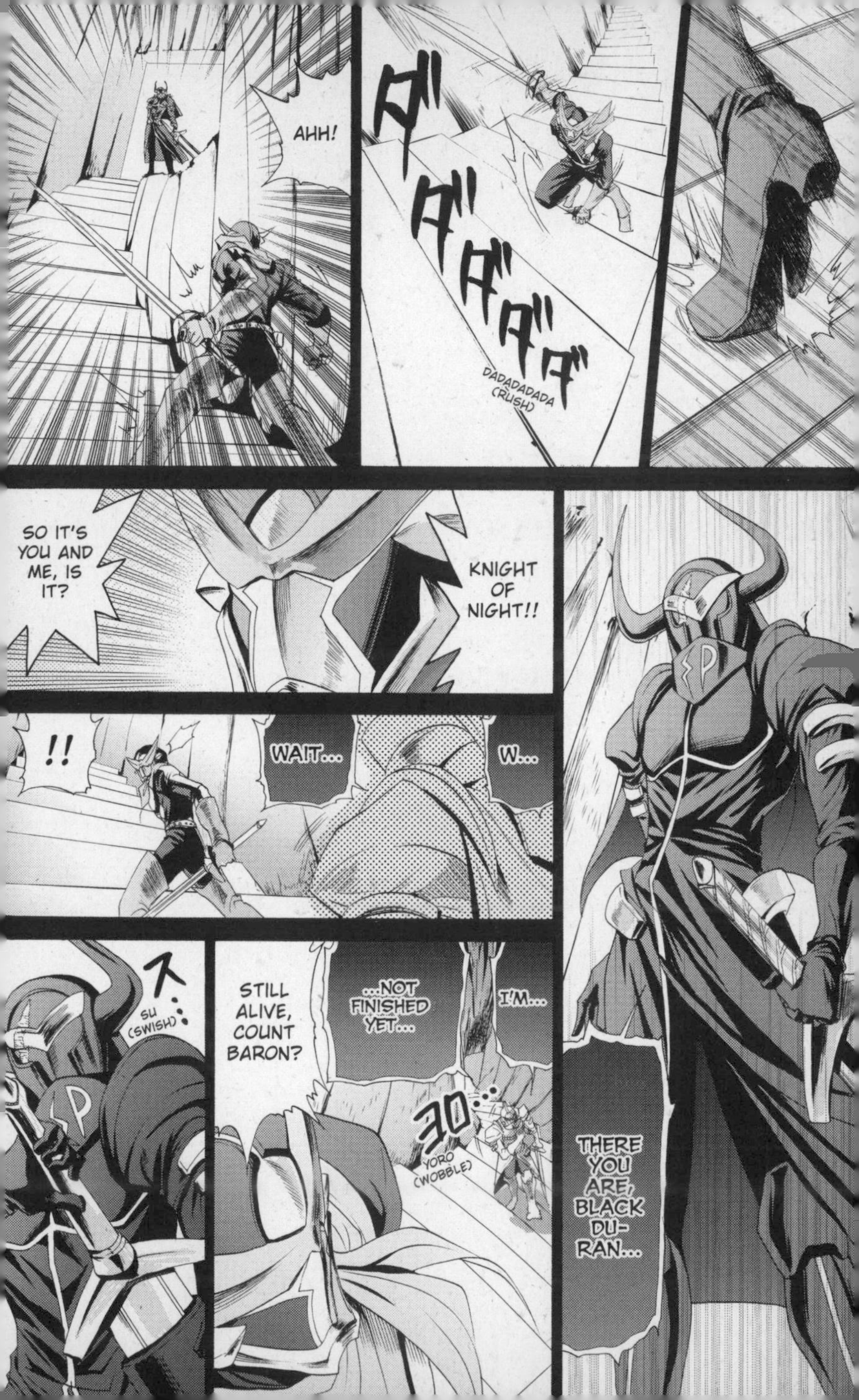
ダダダダ
DADADADADA (RUSH)
AHH!
THERE YOU ARE, BLACK DU-RAN...
KNIGHT OF NIGHT!!
SO IT'S YOU AND ME, IS IT?
W...
WAIT...
!!
I'M...
...NOT FINISHED YET...
ヨロ
YORO (WOBBLE)
STILL ALIVE, COUNT BARON?
ス
SU (SWISH)

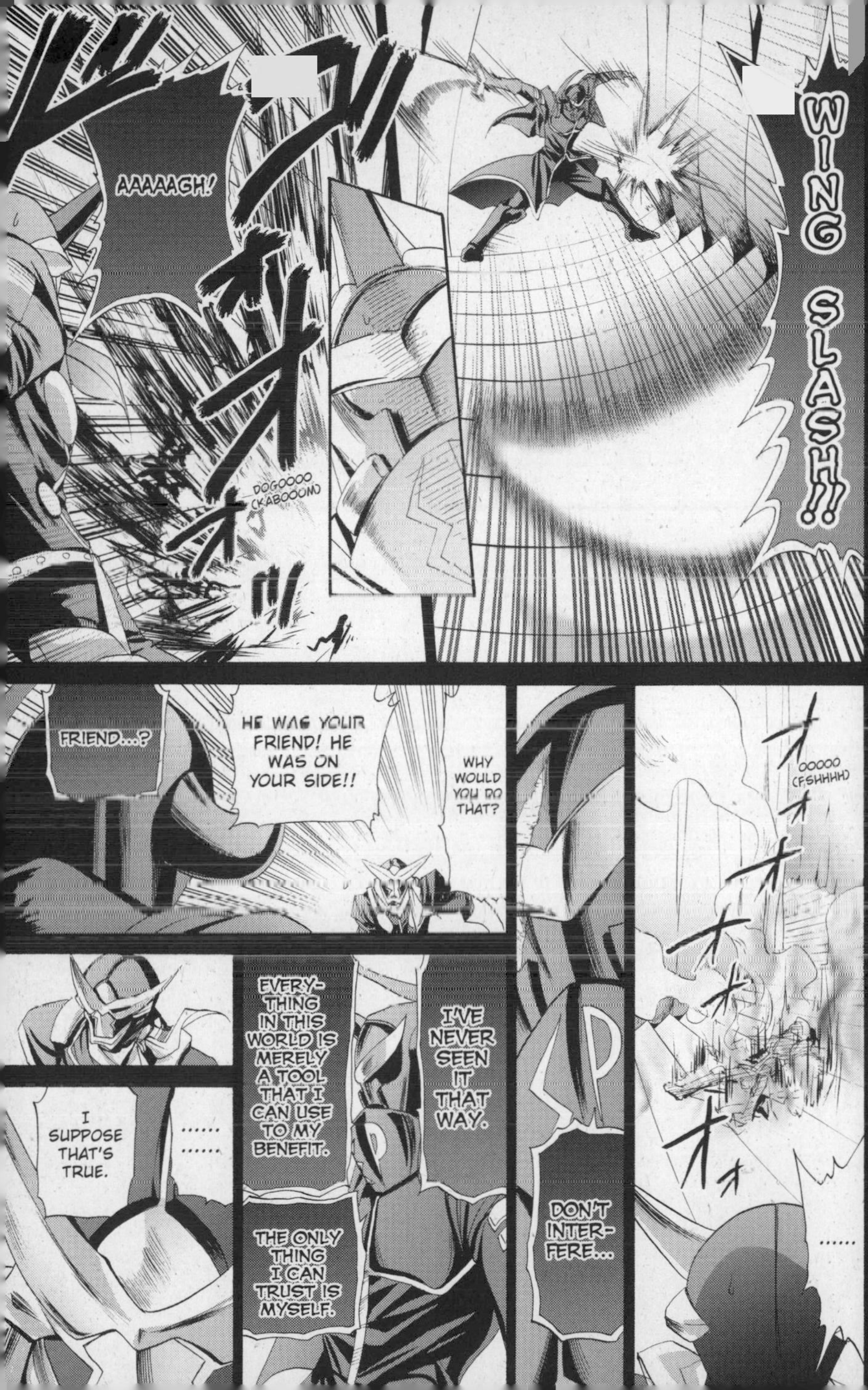

WING SLASH!!
AAAAAGH!
DOGOOOO (KABOOOM)
OOOOO (FSHHHH)
......
DON'T INTERFERE...
WHY WOULD YOU DO THAT?
HE WAS YOUR FRIEND! HE WAS ON YOUR SIDE!!
FRIEND...?
I'VE NEVER SEEN IT THAT WAY.
EVERYTHING IN THIS WORLD IS MERELY A TOOL THAT I CAN USE TO MY BENEFIT.
THE ONLY THING I CAN TRUST IS MYSELF.
......
......
I SUPPOSE THAT'S TRUE.

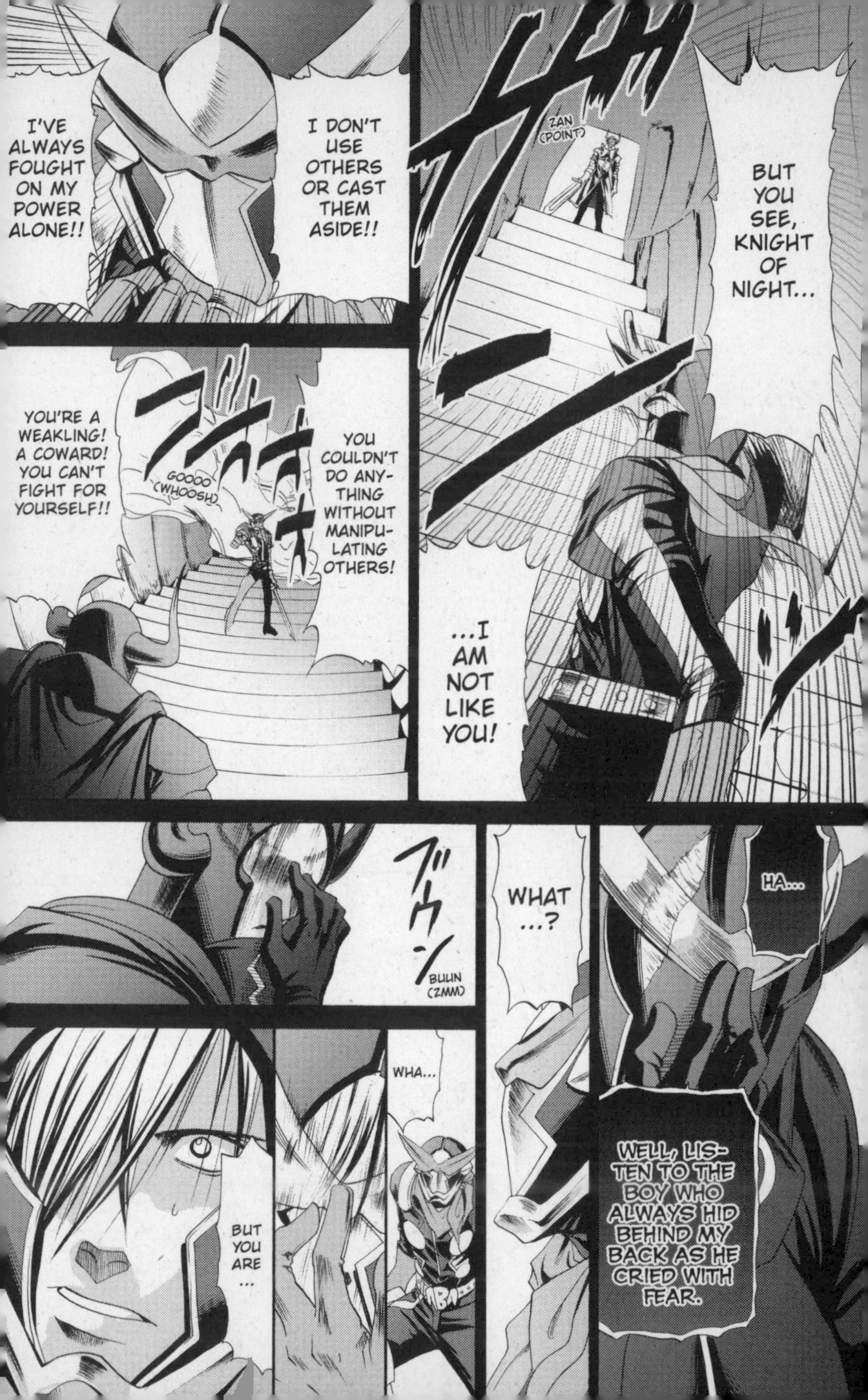
ZAN (POINT)
BUT YOU SEE, KNIGHT OF NIGHT...
...I AM NOT LIKE YOU!
I DON'T USE OTHERS OR CAST THEM ASIDE!!
I'VE ALWAYS FOUGHT ON MY POWER ALONE!!
YOU COULDN'T DO ANY-THING WITHOUT MANIPU-LATING OTHERS!
GOOOO (WHOOSH)
YOU'RE A WEAKLING! A COWARD! YOU CAN'T FIGHT FOR YOURSELF!!
HA...
WELL, LIS-TEN TO THE BOY WHO ALWAYS HID BEHIND MY BACK AS HE CRIED WITH FEAR.
WHAT ...?
BUUN (ZMMM)
WHA...
BUT YOU ARE ...

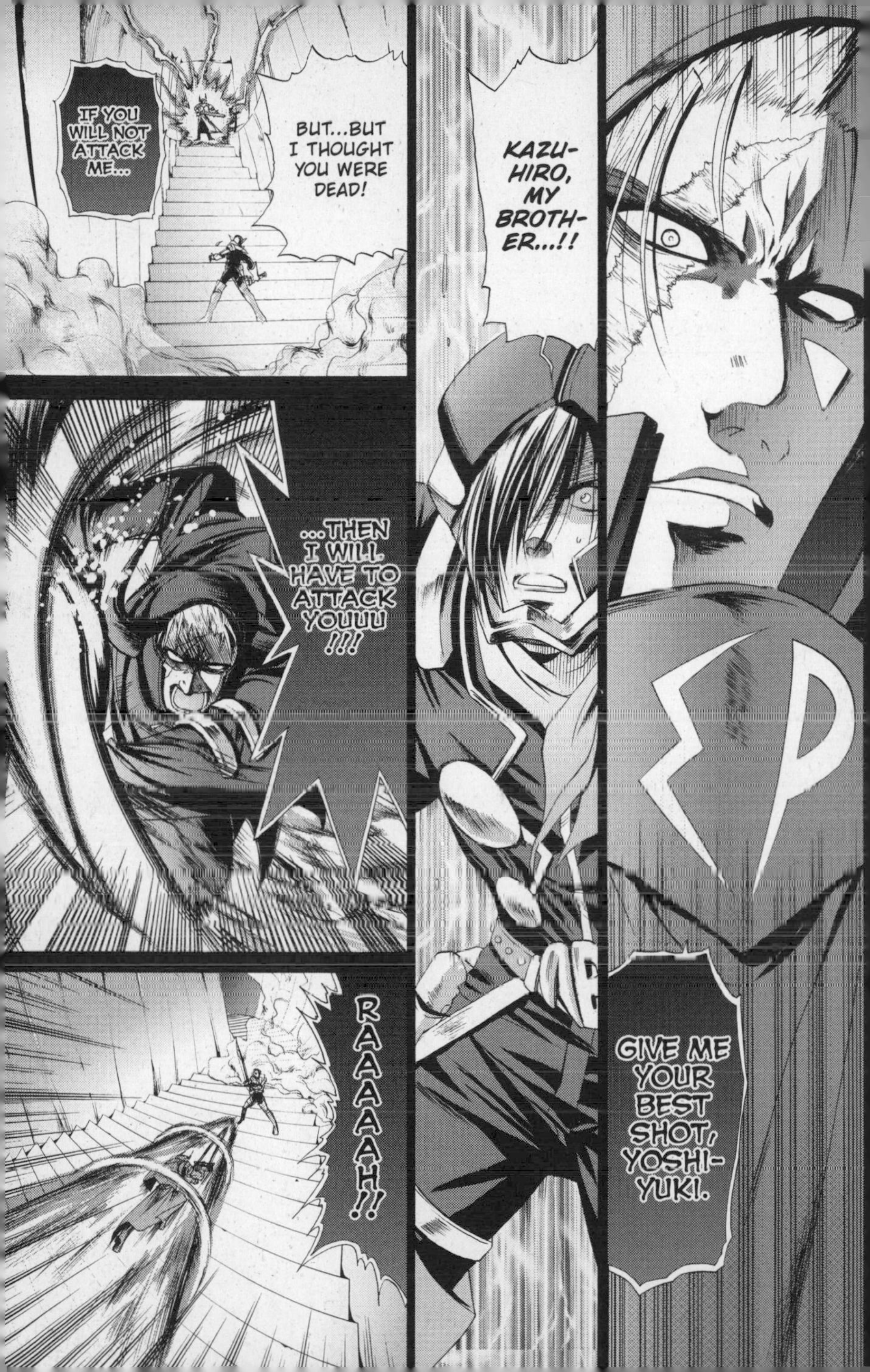
GIVE ME YOUR BEST SHOT, YOSHI-YUKI.
KAZU-HIRO, MY BROTH-ER...!!
BUT...BUT I THOUGHT YOU WERE DEAD!
IF YOU WILL NOT ATTACK ME...
...THEN I WILL HAVE TO ATTACK YOUUU!!!
RAAAAAAH!!

CHAPTER 83
TERAMOTO AND THE FINAL REQUEST

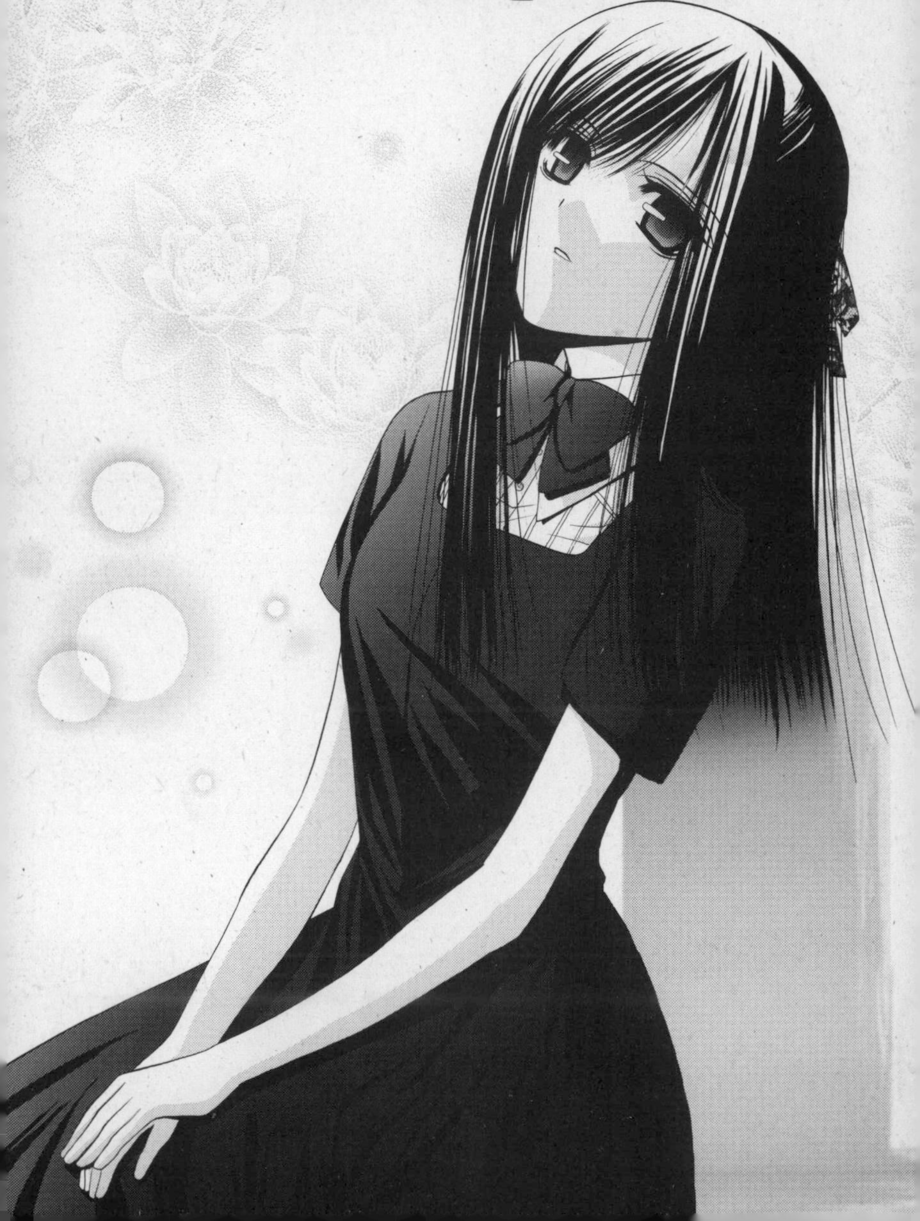

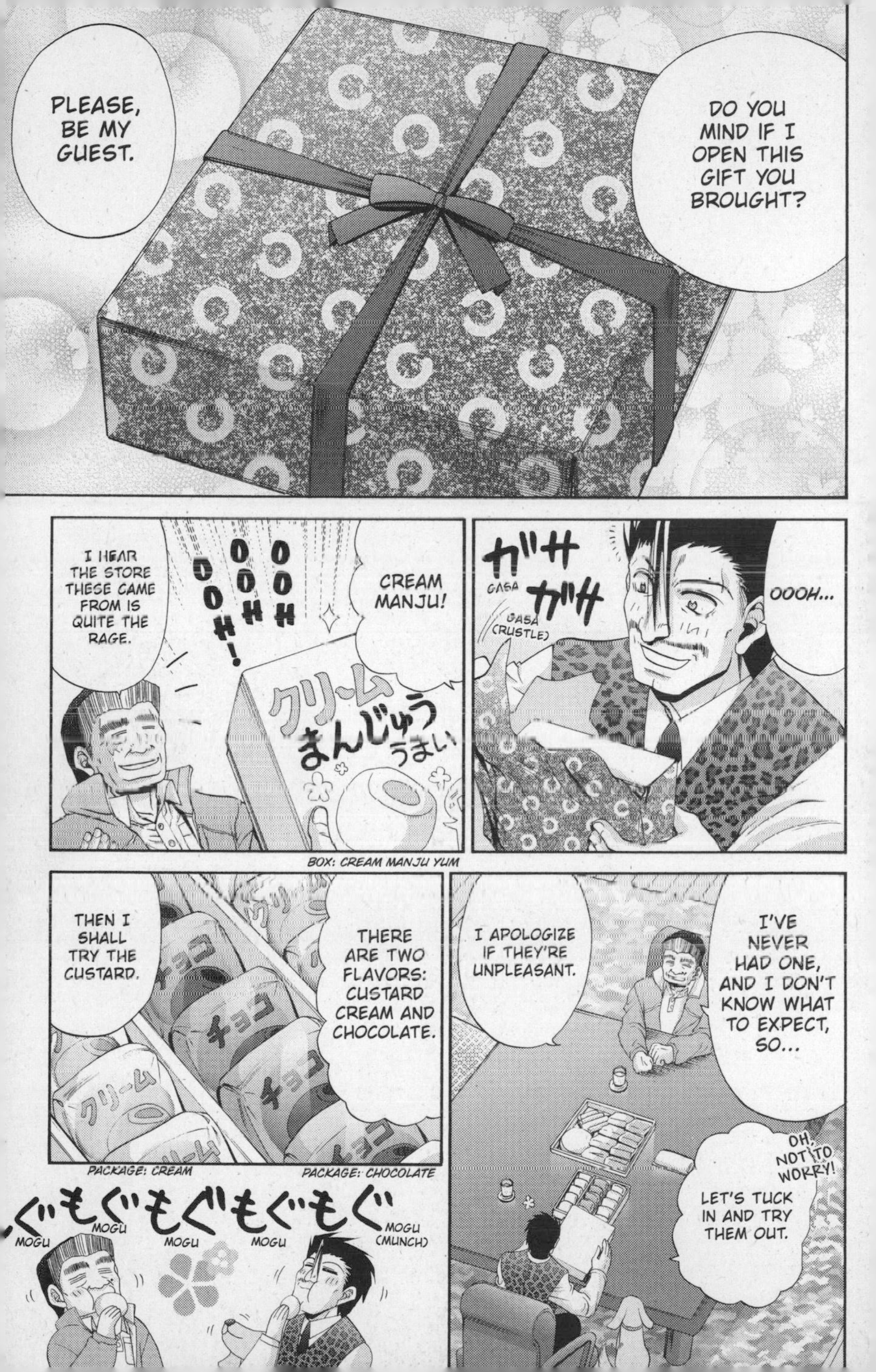
DO YOU MIND IF I OPEN THIS GIFT YOU BROUGHT?
PLEASE, BE MY GUEST.
ガサ ガサ
GASA GASA (RUSTLE)
OOOH...
CREAM MANJU!
OOOOH!
I HEAR THE STORE THESE CAME FROM IS QUITE THE RAGE.
クリーム まんじゅう うまい
BOX: CREAM MANJU YUM
I'VE NEVER HAD ONE, AND I DON'T KNOW WHAT TO EXPECT, SO...
I APOLOGIZE IF THEY'RE UNPLEASANT.
OH, NOT TO WORRY!
LET'S TUCK IN AND TRY THEM OUT.
THERE ARE TWO FLAVORS: CUSTARD CREAM AND CHOCOLATE.
THEN I SHALL TRY THE CUSTARD.
PACKAGE: CREAM
PACKAGE: CHOCOLATE
もぐもぐもぐもぐもぐ
MOGU MOGU MOGU MOGU MOGU (MUNCH)

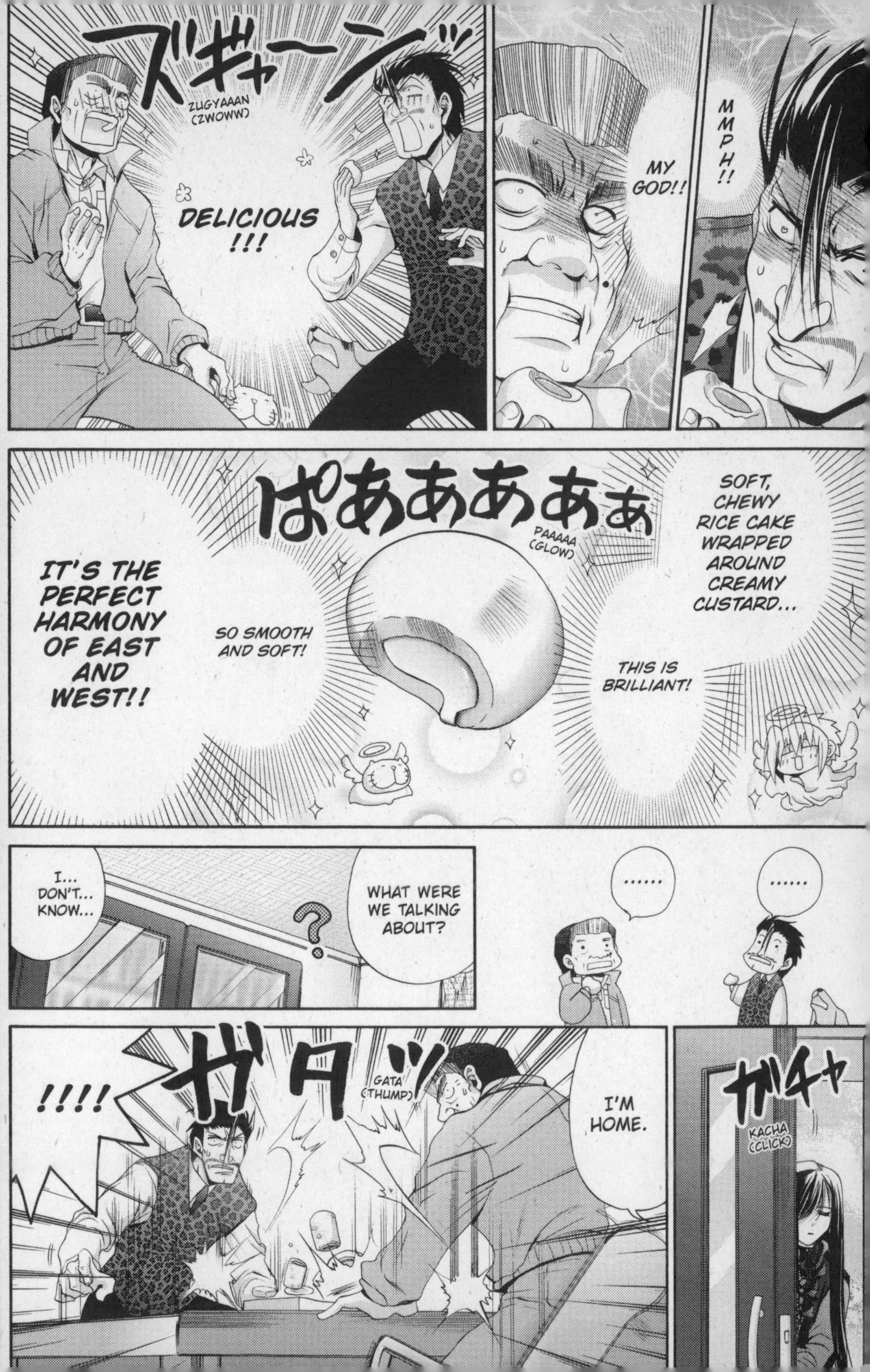
MMPH!!
MY GOD!!
ズギャーン
ZUGYAAAN (ZWOWW)
DELICIOUS!!!
ぱあああああ
PAAAAA (GLOW)
SOFT, CHEWY RICE CAKE WRAPPED AROUND CREAMY CUSTARD...
THIS IS BRILLIANT!
SO SMOOTH AND SOFT!
IT'S THE PERFECT HARMONY OF EAST AND WEST!!
......
......
WHAT WERE WE TALKING ABOUT?
I... DON'T... KNOW...
ガチャ
KACHA (CLICK)
I'M HOME.
ガタッ
GATA (THUMP)
!!!!

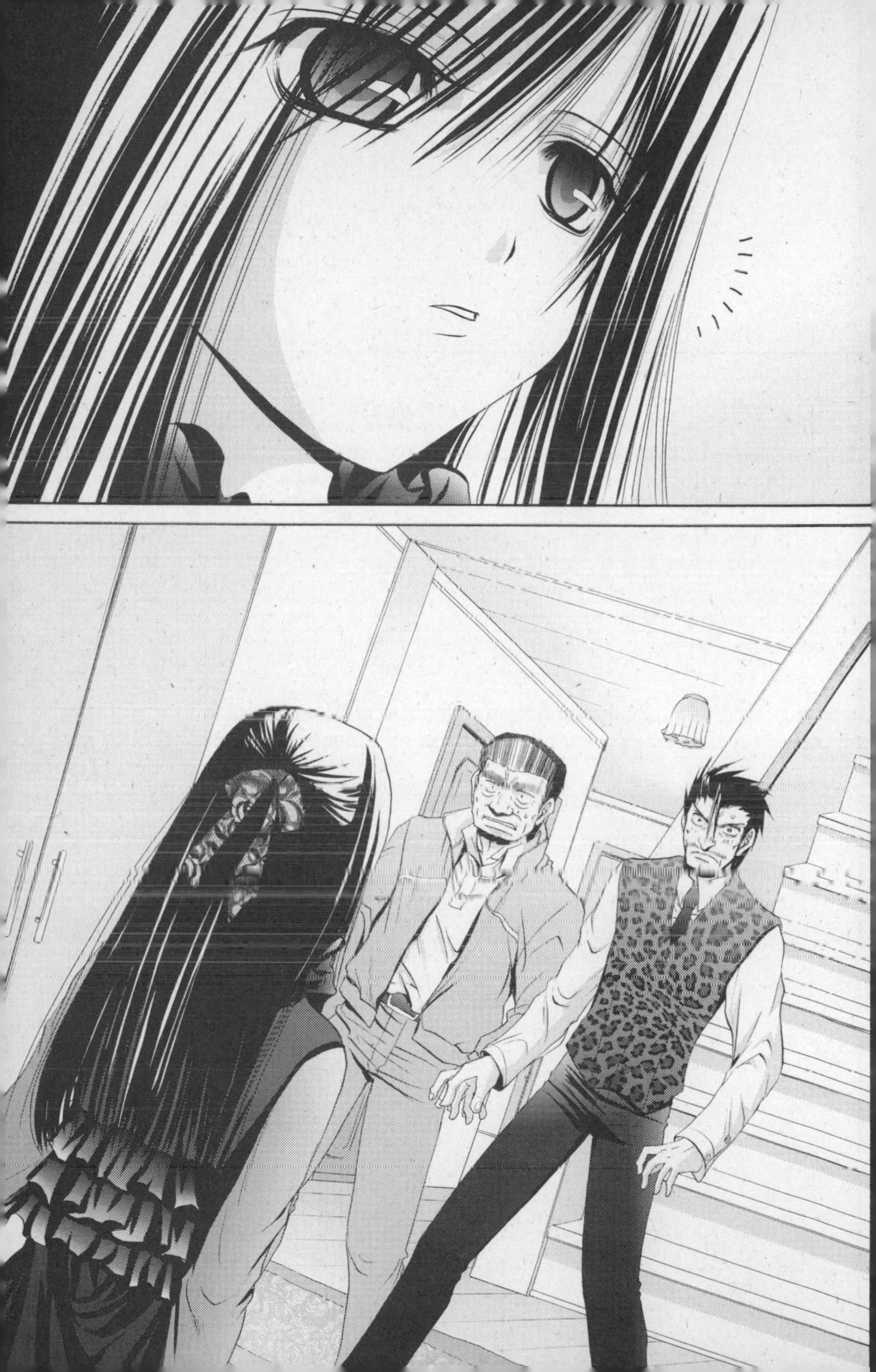

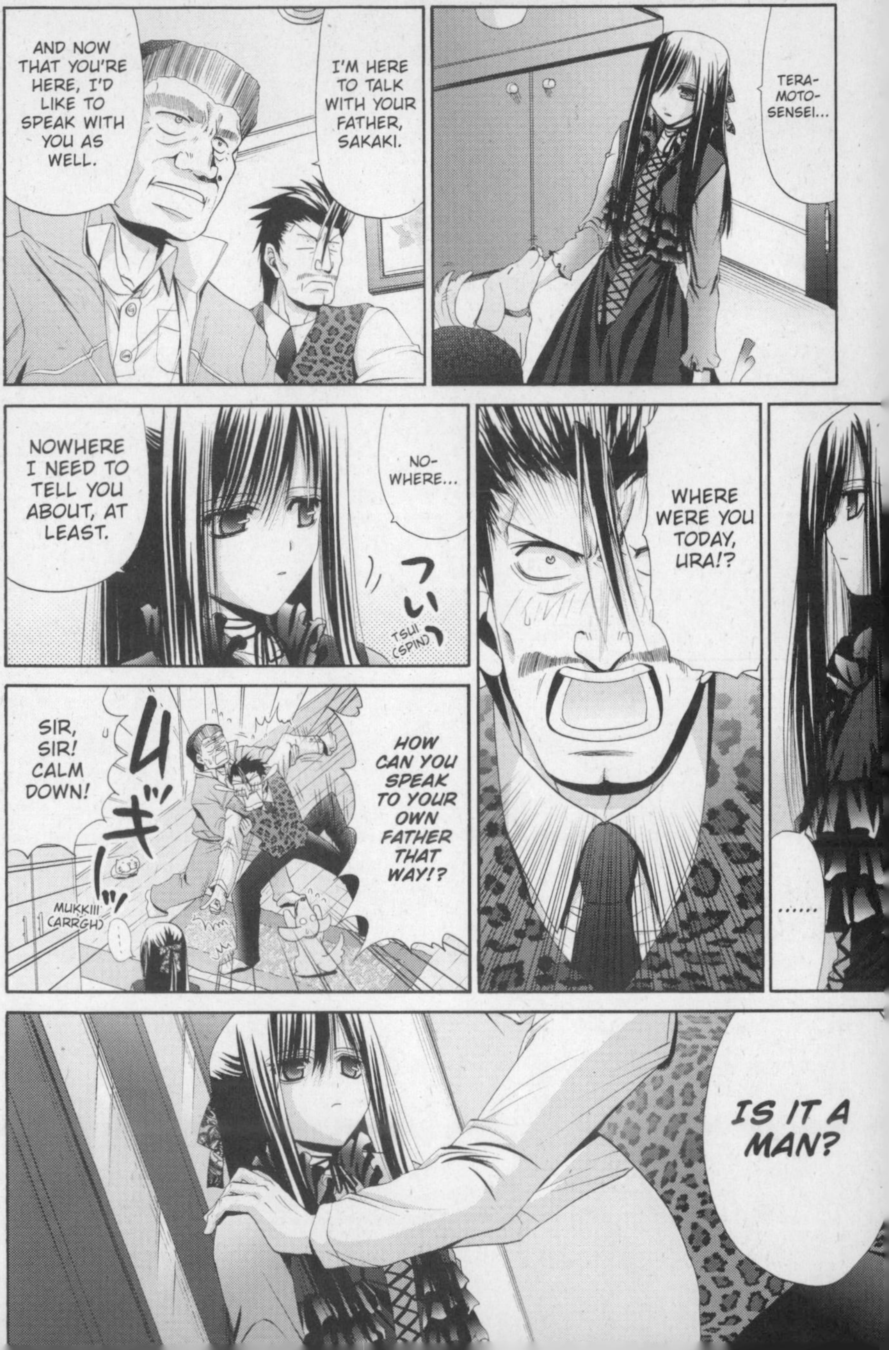
TERA-MOTO-SENSEI...
I'M HERE TO TALK WITH YOUR FATHER, SAKAKI.
AND NOW THAT YOU'RE HERE, I'D LIKE TO SPEAK WITH YOU AS WELL.
......
WHERE WERE YOU TODAY, URA!?
NO-WHERE...
NOWHERE I NEED TO TELL YOU ABOUT, AT LEAST.
TSUI (SPIN)
HOW CAN YOU SPEAK TO YOUR OWN FATHER THAT WAY!?
SIR, SIR! CALM DOWN!
MUKKIII (ARRGH)
IS IT A MAN?

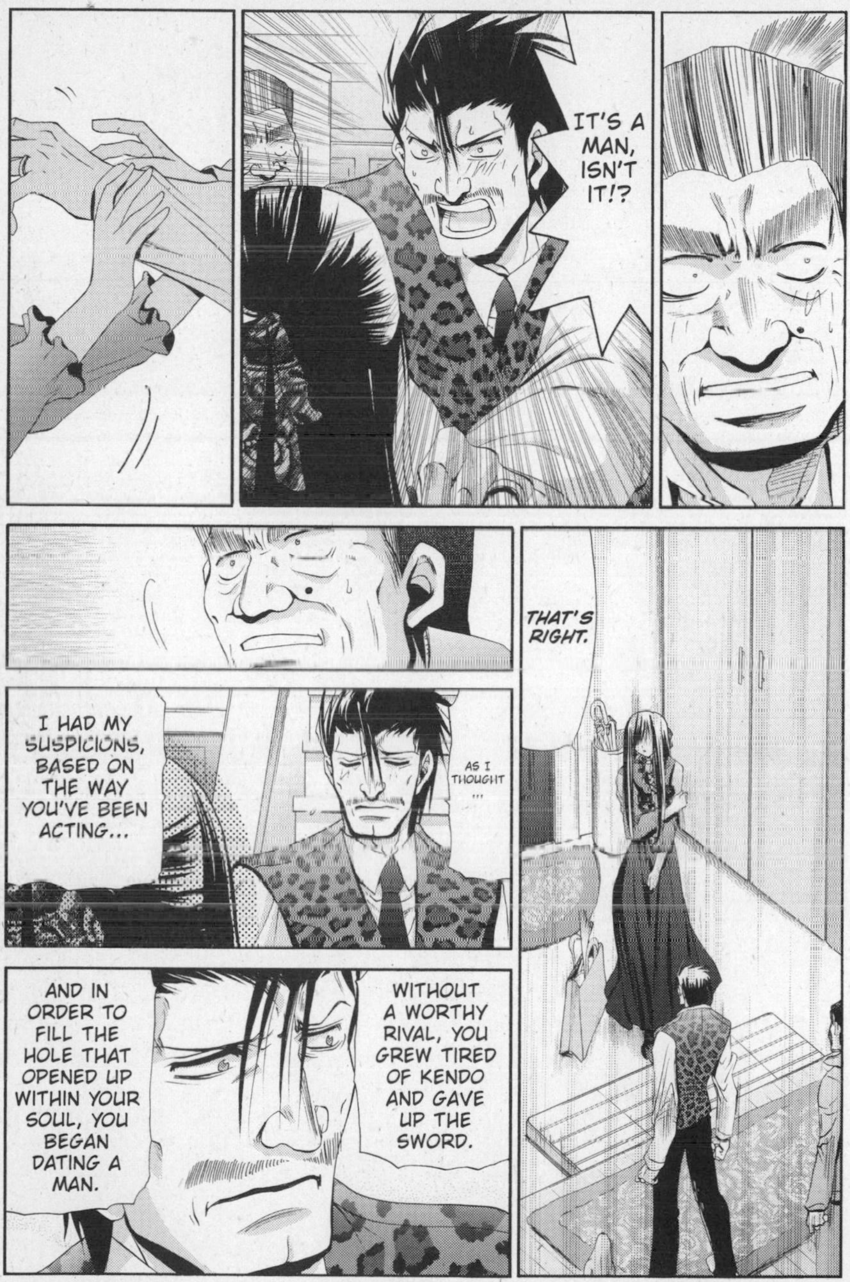
IT'S A MAN, ISN'T IT!?
THAT'S RIGHT.
AS I THOUGHT...
I HAD MY SUSPICIONS, BASED ON THE WAY YOU'VE BEEN ACTING...
WITHOUT A WORTHY RIVAL, YOU GREW TIRED OF KENDO AND GAVE UP THE SWORD.
AND IN ORDER TO FILL THE HOLE THAT OPENED UP WITHIN YOUR SOUL, YOU BEGAN DATING A MAN.

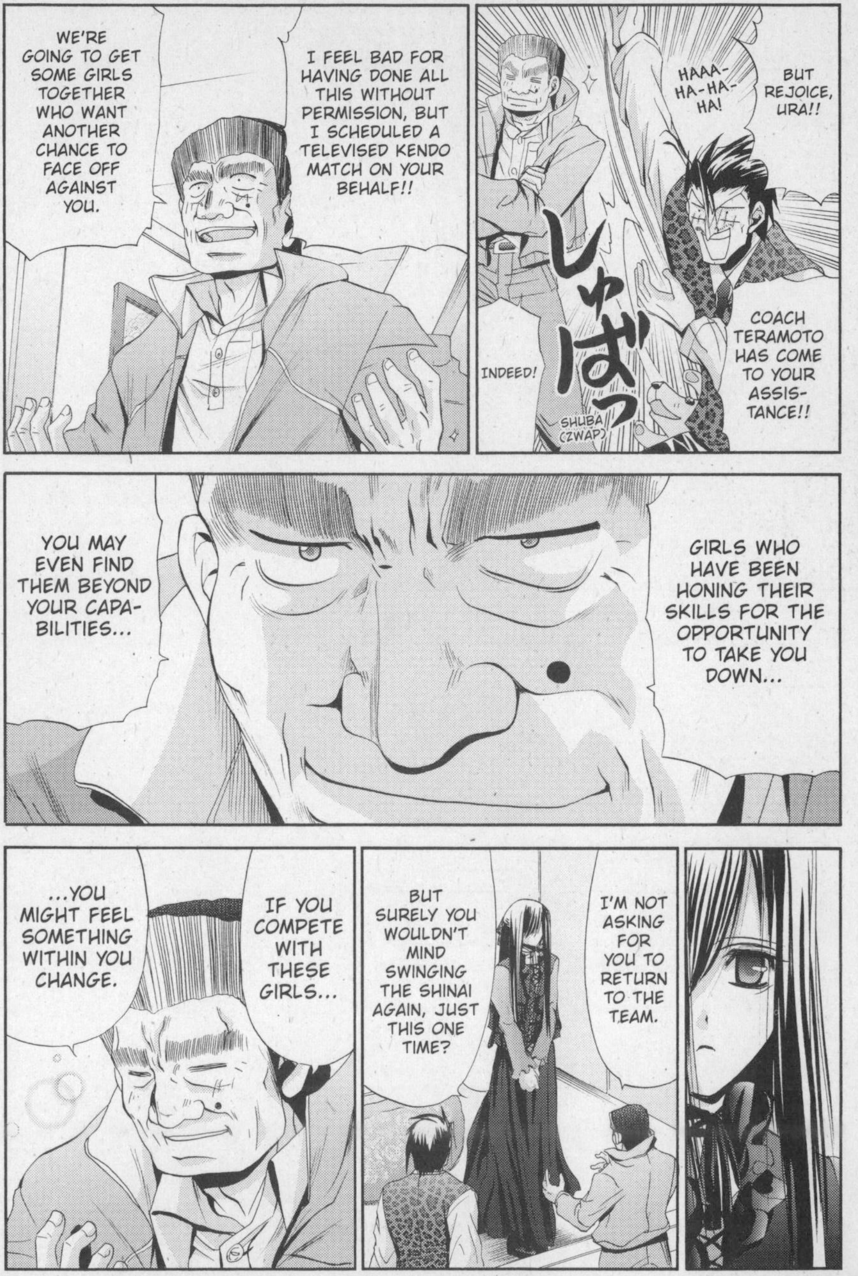
BUT REJOICE, URA!!
HAAA-HA-HA-HA!
COACH TERAMOTO HAS COME TO YOUR ASSISTANCE!!
しゅばっ
SHUBA (ZWAP)
INDEED!
I FEEL BAD FOR HAVING DONE ALL THIS WITHOUT PERMISSION, BUT I SCHEDULED A TELEVISED KENDO MATCH ON YOUR BEHALF!!
WE'RE GOING TO GET SOME GIRLS TOGETHER WHO WANT ANOTHER CHANCE TO FACE OFF AGAINST YOU.
GIRLS WHO HAVE BEEN HONING THEIR SKILLS FOR THE OPPORTUNITY TO TAKE YOU DOWN...
YOU MAY EVEN FIND THEM BEYOND YOUR CAPABILITIES...
I'M NOT ASKING FOR YOU TO RETURN TO THE TEAM.
BUT SURELY YOU WOULDN'T MIND SWINGING THE SHINAI AGAIN, JUST THIS ONE TIME?
IF YOU COMPETE WITH THESE GIRLS...
...YOU MIGHT FEEL SOMETHING WITHIN YOU CHANGE.

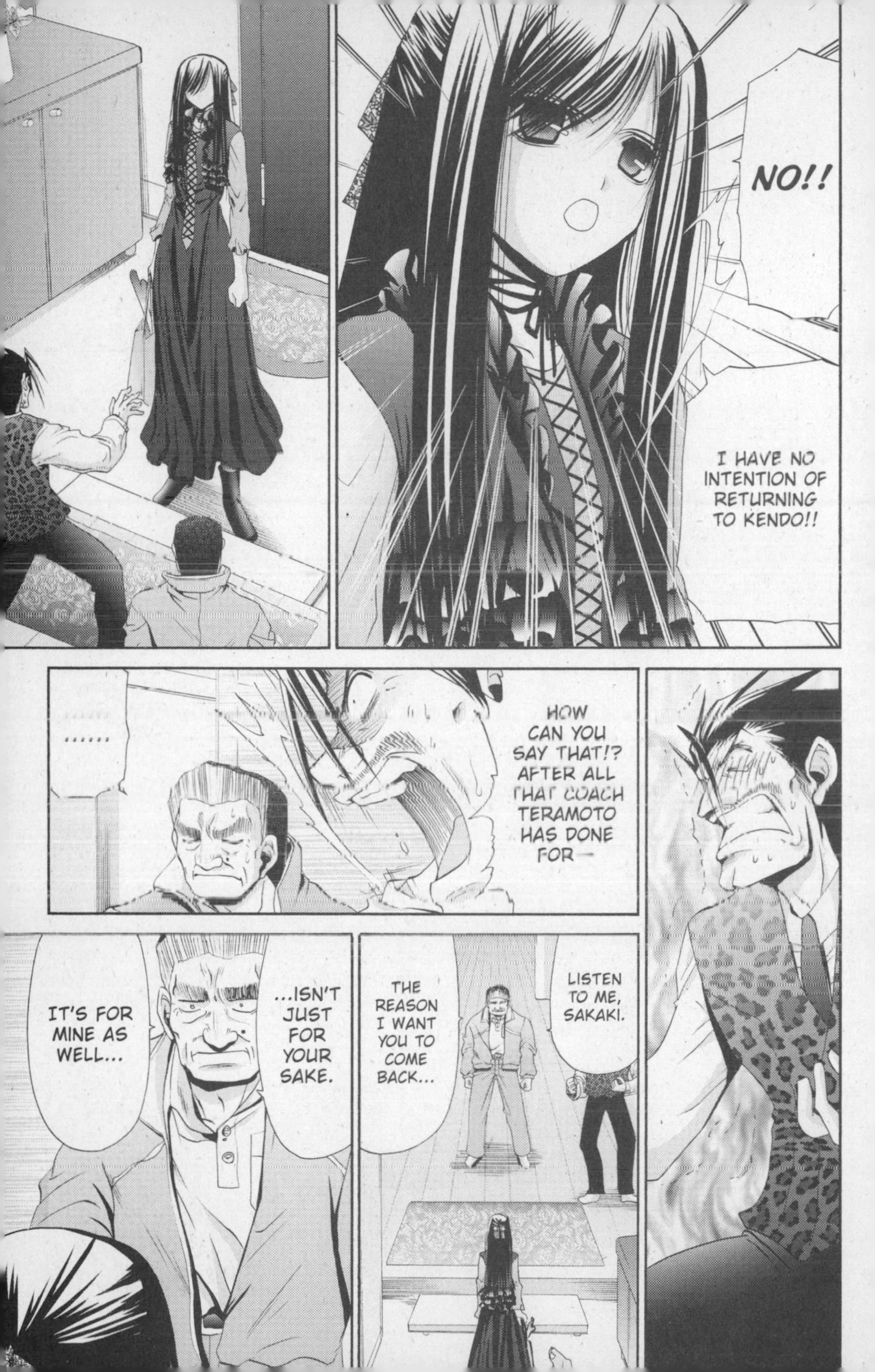
NO!!
I HAVE NO INTENTION OF RETURNING TO KENDO!!
HOW CAN YOU SAY THAT!? AFTER ALL THAT COACH TERAMOTO HAS DONE FOR—
......
LISTEN TO ME, SAKAKI.
THE REASON I WANT YOU TO COME BACK...
...ISN'T JUST FOR YOUR SAKE.
IT'S FOR MINE AS WELL...

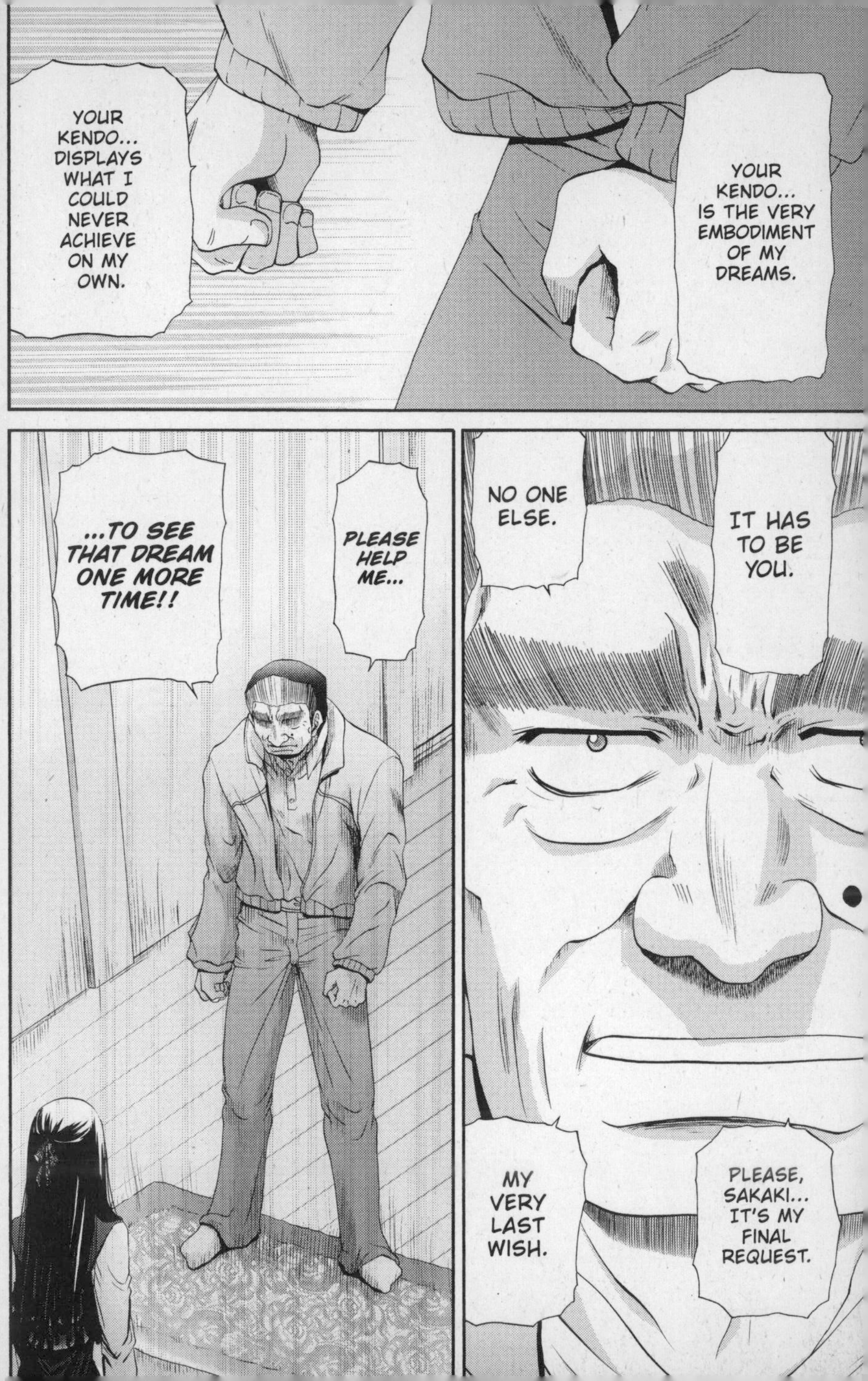
YOUR KENDO... IS THE VERY EMBODIMENT OF MY DREAMS.
YOUR KENDO... DISPLAYS WHAT I COULD NEVER ACHIEVE ON MY OWN.
IT HAS TO BE YOU.
NO ONE ELSE.
PLEASE, SAKAKI... IT'S MY FINAL REQUEST.
MY VERY LAST WISH.
PLEASE HELP ME...
...TO SEE THAT DREAM ONE MORE TIME!!

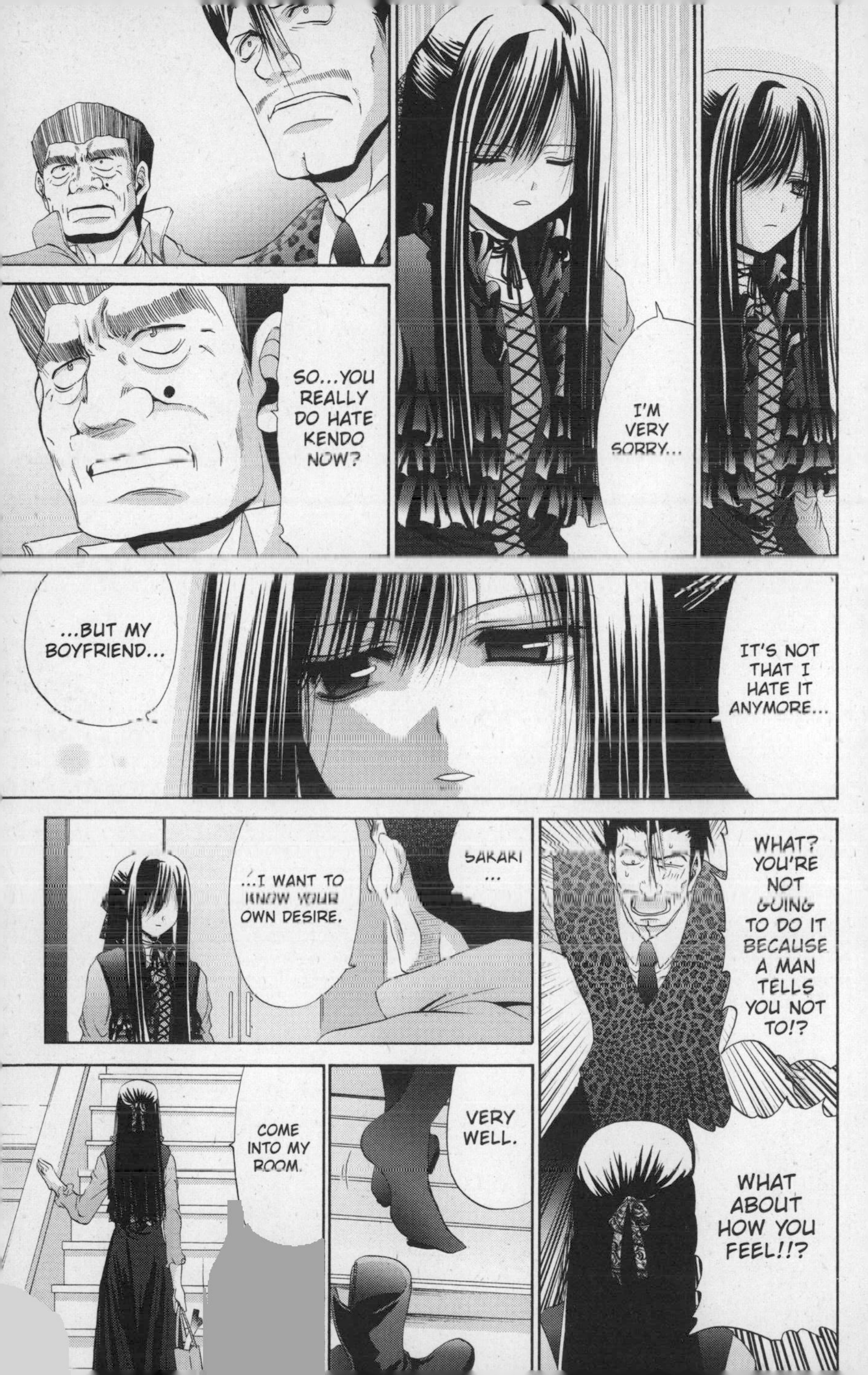
I'M VERY SORRY...
SO...YOU REALLY DO HATE KENDO NOW?
IT'S NOT THAT I HATE IT ANYMORE...
...BUT MY BOYFRIEND...
WHAT? YOU'RE NOT GOING TO DO IT BECAUSE A MAN TELLS YOU NOT TO!?
SAKAKI ...
...I WANT TO KNOW YOUR OWN DESIRE.
WHAT ABOUT HOW YOU FEEL!!?
VERY WELL.
COME INTO MY ROOM.

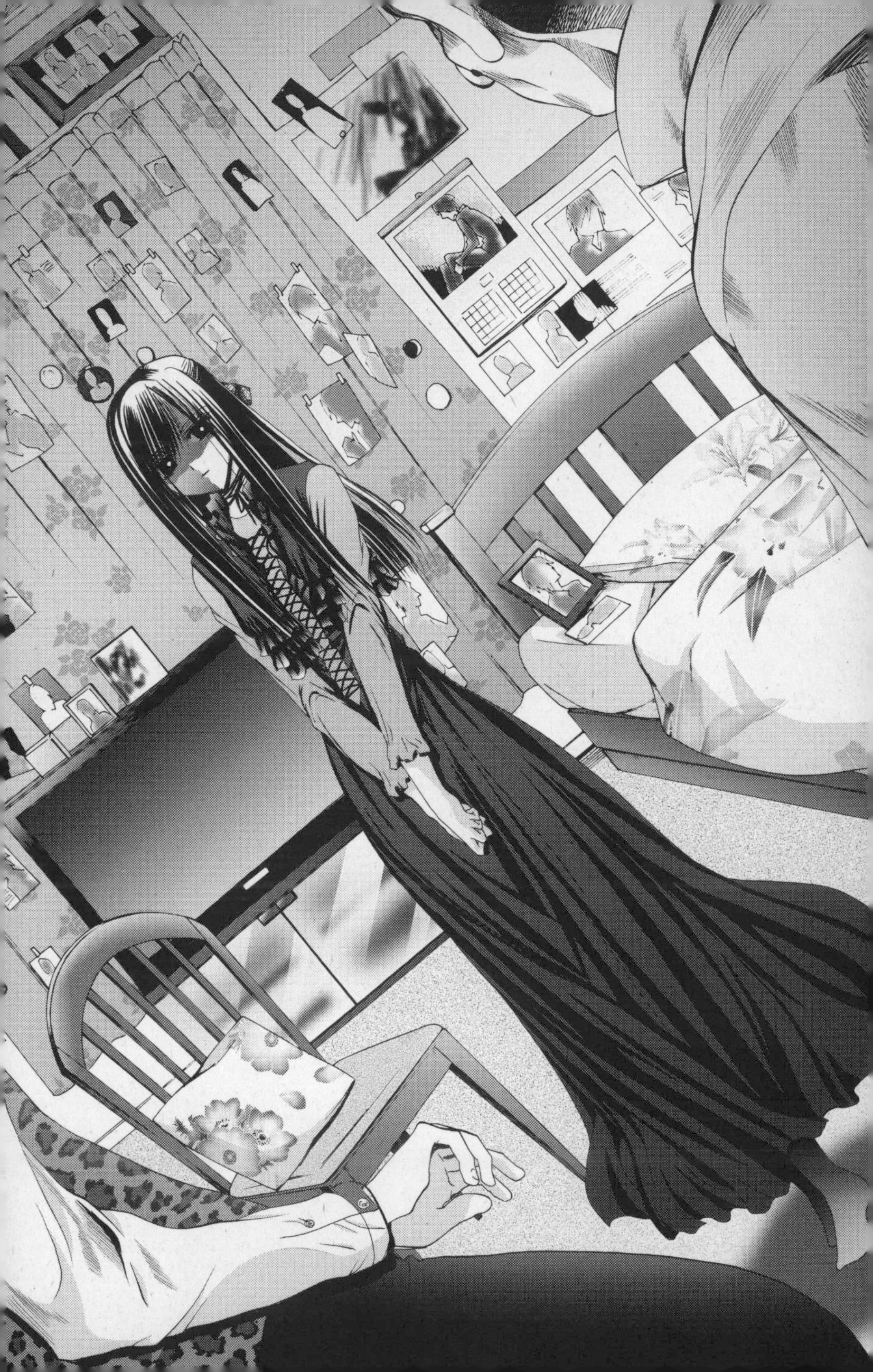

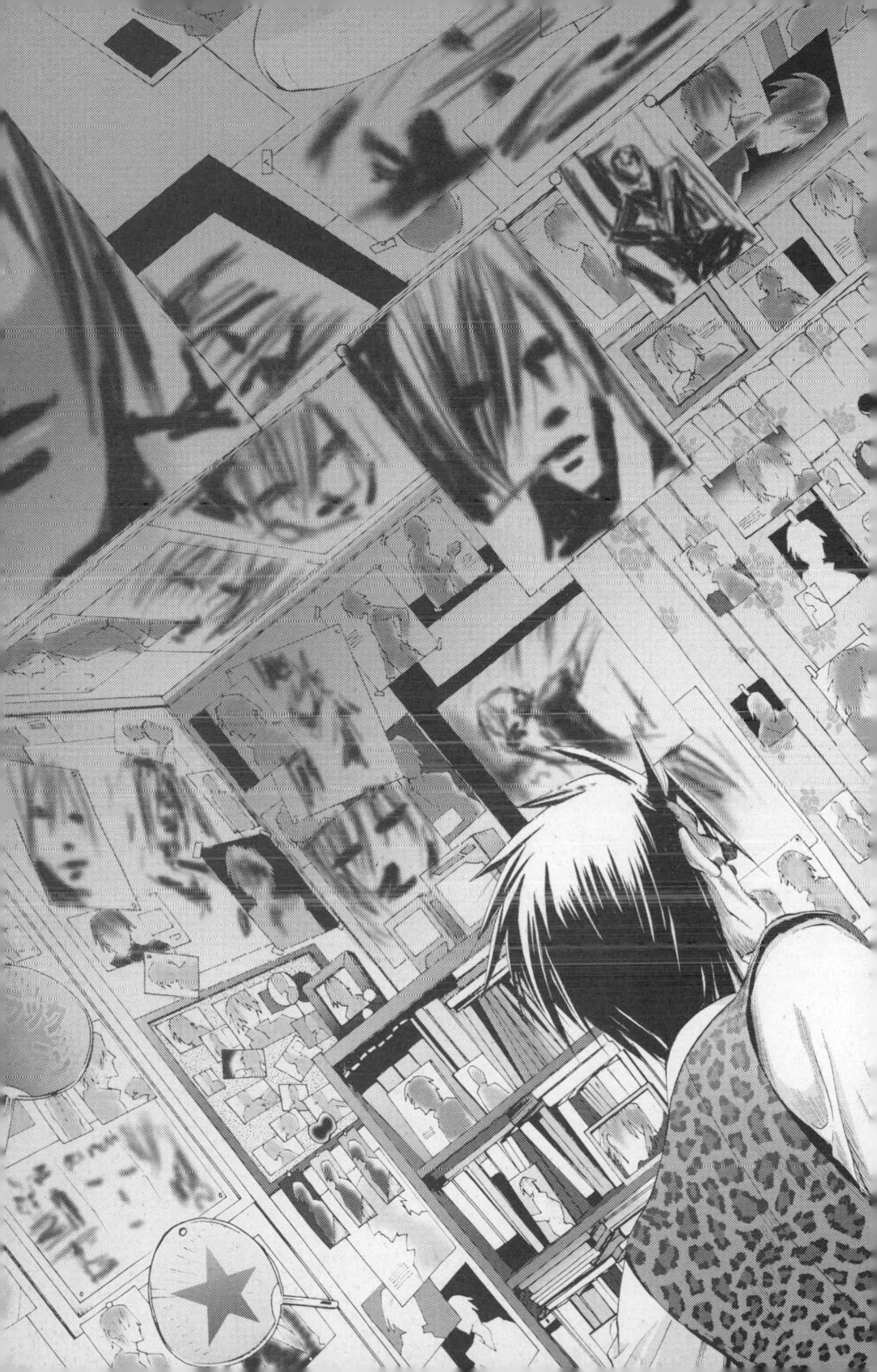

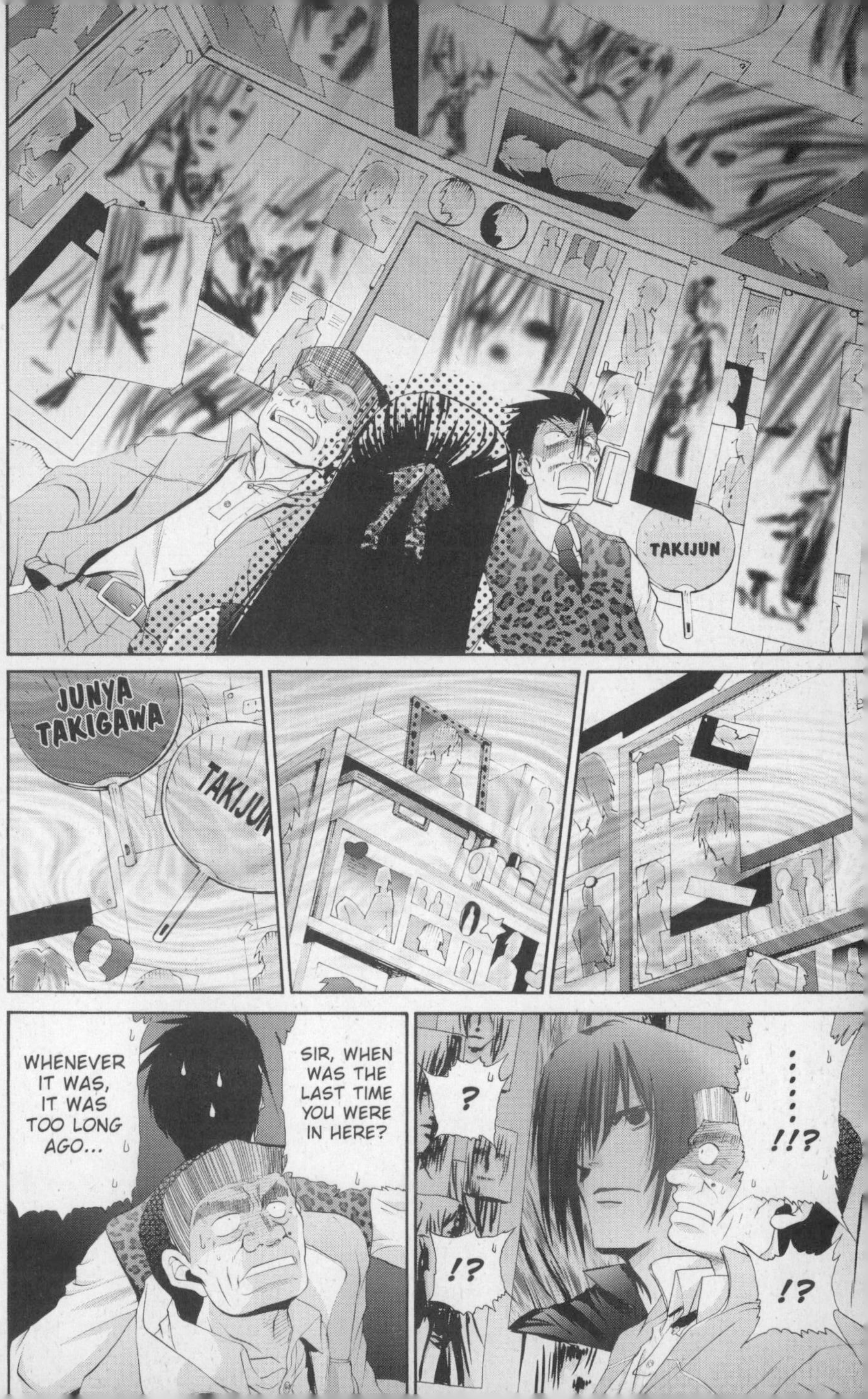
TAKIJUN
JUNYA TAKIGAWA
TAKIJUN
......
!!?
?
!?
!?
SIR, WHEN WAS THE LAST TIME YOU WERE IN HERE?
WHENEVER IT WAS, IT WAS TOO LONG AGO...

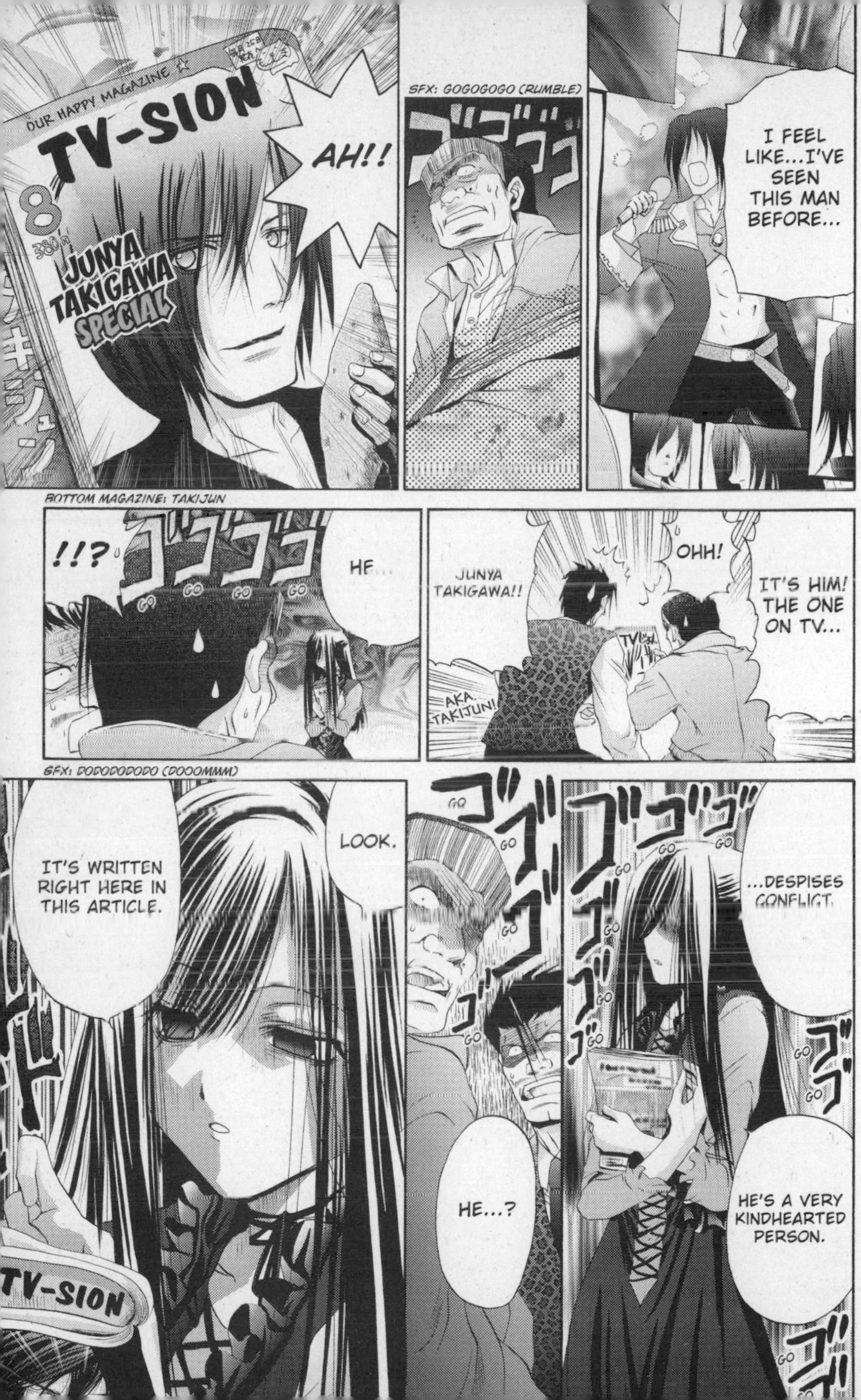
I FEEL LIKE...I'VE SEEN THIS MAN BEFORE...
SFX: GOGOGOGO (RUMBLE)
AH!!
OUR HAPPY MAGAZINE ☆
TV-SION
8
JUNYA TAKIGAWA SPECIAL
BOTTOM MAGAZINE: TAKIJUN
OHH!
IT'S HIM! THE ONE ON TV...
JUNYA TAKIGAWA!!
AKA. TAKIJUN!
HE...
!!?
GO GO GO GO
SFX: DODODODODO (DOOOMMM)
...DESPISES CONFLICT.
HE'S A VERY KINDHEARTED PERSON.
HE...?
LOOK.
IT'S WRITTEN RIGHT HERE IN THIS ARTICLE.
TV-SION

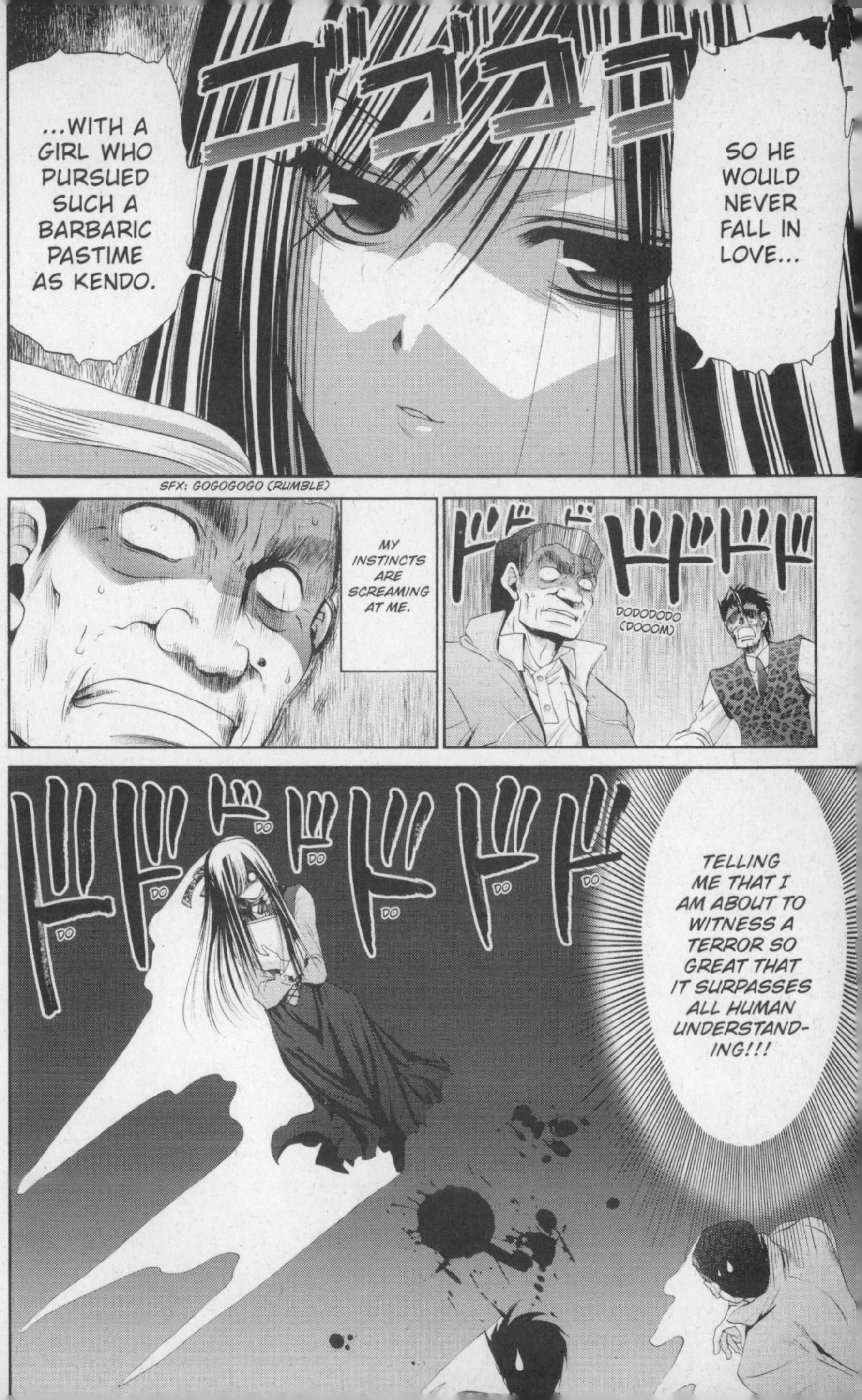
SO HE WOULD NEVER FALL IN LOVE...
...WITH A GIRL WHO PURSUED SUCH A BARBARIC PASTIME AS KENDO.
SFX: GOGOGOGO (RUMBLE)
DODODODO (DOOOM)
MY INSTINCTS ARE SCREAMING AT ME.
DO DO DO DO DO DO DO
TELLING ME THAT I AM ABOUT TO WITNESS A TERROR SO GREAT THAT IT SURPASSES ALL HUMAN UNDERSTAND-ING!!!

BAMBOO BLADE

バンブーブレード

BAMBOO BLADE
バンブーブレード

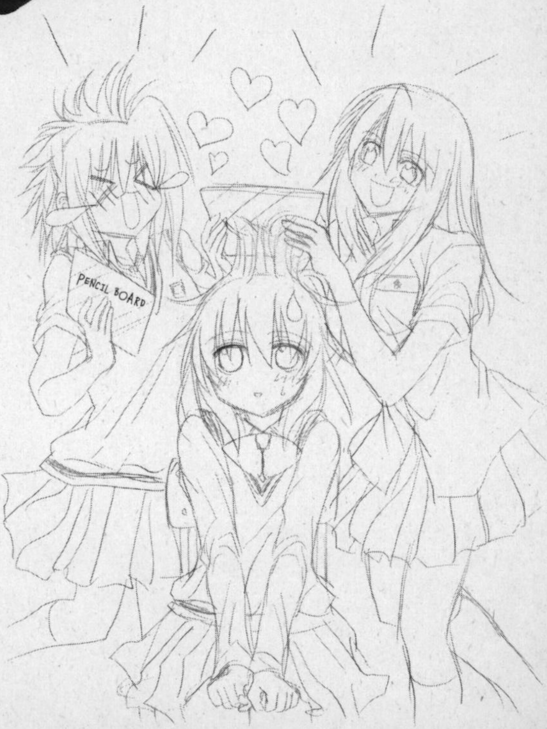
PENCIL BOARD

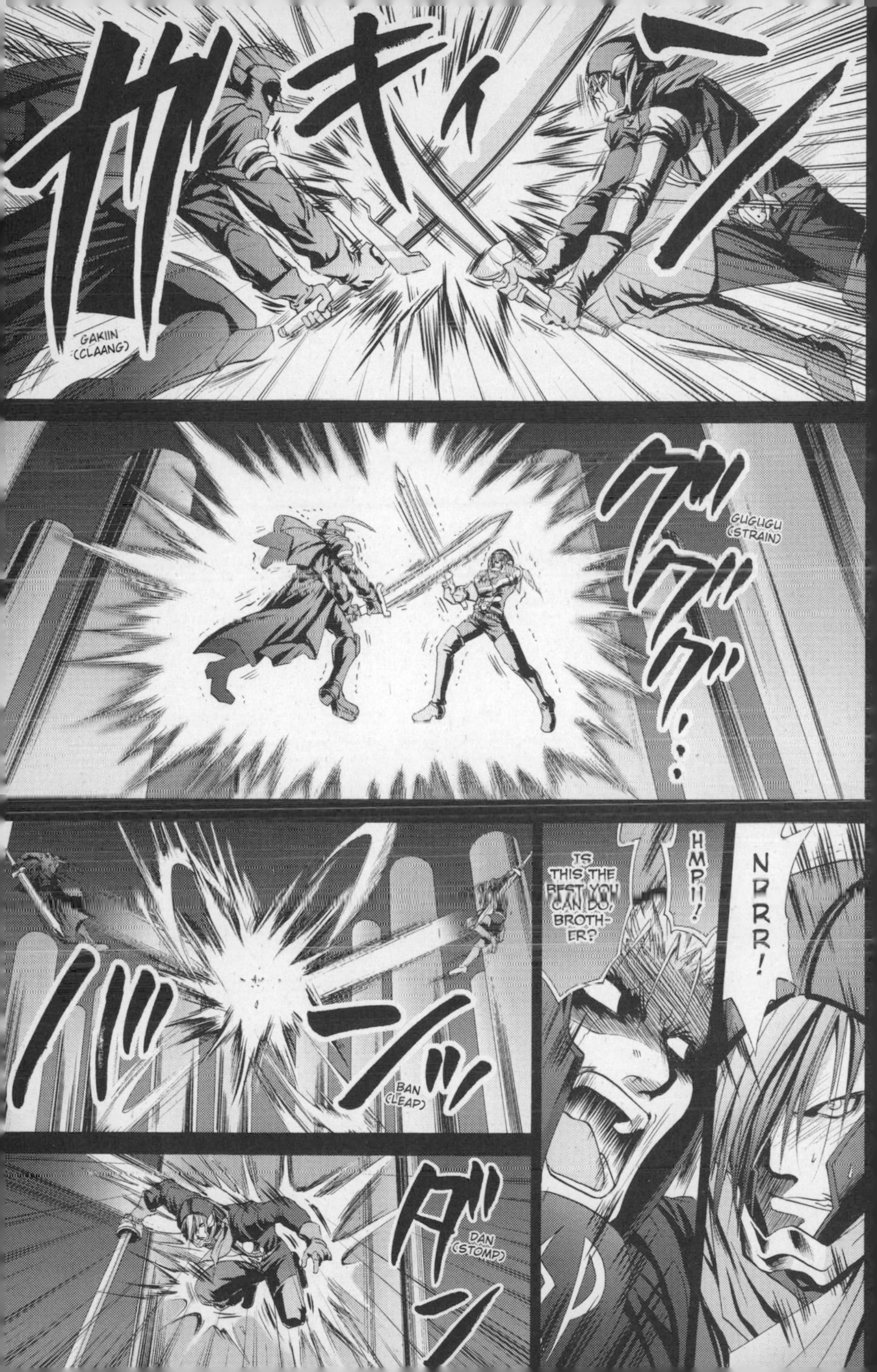
GAKIIN (CLAANG)
GUGUGU (STRAIN)
NRRR!
HMP!!!
IS THIS THE BEST YOU CAN DO, BROTHER?
BAN (LEAP)
DAN (STOMP)

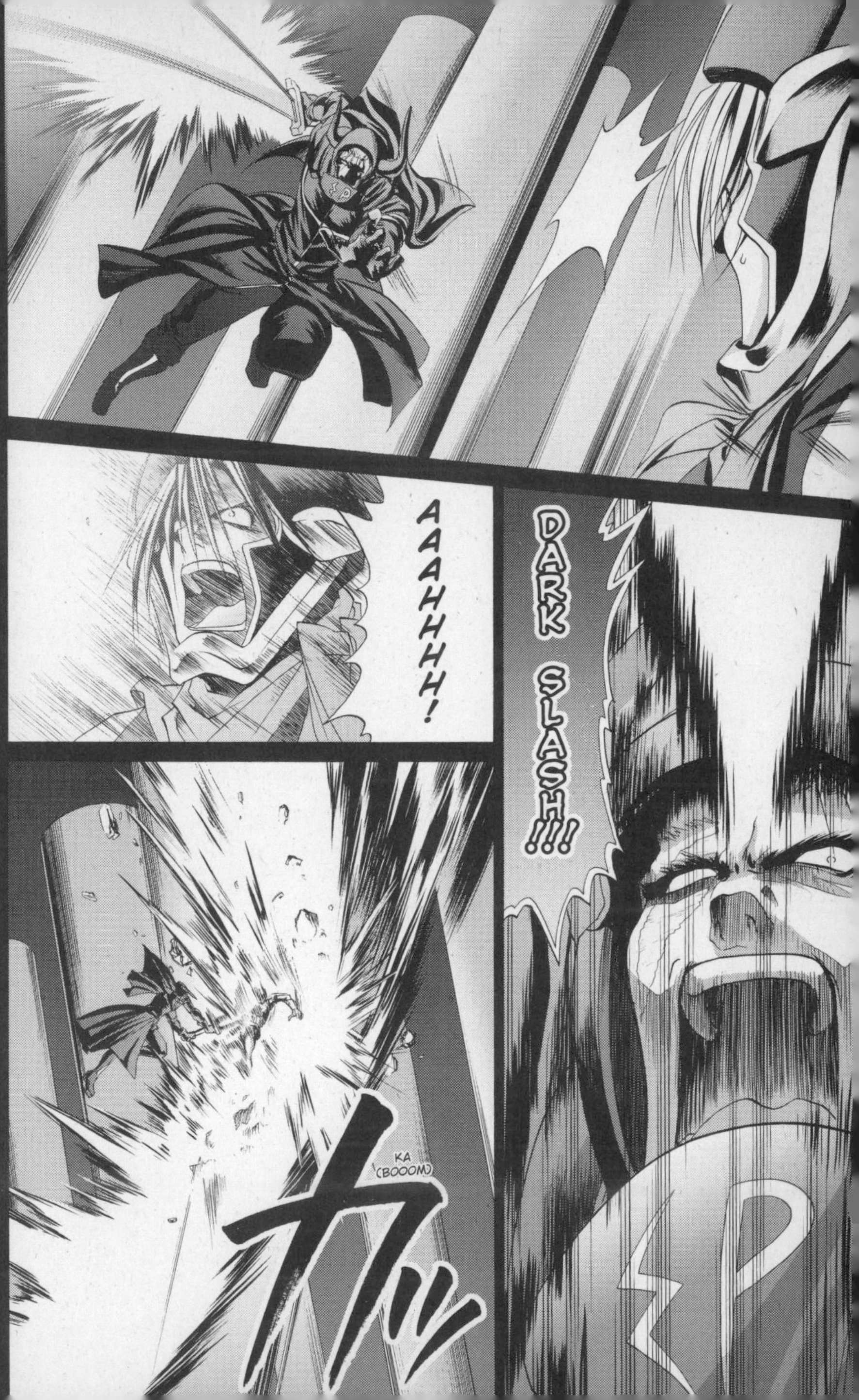
DARK SLASH!!!
AAAHHHH!
KA
(BOOOM)

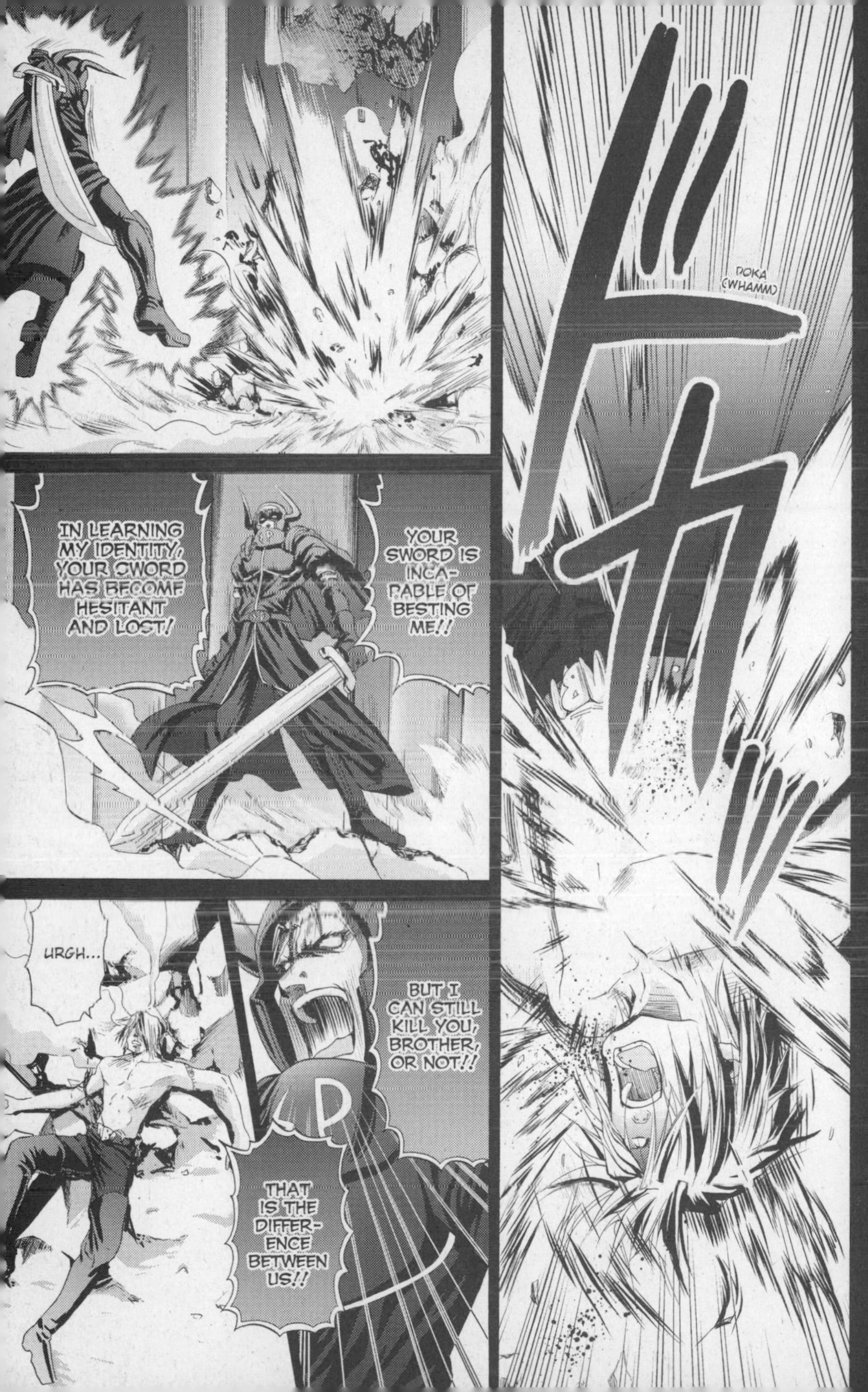
DOKA (WHAMM)
YOUR SWORD IS INCA-PABLE OF BESTING ME!!
IN LEARNING MY IDENTITY, YOUR SWORD HAS BECOME HESITANT AND LOST!
BUT I CAN STILL KILL YOU, BROTHER OR NOT!!
URGH...
THAT IS THE DIFFER-ENCE BETWEEN US!!

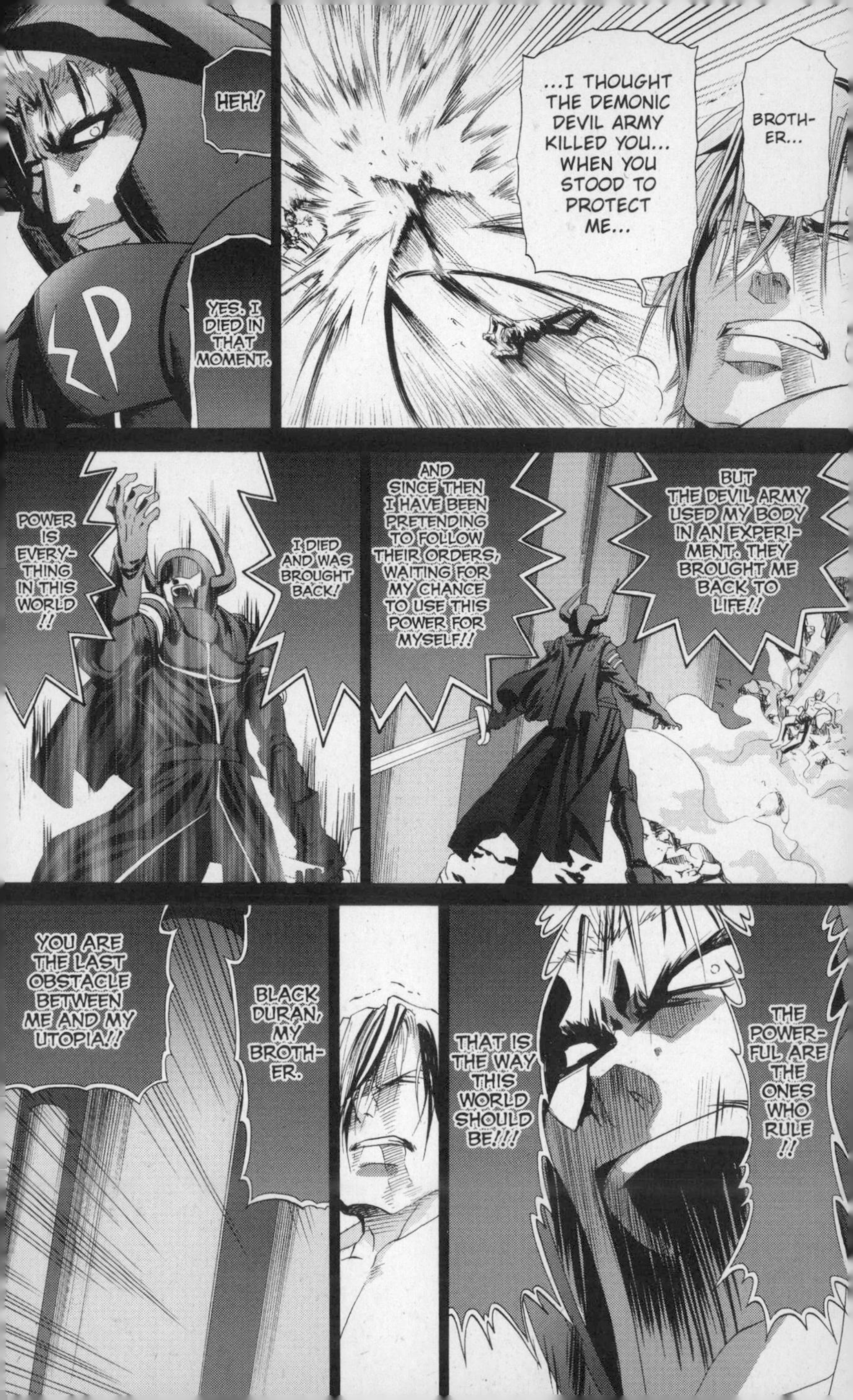
BROTHER...
...I THOUGHT THE DEMONIC DEVIL ARMY KILLED YOU... WHEN YOU STOOD TO PROTECT ME...
HEH!
YES. I DIED IN THAT MOMENT.
BUT THE DEVIL ARMY USED MY BODY IN AN EXPERIMENT. THEY BROUGHT ME BACK TO LIFE!!
AND SINCE THEN I HAVE BEEN PRETENDING TO FOLLOW THEIR ORDERS, WAITING FOR MY CHANCE TO USE THIS POWER FOR MYSELF!!
I DIED AND WAS BROUGHT BACK!
POWER IS EVERYTHING IN THIS WORLD!!
THE POWERFUL ARE THE ONES WHO RULE!!
THAT IS THE WAY THIS WORLD SHOULD BE!!!
BLACK DURAN, MY BROTHER.
YOU ARE THE LAST OBSTACLE BETWEEN ME AND MY UTOPIA!!

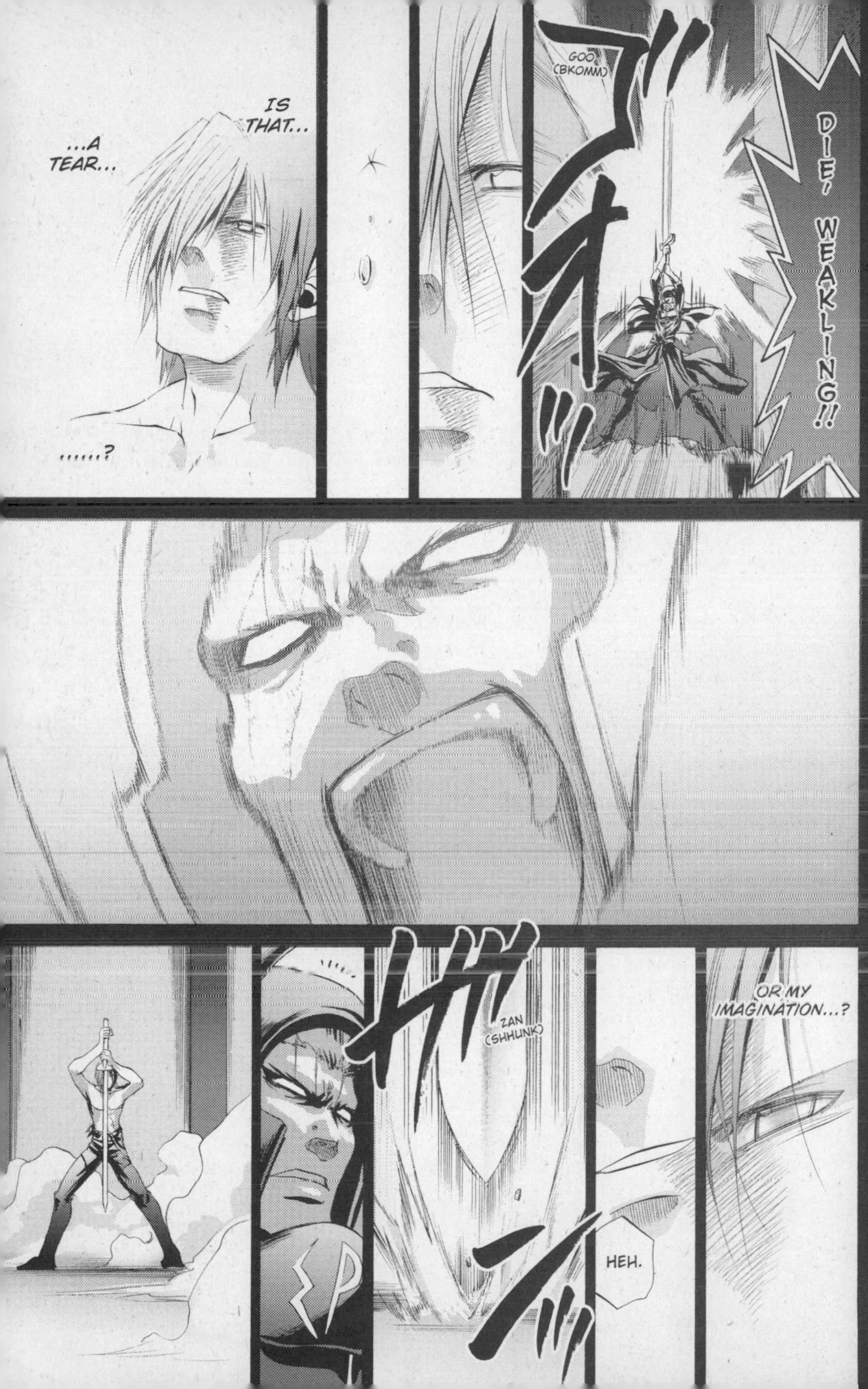
DIE, WEAKLING!!
GOO (BKOMM)
IS THAT...
...A TEAR...
......?
OR MY IMAGINATION...?
HEH.
ZAN (SHHUNK)

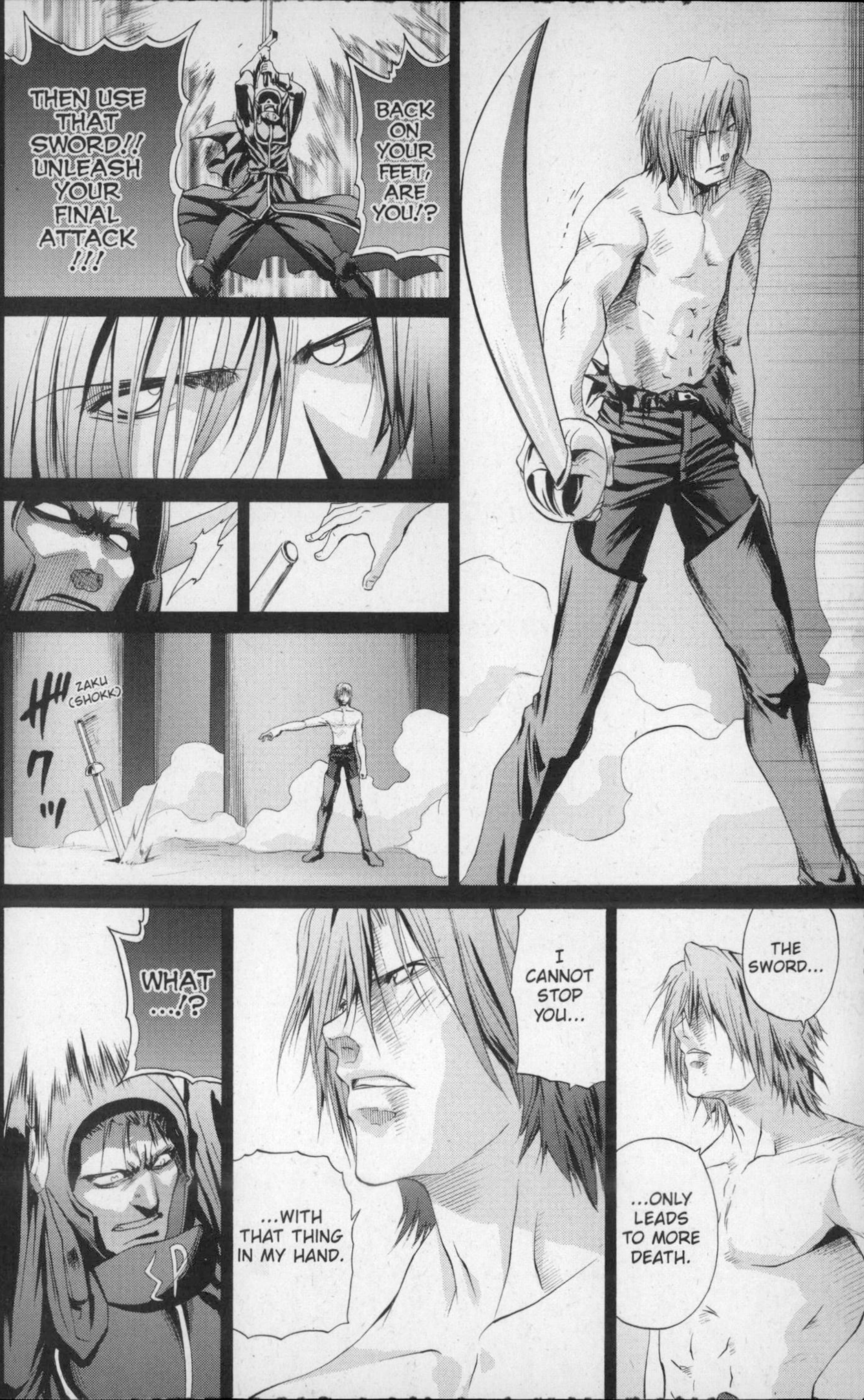
BACK ON YOUR FEET, ARE YOU!?
THEN USE THAT SWORD!! UNLEASH YOUR FINAL ATTACK!!!
ZAKU (SHOKK)
THE SWORD...
...ONLY LEADS TO MORE DEATH.
I CANNOT STOP YOU...
...WITH THAT THING IN MY HAND.
WHAT ...!?

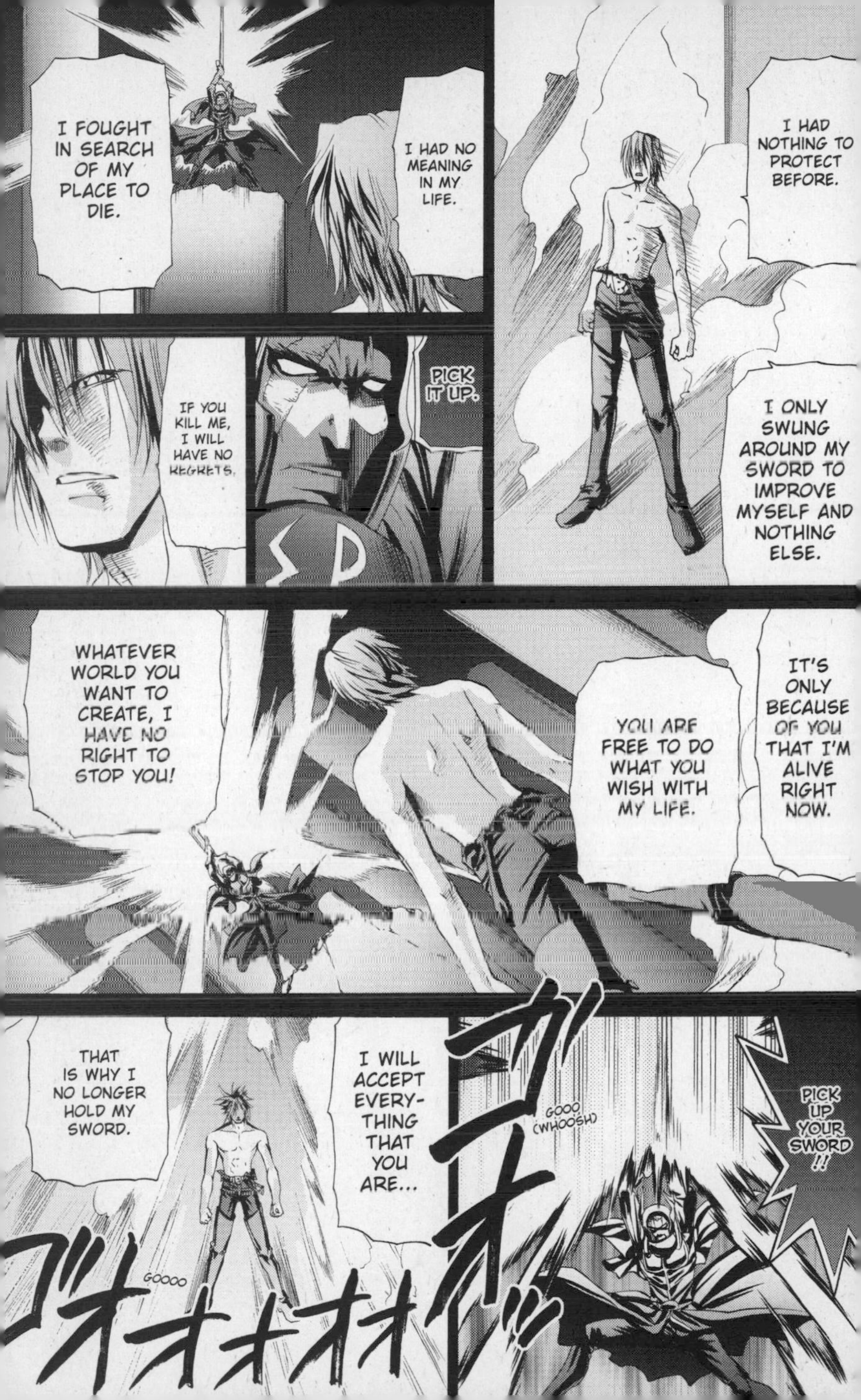
I HAD NOTHING TO PROTECT BEFORE.
I ONLY SWUNG AROUND MY SWORD TO IMPROVE MYSELF AND NOTHING ELSE.
I HAD NO MEANING IN MY LIFE.
I FOUGHT IN SEARCH OF MY PLACE TO DIE.
PICK IT UP.
IF YOU KILL ME, I WILL HAVE NO REGRETS.
IT'S ONLY BECAUSE OF YOU THAT I'M ALIVE RIGHT NOW.
YOU ARE FREE TO DO WHAT YOU WISH WITH MY LIFE.
WHATEVER WORLD YOU WANT TO CREATE, I HAVE NO RIGHT TO STOP YOU!
PICK UP YOUR SWORD!!
GOOO (WHOOSH)
I WILL ACCEPT EVERY-THING THAT YOU ARE...
THAT IS WHY I NO LONGER HOLD MY SWORD.
GOOOO

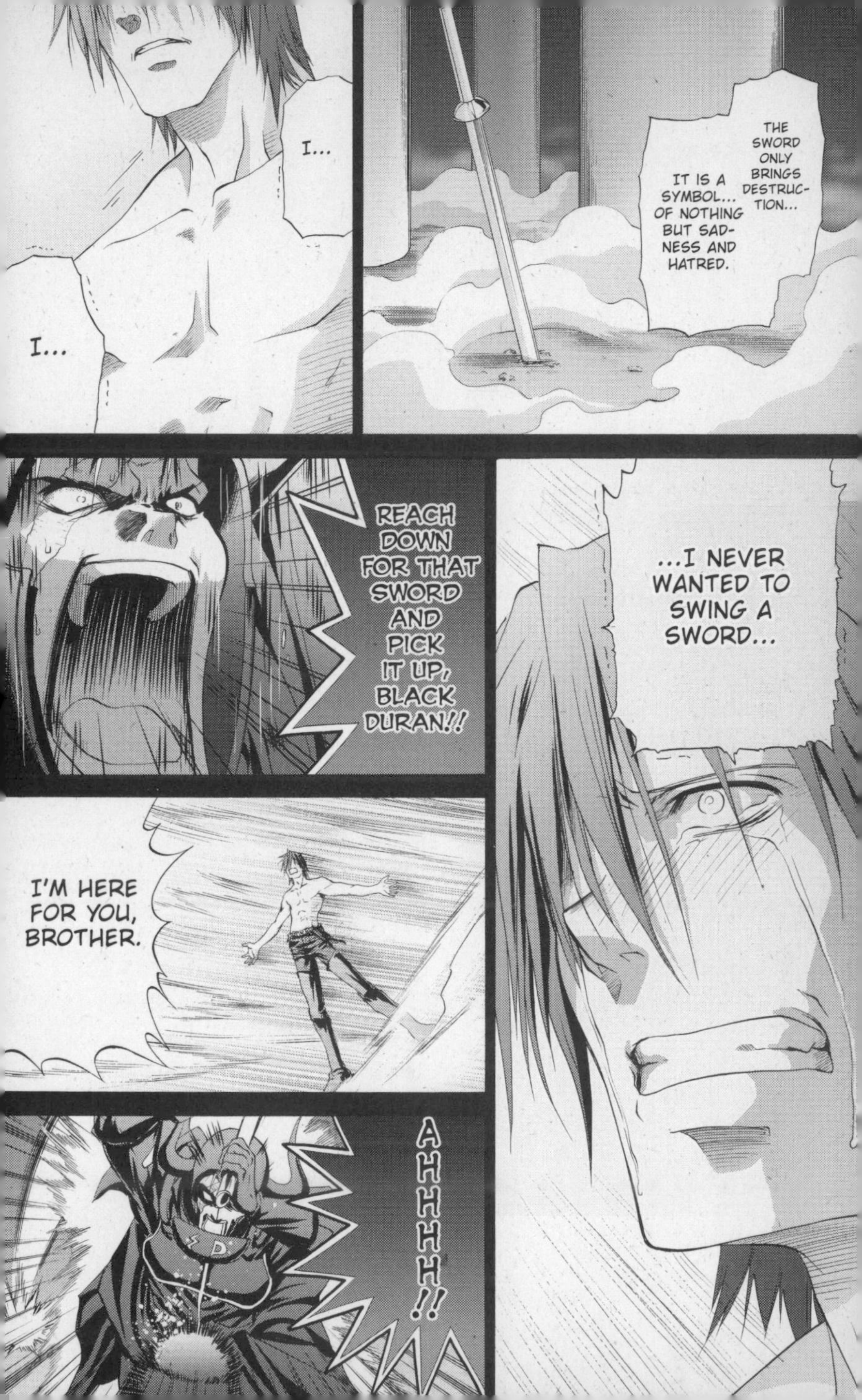
THE SWORD ONLY BRINGS DESTRUCTION...
IT IS A SYMBOL... OF NOTHING BUT SADNESS AND HATRED.
I...
I...
...I NEVER WANTED TO SWING A SWORD...
REACH DOWN FOR THAT SWORD AND PICK IT UP, BLACK DURAN!!
I'M HERE FOR YOU, BROTHER.
AHHHHH!!

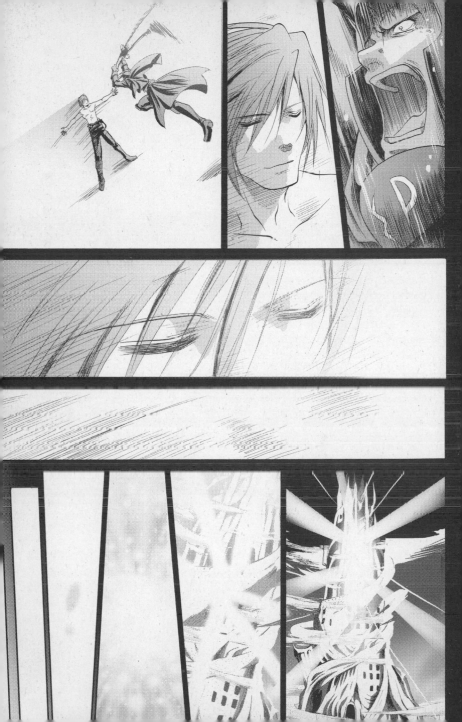

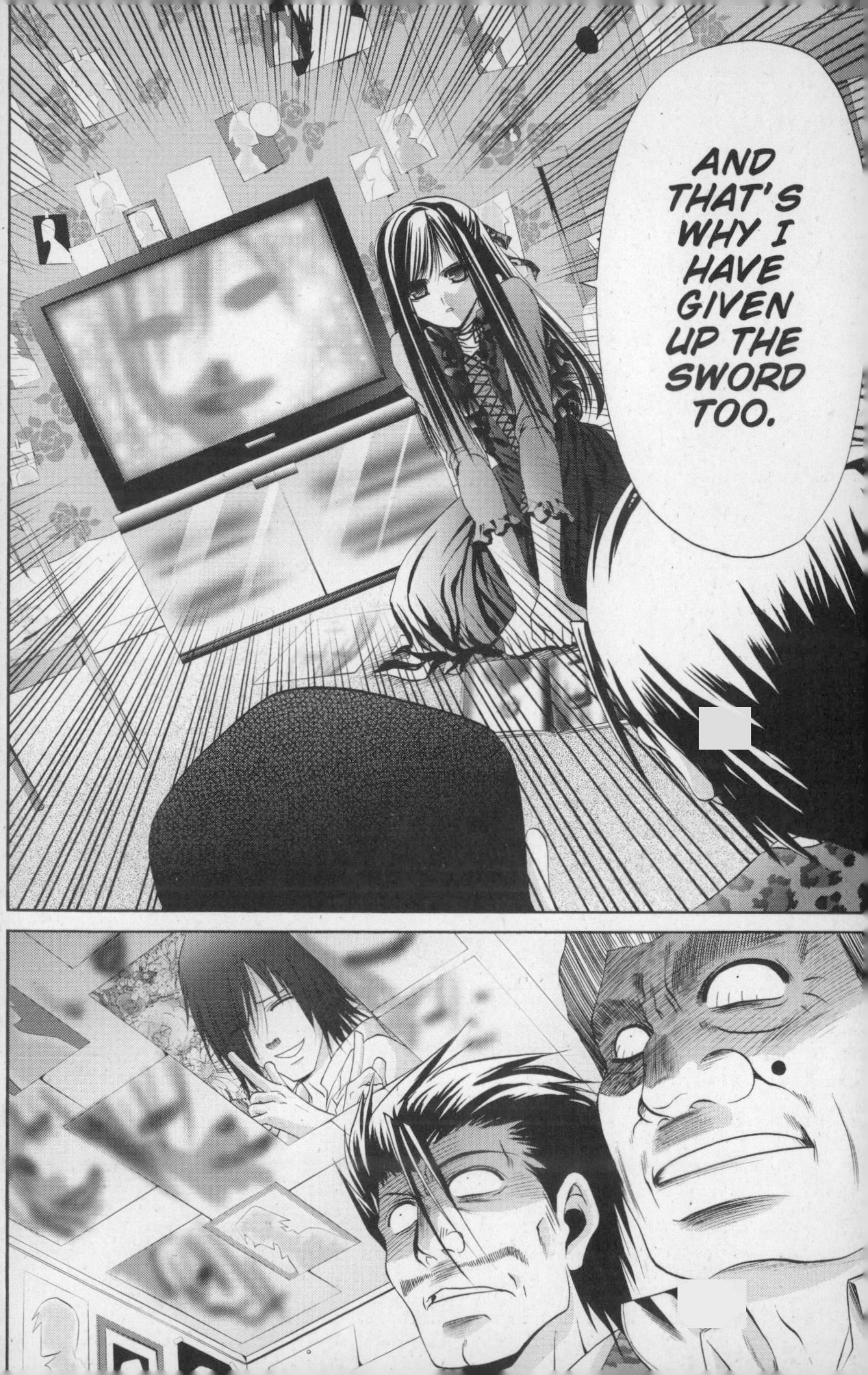
AND THAT'S WHY I HAVE GIVEN UP THE SWORD TOO.

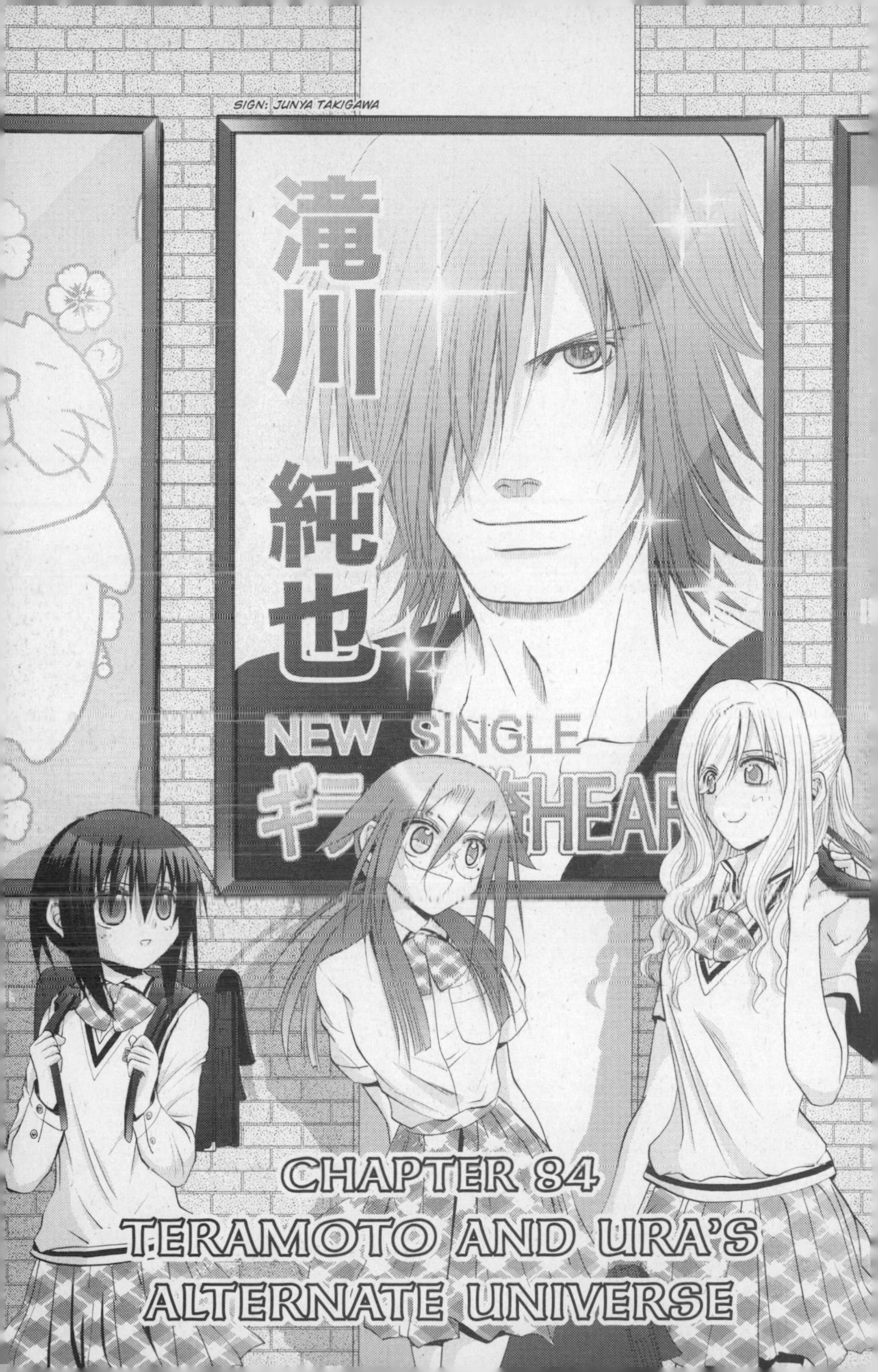
SIGN: JUNYA TAKIGAWA
滝川純也
NEW SINGLE
CHAPTER 84
TERAMOTO AND URA'S ALTERNATE UNIVERSE

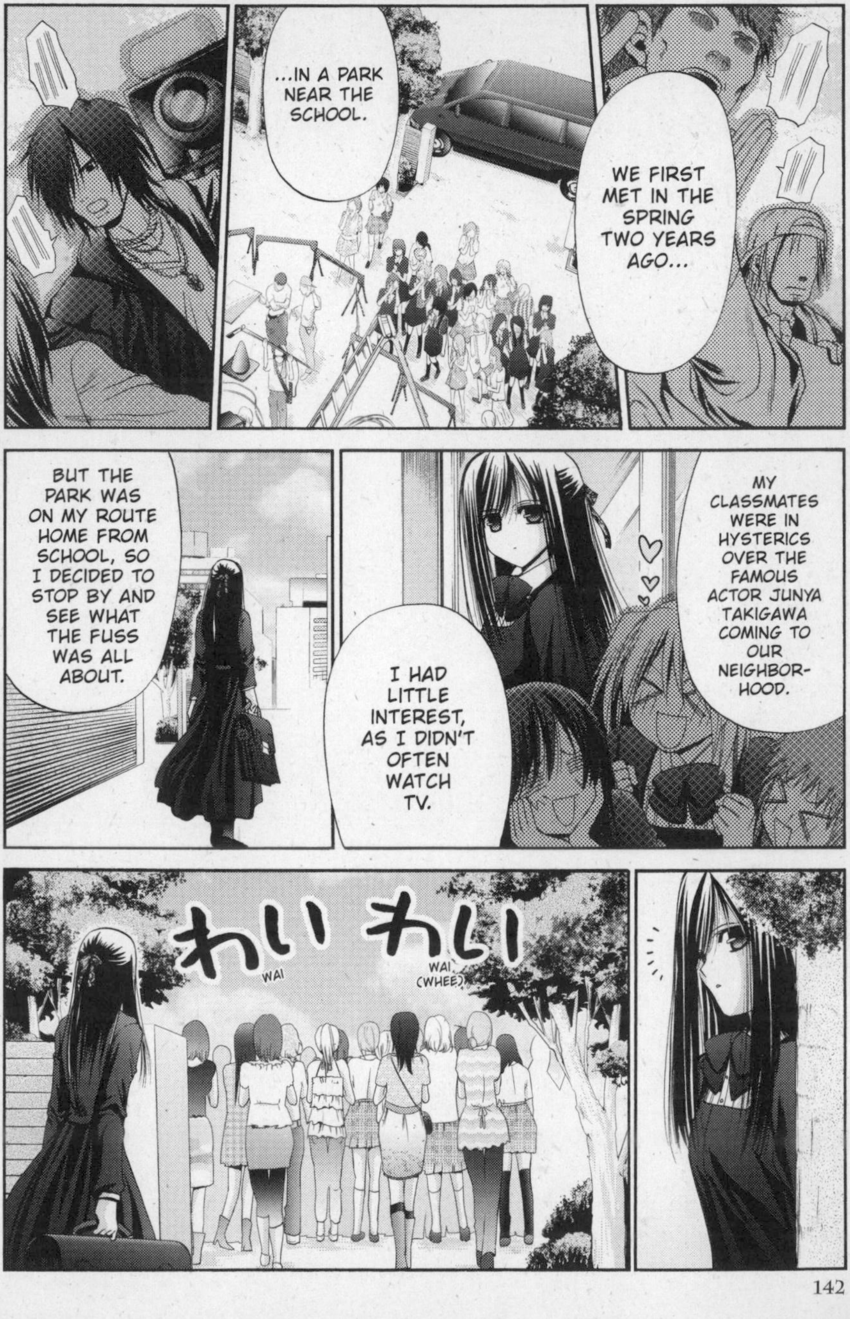
WE FIRST MET IN THE SPRING TWO YEARS AGO...
...IN A PARK NEAR THE SCHOOL.
MY CLASSMATES WERE IN HYSTERICS OVER THE FAMOUS ACTOR JUNYA TAKIGAWA COMING TO OUR NEIGHBOR-HOOD.
I HAD LITTLE INTEREST, AS I DIDN'T OFTEN WATCH TV.
BUT THE PARK WAS ON MY ROUTE HOME FROM SCHOOL, SO I DECIDED TO STOP BY AND SEE WHAT THE FUSS WAS ALL ABOUT.
わい わい
WAI
WAI (WHEE)

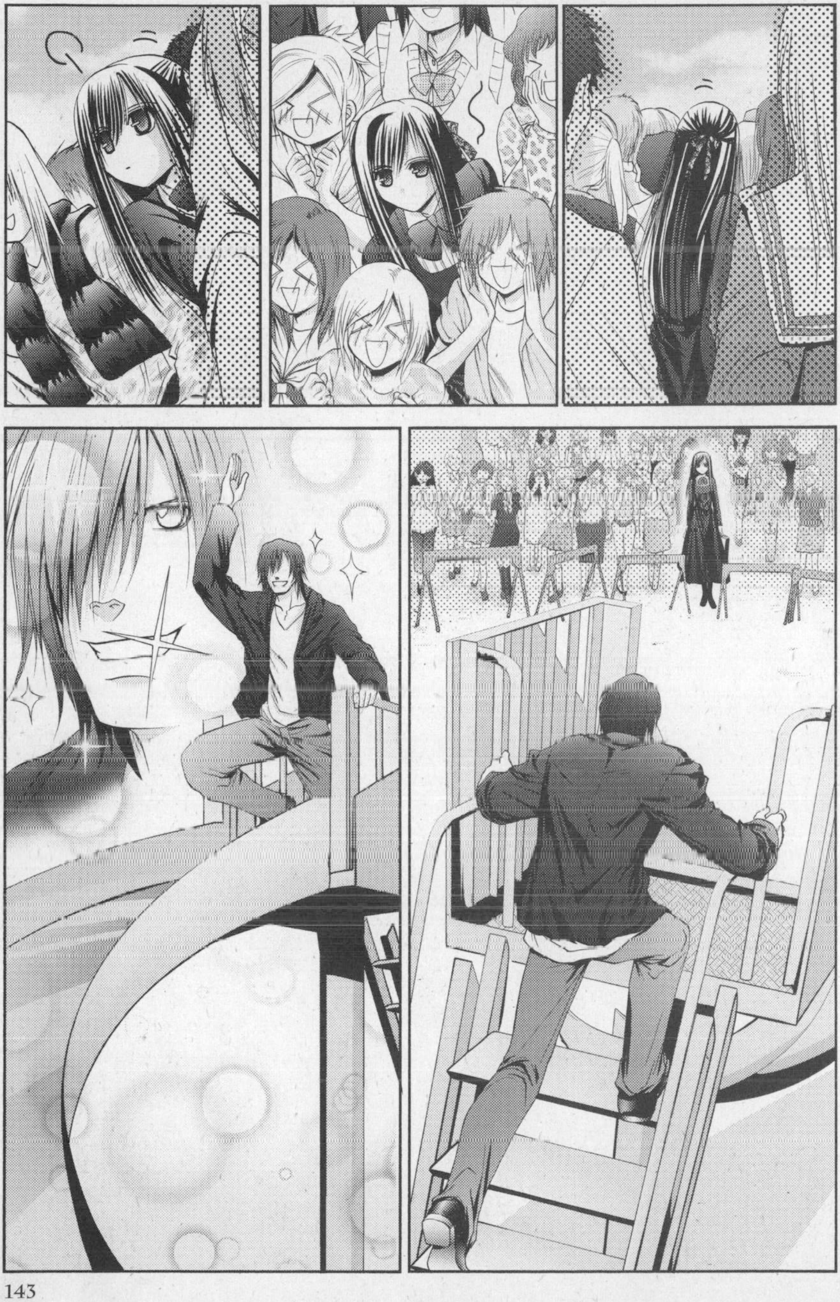

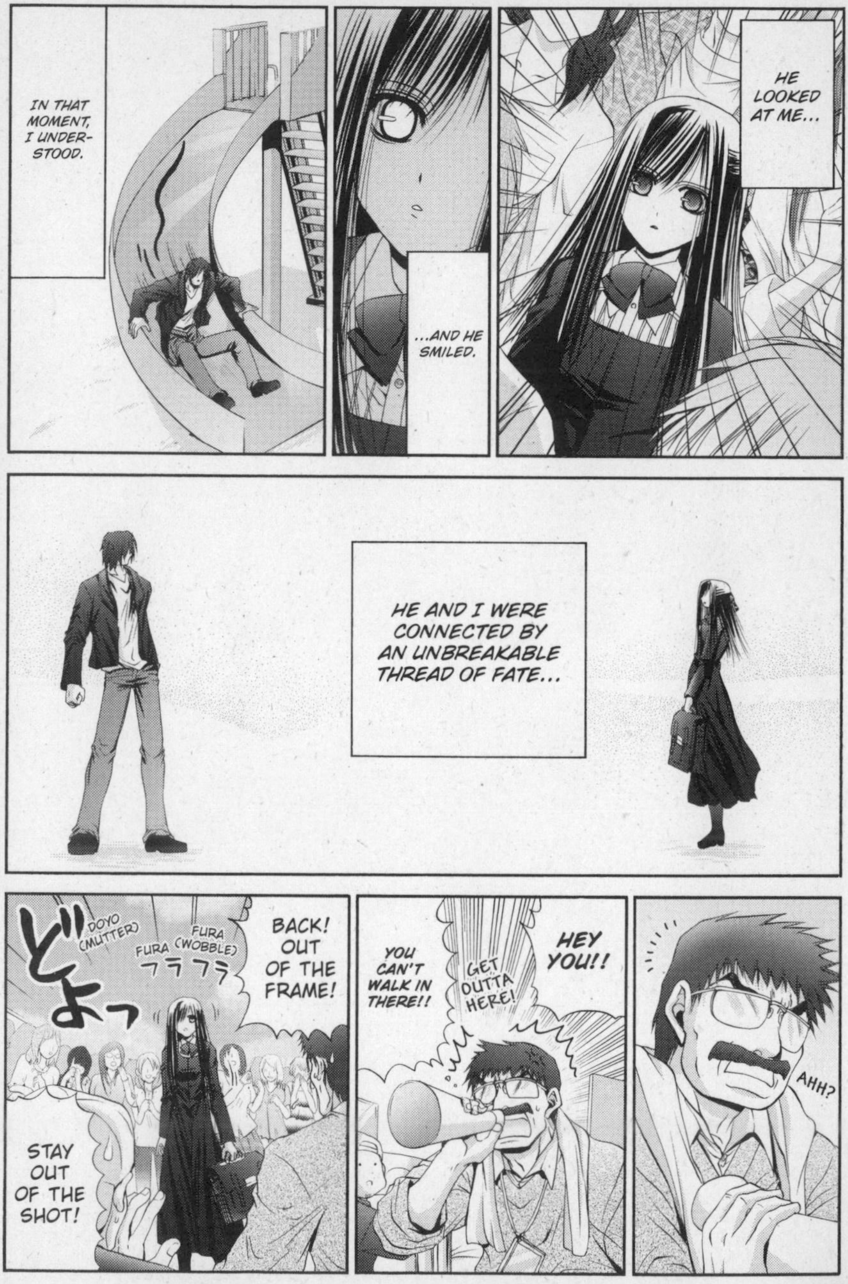
HE LOOKED AT ME...
...AND HE SMILED.
IN THAT MOMENT, I UNDERSTOOD.
HE AND I WERE CONNECTED BY AN UNBREAKABLE THREAD OF FATE...
AHH?
HEY YOU!!
GET OUTTA HERE!
YOU CAN'T WALK IN THERE!!
BACK! OUT OF THE FRAME!
FURA FURA (WOBBLE)
フラフラ
DOYO (MUTTER)
どよっ
STAY OUT OF THE SHOT!

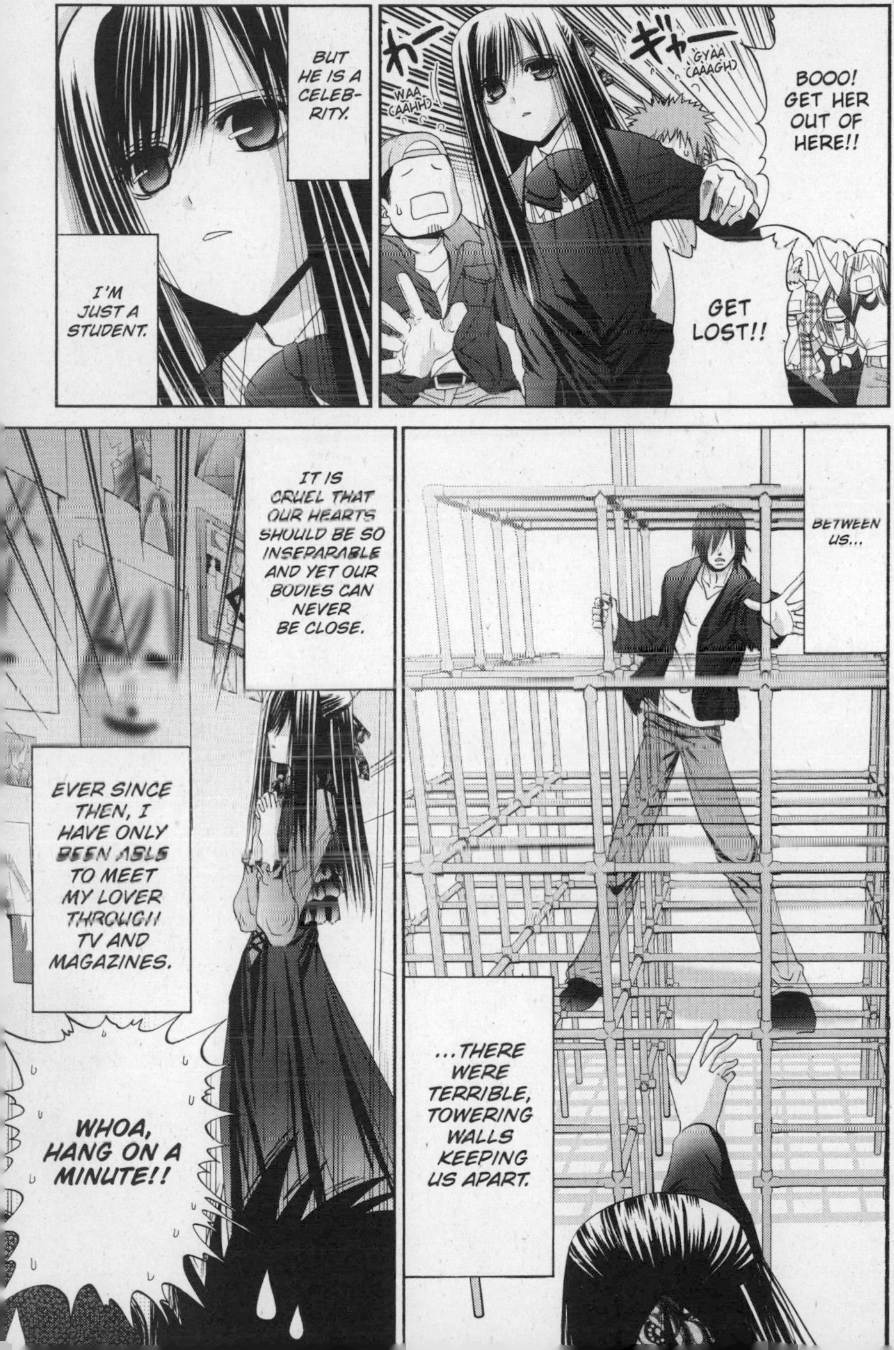
ギャー
GYAA (AAAGH)
BOOO! GET HER OUT OF HERE!!
わー
WAA (AAHH)
GET LOST!!
BUT HE IS A CELEBRITY.
I'M JUST A STUDENT.
BETWEEN US...
...THERE WERE TERRIBLE, TOWERING WALLS KEEPING US APART.
IT IS CRUEL THAT OUR HEARTS SHOULD BE SO INSEPARABLE AND YET OUR BODIES CAN NEVER BE CLOSE.
EVER SINCE THEN, I HAVE ONLY BEEN ABLE TO MEET MY LOVER THROUGH TV AND MAGAZINES.
WHOA, HANG ON A MINUTE!!

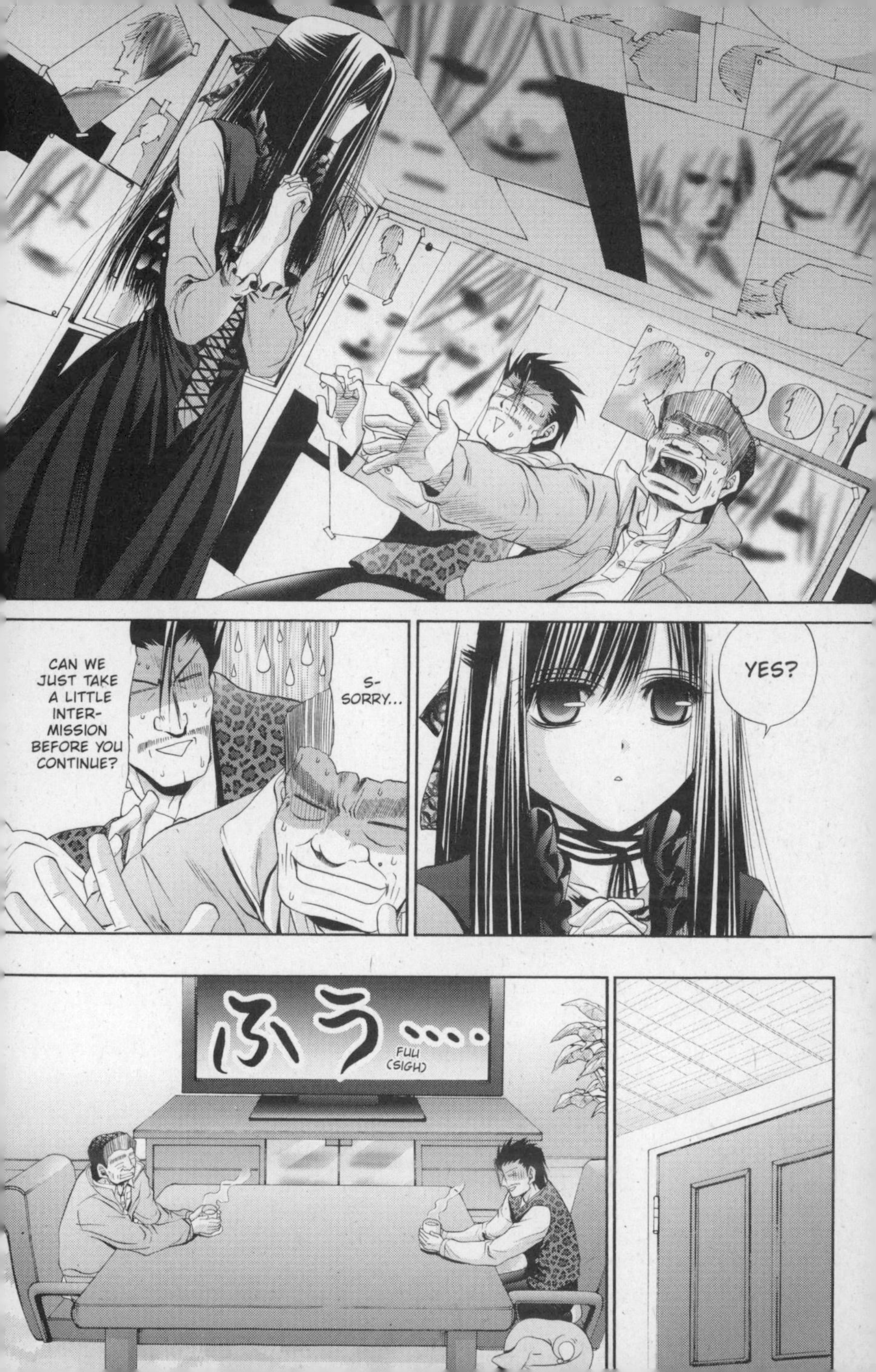
YES?
S-SORRY...
CAN WE JUST TAKE A LITTLE INTERMISSION BEFORE YOU CONTINUE?
ふう….
FUU (SIGH)

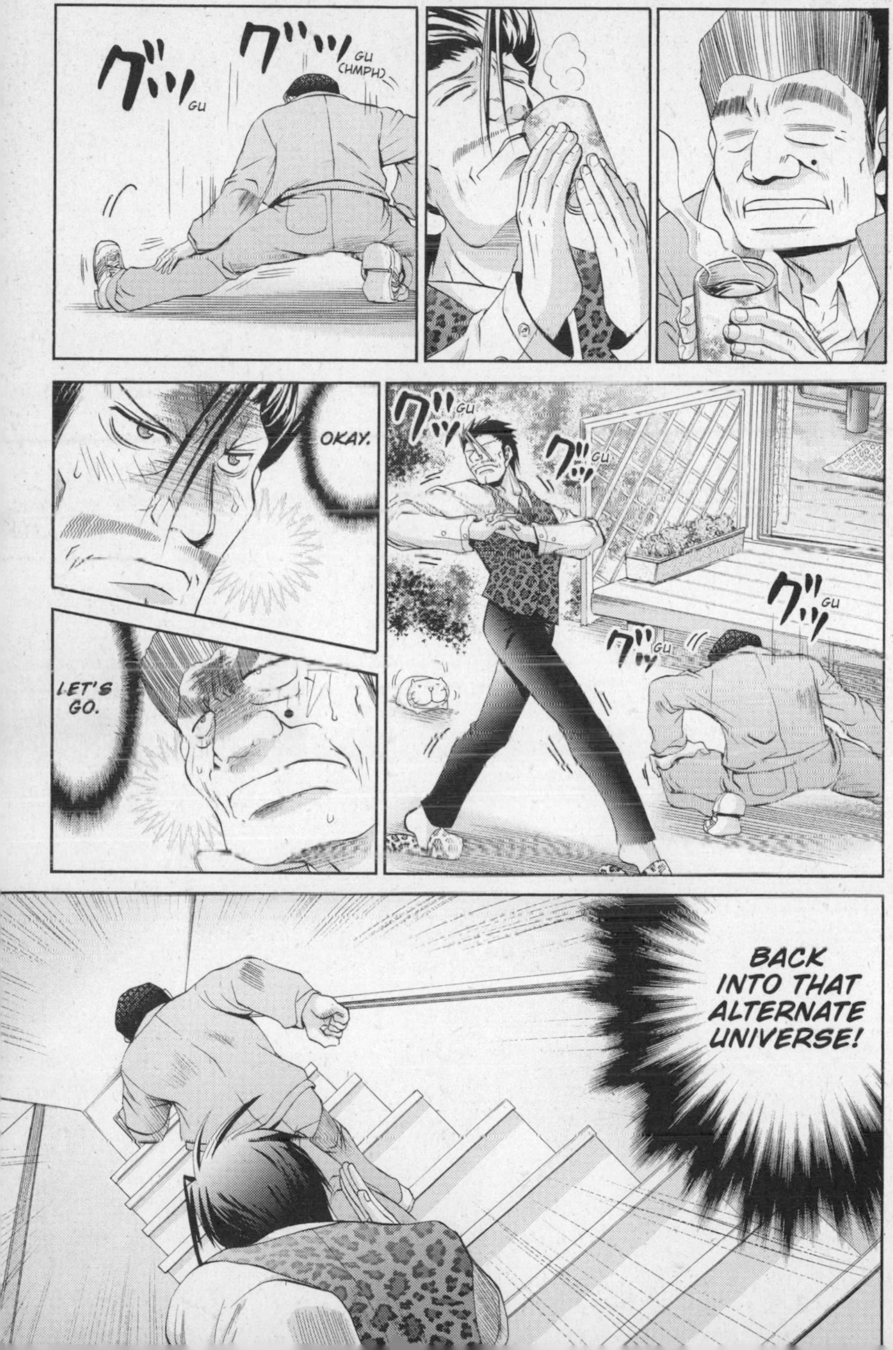
グッ GU (HMPH)
グッ GU
グッ GU
グッ GU
グッ GU
グッ GU
OKAY.
LET'S GO.
BACK INTO THAT ALTERNATE UNIVERSE!

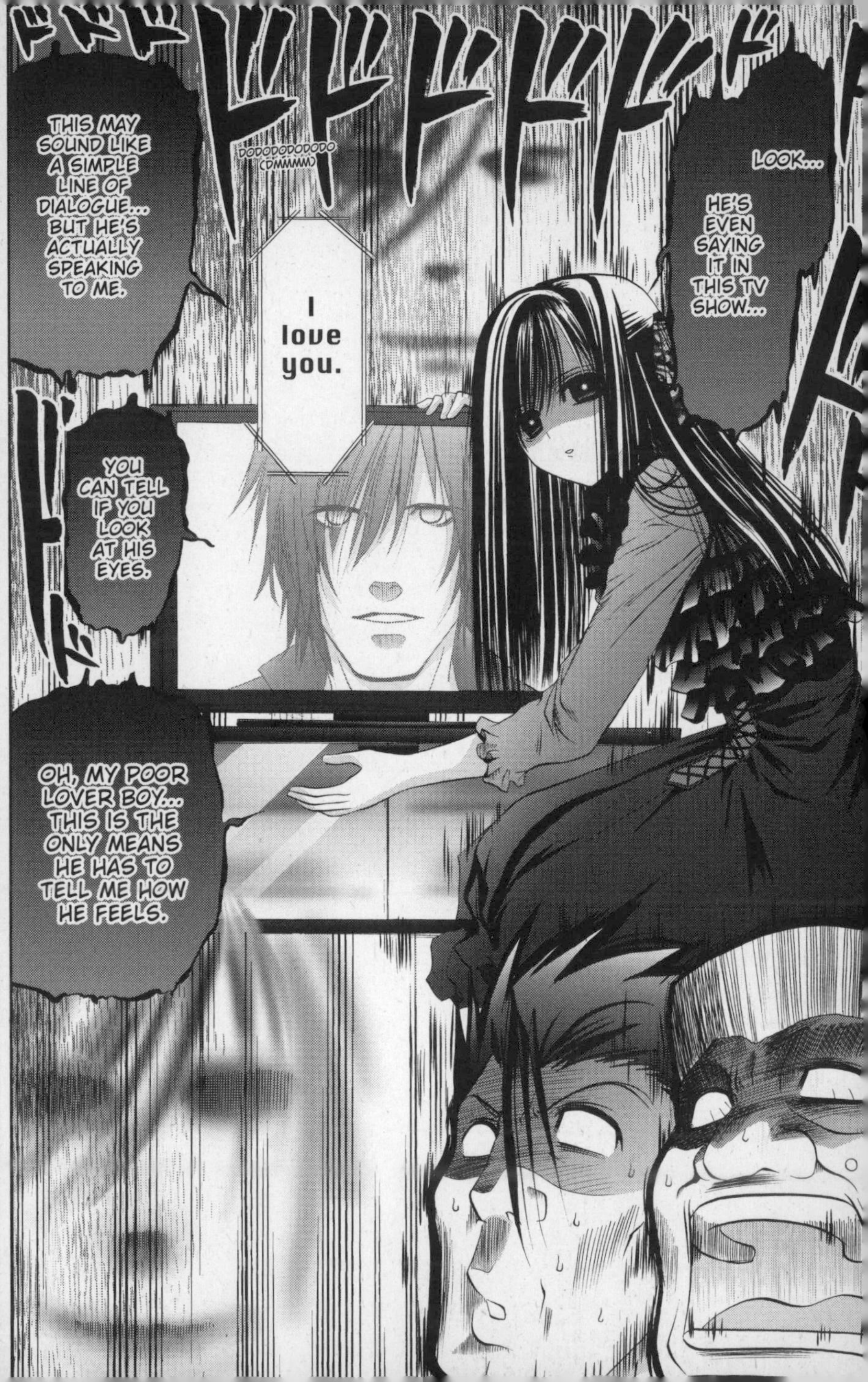
LOOK...
HE'S EVEN SAYING IT IN THIS TV SHOW...
DODODODODODO (DMMMMM)
THIS MAY SOUND LIKE A SIMPLE LINE OF DIALOGUE... BUT HE'S ACTUALLY SPEAKING TO ME.
I love you.
YOU CAN TELL IF YOU LOOK AT HIS EYES.
OH, MY POOR LOVER BOY... THIS IS THE ONLY MEANS HE HAS TO TELL ME HOW HE FEELS.

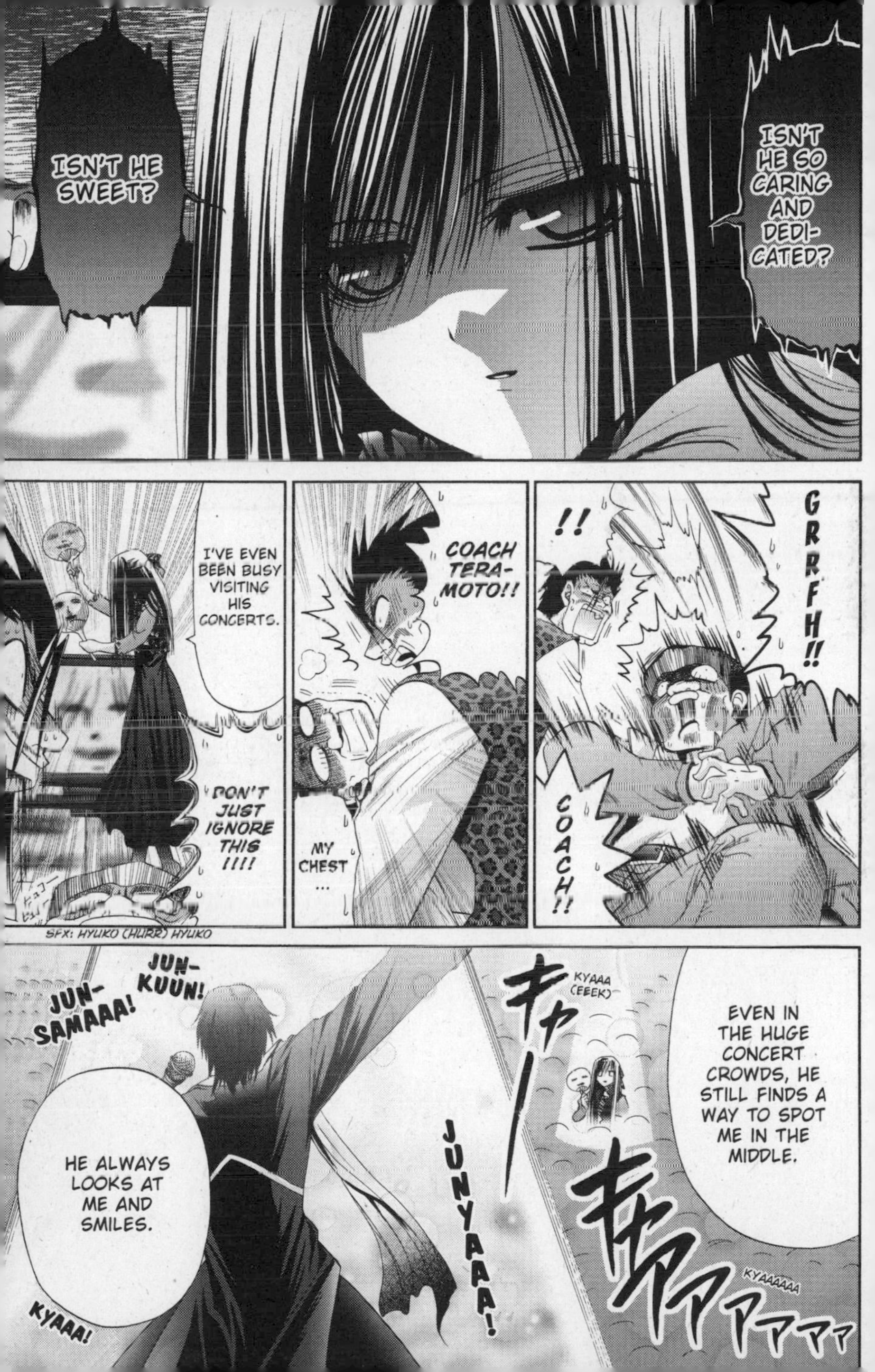
ISN'T HE SO CARING AND DEDI-CATED?
ISN'T HE SWEET?
GRRFH!!
!!
COACH!!
COACH TERA-MOTO!!
MY CHEST ...
I'VE EVEN BEEN BUSY VISITING HIS CONCERTS.
DON'T JUST IGNORE THIS !!!!
SFX: HYUKO (HURR) HYUKO
EVEN IN THE HUGE CONCERT CROWDS, HE STILL FINDS A WAY TO SPOT ME IN THE MIDDLE.
キャー
KYAAA (EEEK)
キャアアアアア
KYAAAAAA
JUNYAAAA!
JUN-KUUN!
JUN-SAMAAA!
HE ALWAYS LOOKS AT ME AND SMILES.
KYAAA!

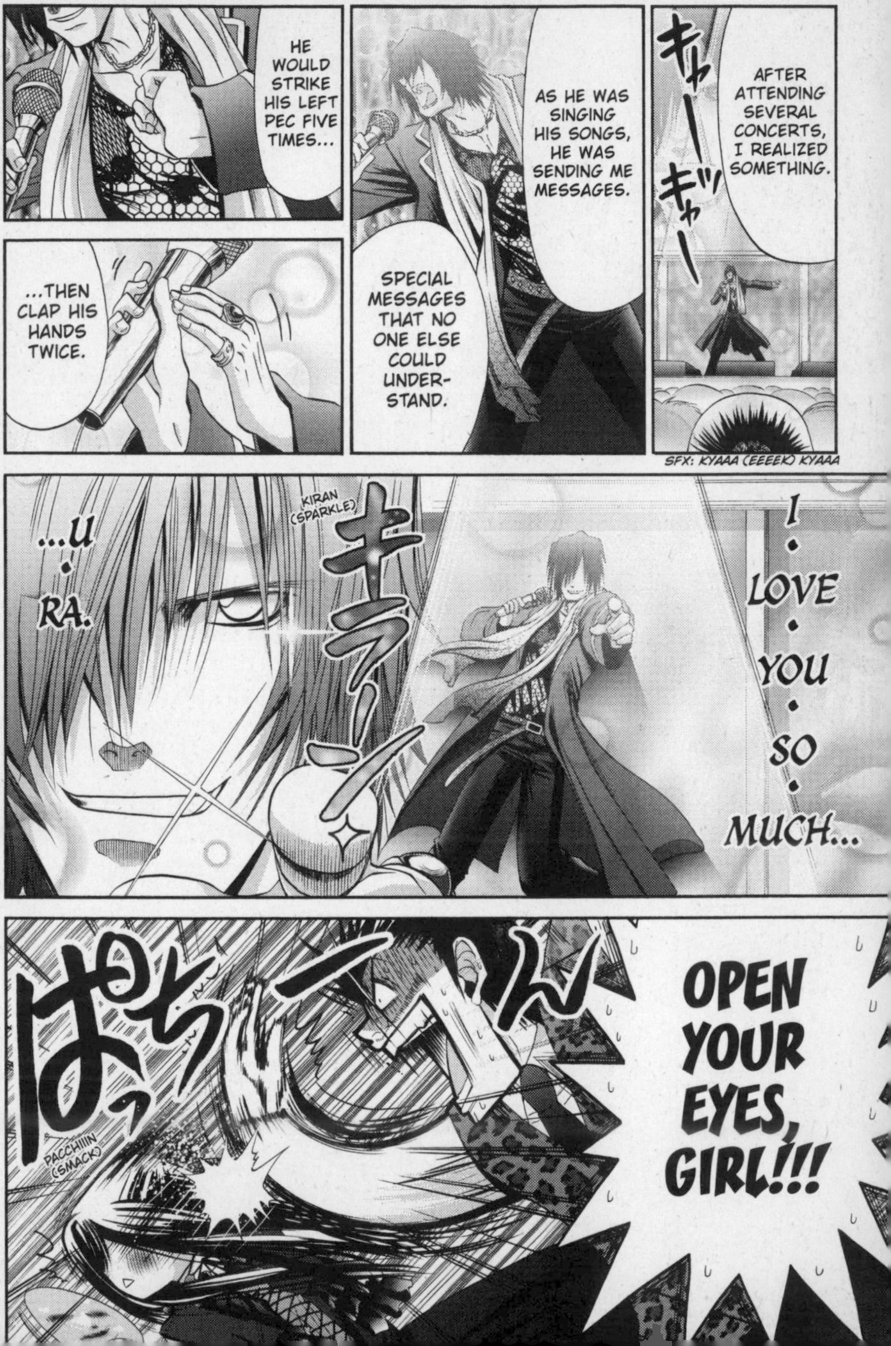

AFTER ATTENDING SEVERAL CONCERTS, I REALIZED SOMETHING.
SFX: KYAAA (EEEEK) KYAAA
AS HE WAS SINGING HIS SONGS, HE WAS SENDING ME MESSAGES.
SPECIAL MESSAGES THAT NO ONE ELSE COULD UNDER-STAND.
HE WOULD STRIKE HIS LEFT PEC FIVE TIMES...
...THEN CLAP HIS HANDS TWICE.
I • LOVE • YOU • SO • MUCH...
KIRAN (SPARKLE)
...U • RA.
OPEN YOUR EYES, GIRL!!!
PACCHIIN (SMACK)

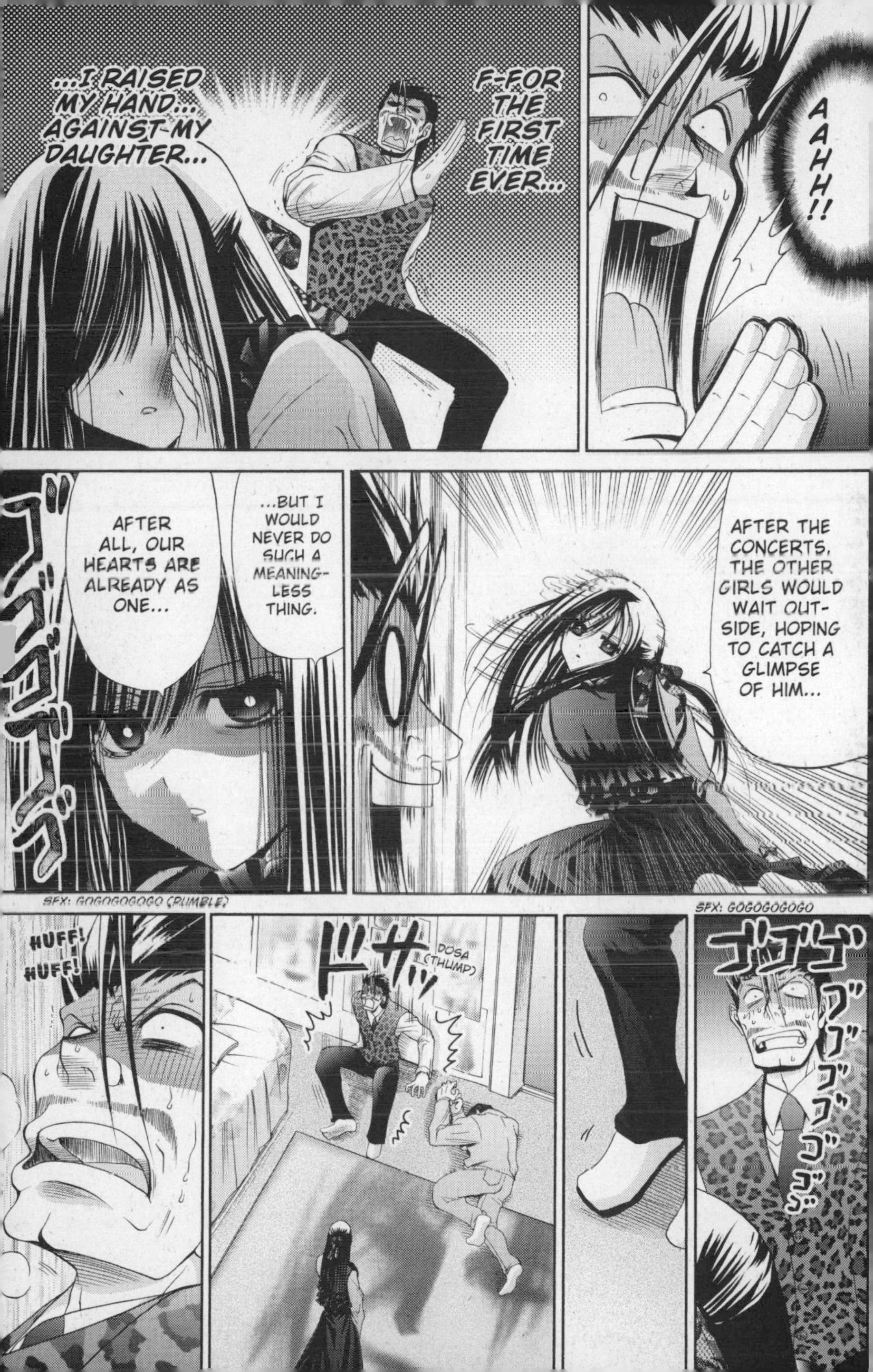
AAAHH!!
F-FOR THE FIRST TIME EVER...
...I RAISED MY HAND... AGAINST MY DAUGHTER...
AFTER THE CONCERTS, THE OTHER GIRLS WOULD WAIT OUTSIDE, HOPING TO CATCH A GLIMPSE OF HIM...
...BUT I WOULD NEVER DO SUCH A MEANINGLESS THING.
AFTER ALL, OUR HEARTS ARE ALREADY AS ONE...
SFX: GOGOGOGOGO
SFX: GOGOGOGOGO (RUMBLE)
ドサッ
DOSA (THUMP)
HUFF! HUFF!

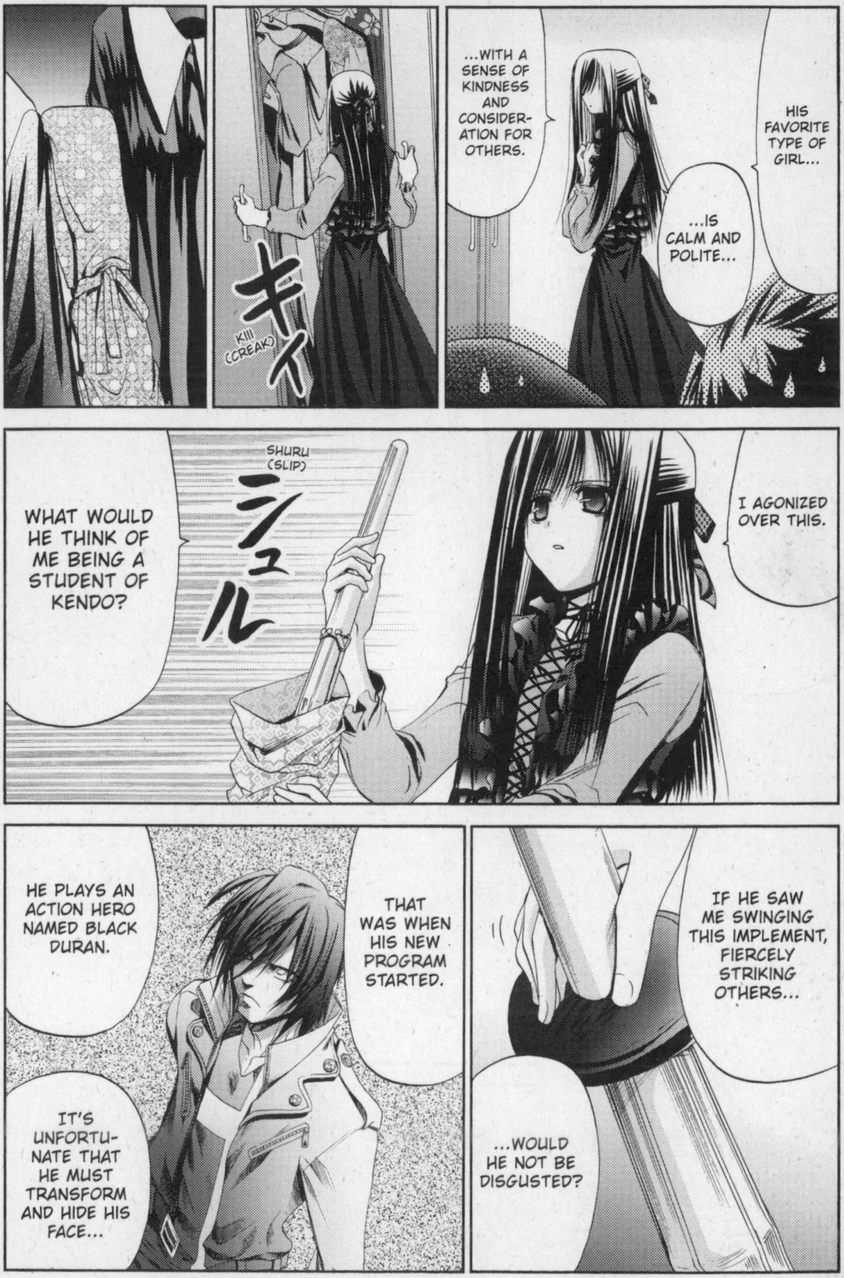
HIS FAVORITE TYPE OF GIRL...
...IS CALM AND POLITE...
...WITH A SENSE OF KINDNESS AND CONSIDER-ATION FOR OTHERS.
キイ
KIII (CREAK)
I AGONIZED OVER THIS.
シュル
SHURU (SLIP)
WHAT WOULD HE THINK OF ME BEING A STUDENT OF KENDO?
IF HE SAW ME SWINGING THIS IMPLEMENT, FIERCELY STRIKING OTHERS...
...WOULD HE NOT BE DISGUSTED?
THAT WAS WHEN HIS NEW PROGRAM STARTED.
HE PLAYS AN ACTION HERO NAMED BLACK DURAN.
IT'S UNFORTU-NATE THAT HE MUST TRANSFORM AND HIDE HIS FACE...

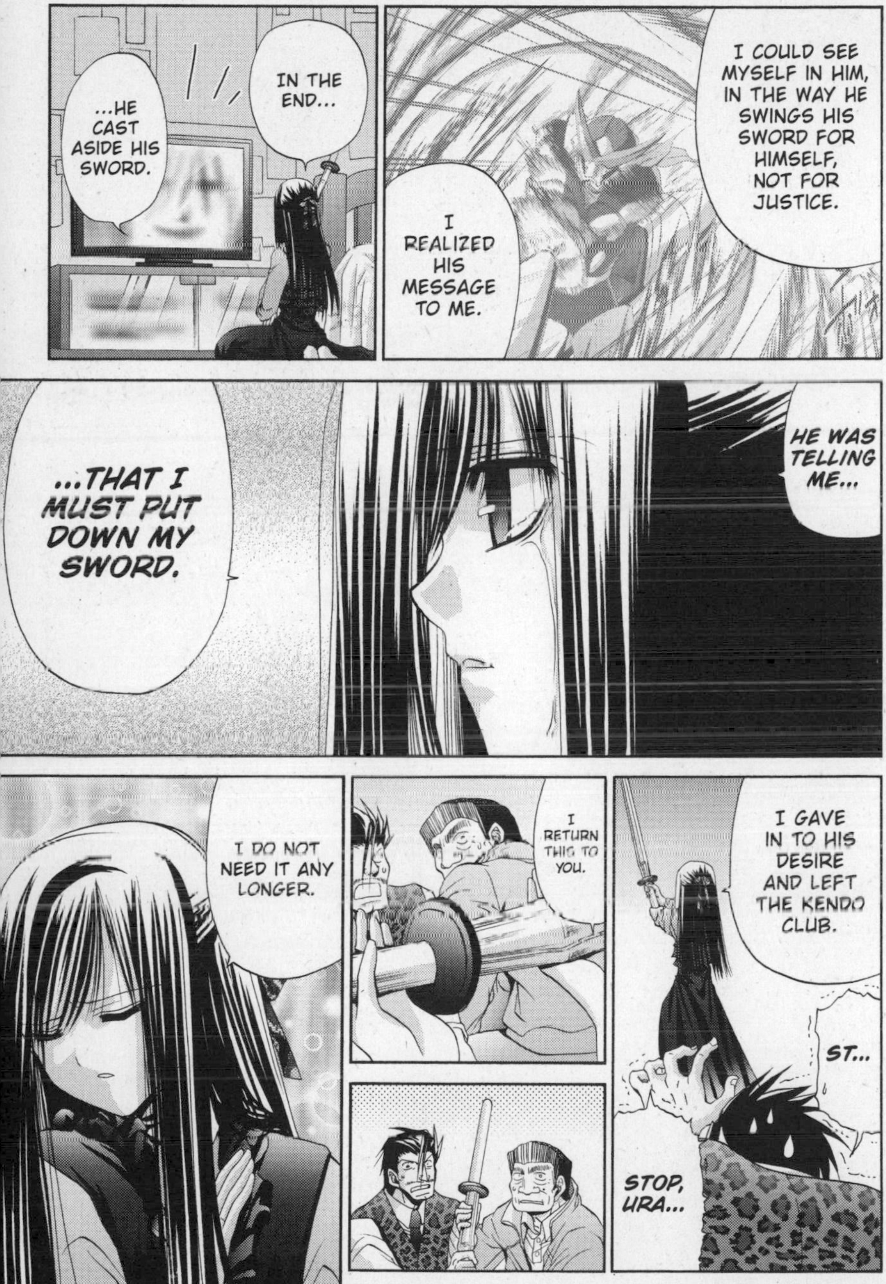
I COULD SEE MYSELF IN HIM, IN THE WAY HE SWINGS HIS SWORD FOR HIMSELF, NOT FOR JUSTICE.
I REALIZED HIS MESSAGE TO ME.
IN THE END...
...HE CAST ASIDE HIS SWORD.
HE WAS TELLING ME...
...THAT I MUST PUT DOWN MY SWORD.
I GAVE IN TO HIS DESIRE AND LEFT THE KENDO CLUB.
ST...
STOP, URA...
I RETURN THIS TO YOU.
I DO NOT NEED IT ANY LONGER.

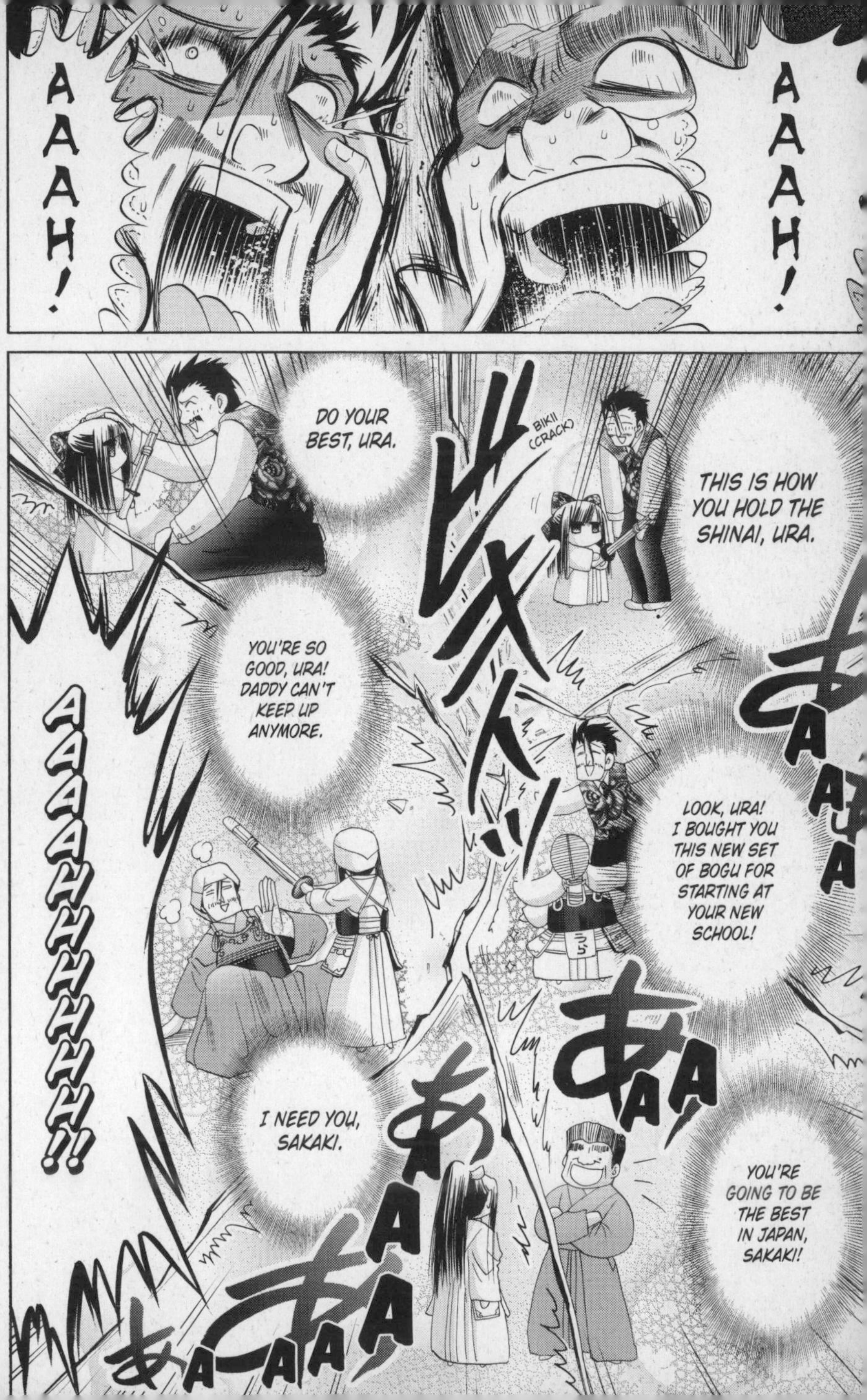
AAAAH!
AAAAH!
THIS IS HOW YOU HOLD THE SHINAI, URA.
BIKII (CRACK)
ビキッ
DO YOUR BEST, URA.
LOOK, URA! I BOUGHT YOU THIS NEW SET OF BOGU FOR STARTING AT YOUR NEW SCHOOL!
YOU'RE SO GOOD, URA! DADDY CAN'T KEEP UP ANYMORE.
YOU'RE GOING TO BE THE BEST IN JAPAN, SAKAKI!
I NEED YOU, SAKAKI.
AAAAAHHHHHHH!!

BAMBOO BLADE
バンブーブレード

BAMBOO BLADE
バンブーブレード

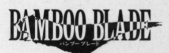

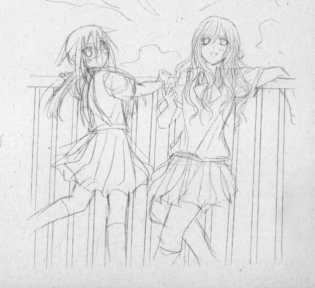

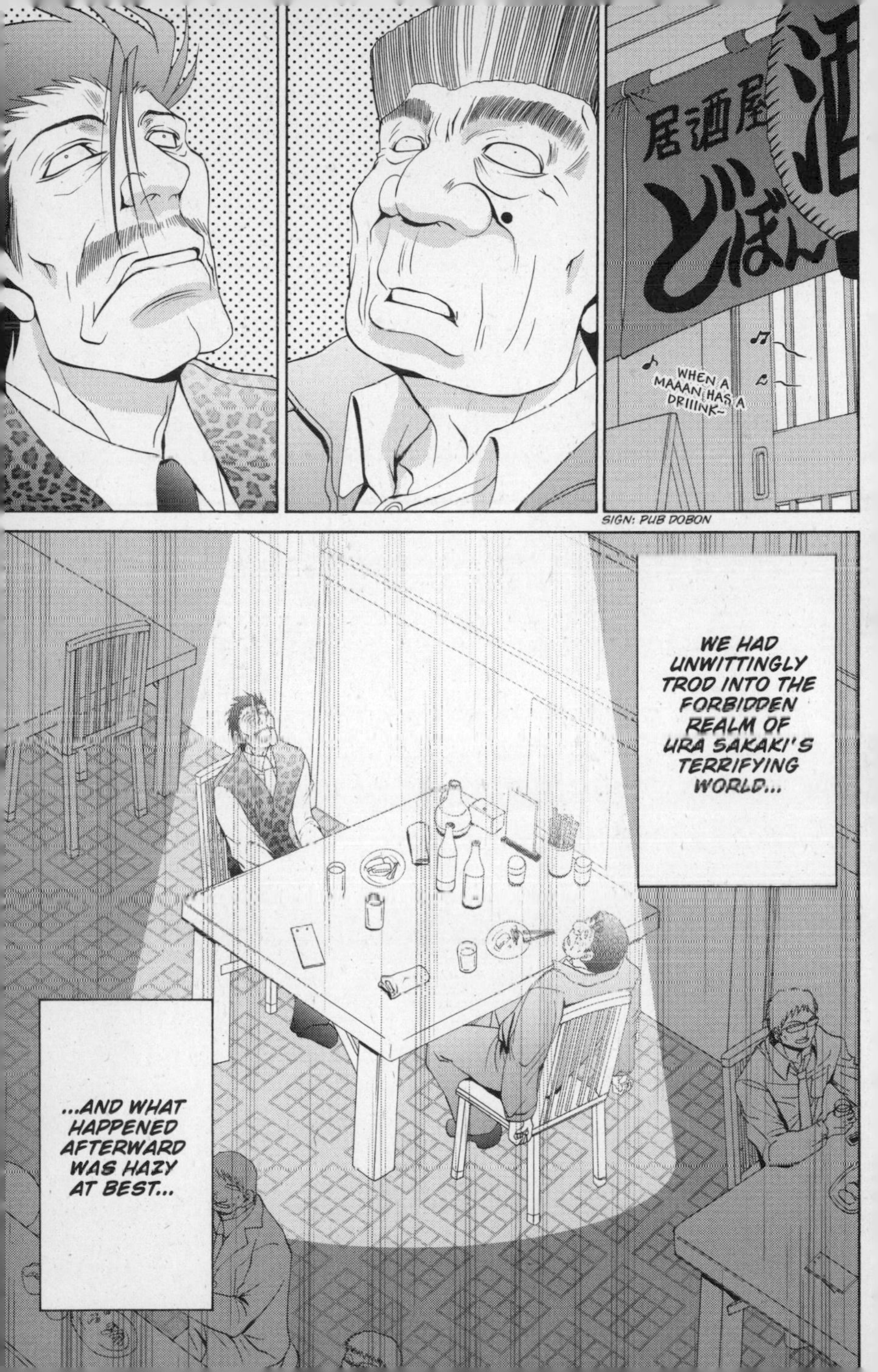
居酒屋
どぼん
♪ WHEN A MAAAN HAS A DRIIINK~ ♪
SIGN: PUB DOBON
WE HAD UNWITTINGLY TROD INTO THE FORBIDDEN REALM OF URA SAKAKI'S TERRIFYING WORLD...
...AND WHAT HAPPENED AFTERWARD WAS HAZY AT BEST...

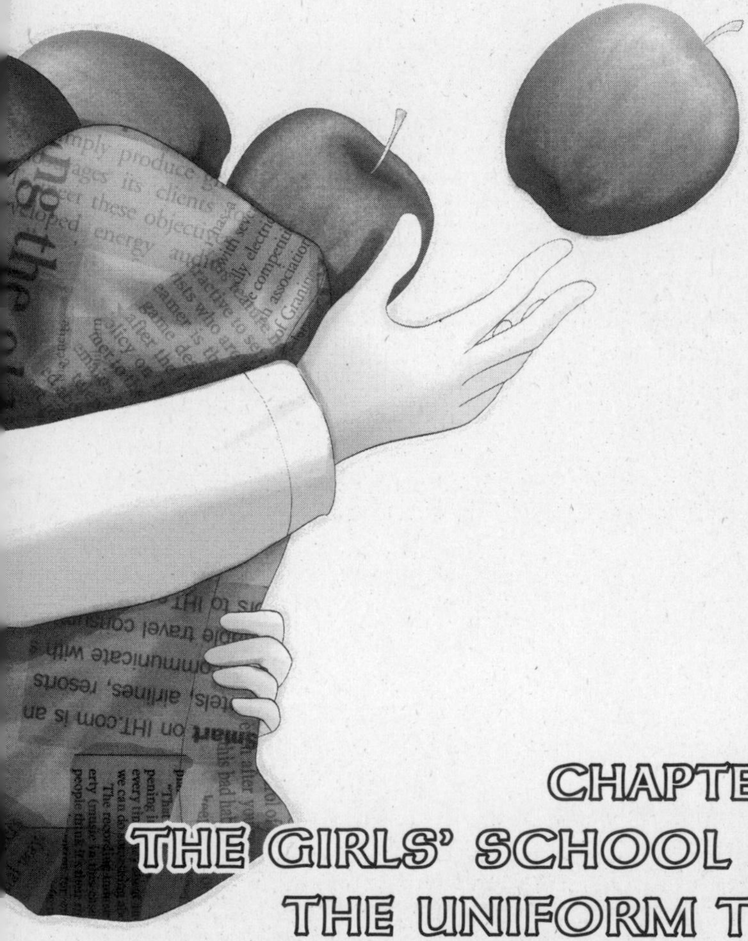

CHAPTER 85
THE GIRLS' SCHOOL AND THE UNIFORM THIEF

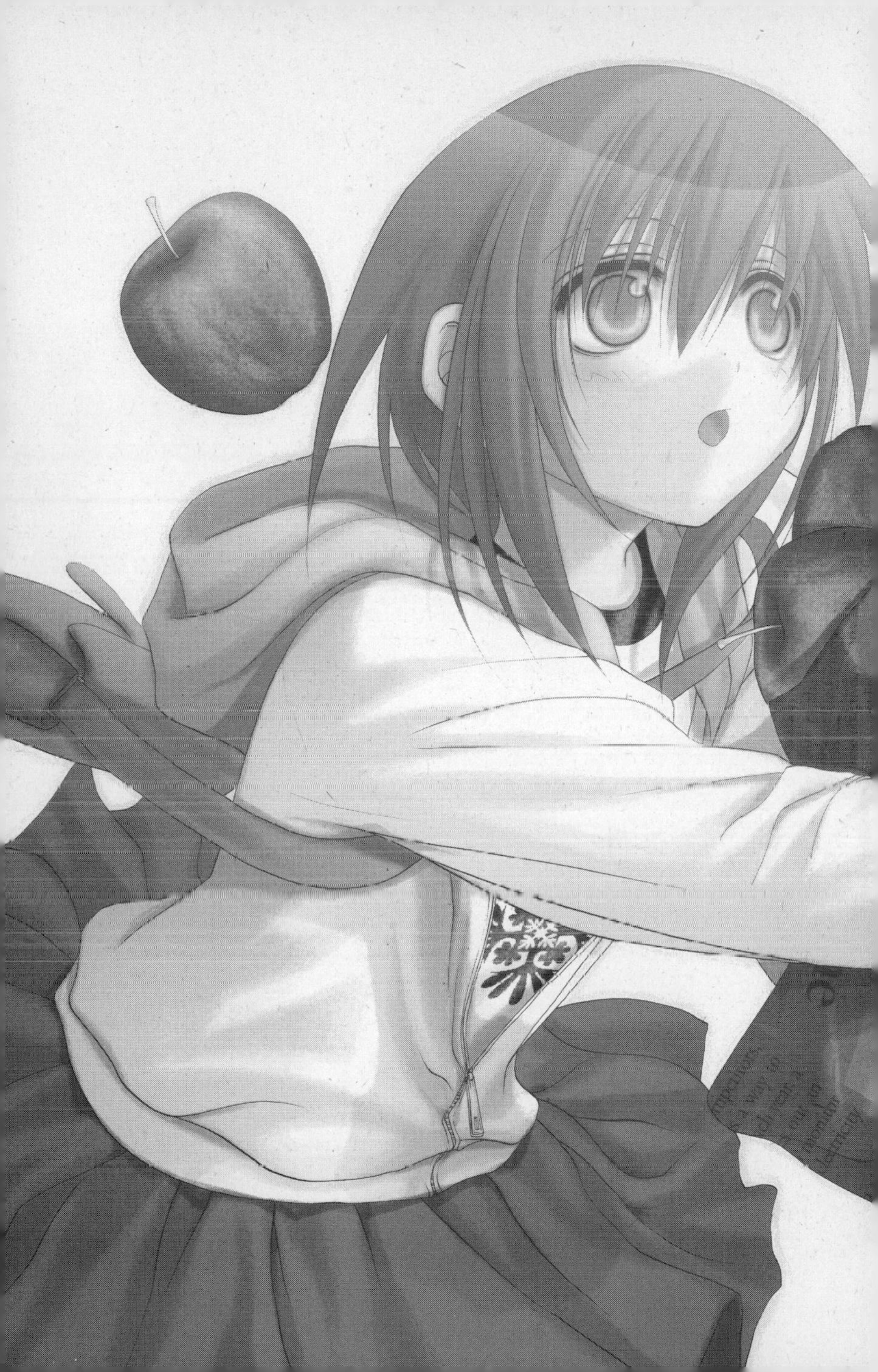

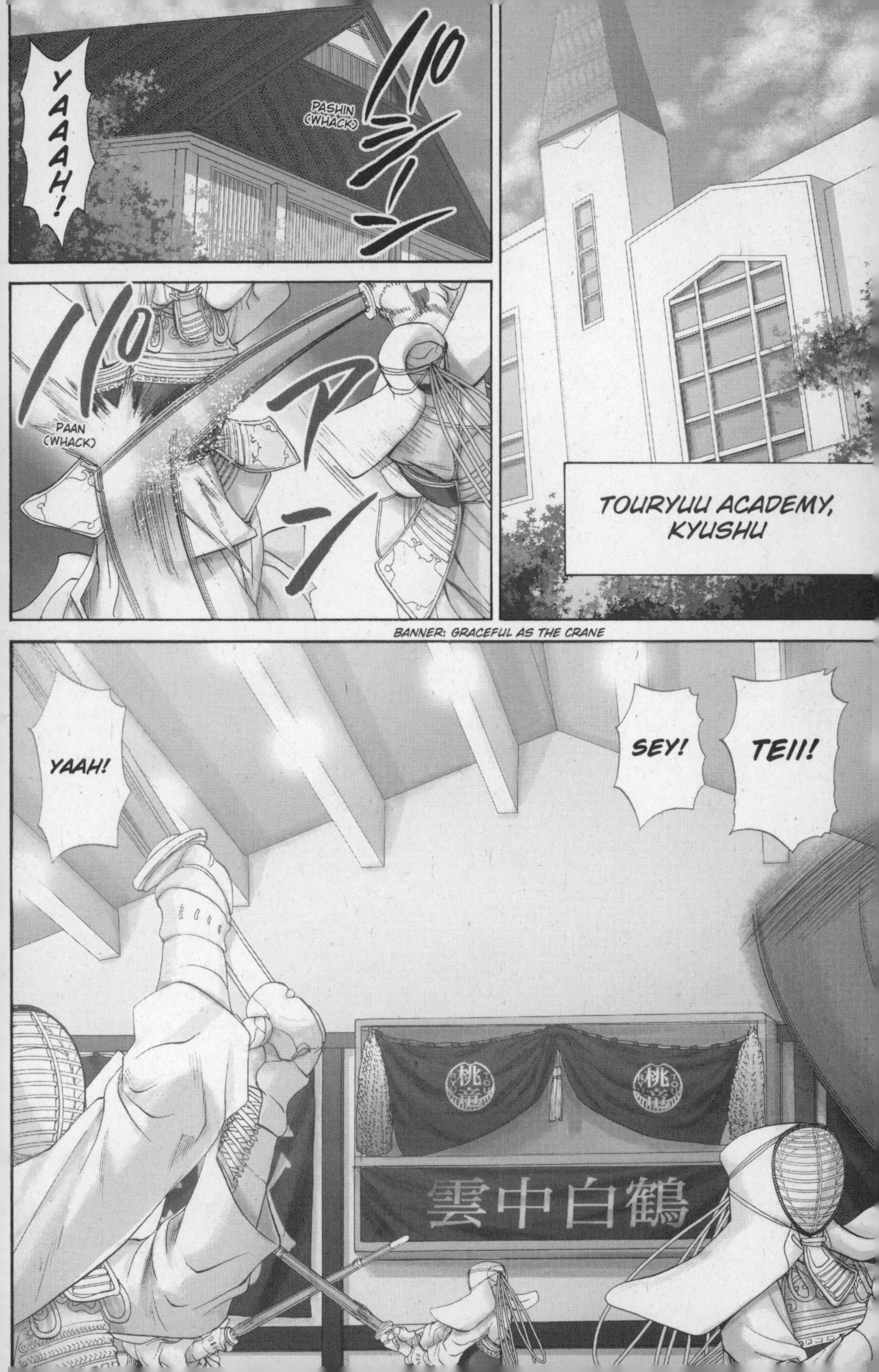
TOURYUU ACADEMY, KYUSHU
PASHIN (WHACK)
YAAAH!
PAAN (WHACK)
BANNER: GRACEFUL AS THE CRANE
TEII!
SEY!
YAAH!
雲中白鶴

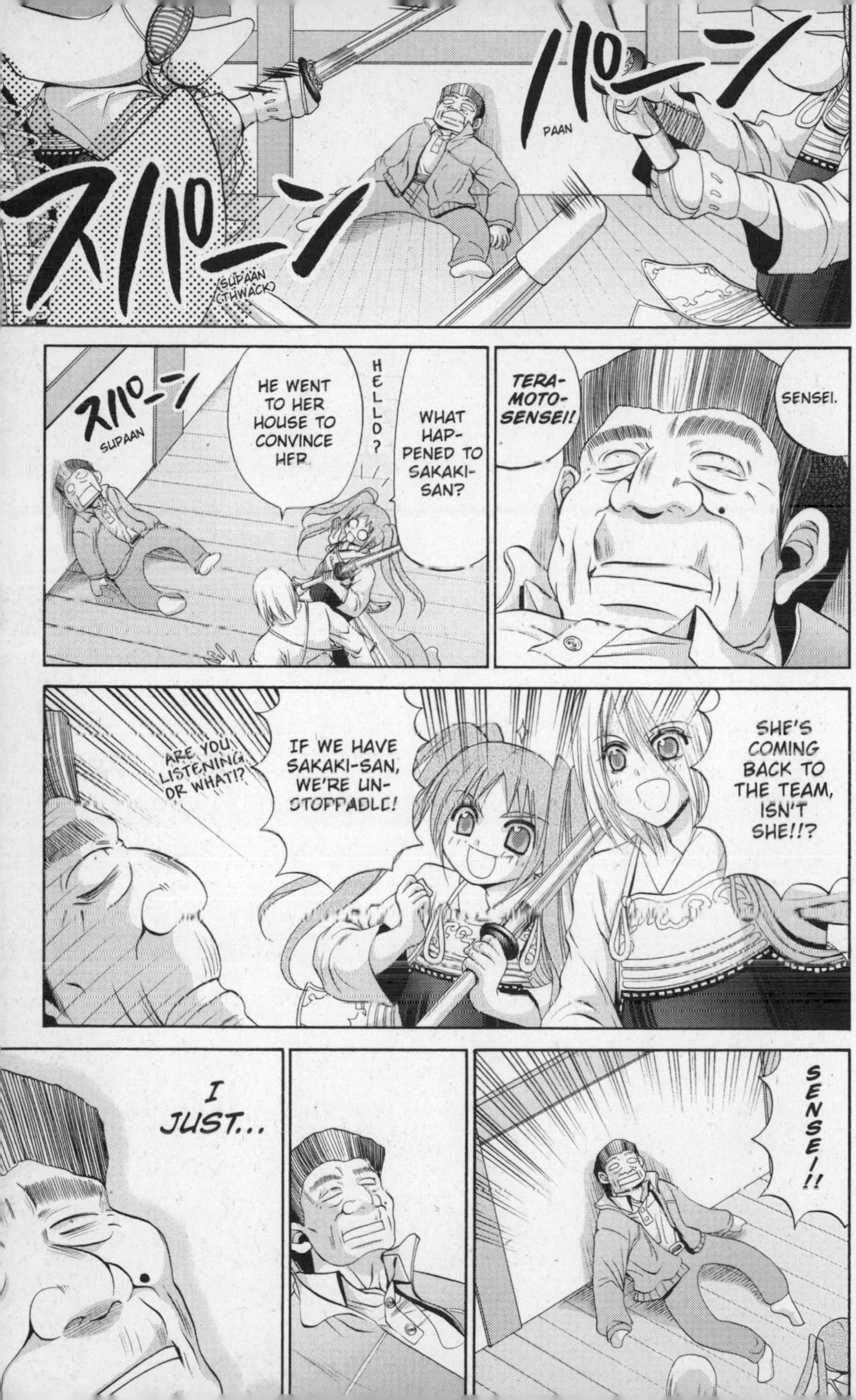
パーン
PAAN
スパーン
(SUPAAN (THWACK)
SENSEI.
TERA-MOTO-SENSEI!!
WHAT HAP-PENED TO SAKAKI-SAN?
HELLO?
HE WENT TO HER HOUSE TO CONVINCE HER.
スパーン
SUPAAN
SHE'S COMING BACK TO THE TEAM, ISN'T SHE!!?
IF WE HAVE SAKAKI-SAN, WE'RE UN-STOPPABLE!
ARE YOU LISTENING OR WHAT!?
SENSEI!!
I JUST...

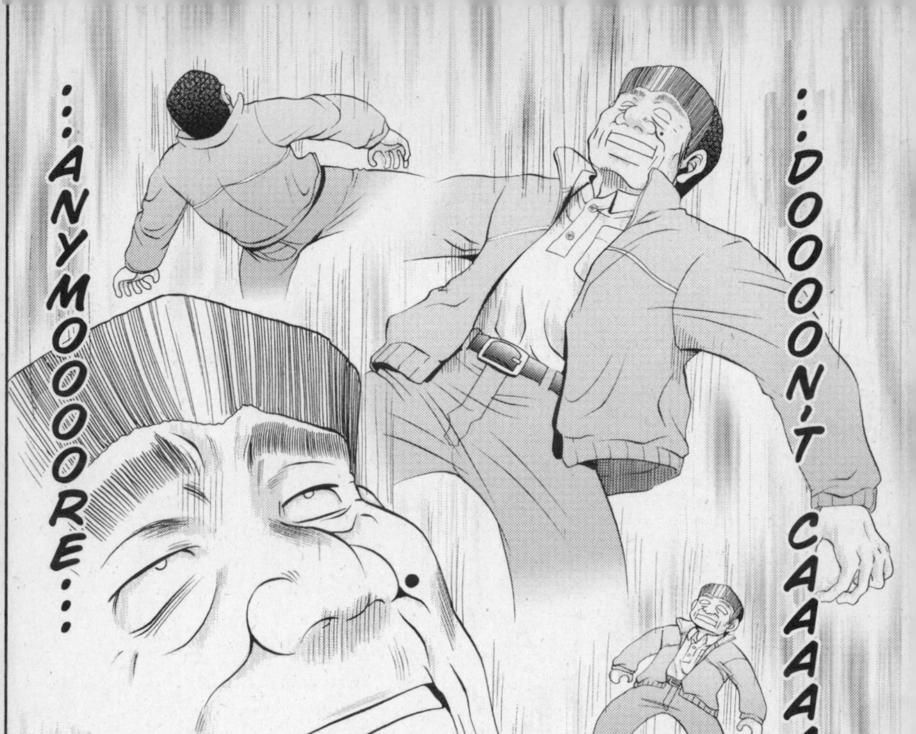
...DOOOOON'T CAAAAARE...
...ANYMOOOORE...

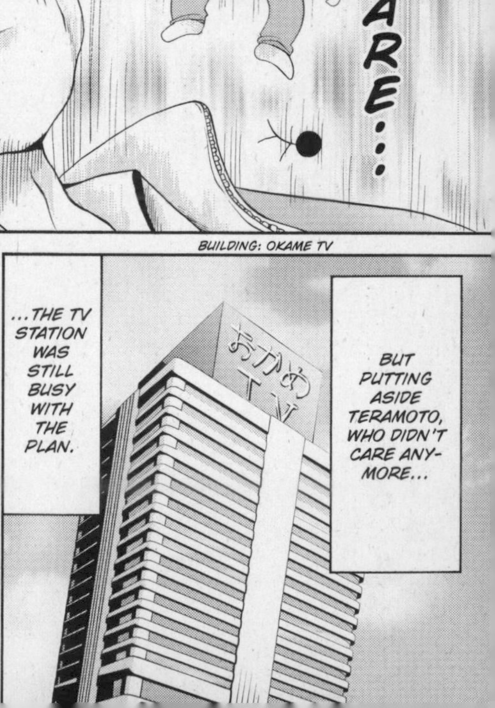
BUILDING: OKAME TV
BUT PUTTING ASIDE TERAMOTO, WHO DIDN'T CARE ANY-MORE...
...THE TV STATION WAS STILL BUSY WITH THE PLAN.

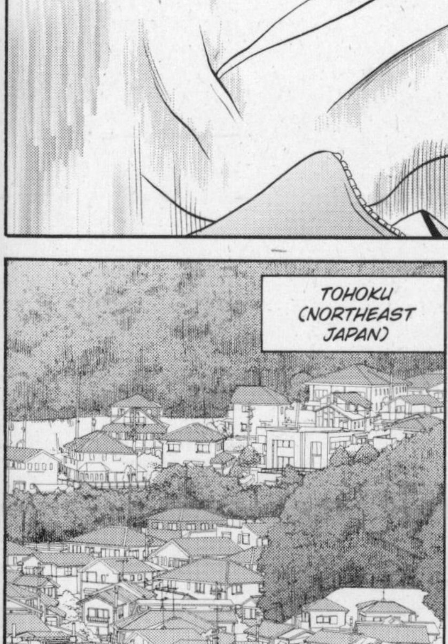
TOHOKU (NORTHEAST JAPAN)

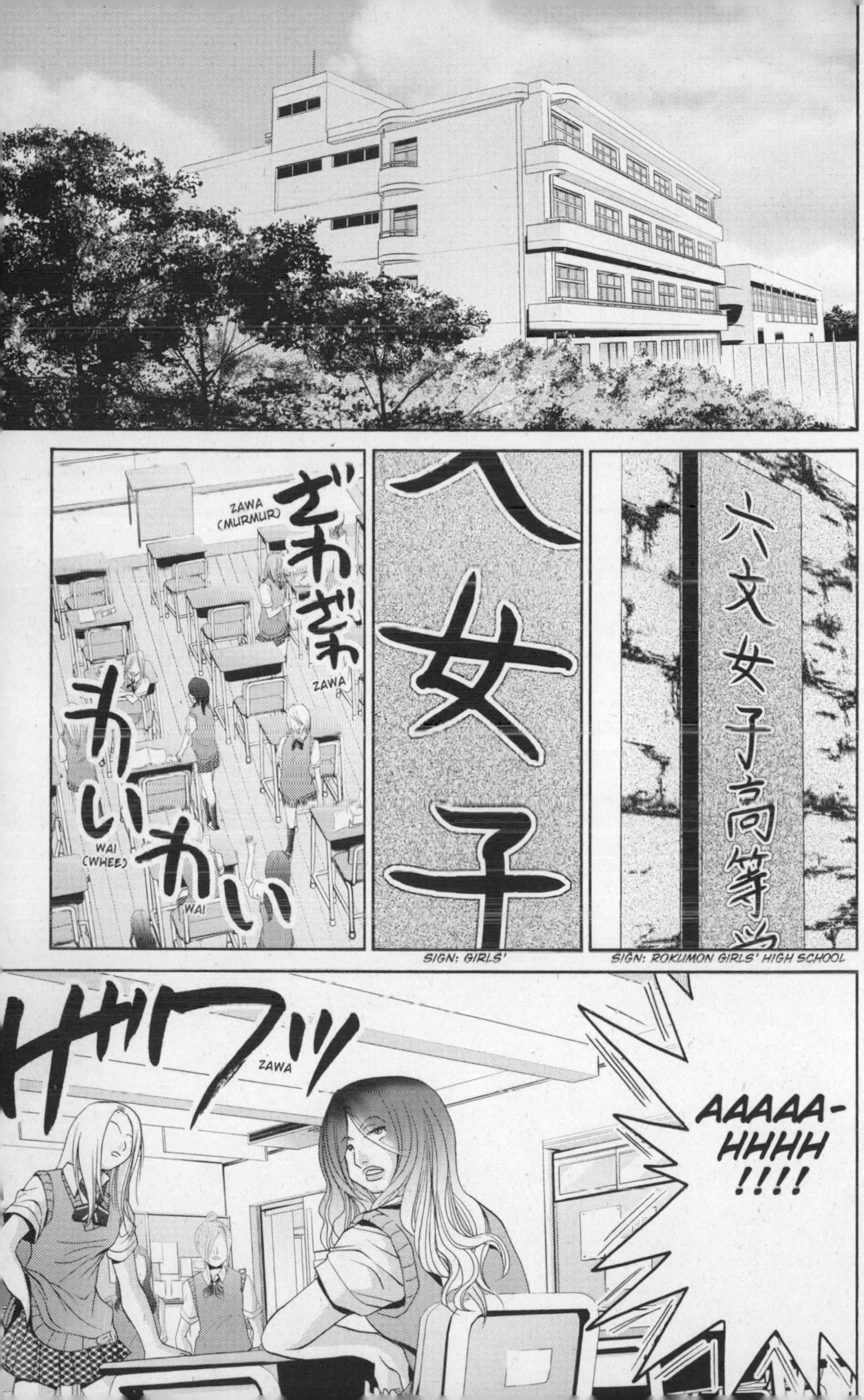
六文女子高等学
SIGN: ROKUMON GIRLS' HIGH SCHOOL
女子
SIGN: GIRLS'
ZAWA (MURMUR)
ZAWA
WAI (WHEE)
WAI
ZAWA
AAAAA-HHHH!!!!

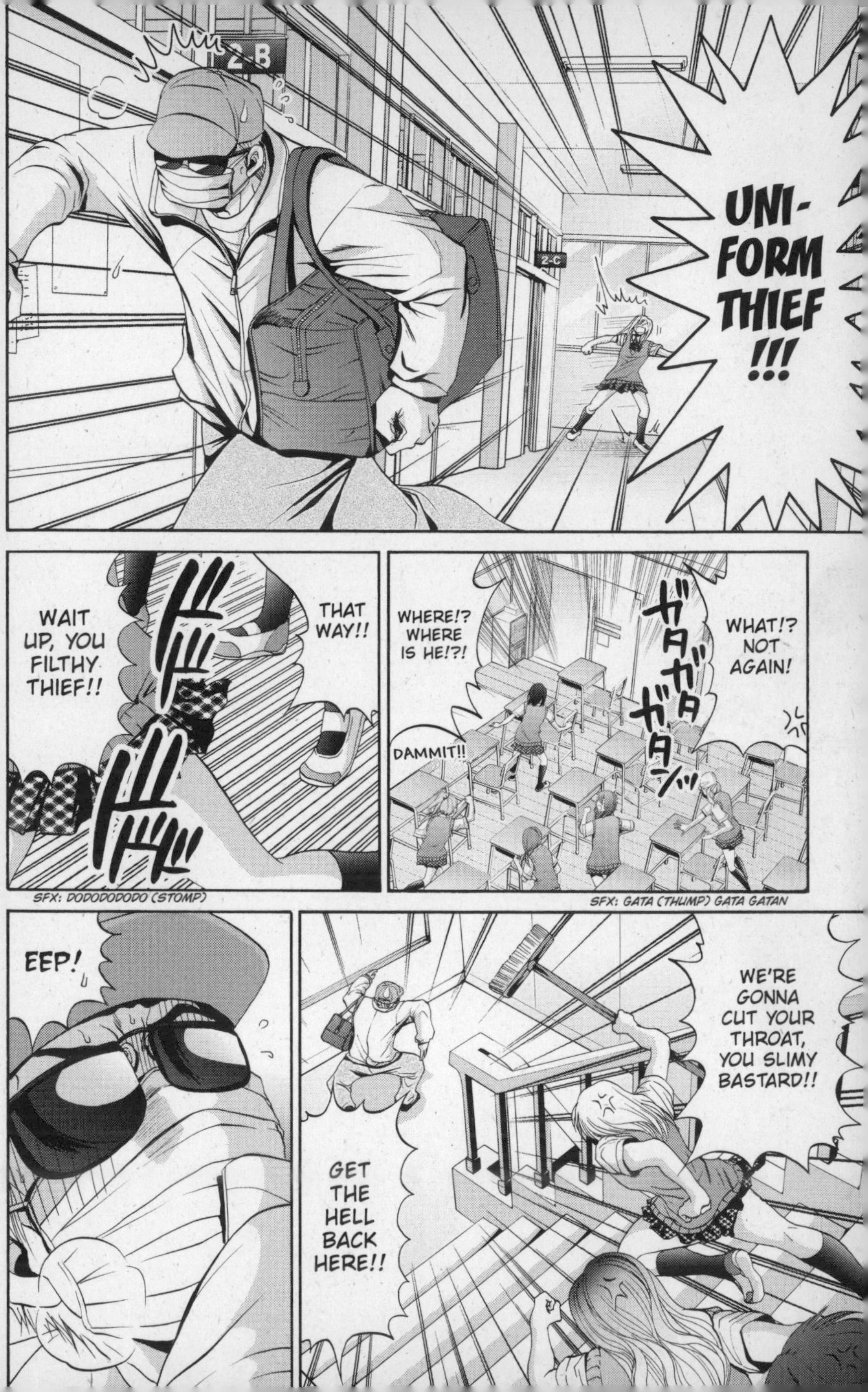
UNI-FORM THIEF!!!
WHAT!? NOT AGAIN!
WHERE!? WHERE IS HE!?!
DAMMIT!!
SFX: GATA (THUMP) GATA GATAN
THAT WAY!!
WAIT UP, YOU FILTHY THIEF!!
SFX: DODODODODO (STOMP)
WE'RE GONNA CUT YOUR THROAT, YOU SLIMY BASTARD!!
GET THE HELL BACK HERE!!
EEP!

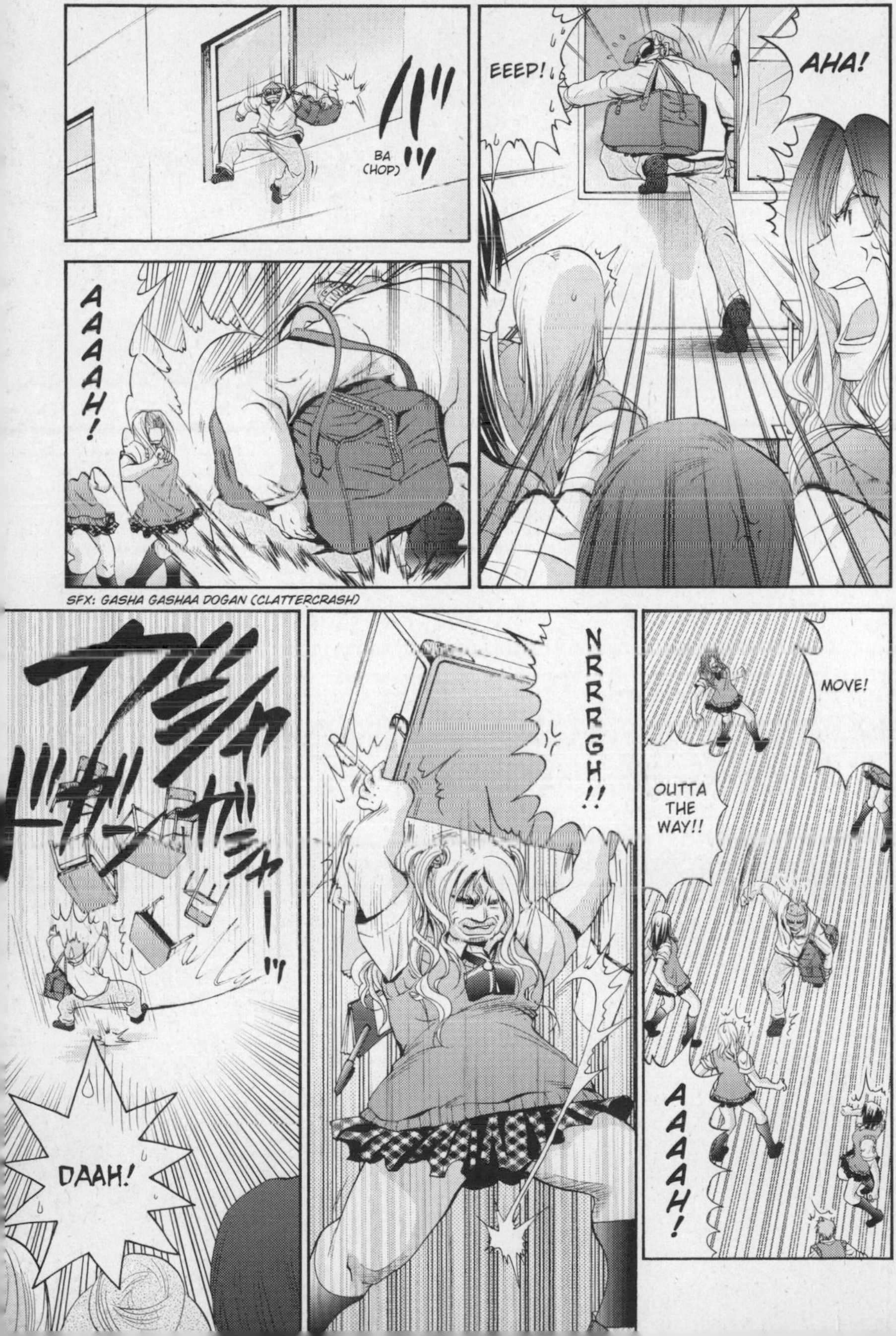
EEEP!
AHA!
BA (HOP)
AAAAAH!
SFX: GASHA GASHAA DOGAN (CLATTERCRASH)
MOVE!
OUTTA THE WAY!!
AAAAAH!
NRRRGH!!
DAAH!

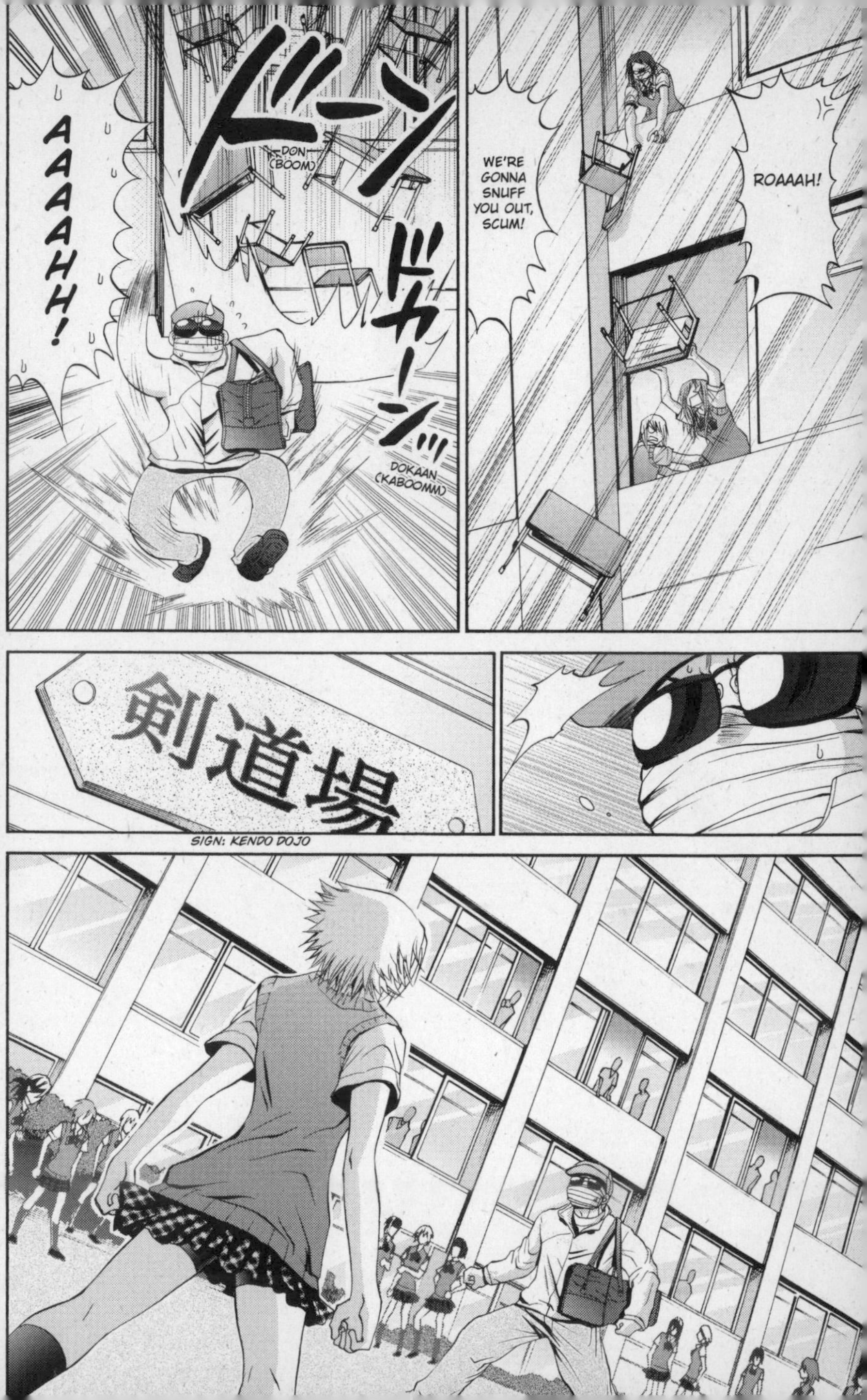
ROAAAH!
WE'RE GONNA SNUFF YOU OUT, SCUM!
ドーン
DON (BOOM)
AAAAHH!
ドカーンッ
DOKAAN (KABOOMM)
剣道場
SIGN: KENDO DOJO

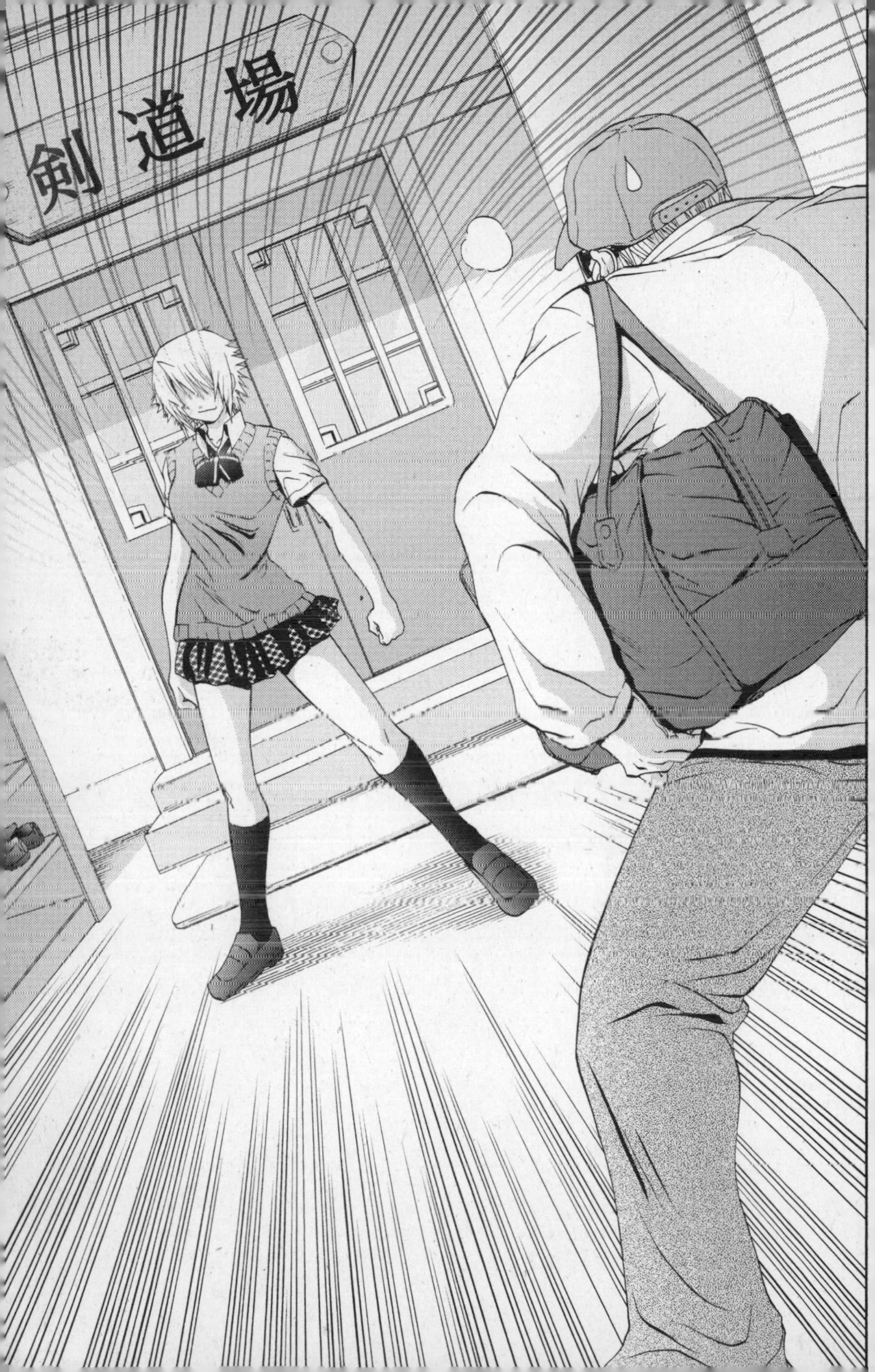
剣道場

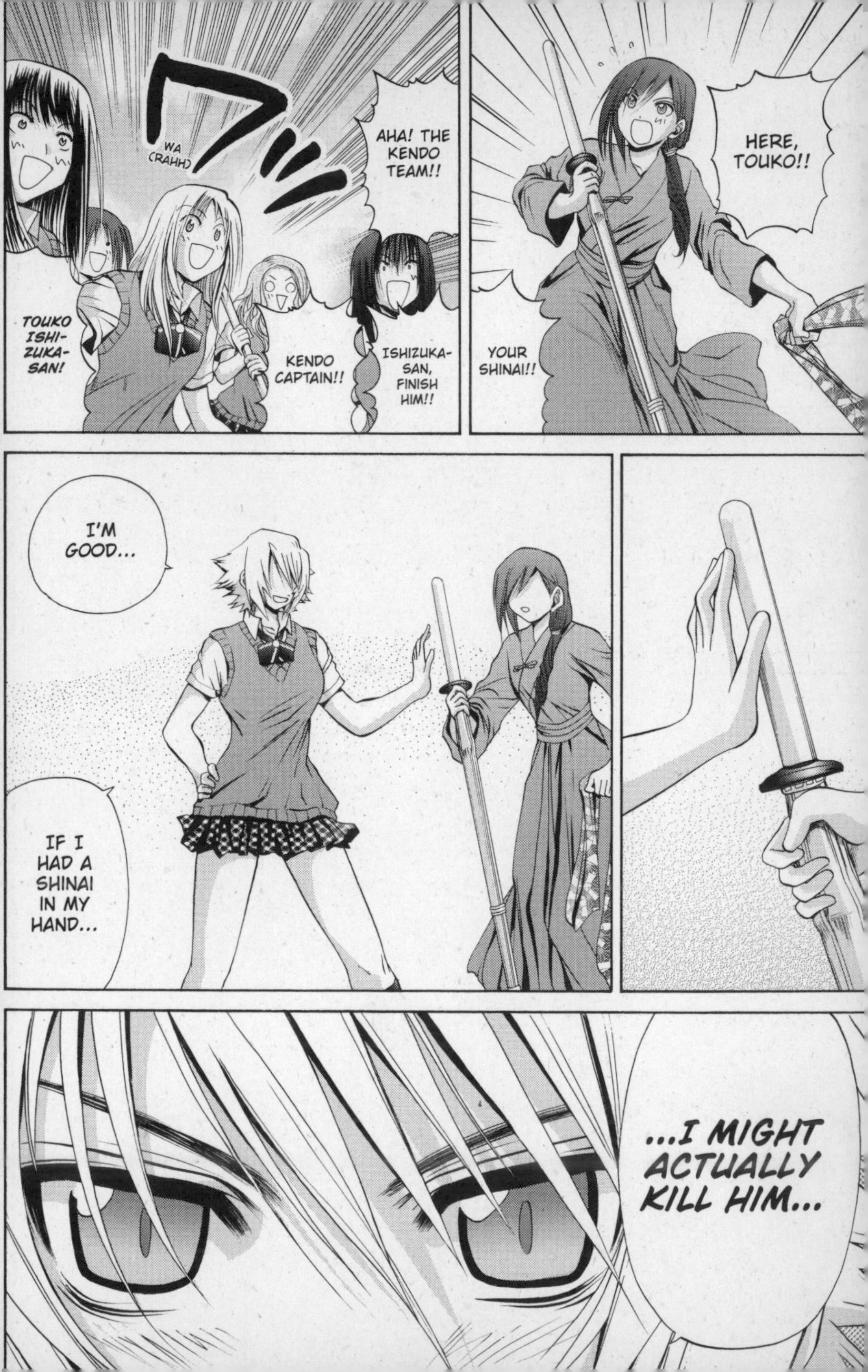
HERE, TOUKO!!
YOUR SHINAI!!
AHA! THE KENDO TEAM!!
WA (RAHH)
ISHIZUKA-SAN, FINISH HIM!!
KENDO CAPTAIN!!
TOUKO ISHIZUKA-SAN!
I'M GOOD...
IF I HAD A SHINAI IN MY HAND...
...I MIGHT ACTUALLY KILL HIM...

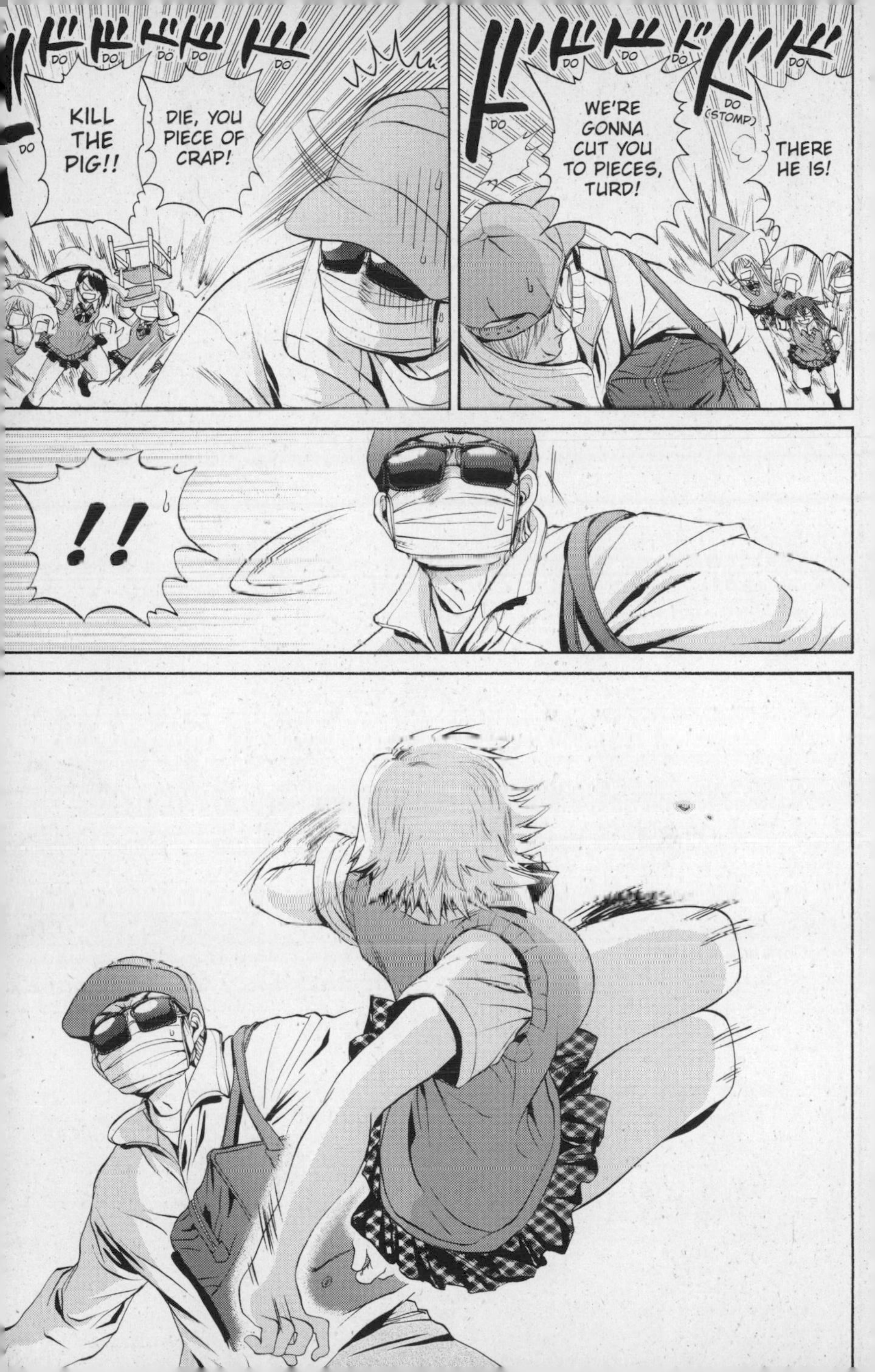
DO DO DO DO DO
THERE HE IS!
DO (STOMP)
WE'RE GONNA CUT YOU TO PIECES, TURD!
DO DO DO DO DO
DIE, YOU PIECE OF CRAP!
KILL THE PIG!!
DO
!!

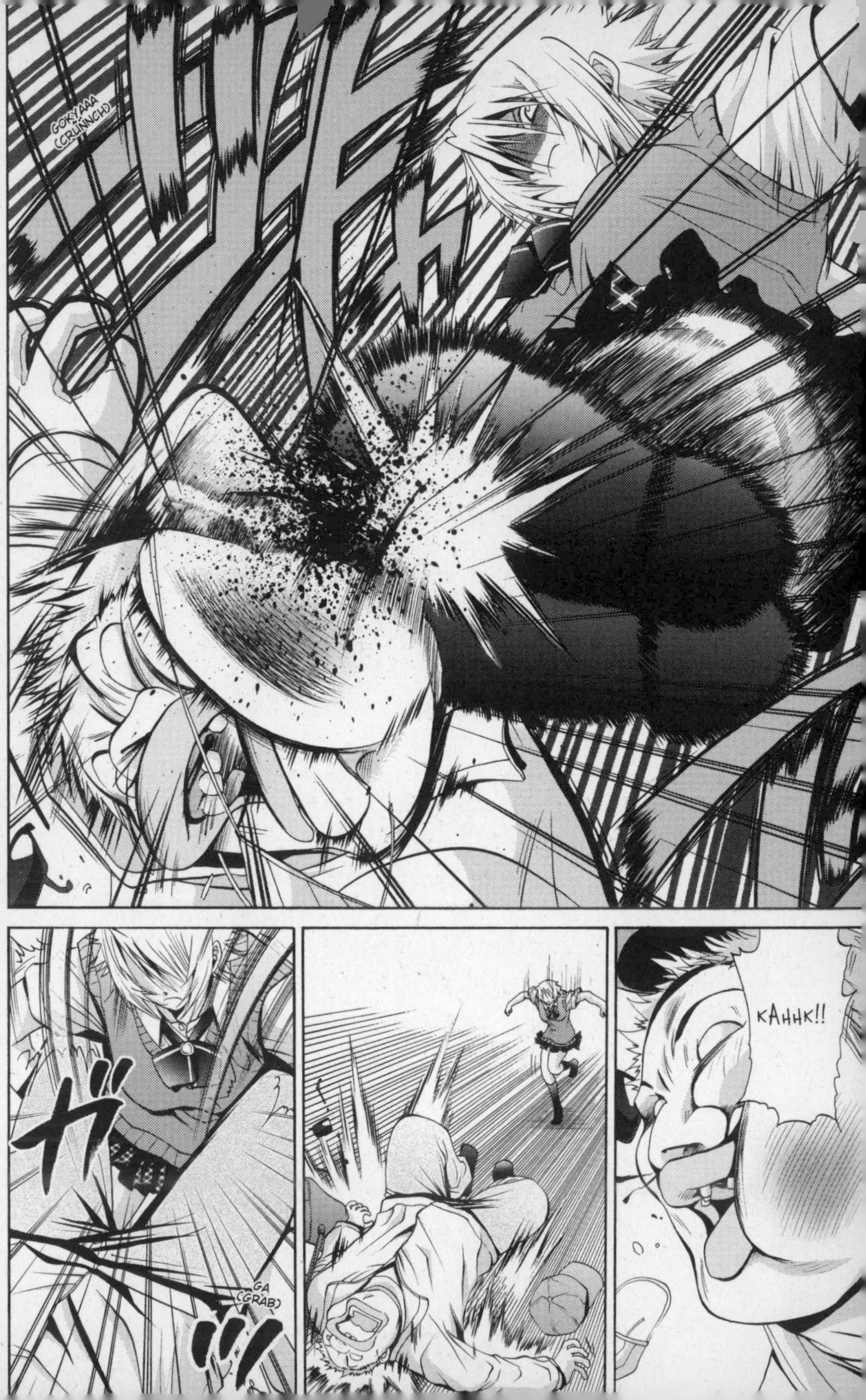
GOKYAAA
(CRUNNCH)
KAHHK!!
GA
(GRAB)

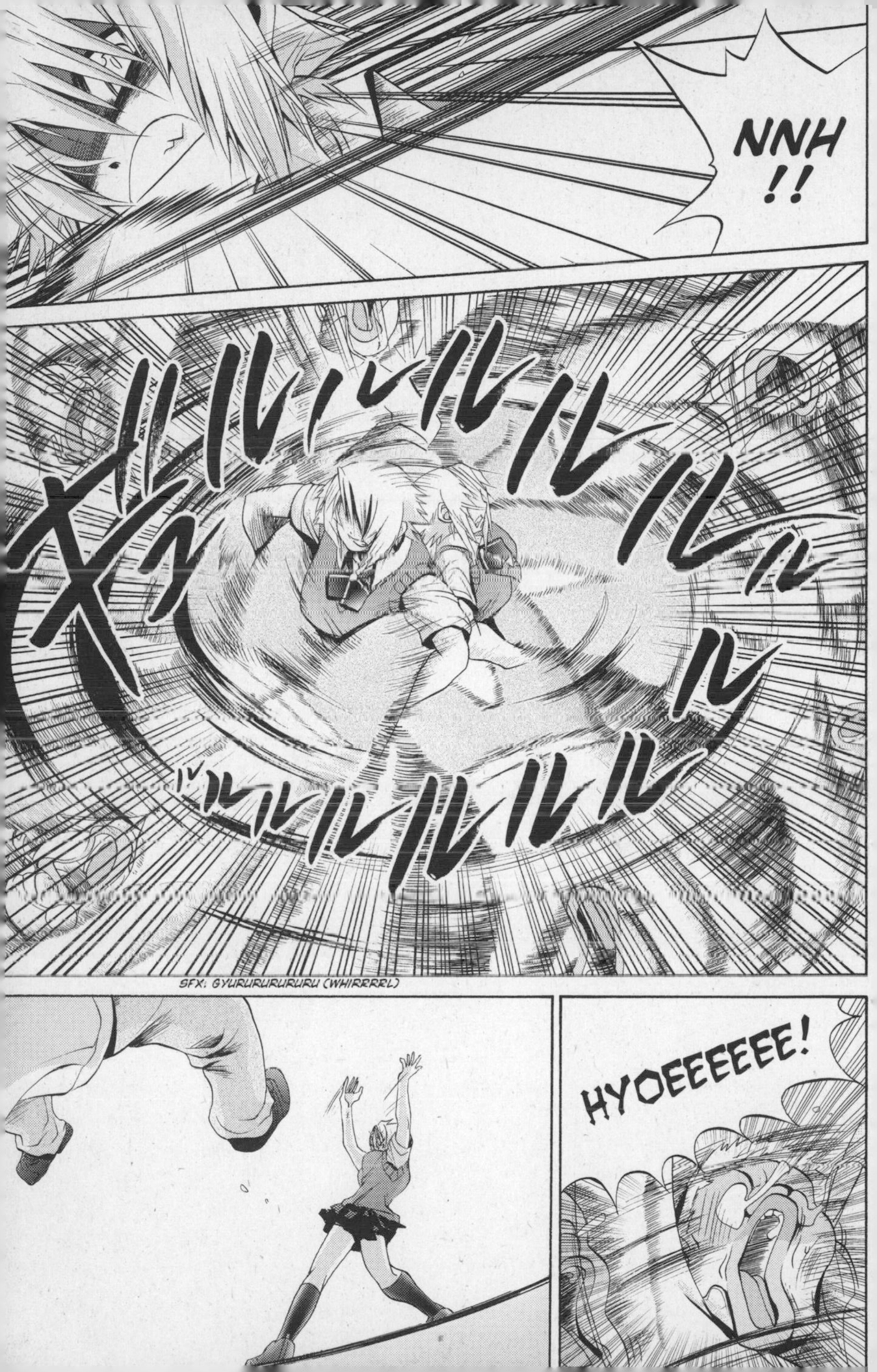
NNH !!
SFX: GYURURURURURU (WHIRRRRL)
HYOEEEEEEE!

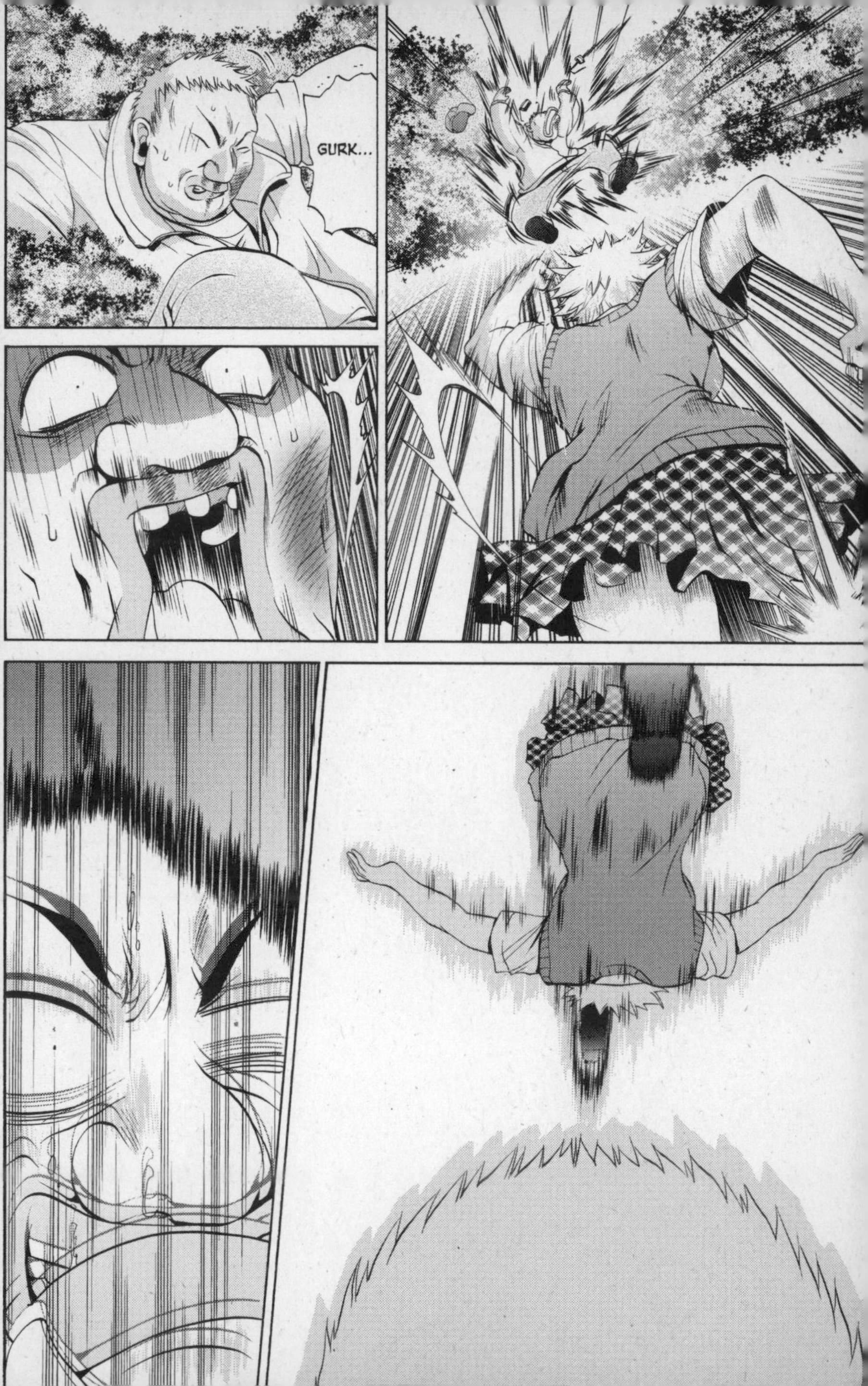
GURK...

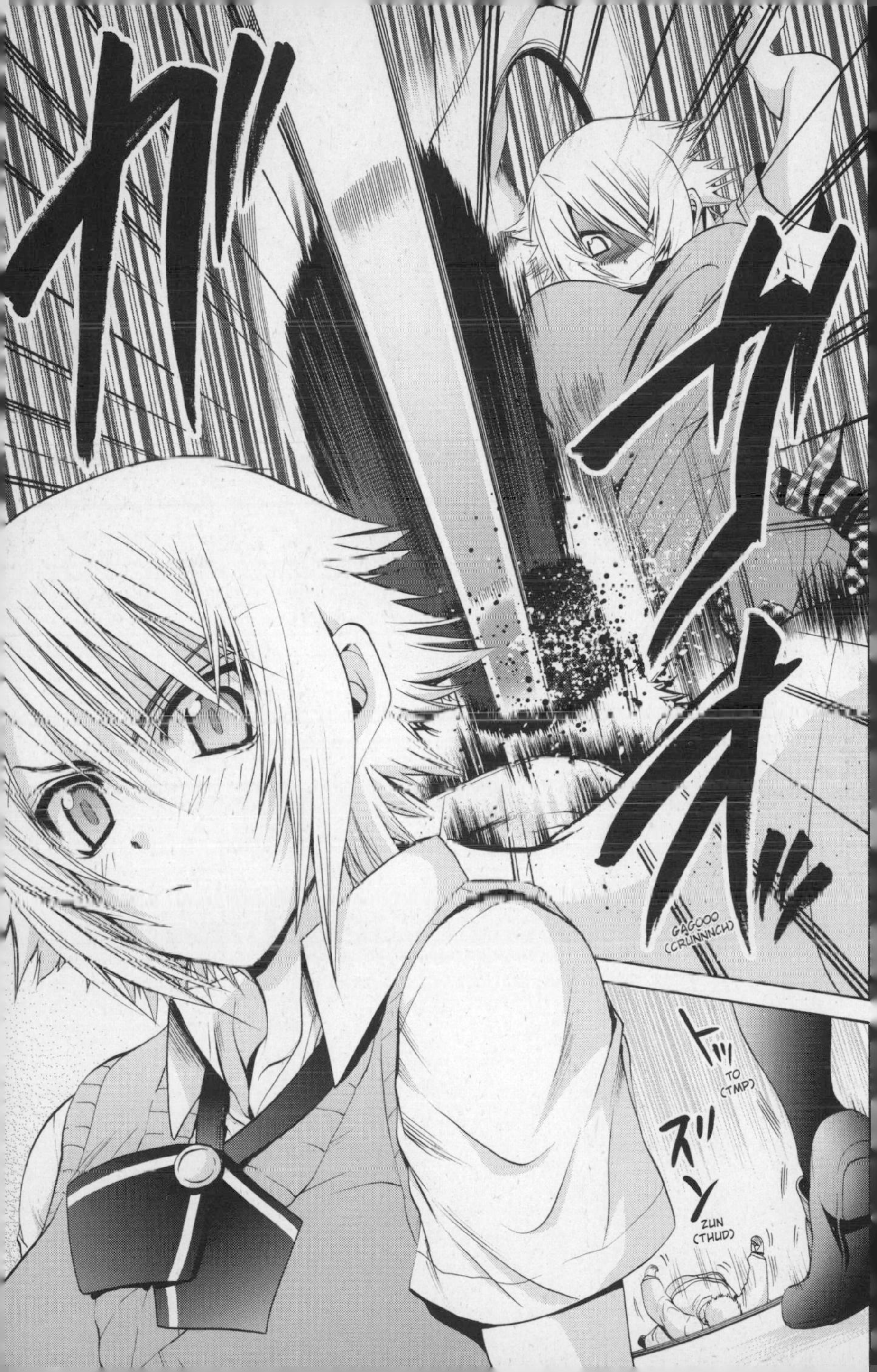
GAGOOO
(CRUNNNCH)
TO
(TMP)
ZUN
(THUD)

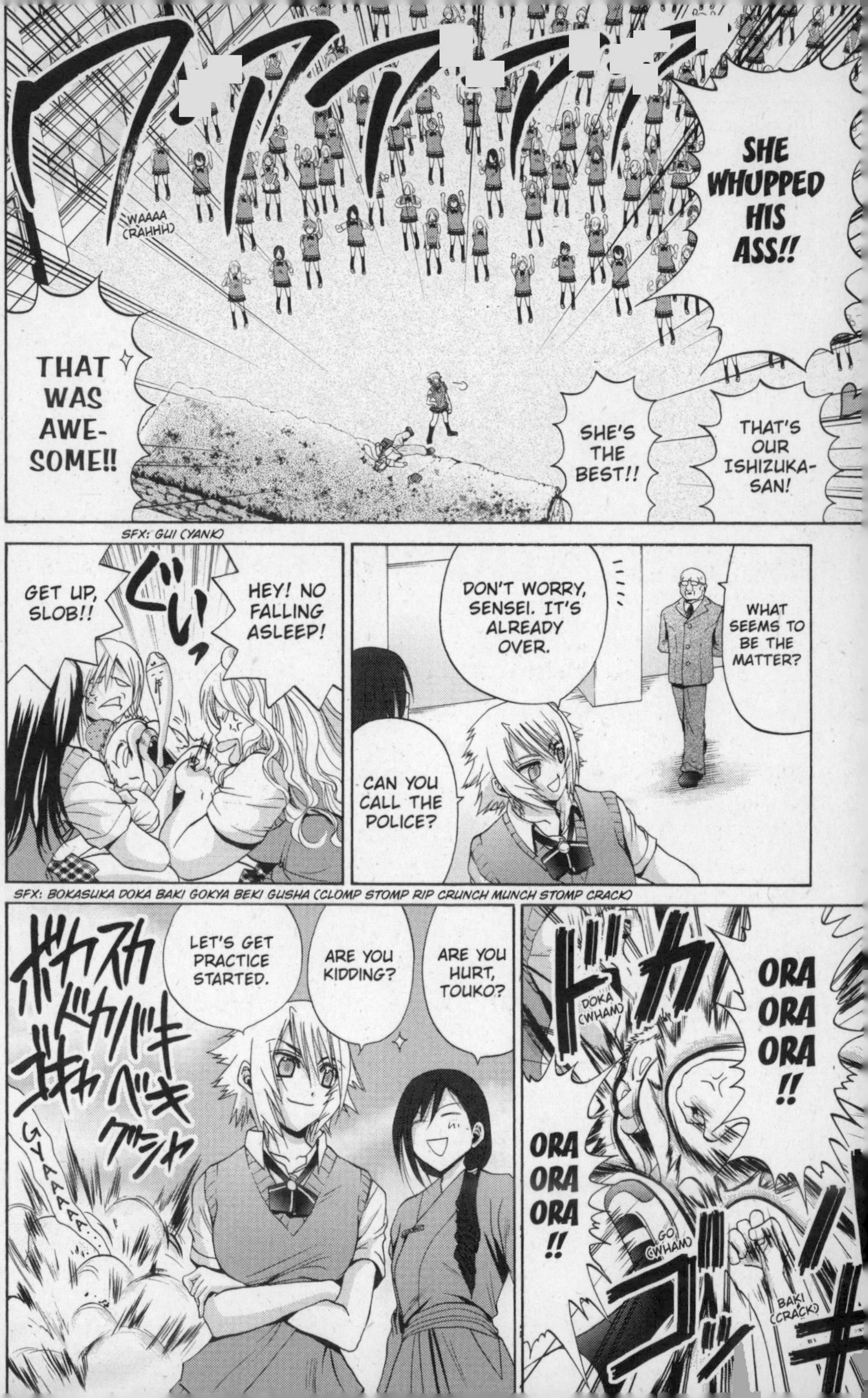
SHE WHUPPED HIS ASS!!
WAAAA (RAHHH)
THAT'S OUR ISHIZUKA-SAN!
SHE'S THE BEST!!
THAT WAS AWESOME!!
SFX: GUI (YANK)
WHAT SEEMS TO BE THE MATTER?
DON'T WORRY, SENSEI. IT'S ALREADY OVER.
CAN YOU CALL THE POLICE?
HEY! NO FALLING ASLEEP!
GET UP, SLOB!!
SFX: BOKASUKA DOKA BAKI GOKYA BEKI GUSHA (CLOMP STOMP RIP CRUNCH MUNCH STOMP CRACK)
ORA ORA ORA!!
DOKA (WHAM)
ORA ORA ORA!!
GO (WHAM)
BAKI (CRACK)
ARE YOU HURT, TOUKO?
ARE YOU KIDDING?
LET'S GET PRACTICE STARTED.
GYAAAAA...

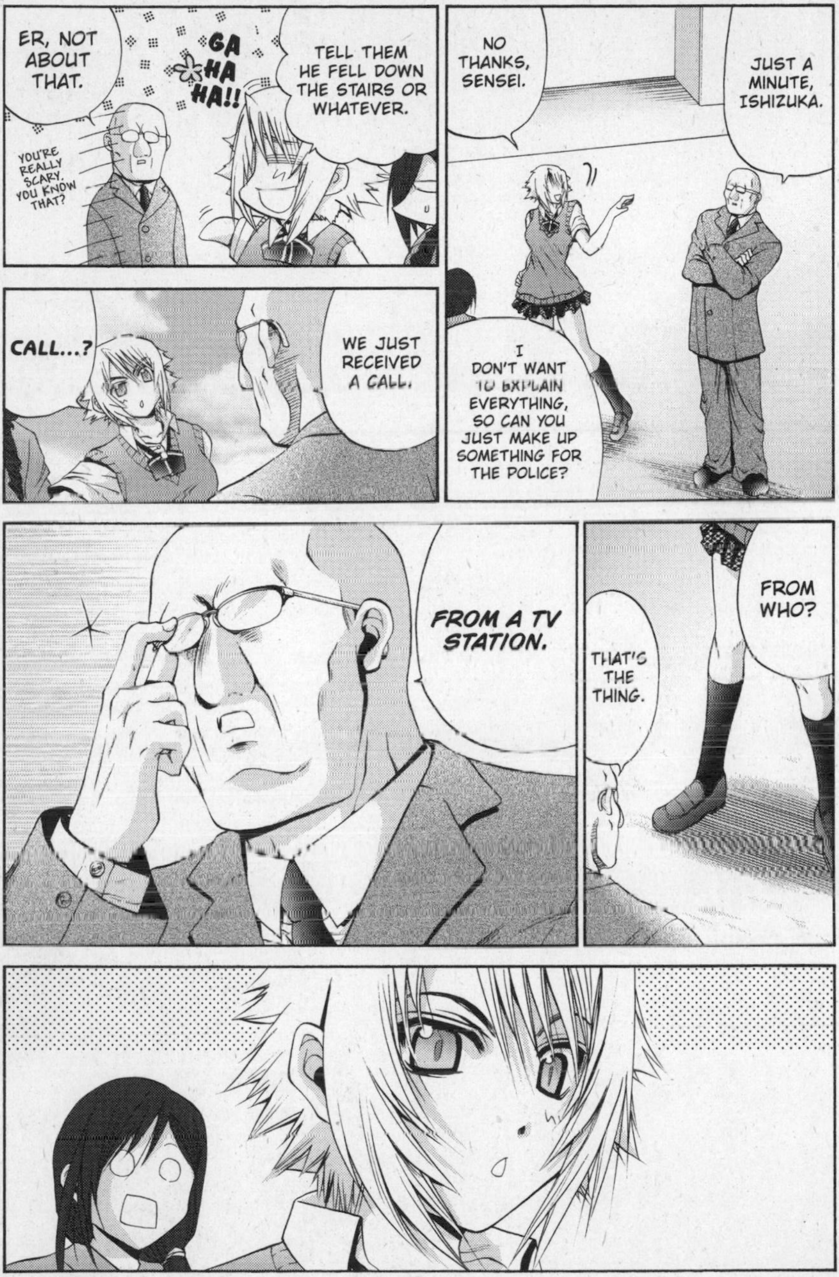

JUST A MINUTE, ISHIZUKA.
NO THANKS, SENSEI.
I DON'T WANT TO EXPLAIN EVERYTHING, SO CAN YOU JUST MAKE UP SOMETHING FOR THE POLICE?
TELL THEM HE FELL DOWN THE STAIRS OR WHATEVER.
GA HA HA!!
ER, NOT ABOUT THAT.
YOU'RE REALLY SCARY, YOU KNOW THAT?
WE JUST RECEIVED A CALL.
CALL...?
FROM WHO?
THAT'S THE THING.
FROM A TV STATION.

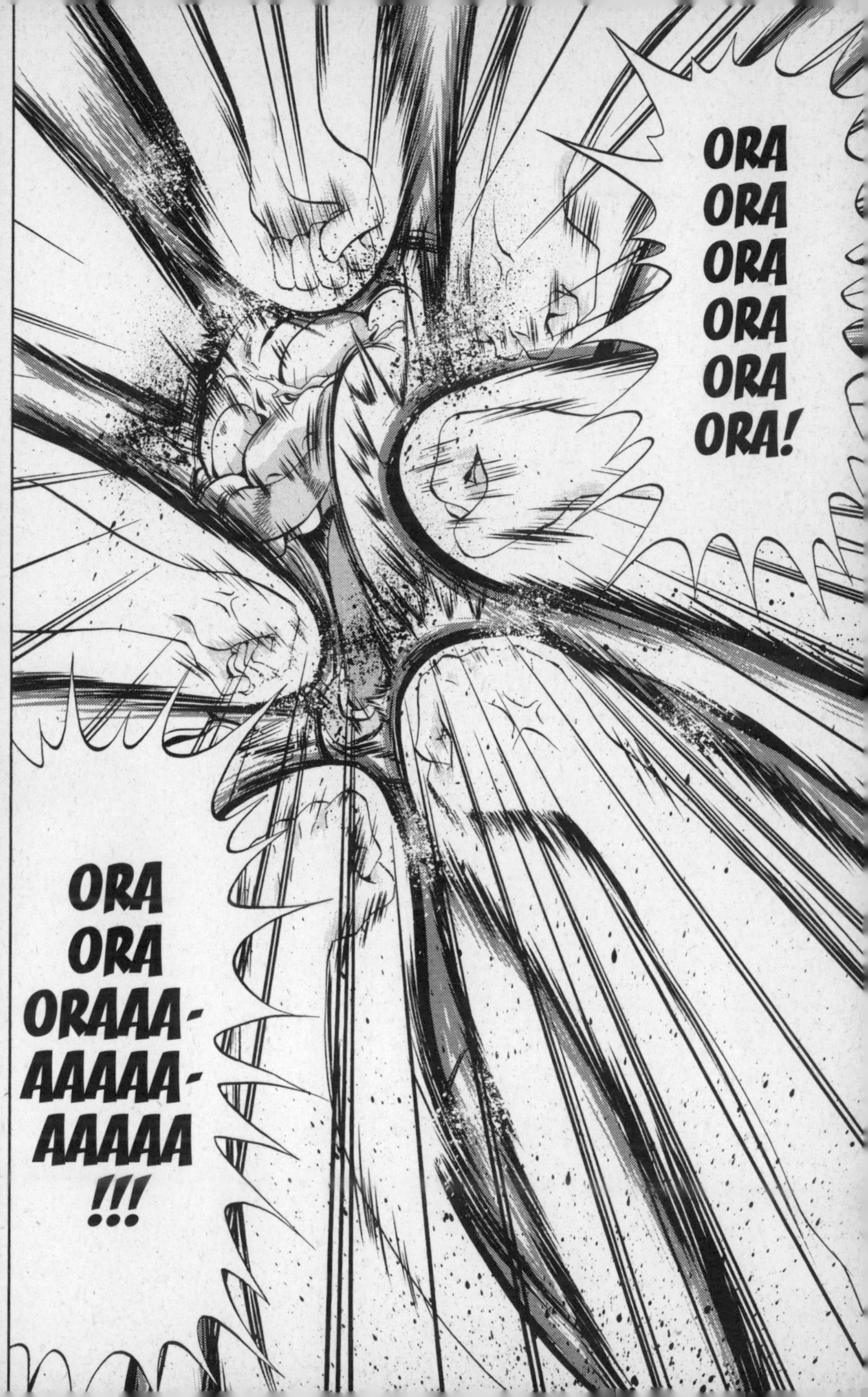
ORA ORA ORA ORA ORA ORA!
ORA ORA ORAAA-AAAAA-AAAAA!!!

BAMBOO BLADE

バンブーブレード

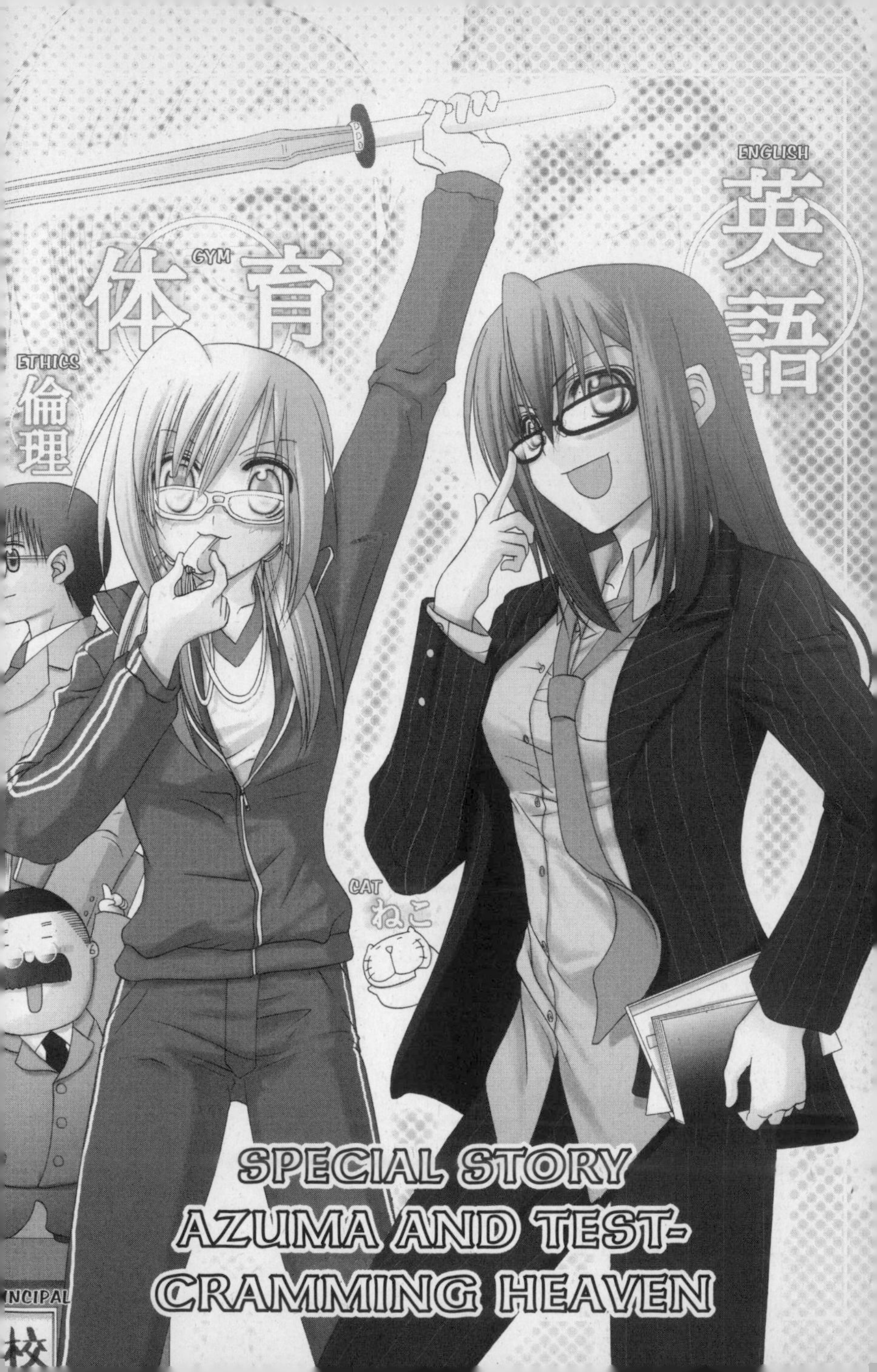
ENGLISH
英語
GYM
体育
ETHICS
倫理
CAT
ねこ
NCIPAL
校
SPECIAL STORY
AZUMA AND TEST-
CRAMMING HEAVEN

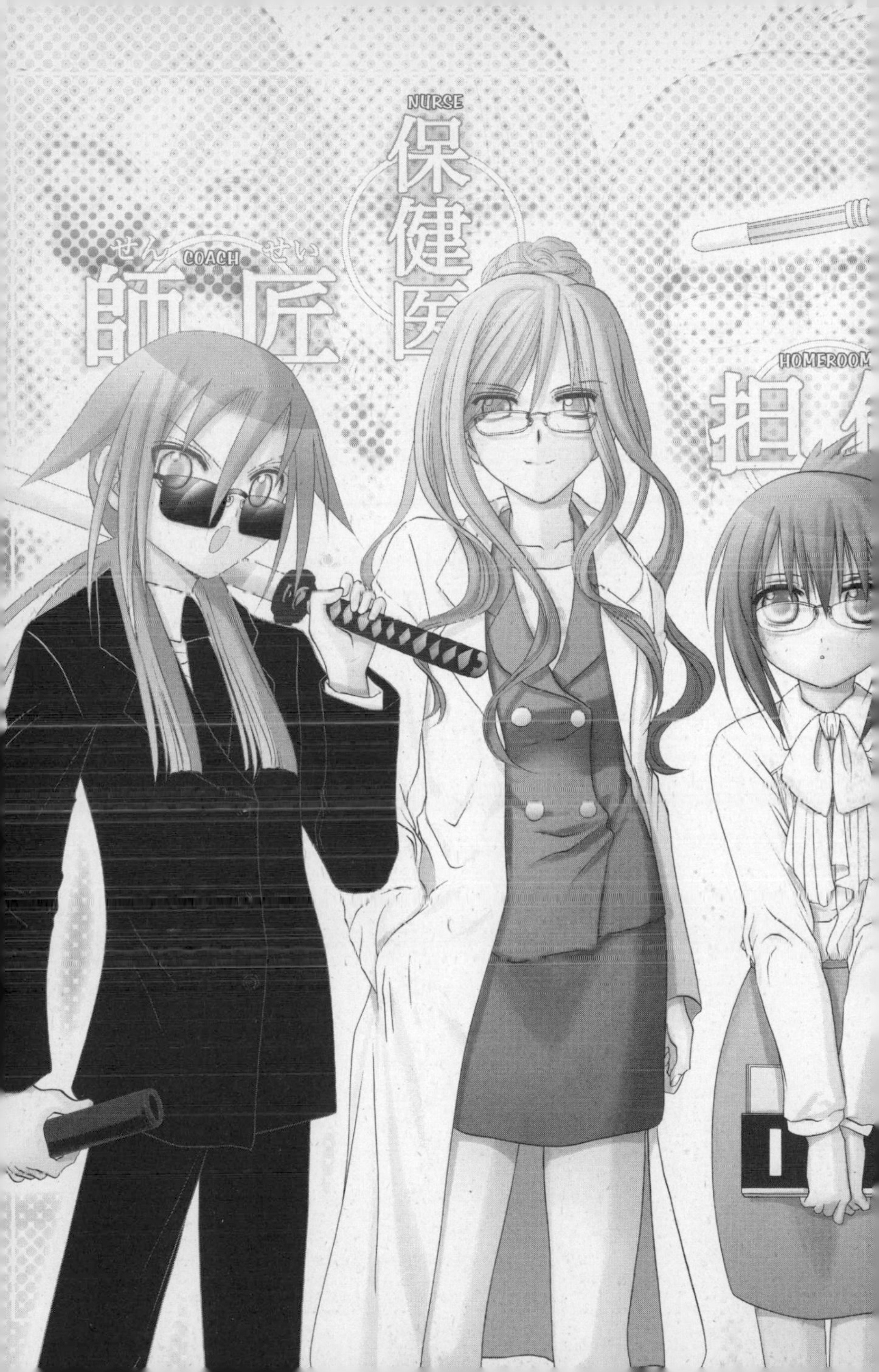
HOMEROOM
担
NURSE
保健医
COACH
師匠（せんせい）

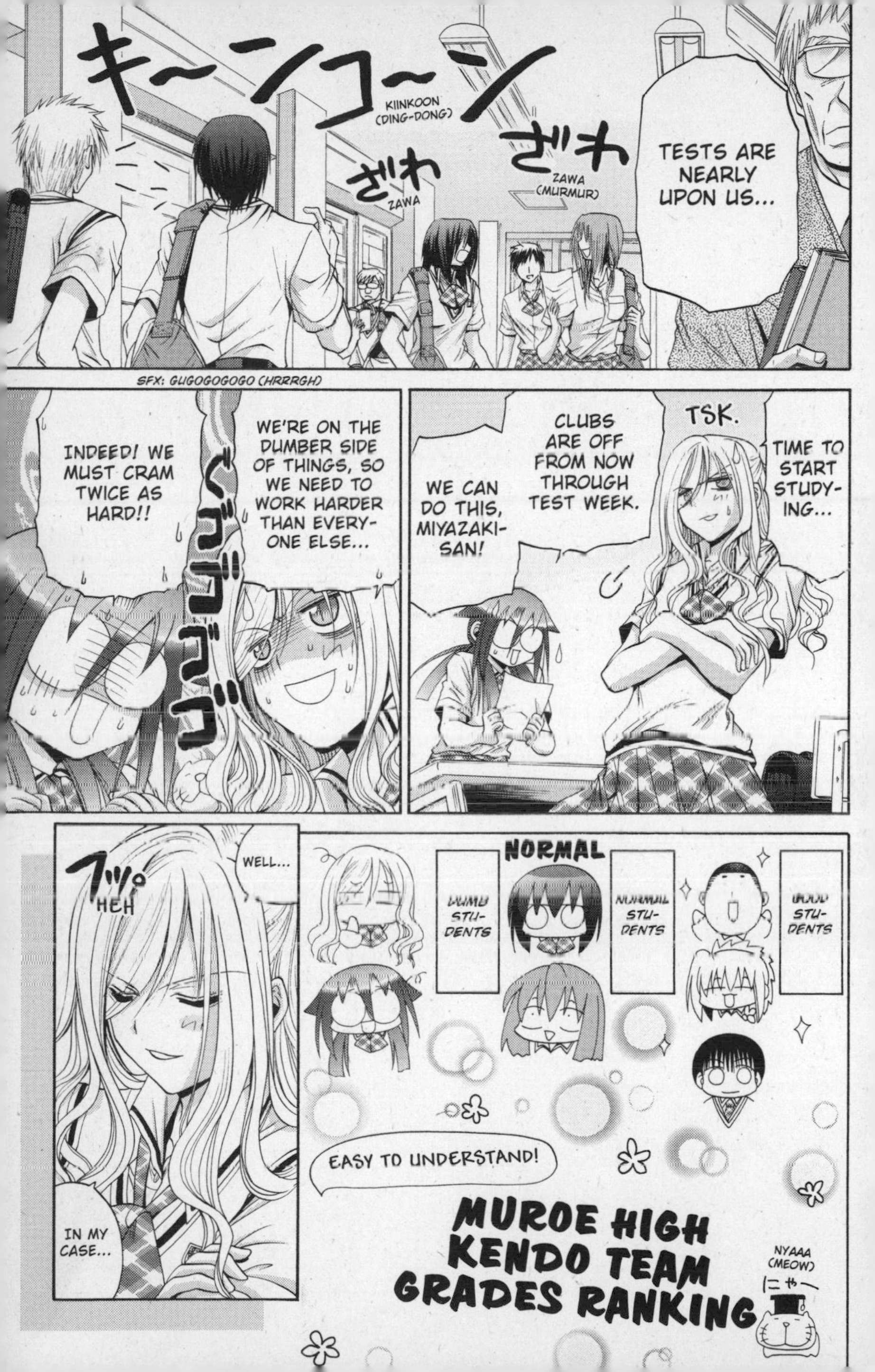

キ~ンコ~ン
KIINKOON (DING-DONG)
ざわ
ZAWA (MURMUR)
ざわ
ZAWA
TESTS ARE NEARLY UPON US...
SFX: GUGOGOGOGO (HRRRGH)
TSK.
TIME TO START STUDYING...
CLUBS ARE OFF FROM NOW THROUGH TEST WEEK.
WE CAN DO THIS, MIYAZAKI-SAN!
WE'RE ON THE DUMBER SIDE OF THINGS, SO WE NEED TO WORK HARDER THAN EVERYONE ELSE...
INDEED! WE MUST CRAM TWICE AS HARD!!
ぐゴゴゴゴ
GOOD STUDENTS
NORMAL
NORMAL STUDENTS
DUMB STUDENTS
EASY TO UNDERSTAND!
MUROE HIGH KENDO TEAM GRADES RANKING
NYAAA (MEOW)
にゃー
WELL...
フッ
HEH
IN MY CASE...

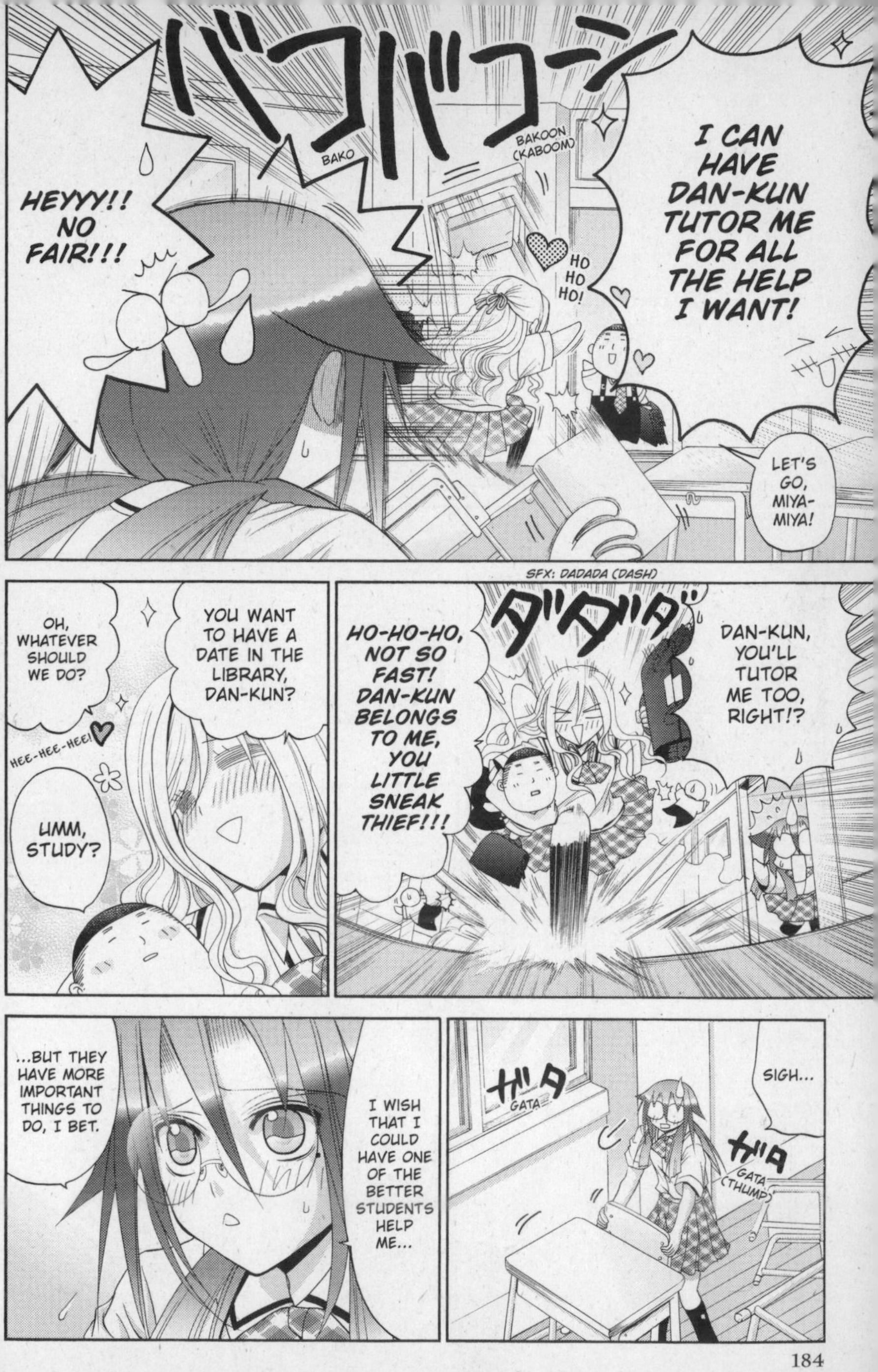

I CAN HAVE DAN-KUN TUTOR ME FOR ALL THE HELP I WANT!
バコバコーン
BAKOON (KABOOM)
HO HO HO!
BAKO
LET'S GO, MIYA-MIYA!
HEYYY!! NO FAIR!!!
DAN-KUN, YOU'LL TUTOR ME TOO, RIGHT!?
ダダダ
SFX: DADADA (DASH)
HO-HO-HO, NOT SO FAST! DAN-KUN BELONGS TO ME, YOU LITTLE SNEAK THIEF!!!
YOU WANT TO HAVE A DATE IN THE LIBRARY, DAN-KUN?
OH, WHATEVER SHOULD WE DO?
HEE-HEE-HEE!
UMM, STUDY?
SIGH...
ガタ
GATA
ガタ
GATA (THUMP)
I WISH THAT I COULD HAVE ONE OF THE BETTER STUDENTS HELP ME...
...BUT THEY HAVE MORE IMPORTANT THINGS TO DO, I BET.

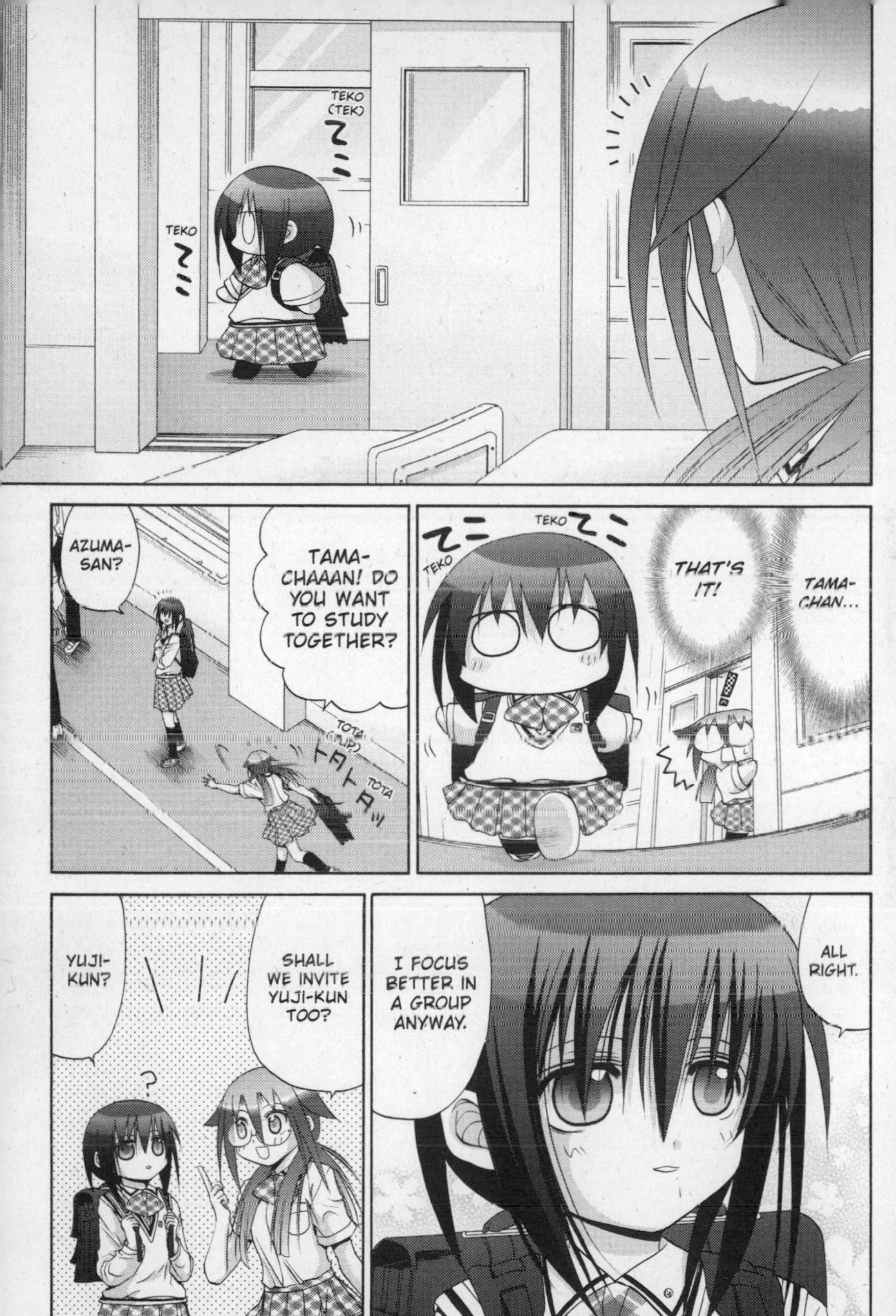
TEKO (TEK)
TEKO
TAMA-CHAN...
THAT'S IT!
TEKO
TEKO
TAMA-CHAAAN! DO YOU WANT TO STUDY TOGETHER?
AZUMA-SAN?
TOTA (SLIP)
TOTA
ALL RIGHT.
I FOCUS BETTER IN A GROUP ANYWAY.
SHALL WE INVITE YUJI-KUN TOO?
YUJI-KUN?

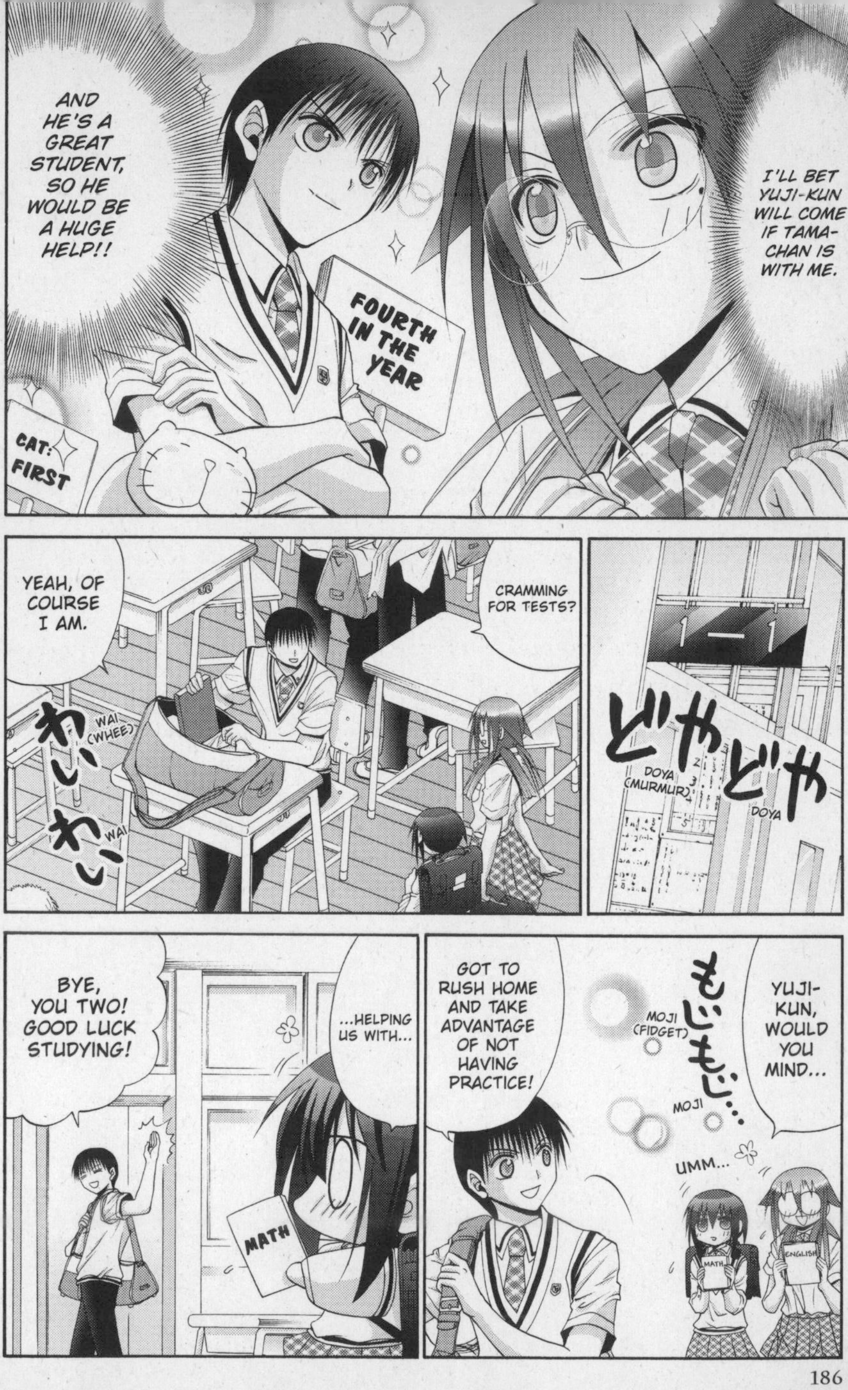
I'LL BET YUJI-KUN WILL COME IF TAMA-CHAN IS WITH ME.
AND HE'S A GREAT STUDENT, SO HE WOULD BE A HUGE HELP!!
FOURTH IN THE YEAR
CAT: FIRST
どやどや
DOYA (MURMUR)
DOYA
1—1
CRAMMING FOR TESTS?
YEAH, OF COURSE I AM.
わいわい
WAI (WHEE)
WAI
YUJI-KUN, WOULD YOU MIND...
もじもじ...
MOJI (FIDGET)
MOJI
GOT TO RUSH HOME AND TAKE ADVANTAGE OF NOT HAVING PRACTICE!
UMM...
ENGLISH
MATH
...HELPING US WITH...
MATH
BYE, YOU TWO! GOOD LUCK STUDYING!

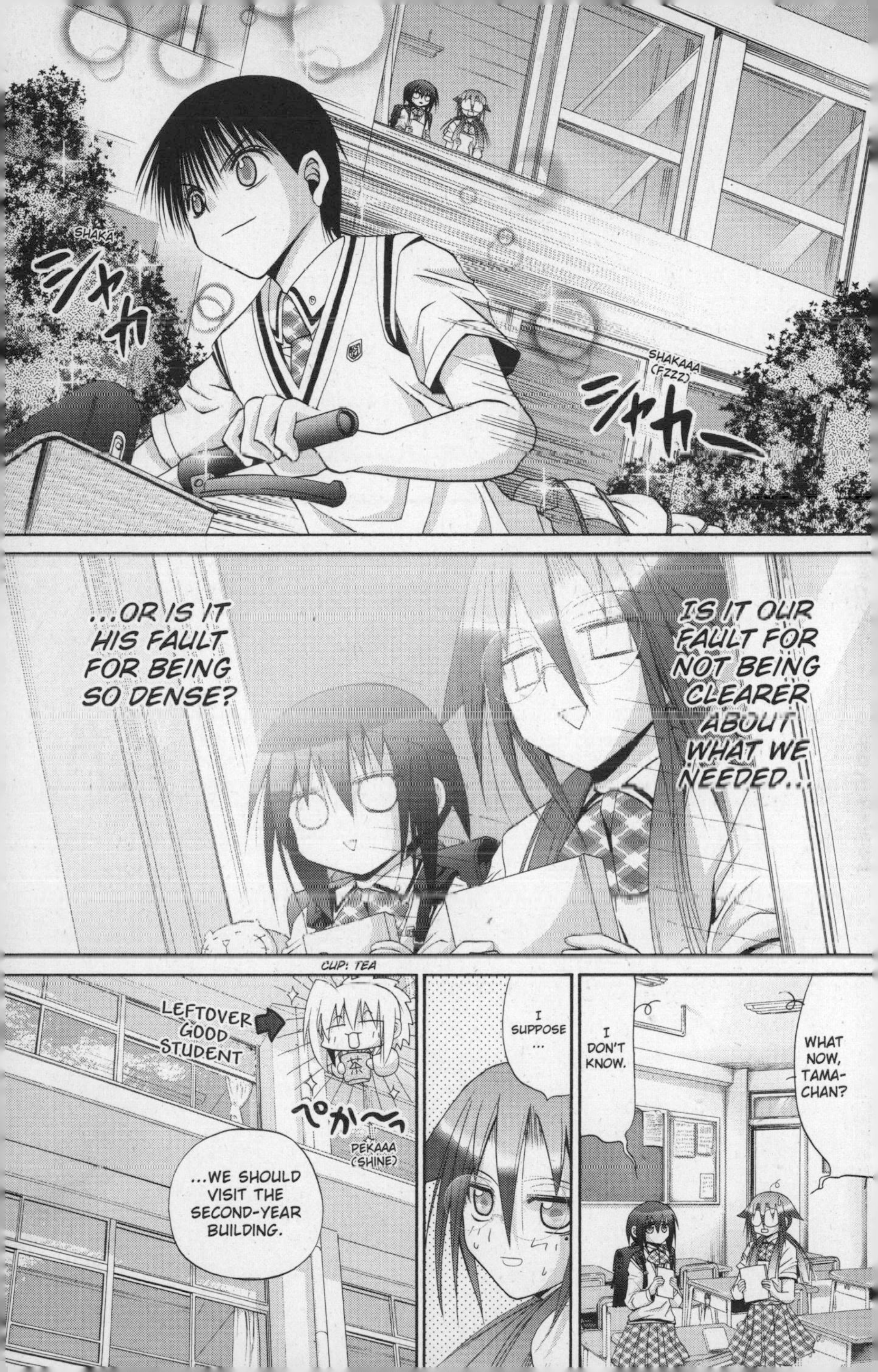
シャカ
SHAKA
シャカー
SHAKAAA (FZZZ)
IS IT OUR FAULT FOR NOT BEING CLEARER ABOUT WHAT WE NEEDED...
...OR IS IT HIS FAULT FOR BEING SO DENSE?
WHAT NOW, TAMA-CHAN?
I DON'T KNOW.
I SUPPOSE ...
CUP: TEA
LEFTOVER GOOD STUDENT
茶
ぺか〜っ
PEKAAA (SHINE)
...WE SHOULD VISIT THE SECOND-YEAR BUILDING.

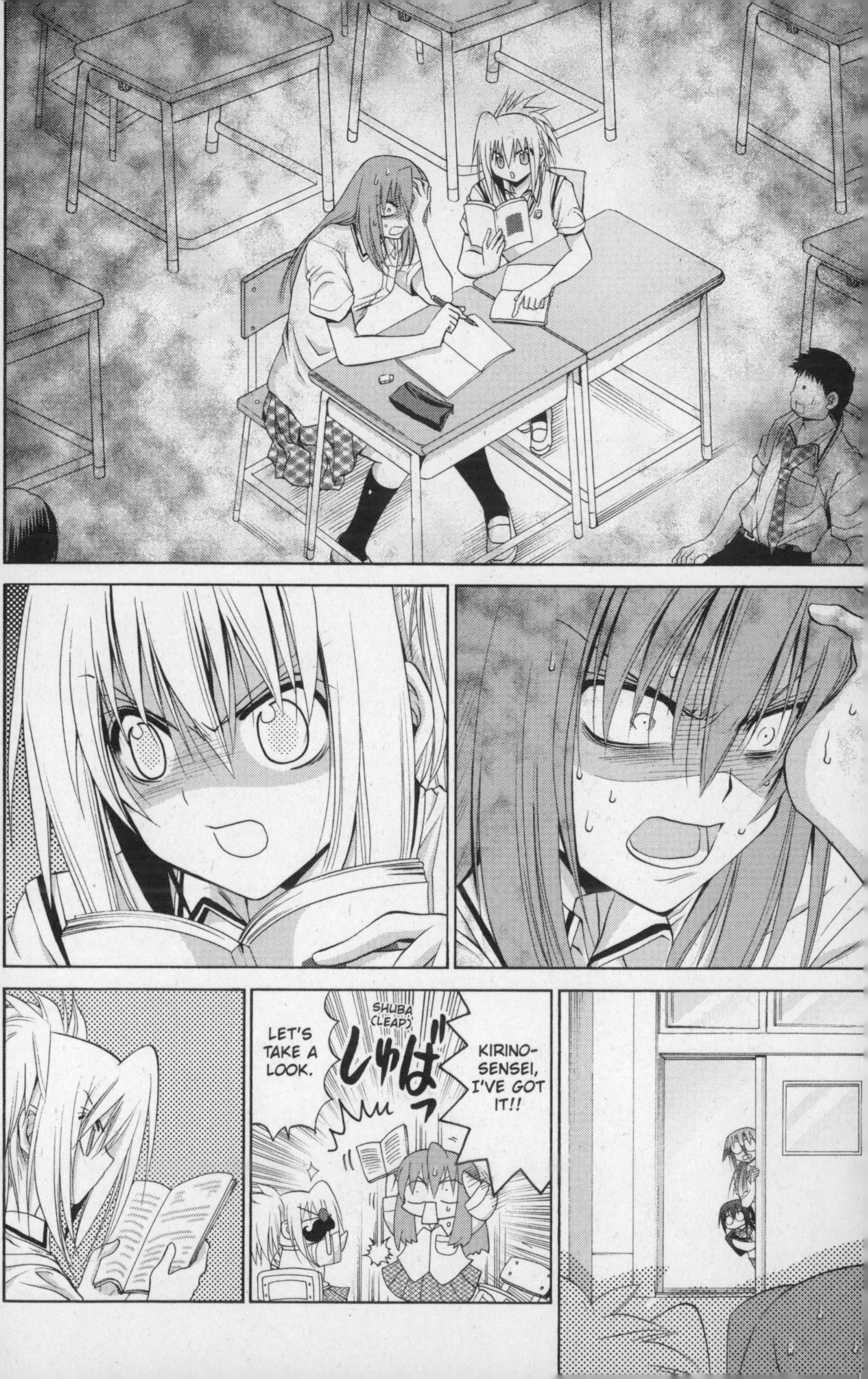

SHUBA (LEAP)
しゅばっ
KIRINO-SENSEI, I'VE GOT IT!!
LET'S TAKE A LOOK.

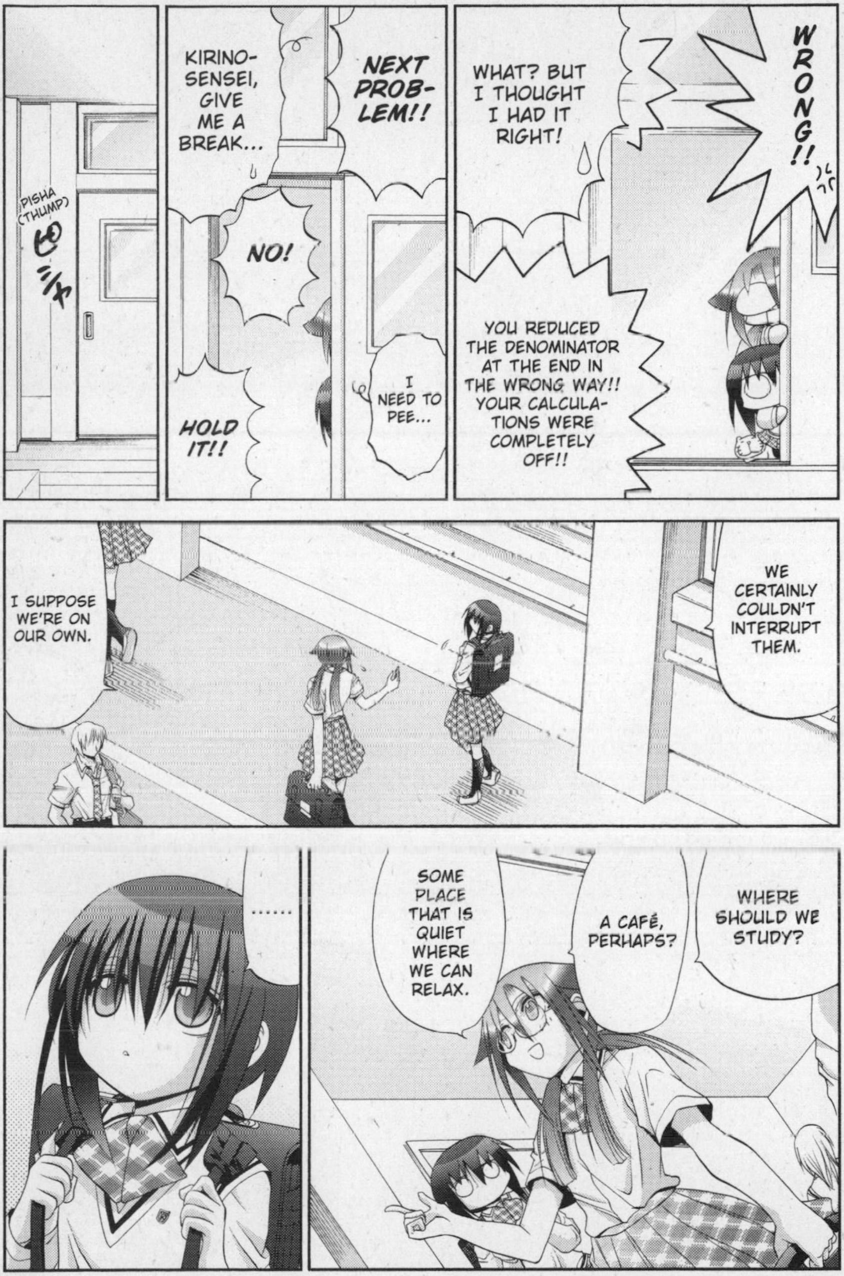
WRONG!!
WHAT? BUT I THOUGHT I HAD IT RIGHT!
YOU REDUCED THE DENOMINATOR AT THE END IN THE WRONG WAY!! YOUR CALCULATIONS WERE COMPLETELY OFF!!
NEXT PROBLEM!!
KIRINO-SENSEI, GIVE ME A BREAK...
NO!
I NEED TO PEE...
HOLD IT!!
PISHA (THUMP)
ピシャ
WE CERTAINLY COULDN'T INTERRUPT THEM.
I SUPPOSE WE'RE ON OUR OWN.
WHERE SHOULD WE STUDY?
A CAFÉ, PERHAPS?
SOME PLACE THAT IS QUIET WHERE WE CAN RELAX.
......

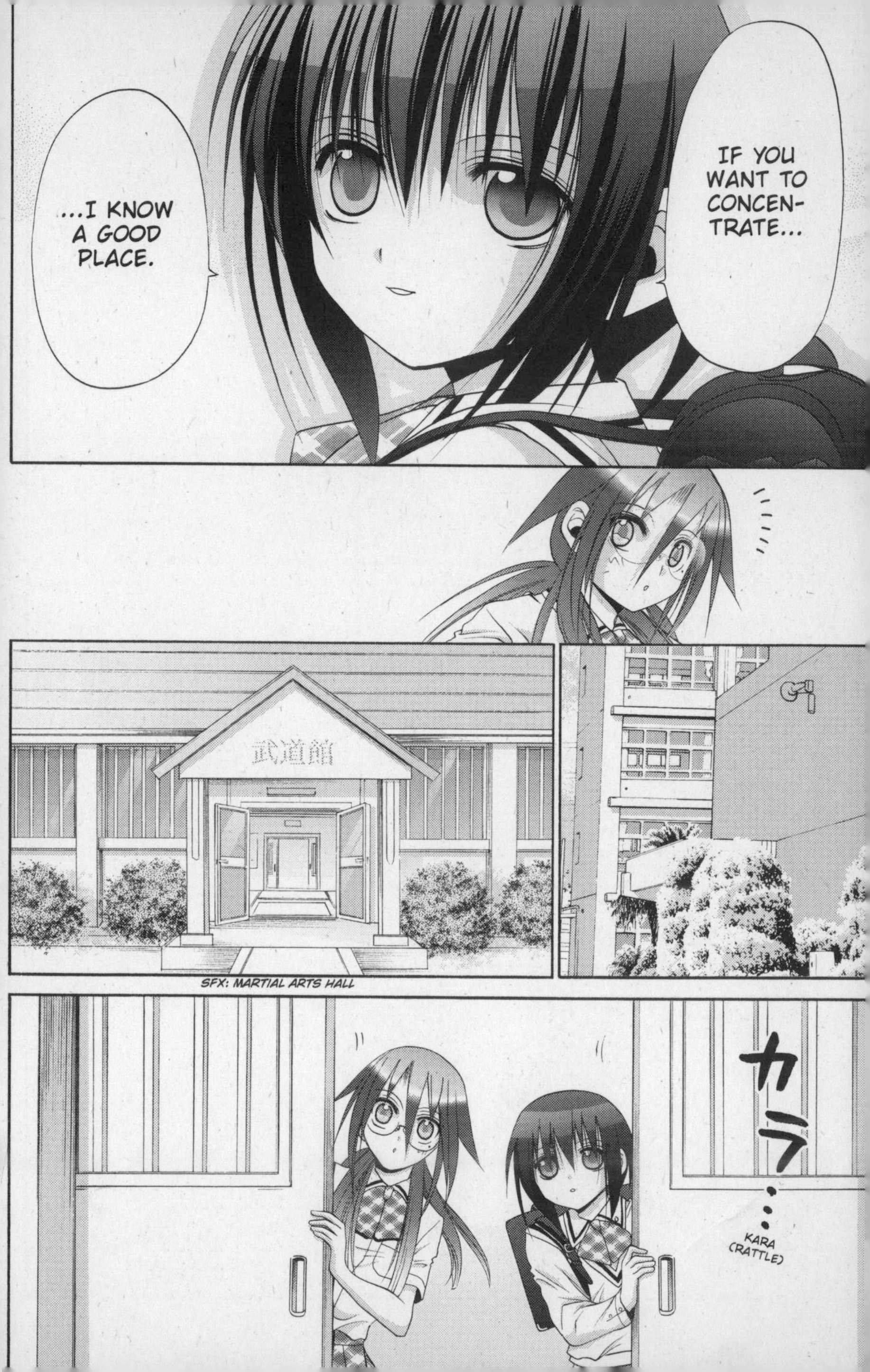
IF YOU WANT TO CONCEN-TRATE...
...I KNOW A GOOD PLACE.
武道館
SFX: MARTIAL ARTS HALL
カラ…
KARA (RATTLE)

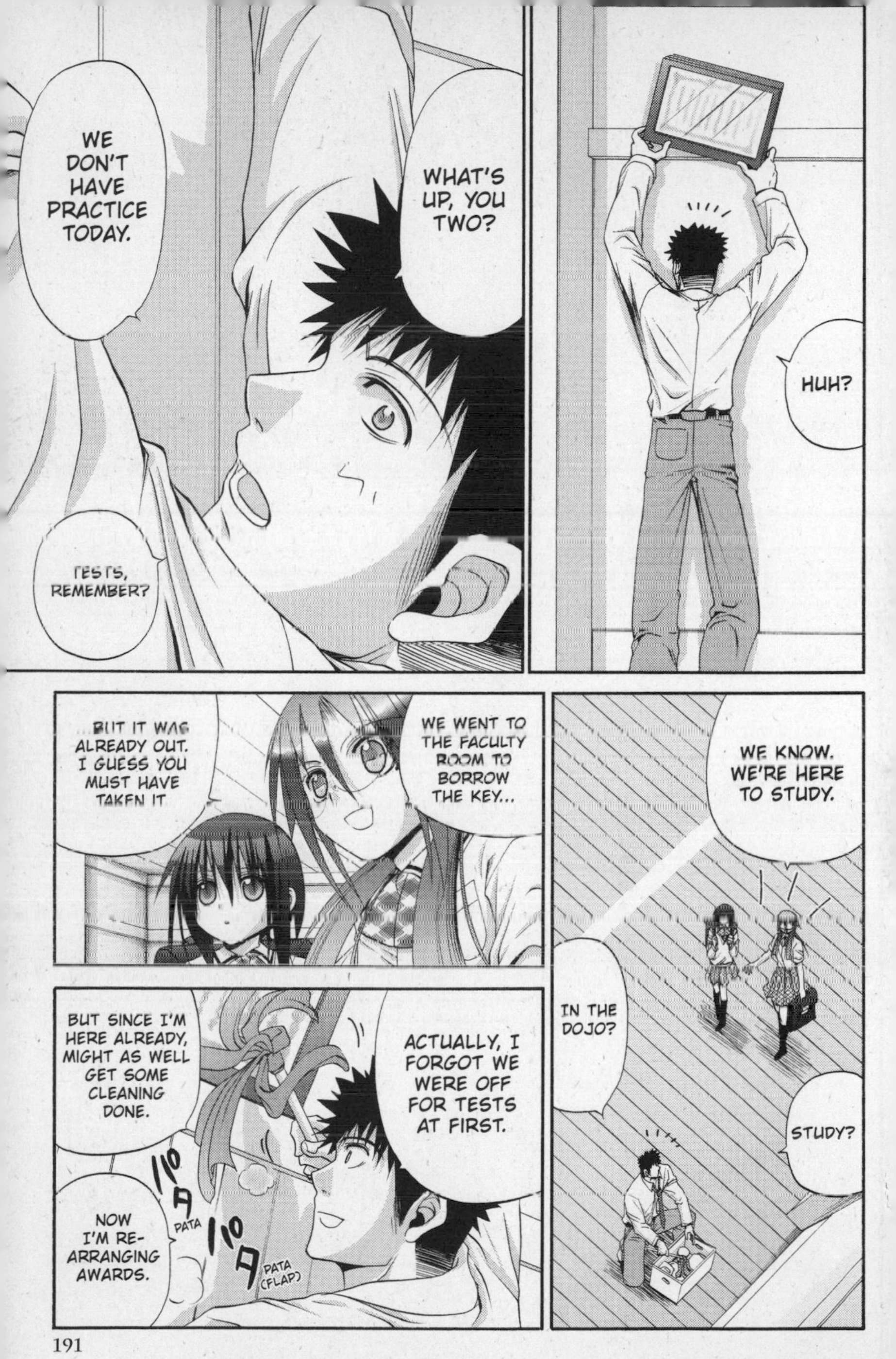
HUH?
WHAT'S UP, YOU TWO?
WE DON'T HAVE PRACTICE TODAY.
TESTS, REMEMBER?
WE KNOW. WE'RE HERE TO STUDY.
IN THE DOJO?
STUDY?
WE WENT TO THE FACULTY ROOM TO BORROW THE KEY...
...BUT IT WAS ALREADY OUT. I GUESS YOU MUST HAVE TAKEN IT.
ACTUALLY, I FORGOT WE WERE OFF FOR TESTS AT FIRST.
BUT SINCE I'M HERE ALREADY, MIGHT AS WELL GET SOME CLEANING DONE.
パタ PATA
パタ PATA (FLAP)
NOW I'M RE-ARRANGING AWARDS.

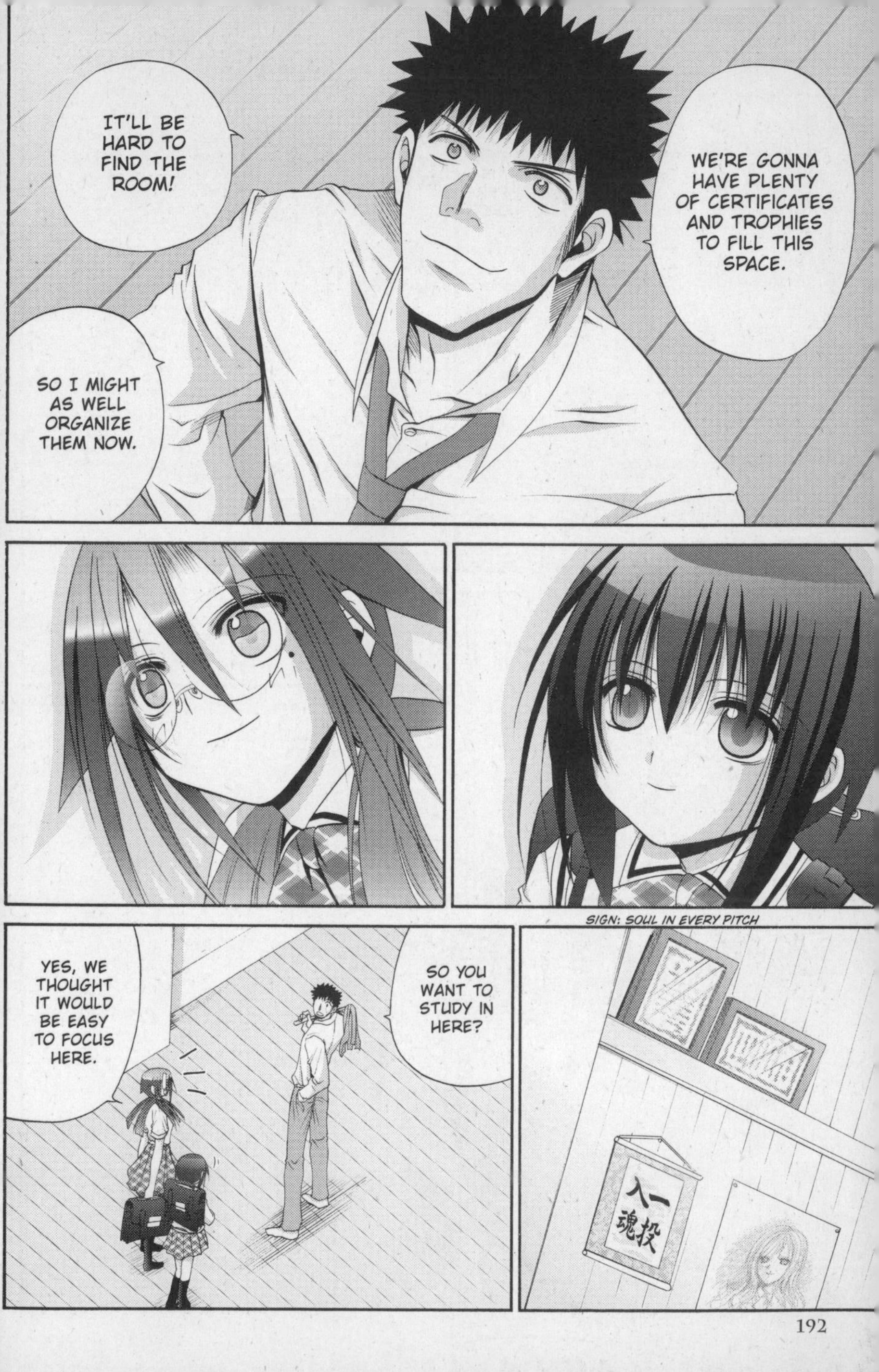
WE'RE GONNA HAVE PLENTY OF CERTIFICATES AND TROPHIES TO FILL THIS SPACE.
IT'LL BE HARD TO FIND THE ROOM!
SO I MIGHT AS WELL ORGANIZE THEM NOW.
SIGN: SOUL IN EVERY PITCH
一投入魂
SO YOU WANT TO STUDY IN HERE?
YES, WE THOUGHT IT WOULD BE EASY TO FOCUS HERE.

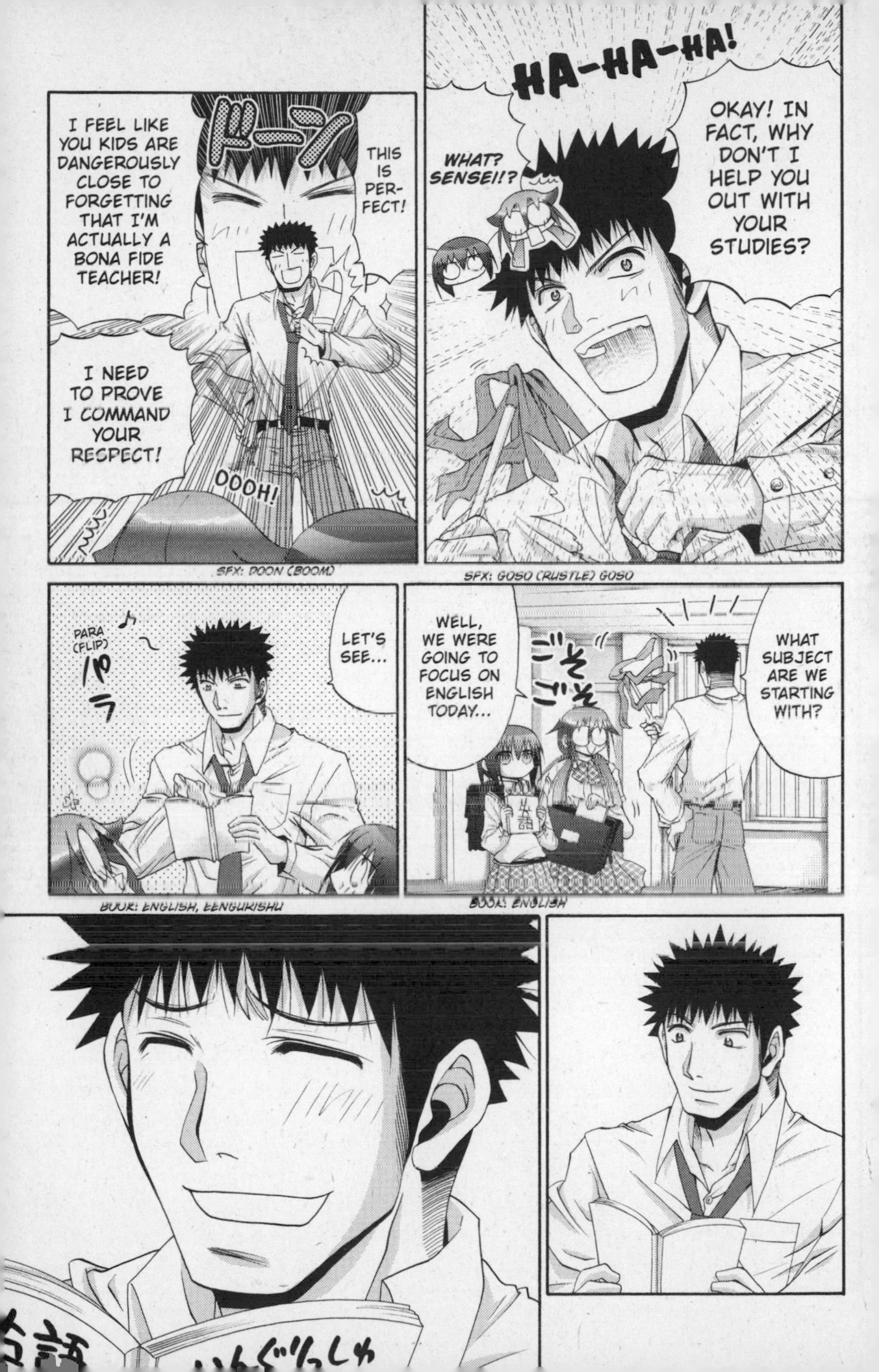
HA-HA-HA-HA!
OKAY! IN FACT, WHY DON'T I HELP YOU OUT WITH YOUR STUDIES?
WHAT? SENSEI!?
SFX: GOSO (RUSTLE) GOSO
I FEEL LIKE YOU KIDS ARE DANGEROUSLY CLOSE TO FORGETTING THAT I'M ACTUALLY A BONA FIDE TEACHER!
THIS IS PER-FECT!
I NEED TO PROVE I COMMAND YOUR RESPECT!
OOOH!
SFX: DOON (BOOM)
WHAT SUBJECT ARE WE STARTING WITH?
WELL, WE WERE GOING TO FOCUS ON ENGLISH TODAY...
BOOK: ENGLISH
LET'S SEE...
PARA (FLIP)
BOOK: ENGLISH, EENGURISHU

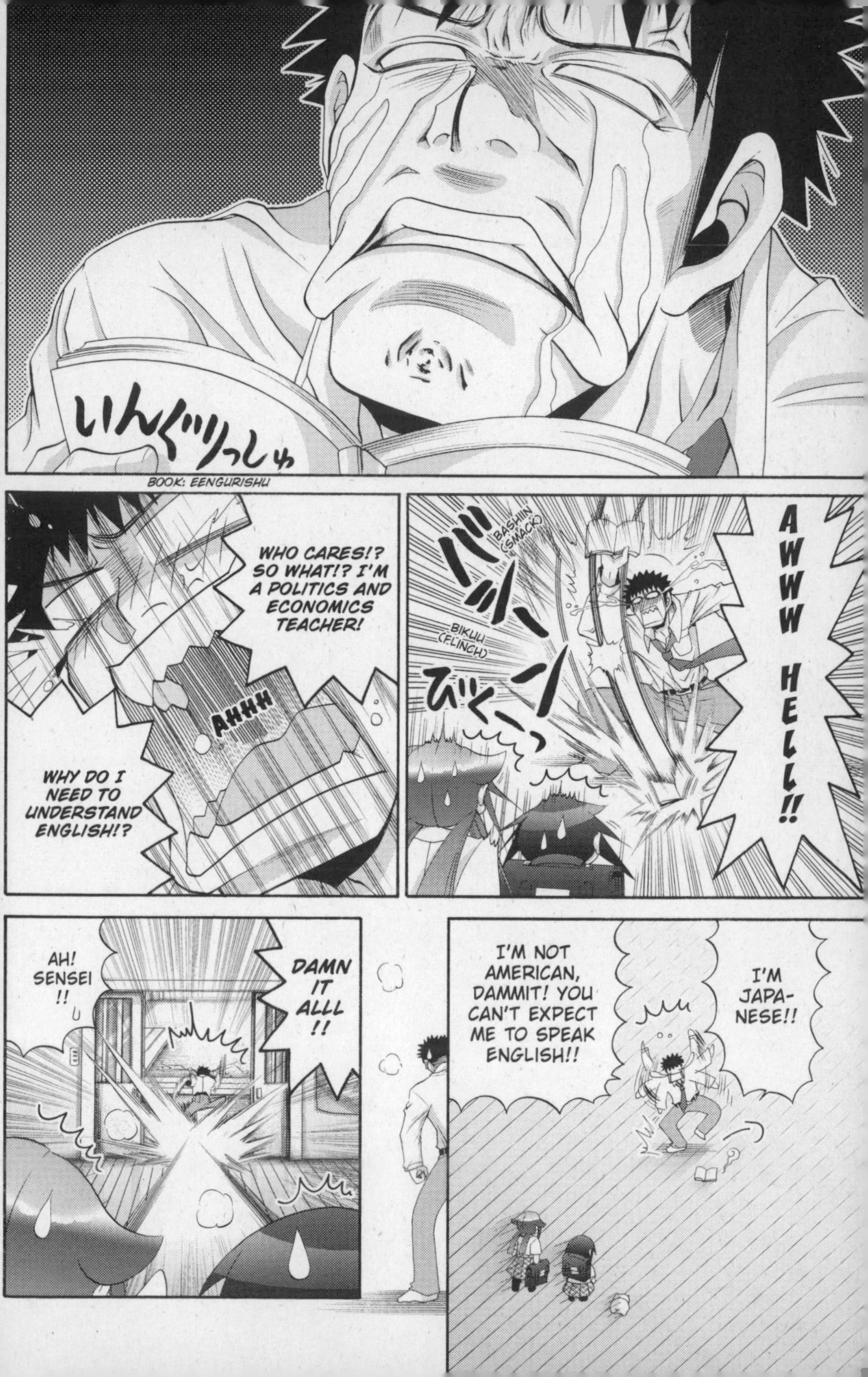
いんぐりっしゅ
BOOK: EENGURISHU
AWWW HELL!!
バシーン
BASHIN (SMACK)
BIKUU (FLINCH)
びくーっ
WHO CARES!? SO WHAT!? I'M A POLITICS AND ECONOMICS TEACHER!
AHHH
WHY DO I NEED TO UNDERSTAND ENGLISH!?
I'M JAPA-NESE!!
I'M NOT AMERICAN, DAMMIT! YOU CAN'T EXPECT ME TO SPEAK ENGLISH!!
DAMN IT ALLL!!
AH! SENSEI!!

TRANSLATION NOTES

Common Honorifics
No honorific: Indicates familiarity or closeness; if used without permission or reason, addressing someone in this manner would constitute an insult.
-san: The Japanese equivalent of Mr./Mrs./Miss. If a situation calls for politeness, this is the fail-safe honorific.
-sama: Conveys great respect; may also indicate that the social status of the speaker is lower than that of the addressee.
-kun: Used most often when referring to boys, this indicates affection or familiarity. Occasionally used by older men among their peers, but it may also be used by anyone referring to a person of lower standing.
-chan: An affectionate honorific indicating familiarity used mostly in reference to girls; also used in reference to cute persons or animals of either gender.
-senpai: Used as a suffix or alone to address one's upperclassmen.
kouhai: The opposite of *senpai*, used to address younger schoolmates or team members.
-sensei: A respectful term for teachers, artists, or high-level professionals.

Page 23
Bromide: A high-quality, usually promotional photograph of a celebrity. The name is based on the term "bromide paper," a type of photograph paper that contains the chemical bromide. These glossy photos were first advertised in Japan using the term bromide, and the name stuck, even when actual bromide paper isn't used.

Page 29
Shamoji: A large, flat paddle used specifically for stirring and serving rice.

Page 38
Hoichi the Earless: A figure from Japanese mythology, Hoichi the Earless was a blind minstrel haunted by ghosts that tricked him into thinking he was performing music for a feudal lord every night. When a priest discovered the treachery, he painted the kanji for a protective sutra all over Hoichi's body, only forgetting to cover his ears. When Hoichi was next visited by the ghosts and the sutra protected his body, they ripped off his exposed ears in rage.

Page 43
Ochugen: A gift-giving occasion centered around July 15th. Gifts are delivered to people to whom the giver owes a formal or personal debt, such as a physician, a teacher, a helpful relative, etc. Perhaps *Ochugen Cop* is a hard-boiled detective who never forgets to display his appreciation.

Page 53
Gyokuryuuki: A famous, real-life high school kendo meet that is held annually in the city of Fukuoka in Kyushu. The Shouryuuki meet depicted in Volume 1 of *Bamboo Blade* was originally an homage to this tournament.

Page 115
Manju: A traditional confection consisting of a rounded, steamed bun made of flour and rice powder with a sweet filling inside, typically a sweet red bean paste (*anko*).

Page 126
Takijun: In Japanese, nicknames given to people, bands, TV shows, games, anime, and so on are often abbreviated in a way that takes the first syllable or two of each word into a short and catchy phrase. The "Takijun" shown here is easy to understand when you see the name Junya Takigawa placed in its original Japanese order of family name first and given name last: **Taki**-gawa **Jun**-ya. (The show *Burnish Academy* is the same deal: it's an abbreviation of the fictional comedy duo that hosts it, **Burni**-ng Da-**sh**.)

BAMBOO BLADE
バンブーブレード

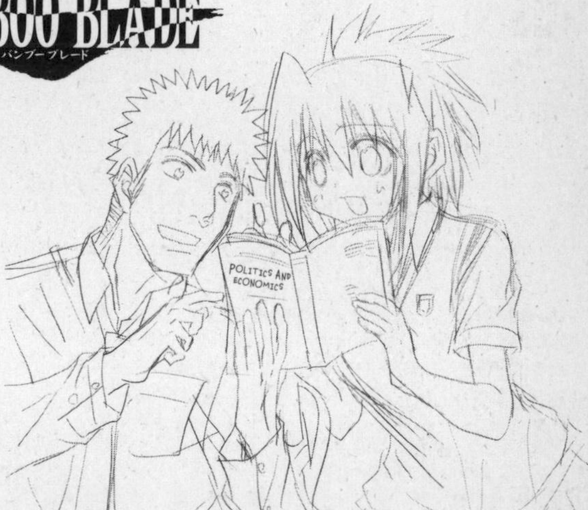
POLITICS AND
ECONOMICS

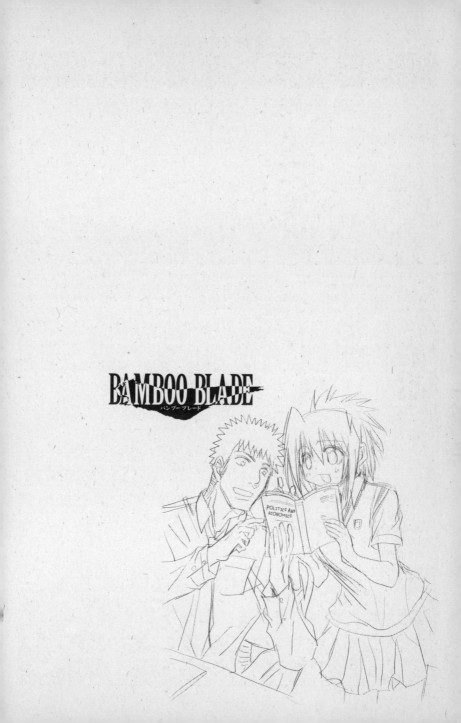

OMAKE MANGA THEATER ❶

SAYAKO AND THE RETURN OF THE FAMILY MEETING

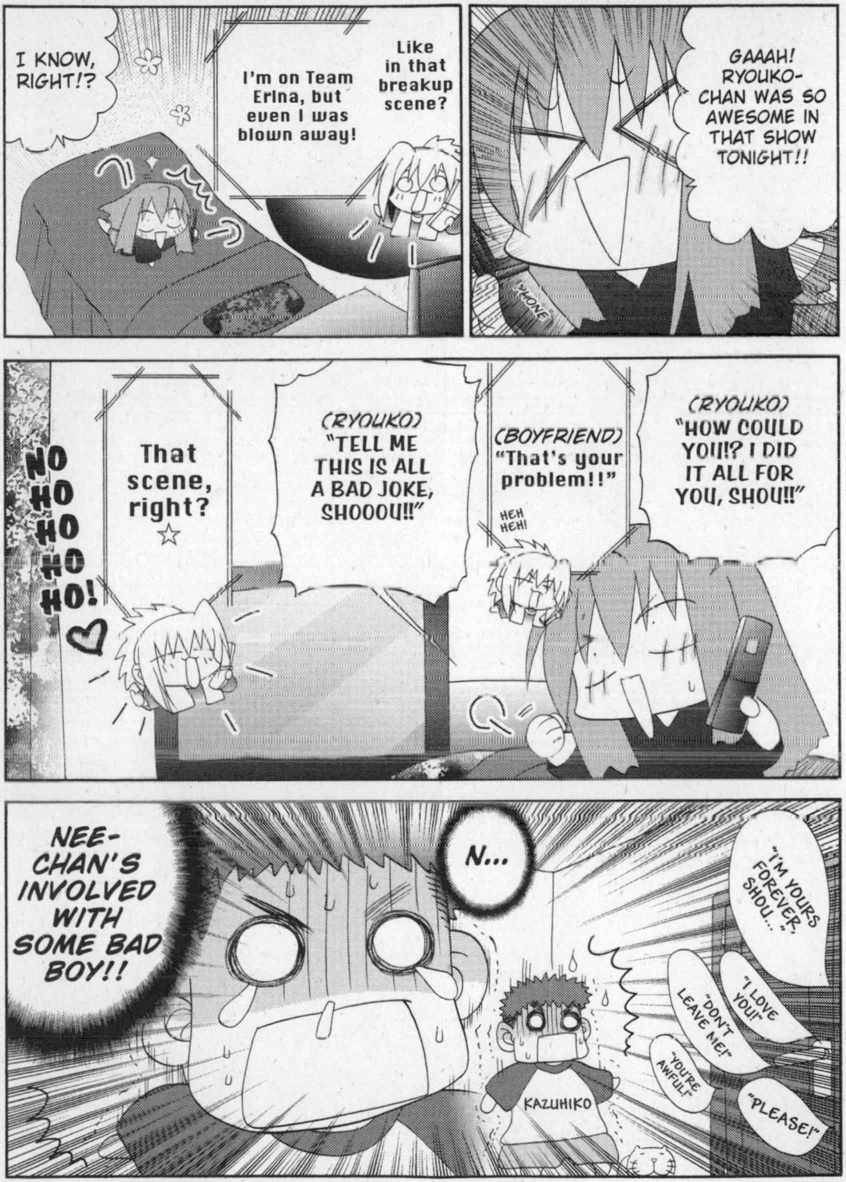
GAAAH! RYOUKO-CHAN WAS SO AWESOME IN THAT SHOW TONIGHT!!
Like in that breakup scene?
I'm on Team Erina, but even I was blown away!
I KNOW, RIGHT!?
(RYOUKO) "HOW COULD YOU!? I DID IT ALL FOR YOU, SHOU!!"
(BOYFRIEND) "That's your problem!!"
HEH HEH!
(RYOUKO) "TELL ME THIS IS ALL A BAD JOKE, SHOOOU!!"
That scene, right? ☆
NO HO HO HO HO HO! ♥
"I'M YOURS FOREVER, SHOU..."
"I LOVE YOU!"
"DON'T LEAVE ME!"
"PLEASE!"
"YOU'RE AWFUL!"
N...
NEE-CHAN'S INVOLVED WITH SOME BAD BOY!!
KAZUHIKO

OMAKE MANGA THEATER ❷

SATORI AND THE UNREMOVABLE MEMO

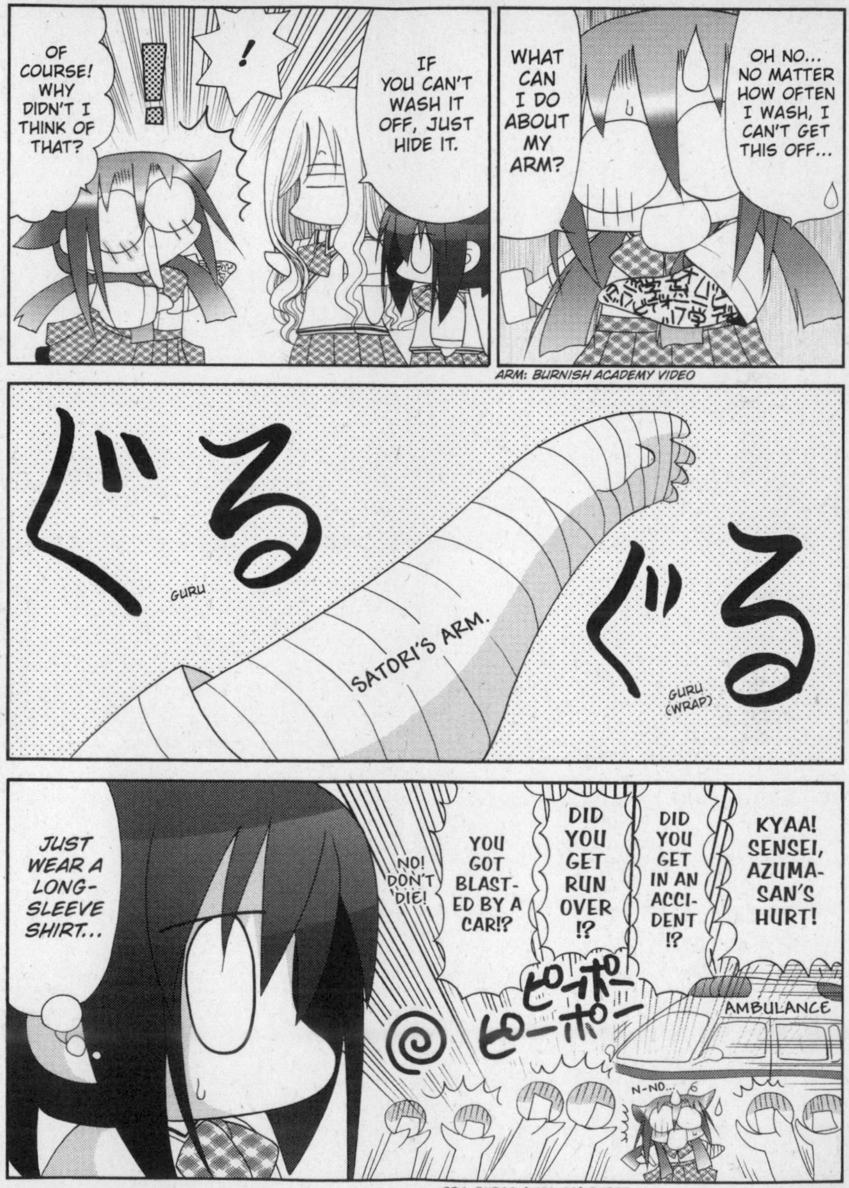
OH NO... NO MATTER HOW OFTEN I WASH, I CAN'T GET THIS OFF...
WHAT CAN I DO ABOUT MY ARM?
IF YOU CAN'T WASH IT OFF, JUST HIDE IT.
!
OF COURSE! WHY DIDN'T I THINK OF THAT?
ぐる
GURU (WRAP)
SATORI'S ARM.
ぐる
GURU
KYAA! SENSEI, AZUMA-SAN'S HURT!
DID YOU GET IN AN ACCIDENT!?
DID YOU GET RUN OVER!?
YOU GOT BLASTED BY A CAR!?
NO! DON'T DIE!
AMBULANCE
ピーポーピーポー
N-NO...
JUST WEAR A LONG-SLEEVE SHIRT...

ARM: BURNISH ACADEMY VIDEO

SFX: PIIPOO (WEE-OO) PIIPOO

OMAKE MANGA THEATER ③

FATHER AND DAUGHTER'S COOKING

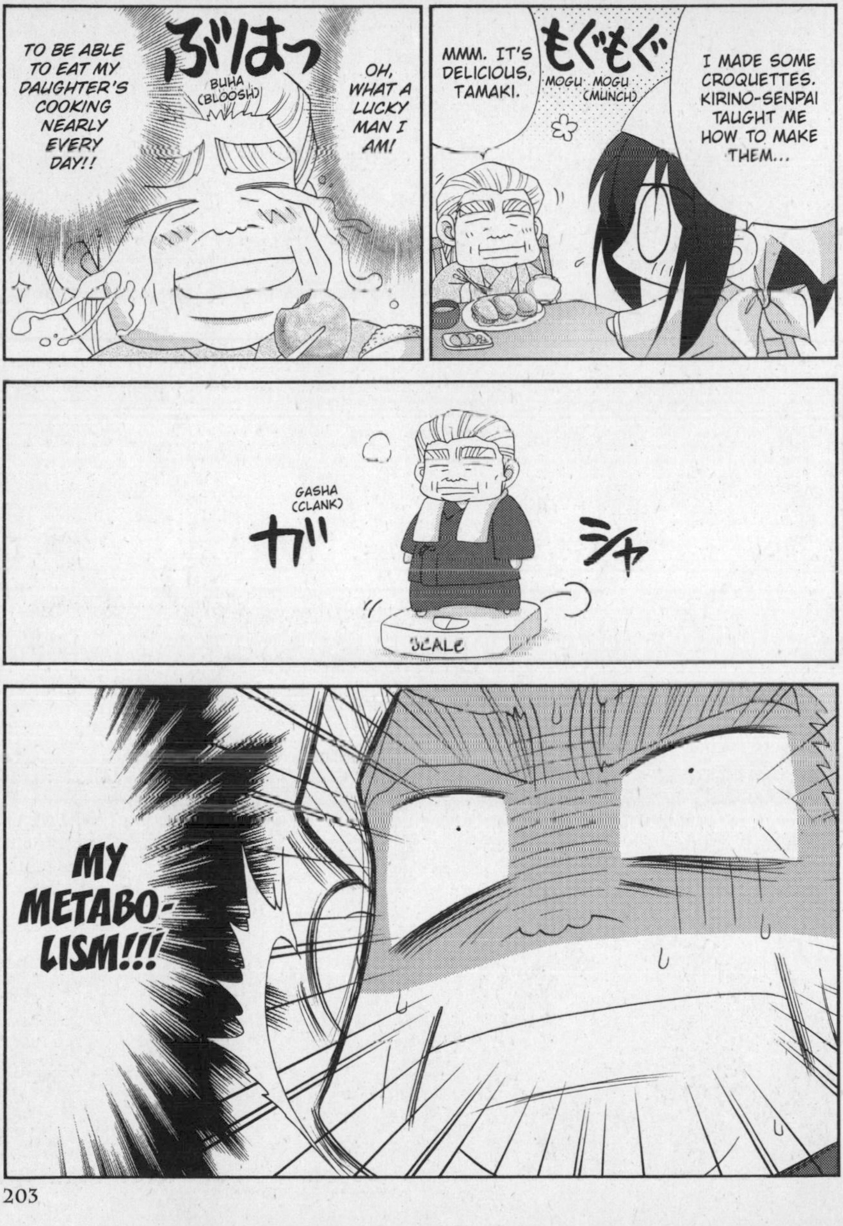
I MADE SOME CROQUETTES. KIRINO-SENPAI TAUGHT ME HOW TO MAKE THEM...
もぐもぐ
MOGU MOGU (MUNCH)
MMM. IT'S DELICIOUS, TAMAKI.
ぶはっ
BUHA (BLOOSH)
OH, WHAT A LUCKY MAN I AM!
TO BE ABLE TO EAT MY DAUGHTER'S COOKING NEARLY EVERY DAY!!
ガシャ
GASHA (CLANK)
SCALE
MY METABO-LISM!!!

OMAKE MANGA THEATER ④

TERAMOTO-SENSEI AND THE BAD STUDENTS

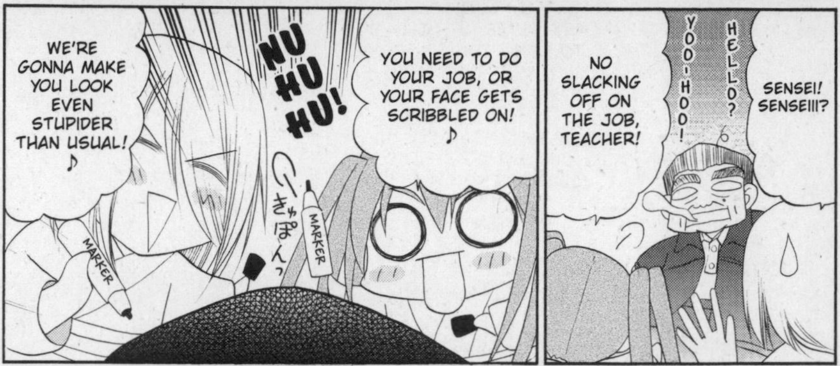
SENSEI! SENSEIII?
HELLO?
YOO-HOO!
NO SLACKING OFF ON THE JOB, TEACHER!
YOU NEED TO DO YOUR JOB, OR YOUR FACE GETS SCRIBBLED ON! ♪
NU HU HU!
きゅぽんっ
MARKER
WE'RE GONNA MAKE YOU LOOK EVEN STUPIDER THAN USUAL! ♪
MARKER

SFX: KYUPON (POP)

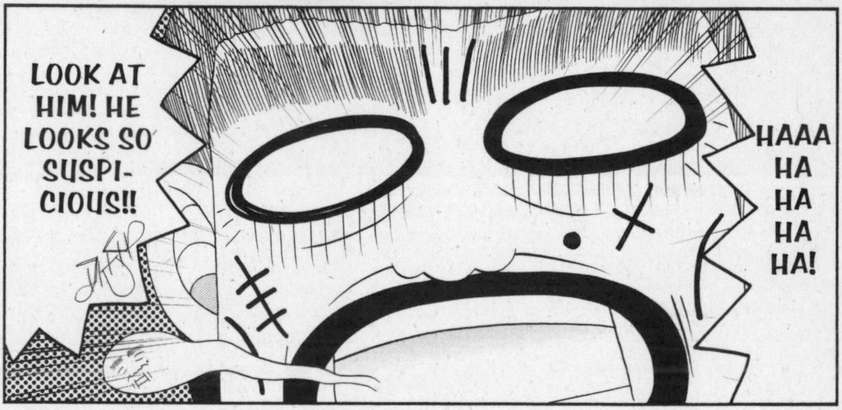
HAAA HA HA HA HA!
LOOK AT HIM! HE LOOKS SO SUSPI-CIOUS!!

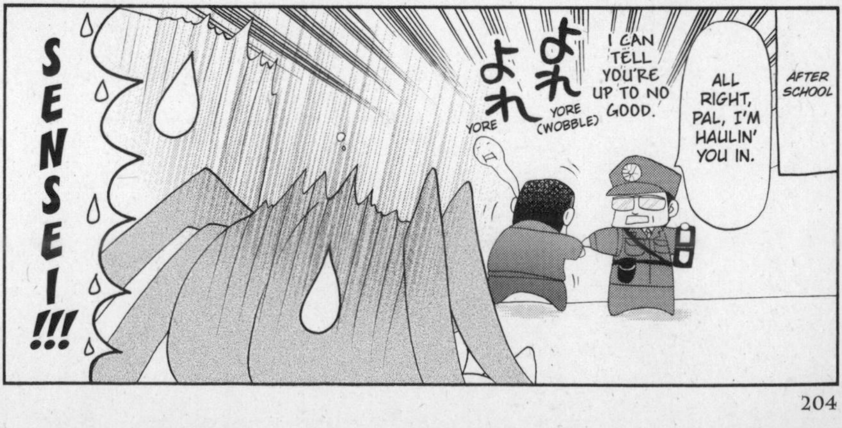
AFTER SCHOOL
ALL RIGHT, PAL, I'M HAULIN' YOU IN.
I CAN TELL YOU'RE UP TO NO GOOD.
よれ よれ
YORE YORE (WOBBLE)
SENSEI!!!

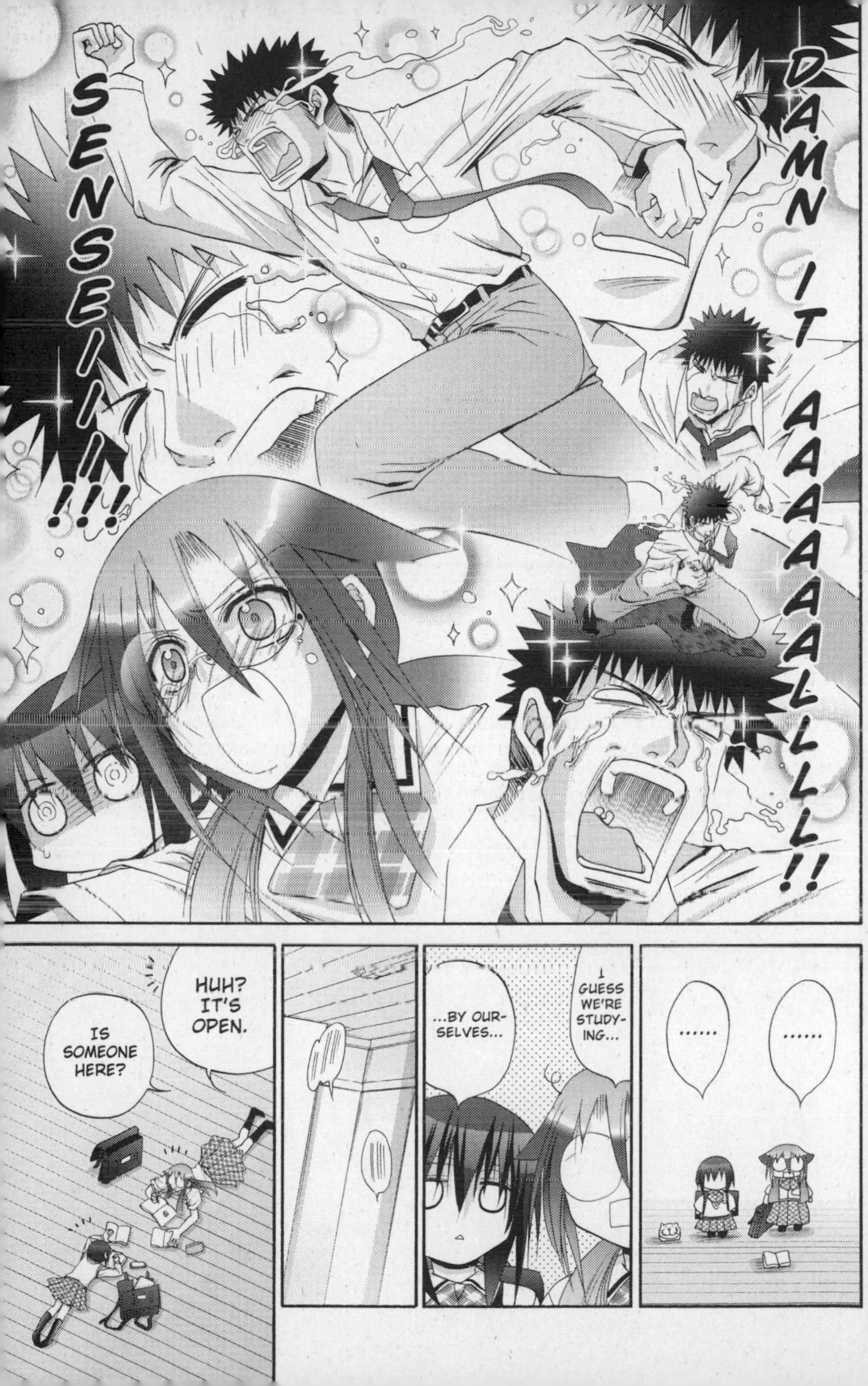
DAMN IT AAAAAALLLL!!
SENSEIII!!!
......
......
I GUESS WE'RE STUDYING...
...BY OURSELVES...
HUH? IT'S OPEN.
IS SOMEONE HERE?

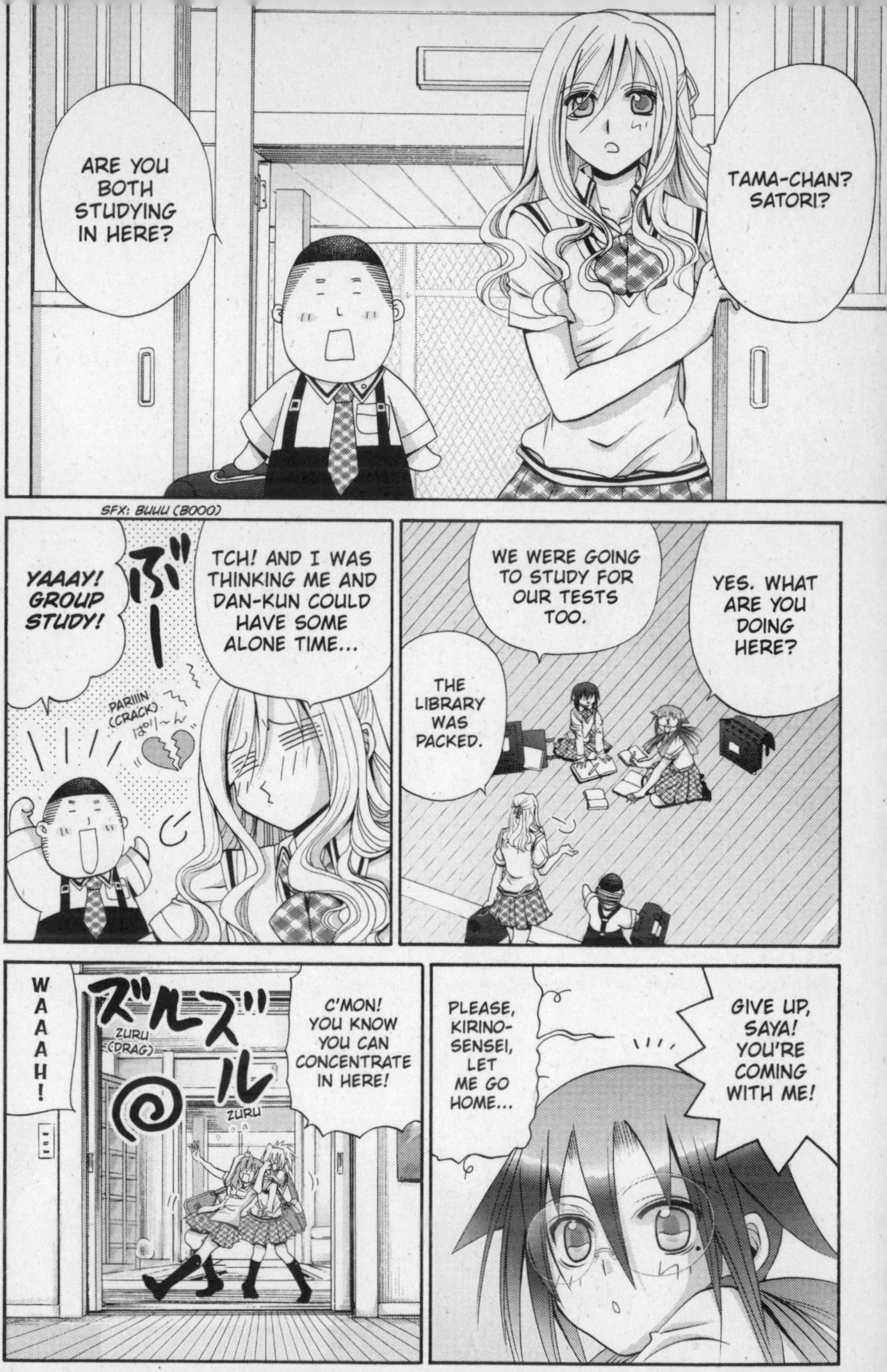
TAMA-CHAN? SATORI?
ARE YOU BOTH STUDYING IN HERE?
YES. WHAT ARE YOU DOING HERE?
WE WERE GOING TO STUDY FOR OUR TESTS TOO.
THE LIBRARY WAS PACKED.
TCH! AND I WAS THINKING ME AND DAN-KUN COULD HAVE SOME ALONE TIME...
ぶー
SFX: BUUU (BOOO)
YAAAY! GROUP STUDY!
PARIIIN (CRACK)
ぱリ～ん
GIVE UP, SAYA! YOU'RE COMING WITH ME!
PLEASE, KIRINO-SENSEI, LET ME GO HOME...
C'MON! YOU KNOW YOU CAN CONCENTRATE IN HERE!
ズルズル
ZURU (DRAG)
ZURU
WAAAAH!

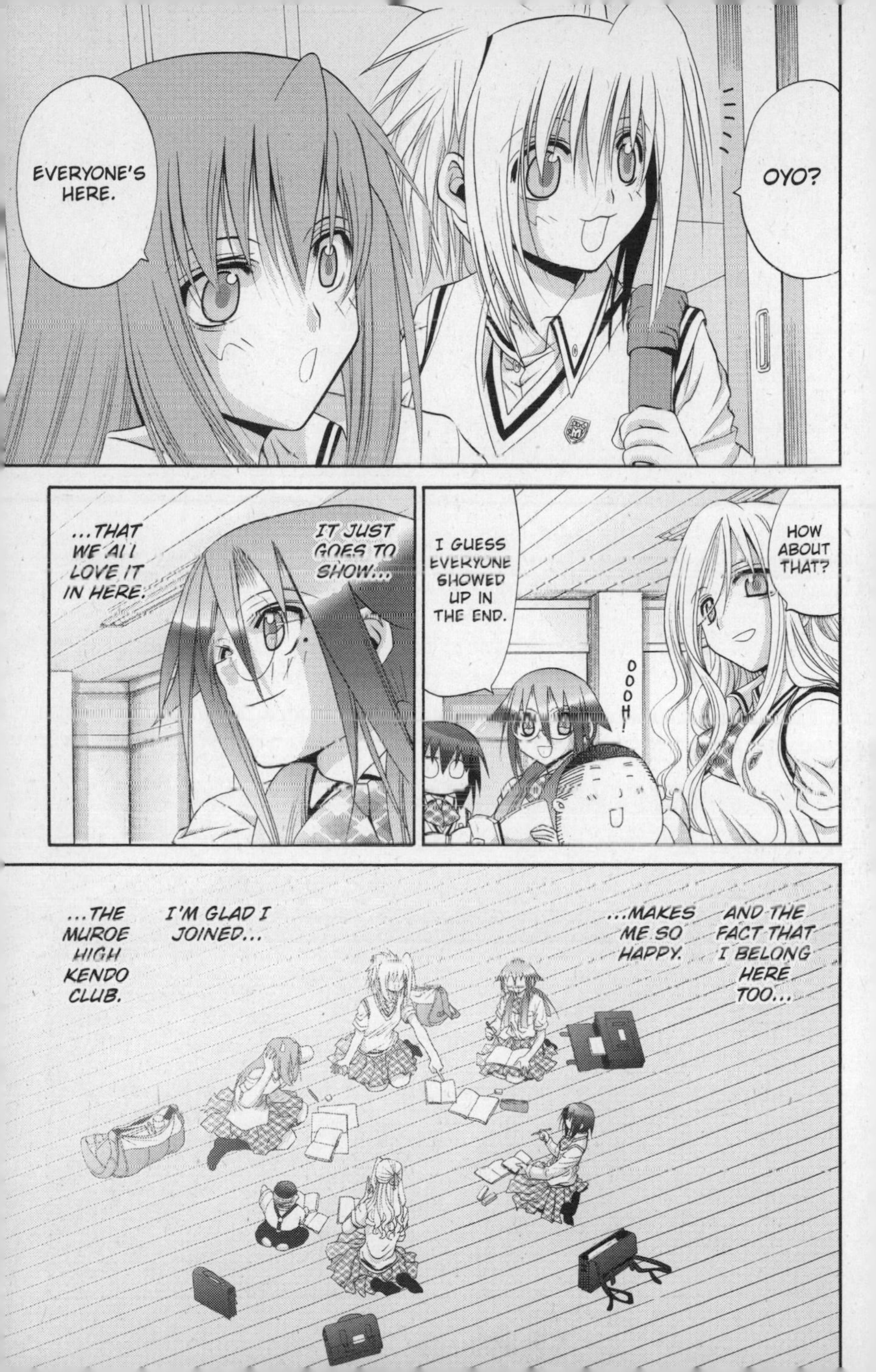
OYO?
EVERYONE'S HERE.
HOW ABOUT THAT?
I GUESS EVERYONE SHOWED UP IN THE END.
OOOH!
IT JUST GOES TO SHOW...
...THAT WE ALL LOVE IT IN HERE.
AND THE FACT THAT I BELONG HERE TOO...
...MAKES ME SO HAPPY.
I'M GLAD I JOINED...
...THE MUROE HIGH KENDO CLUB.

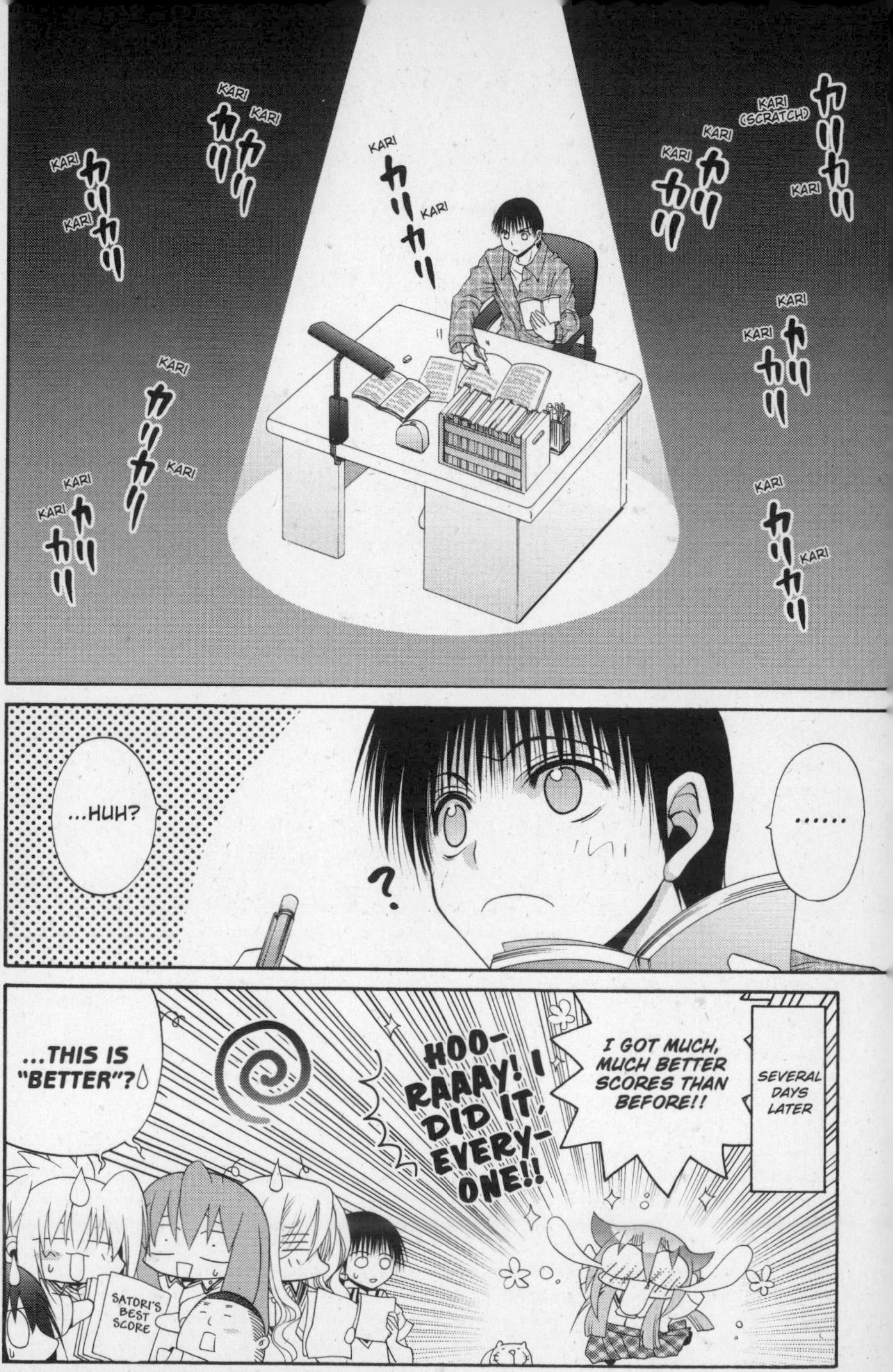
KARI (SCRATCH)
カリカリ
KARI
KARI
カリカリ
KARI
KARI
カリカリ
KARI
KARI
カリカリ
KARI
KARI
カリカリ
KARI
KARI
カリカリ
KARI
KARI
カリカリ
KARI
KARI
カリカリ
KARI
KARI
カリカリ
KARI
KARI
カリカリ
......
...HUH?
SEVERAL DAYS LATER
I GOT MUCH, MUCH BETTER SCORES THAN BEFORE!!
HOO-RAAAY! I DID IT, EVERY-ONE!!
...THIS IS "BETTER"?
SATORI'S BEST SCORE

AFTERWORD

THE BAMBOO BLADE THAT YOU SEE IN THESE PAGES IS A COLLABORATION BETWEEN IGARASHI-SENSEI AND I, SO IT ISN'T CREATED WITH COMPLETE AND TOTAL ABANDON. IN THE SERIES WHERE I HANDLE BOTH STORY AND ART, I'M FREE TO DO WHATEVER I FEEL LIKE, BUT *BAMBOO BLADE* AND MY OTHER CURRENT SERIES, *MATERIAL PUZZLE ZERO KREUZ*, ARE DRAWN BY OTHER ARTISTS, SO I DON'T PUT QUITE AS MUCH POISONOUS CYNICISM INTO THEM. I DO MY BEST NOT TO LOAD THEM WITH SNEAKY, UNPREDICTABLE PLOT TWISTS AND SURREAL GAGS. THE GOAL IS NOT QUITE AS MUCH ABOUT SATISFYING MYSELF AS SATISFYING THE READERS' DESIRES.

THE WORLD AROUND US IS CURRENTLY IN THE WILDLY POPULAR PART OF THE BOOM-AND-BUST CYCLE WITH REGARDS TO OLD MEN, SO IT'S REALLY ONLY NATURAL THAT CHARACTERS LIKE COACH TERAMOTO AND URA'S PAPA BECOME THE FOCUS OF THE STORY, BUT FOR SOME REASON, MY EDITOR STARTED SULKING.

"I HATE THIS. I'VE HAD ENOUGH OF THE OLD MEN. I WANNA SEE GIRLS. DRAW MORE GIRLS."

THIS EDITOR IS A HUGE FAN OF MY MANGA, SO HE TRIES TO SEE WHERE I'M TAKING THE STORY BEFORE ANYONE ELSE. AS I'M DRAWING THE CHAPTER, HE GOES,

"IS IT READY? IS IT READY?"

AND THEN HE STARTS BEGGING FOR DETAILS.

"WHAT'S GOING TO HAPPEN NEXT WITH THIS?"

BUT FINDING OUT AHEAD OF TIME RUINS ALL THE SUSPENSE AND EXCITEMENT, SO WHEN I TELL HIM TO BE PATIENT AND READ IT IN THE MAGAZINE, HE SNAPS AND SCREAMS,

"NO WAY, MAN!"

WHAT'S HIS PROBLEM ANYWAY?

COACH TERAMOTO

I'M TRYING TO FULFILL THE READERS' NEEDS BY PUMPING OUT LOTS OF OLD MEN, BUT SINCE IT IS THANKS TO THIS EDITOR THAT I HAVE A SERIES AT ALL, I FEEL OBLIGED TO SATISFY HIM. IT'S REALLY HARD TO CREATE A GREAT MANGA WHEN YOU'RE STUCK BETWEEN A ROCK AND A HARD PLACE LIKE THIS. I'M WRITING THIS MESSAGE HERE IN THE HOPES THAT YOU ALL UNDERSTAND MY PLIGHT. PLEASE KEEP IT IN MIND AS THE REST OF THE STORY UNFOLDS.

MASAHIRO TOTSUKA

BACKSTAGE AFTERWORD ♥

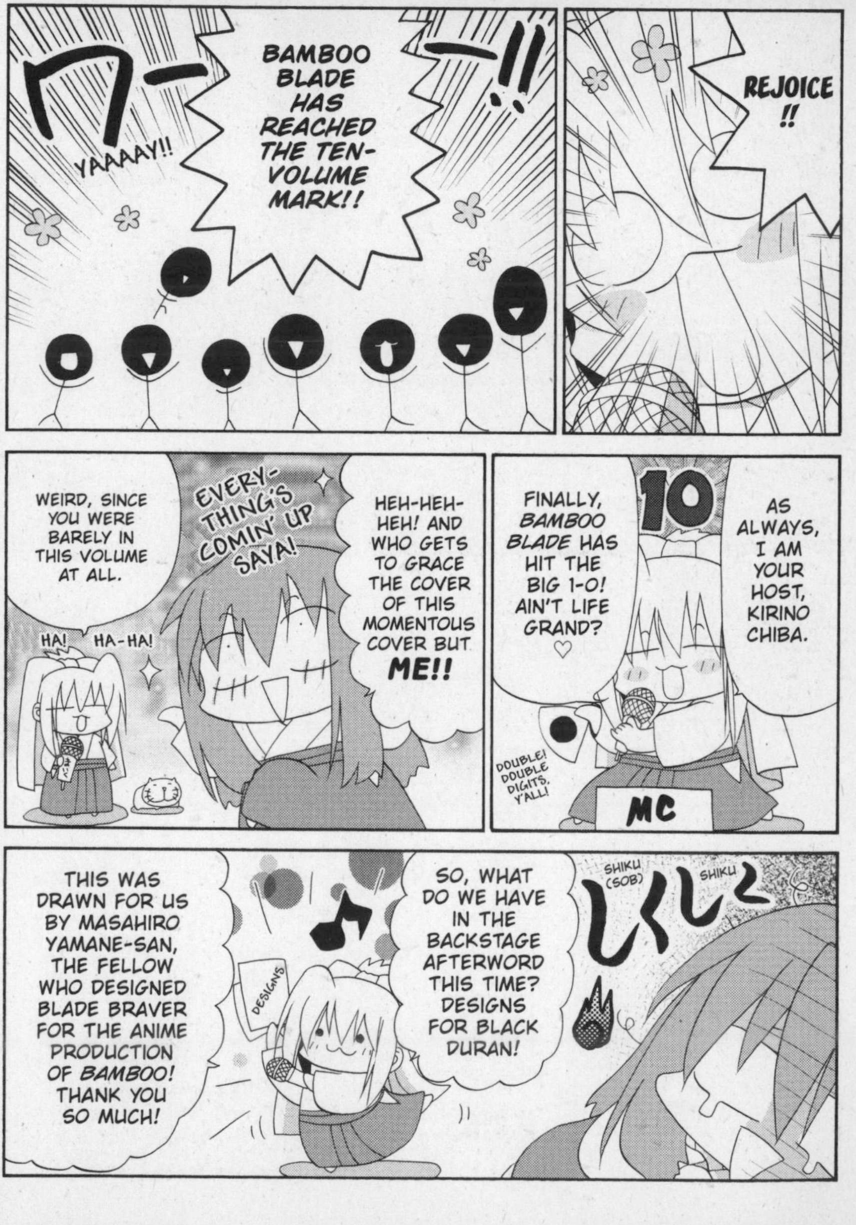
REJOICE!!
ワー ー!!
BAMBOO BLADE HAS REACHED THE TEN-VOLUME MARK!!
YAAAAY!!
AS ALWAYS, I AM YOUR HOST, KIRINO CHIBA.
10
FINALLY, *BAMBOO BLADE* HAS HIT THE BIG 1-O! AIN'T LIFE GRAND? ♡
DOUBLE! DOUBLE DIGITS, Y'ALL!
MC
HEH-HEH-HEH! AND WHO GETS TO GRACE THE COVER OF THIS MOMENTOUS COVER BUT **ME!!**
EVERY-THING'S COMIN' UP SAYA!
WEIRD, SINCE YOU WERE BARELY IN THIS VOLUME AT ALL.
HA! HA-HA!
SHIKU (SOB) SHIKU
しくしく
SO, WHAT DO WE HAVE IN THE BACKSTAGE AFTERWORD THIS TIME? DESIGNS FOR BLACK DURAN!
DESIGNS
THIS WAS DRAWN FOR US BY MASAHIRO YAMANE-SAN, THE FELLOW WHO DESIGNED BLADE BRAVER FOR THE ANIME PRODUCTION OF *BAMBOO*! THANK YOU SO MUCH!

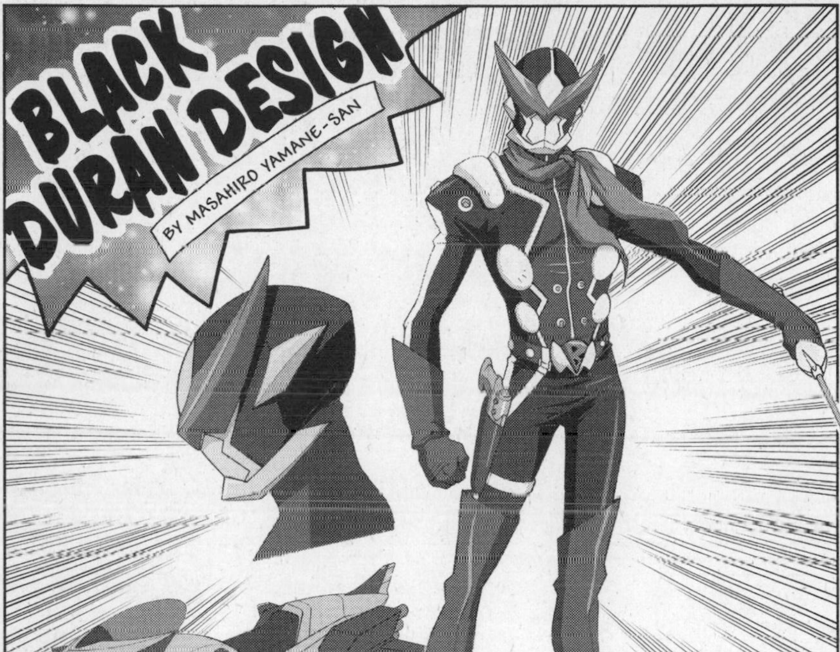
BLACK DURAN DESIGN
BY MASAHIRO YAMANE-SAN

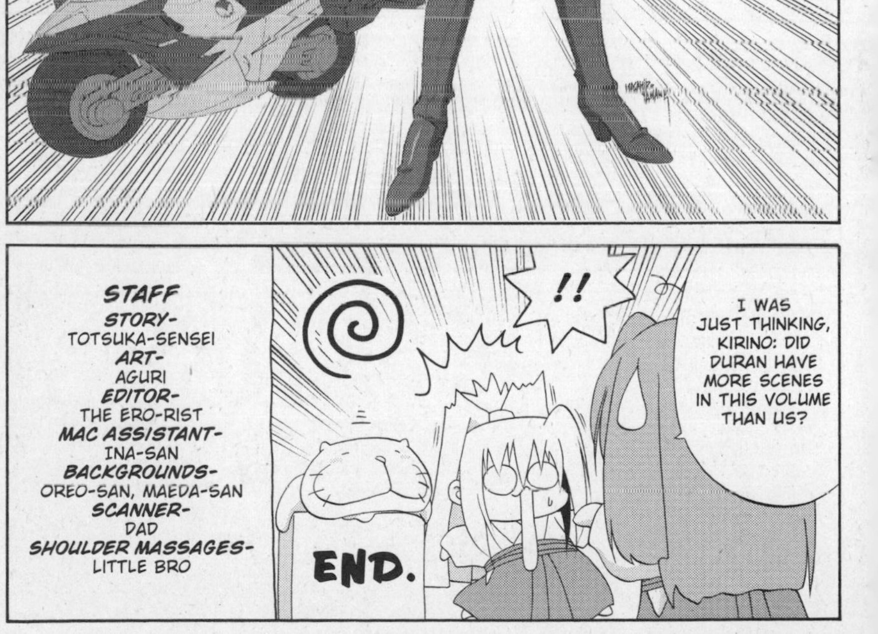
I WAS JUST THINKING, KIRINO: DID DURAN HAVE MORE SCENES IN THIS VOLUME THAN US?
!!
END.

STAFF

STORY-
TOTSUKA-SENSEI
ART-
AGURI
EDITOR-
THE ERO-RIST
MAC ASSISTANT-
INA-SAN
BACKGROUNDS-
OREO-SAN, MAEDA-SAN
SCANNER-
DAD
SHOULDER MASSAGES-
LITTLE BRO